Anthologizing Poe

Perspectives on Edgar Allan Poe

General Editor: Barbara Cantalupo,
Pennsylvania State University, Lehigh Valley

The Perspectives on Poe series includes books on new approaches to Edgar A. Poe, his work and influence; all perspectives—theoretical, historical, biographical, gender studies, source studies, cultural studies, global studies, etc.—are invited.

Titles in This Series

http://inpress.sites.lehigh.edu/

Anthologizing Poe

*Editions, Translations, and
(Trans)National Canons*

Edited by Emron Esplin and
Margarida Vale de Gato

LEHIGH UNIVERSITY PRESS
Bethlehem

Published by Lehigh University Press
Copublished by The Rowman & Littlefield Publishing Group, Inc.
4501 Forbes Boulevard, Suite 200, Lanham, Maryland 20706
www.rowman.com

6 Tinworth Street, London SE11 5AL, United Kingdom

British Library Cataloguing in Publication Information Available

Library of Congress Cataloging-in-Publication Data
Names: Esplin, Emron, editor. | Gato, Margarida Vale de, editor.
Title: Anthologizing Poe : editions, translations, and (trans)national
   canons / edited by Emron Esplin and Margarida Vale de Gato.
Description: Bethlehem : Lehigh University Press ; Lanham, Maryland : The
   Rowman & Littlefield Publishing Group, Inc., [2020] | Series:
   Perspectives on Edgar Allan Poe | Includes bibliographical references
   and index. | Summary: "This book examines the processes of editing and
   anthologizing as innovative contributions to the field of literary
   culture, analyzing how single-author editions and multi-author
   anthologies have created distinct reputations for Edgar Allan Poe. The
   book explores how Poe's editors, anthologizers, and translators continue
   to shape his global images"— Provided by publisher.
Identifiers: LCCN 2020004424 (print) | LCCN 2020004425 (ebook) | ISBN
   9781611462586 (cloth ; alk. paper) | ISBN 9781611462609 (pbk)
   ISBN 9781611462593 (epub)
Subjects: LCSH: Poe, Edgar Allan, 1809-1849—Criticism and interpretation.
   | Anthologies—Editing. | Anthologies—Publishing—United
   States—History. | Anthologies—Publishing—Great Britain—History. |
   Poe, Edgar Allan, 1809-1849—Translations—History and criticism.
Classification: LCC PS2638 .A64 2020 (print) | LCC PS2638 (ebook) | DDC
   818/.309—dc23
LC record available at https://lccn.loc.gov/2020004424
LC ebook record available at https://lccn.loc.gov/2020004425

~

Contents

Part III: Setting Tones and Moods: Genre Anthologies and Audiobooks

Part IV: Wor(l)ding Poe Abroad: Anthologizers, Editors, Illustrators, and Translators

~

Acknowledgments

Like our first co-edited book, *Translated Poe*, this book began with a series of conversations and then came to fruition through the magic of electronic communication and a number of personal meetings between the editors and contributors at various conference venues around the globe. In 2016, we were discussing the possibility of a project on the relationship, or lack thereof, between the fields of American studies and translation studies when Margarida and Alexandra Urakova had a long conversation about Poe, anthologies, and nineteenth-century gift books that made us ask questions about Poe and the anthologizing apparatus—questions that Margarida had already started to ponder in her work on anthologies in Portugal and that synergized with work that Emron had been doing on Poe's reception and presence in Argentina and Spanish America in general. So, we put our other project on the back burner and began to invite scholars to write on specific topics under the larger umbrella of Poe anthologies, collections, editions, and translations.

Most of our communication with our contributors has taken place via email, but we have also been fortunate enough to meet at least once in person with almost all of our contributors through the organization of conference panels on Poe and anthologies. We have met in smaller groups at the 2017 American Literature Association's Annual Conference in Boston; the 2018 Conference of the International Association of Inter-American Studies in Coimbra; the 2018 International Poe & Hawthorne Conference in Kyoto;

the 2019 Modern Language Association's International Symposium in Lisbon; and the 2020 International Conference of the Edgar Allan Poe Spanish Association in Almería. These gatherings have been helpful in the drafting and refining of our chapters, and they have also been rewarding since they have allowed us to meet many colleagues whom we previously knew only by email and attached Word files.

Margarida would like to thank the Centre of English Studies and the School of Arts and Humanities at the Universidade de Lisboa, as well as the Portuguese Foundation for Science and Technology, and Emron would like to thank the College of Humanities, the Department of English, the David M. Kennedy Center for International Studies, the Latin American Studies Program, and the Translation Studies Group (sponsored by the Humanities Center)—all at Brigham Young University—for sponsoring the travel that allowed us to formulate this book in person. We both wish to thank Susan Tane for the travel grants that supported our participation in conferences connected to the Poe Studies Association. We would also like to thank the Department of English at BYU and the Centre for English Studies at the Universidade de Lisboa for providing us with funds to hire Enid Zafran to help us index this book, and we are grateful to Enid for her thorough and timely work. Finally, we would like to thank Barbara Cantalupo, Katherine Crassons, and Tricia J. Moore at Lehigh University Press; Zachary Nycum at Rowman & Littlefield; and the two readers who gave us feedback on our manuscript for their support for this project.

We also need to acknowledge and thank the following copyright holders for permission to cite sources at length and to reproduce images. In chapter 9, the extended quotations from Ray Bradbury's "Usher II" are reprinted by permission of Don Congdon Associates, Inc. © 1950 by Standard Magazines, renewed 1977 by Ray Bradbury. In chapter 12, the two images are photographs by Philip Edward Phillips, with permission from the Boston Athenæum. In chapter 15, we reproduce images with permission from the following entities: the Universidad de Castilla-La Mancha, the Research Group LyA at the Universidad de Castilla-La Mancha, Editorial Juventud, Editorial E.D.A.F., Mercé Calsina (through the Fundació Privada Ramon Calsina), Editorial Vicens-Vives, Joan-Pere Viladecans, and Editorial Anaya—also see the individual illustration captions in the chapter itself. We are grateful to Filipe Abranches for granting us permission to use one of his illustrations from *Obra Poética Completa de Edgar Allan Poe* (2009) for our book's cover art.

We thank our contributors for their diligence and their creativity in helping us craft a book that shows, once again, Poe's global presence and that also reveals the influence and power of the less-heralded individuals of the publishing industry—the anthologizers, editors, and translators who give Poe to the world. Finally, we would like to thank one another, and we express our gratitude to our families for their patience and support. Margarida thanks Patricia Odber de Baubeta for sparking her scholarly interest in anthologies, Paulo Tomé for his perseverance in companionship, and her daughter Alice for helping her learn the freedom of the boundless mother-daughter bond. Emron thanks Marlene for all of her work as a scholar, wife, mother, and friend, and he thanks their children—Moses, Anya, Ansel, Edith, and Simon—for their energy and love.

~

Introduction

Types of Anthologies and Types of Poe

Margarida Vale de Gato and Emron Esplin

Edgar Allan Poe wields more influence in the spheres of literature and popular culture on a world scale than any other U.S. author.[1] This influence, however, does not rely on the quality of Poe's texts alone nor on the compellingly tragic nature of his biography; his reputation and his ubiquitous presence owe much of their longevity to the ways Poe has been interpreted and portrayed by his advocates—other writers, translators, literary critics, literary historians, illustrators, filmmakers, musicians—and packaged by various "professional mediators" (Price 10) in the literary field, especially editors and anthologizers. As our study demonstrates, the division between Poe's advocates and the "professional mediators" who organize his work for consumption by the reading public can be very porous, as many of Poe's most adamant proponents—Charles Baudelaire and Julio Cortázar, for example—also anthologized, edited, and/or translated his works. *Anthologizing Poe: Editions, Translations, and (Trans)National Canons* focuses on the works produced by Poe's anthologizers and editors, both the famous and the lesser-known, whose labor can take place behind the scenes and, as Leah Price points out, often appear in the "scholarly footnotes" or margins of academic discourse rather than in the "critical text" even though editions and anthologies help to "shape a larger generic system" (10). According to translation studies scholar André Lefevere, anthologizers, just like "translators, critics, and historians . . . are image makers, exerting the power of subversion under the guise of objectivity" (6–7). Poe's editors and anthologizers wield real power,

1

and over the last 170 years, they have crafted and framed the various Poes we recognize, revere, cherish, and critique today.

Unlike Poe—whose works have led to countless adaptations and refractions and to a proliferation of scholarly books and articles—anthologies and the concepts of anthologizing, organizing, collecting, and/or editing an author's work receive relatively little coverage in the literary market or in the scholarly tradition. In the introduction to his 2004 edited volume, *On Anthologies: Politics and Pedagogy*, Jeffrey R. Di Leo notes that "while anthologies are a pervasive and dominant part of academic culture, they have not yet been given sustained analysis by cultural theorists" (6).[2] Most serious treatments of anthologies have appeared in the twenty-first century, and anything approaching what we can now call the field of anthology studies has only emerged over these past two decades, even though the concept of the anthology takes us all the way back to ancient Greece.

It is our aim to contribute to the growing critical conversation around anthologies and other editorial practices of textual organization, and our book builds upon the works of Barbara Mujica, Paul Lauter, and Joseph Csicsila (who examine how anthologies are used for teaching literature); Leah Price, René Audet, Kasia Boddy, Anne Ferry, and Neil Fraistat (who analyze how collections and selections shape the development of the novel, the short story, and poetry as genres); Patricia Anne Odber de Baubeta, Joe Lockard and Jillian Sandell, and Alan Golding (who historicize the roles of anthologies and editorial practices in particular literary traditions); and Teresa Seruya, Lieven D'hulst, Alexandra Assis Rosa, and Maria Lin Moniz (who have put together a volume of essays that explores the interplay between translated and native literary production and how translation functions in anthologies and collections of the nineteenth and twentieth centuries).[3] However, certain types of scholarship are still lacking in the critical dialogue around anthologies and anthological practices. For example, in-depth studies about (or essay collections with diverse perspectives on) the effects and affects of anthologizing and editing as projects of public literacy for a given writer—whether extending the possibilities of interpreting him or her, or cutting up the slices into which the writer is to be consumed—are still missing.[4] The field has yet to produce many book-length projects that bring anthology studies and single-author studies into the same sphere. *Anthologizing Poe* follows this research combination by examining how anthologizers and editors package, repackage, and ultimately create one particularly influential and extremely popular American writer—Poe.

In the field of anthology studies, the actual definition of "anthology" can be more slippery than one would hope. In *Anthologies*, Di Leo claims that "the basic notion of an anthology as a *collection* of writings remains the same. Today an anthology is a collection of connected or interrelated writings that center around a topic. Organizing topics may include themes, disciplines, persona, and historical periods" (3). But he also avers, "In the classroom the term *anthology* tends to be conflated with *collection*, as well as *reader*, *casebook*, and even *textbook*" (4). In *Translation in Anthologies and Collections*, Teresa Seruya and her colleagues point out the circularity in many definitions of the terms anthology and collection:

> The terms anthology and collection are used interchangeably and tautologically in several definitions ("an anthology is a collection. . ." and "a collection is an anthology"), and they are also used to refer to a single volume or to a series of volumes including mainly literary texts, but also music pieces, films or works of art, in general. (3)[5]

We agree with Seruya and her co-editors' belief in the utility of a "prototypical definition of the conceptual core of anthology and neighbouring notions (such as collection, or album) as an 'anthological class,' a dynamic generic construct" (3).

Inspired by the hermeneutic approaches to anthologies, we seek to expand the spectrum of the concept in order to broadly gauge the editorial devices that direct how texts are to be interpreted within larger assemblages, contributing at the same time to situate an author within an artistic community and in the imagination of his or her readers. Accordingly, the different authors in our book analyze various Poe editions (from multivolume attempts at complete works to single-volume "portable" editions); shorter Poe collections (which can also be termed single-author anthologies); genre anthologies (in terms of form—e.g., poetry or short fiction—and in terms of content—e.g., horror/gothic tales, detective stories, science fiction); large multi-author anthologies used in college classrooms (such as the Norton or the Heath); nineteenth-century gift books; illustrated Poe editions; and translated editions, collections, and anthologies from various literary traditions. In short, our study explores how the anthologizing process—choosing which authors and texts to include and exclude; ordering those authors and texts; deciding how to frame the chosen pieces with introductions, epilogues, and other front matter and back matter; determining the scholarly/editorial apparatus that should accompany the primary texts (e.g., footnotes, endnotes, headnotes, a glossary); selecting or commissioning illustrations; and many other decisions—shapes the various images and reputations of Poe that we read for work, read for pleasure, and/or teach to our students.

Anthologizing Poe follows its own anthological design, planned as an edited collection in four sections, each one representing different facets and assumptions of the anthologizing model. The first section covers early prototypes of anthologies and editions that circulated during Poe's life, including projects for which Poe himself served as the editor and/or anthologizer. The second section traces Poe's anthological fate in the Anglophone transatlantic axis (the United Kingdom and the United States). This section examines the best-known editions of Poe in English, and in the case of U.S. literary history, it also places a special focus on the anthology as textbook in the university classroom. The third section explores the significance of programmatic, genre, and theme anthologies that give us Poe the poet, the horror writer, the father of the detective story, and the precursor to modern science fiction. The fourth and final section analyzes translated literary anthologies and editions, contextualizing them in the target regional or national traditions as well as from an interdisciplinary angle that includes the visual arts, while assessing their impact across borders and the interplay between literary promoters over time and areas of influence.

Exclusion, Inclusion, Recuperation, and Relation

Anthologies, in their various types, are both objects of inclusion and exclusion and objects of recuperation and relation. They help to contextualize the industry and history of literature and to deepen our understanding of geopolitics. They reflect shifting literary tastes, while also performing cultural work that projects traits and trends.[6] As Helga Essman and Armin Paul Frank have pointed out, anthologies can be likened to museums in their preservation function. However, unlike the museum, their lack of notoriety thus far in the scholarly field relegates them to a site of resistance and potential subversion, that of a "shadow culture" (68). Moreover, the cognitive operations involved in gathering texts are, on the one hand, discriminatory and contrastive and, on the other, interconnecting and intertextual, enhancing the experience of reading.

The process of anthologizing requires serious decision-making about whom or what to include and exclude, and the anthologizer or editor inevitably excludes much more than she includes because, as Paul Lauter notes via another effective anthology-as-museum metaphor, "one runs out of room: books fall apart, the binding will not hold, the limits are upon us" (29). This ontology of exclusion exerts real power; it creates literary canons, and it affects or even controls whom and what are available to read. Karen Kilcup writes, "Composing an anthology creates a miniature canon, no matter how

resistant the editor is to the vexed notions of goodness and importance. . . .
By definition, what's in is important and good, and what's omitted is at
least potentially questionable" (113). Price goes as far as to argue that
"[a]nthologies are more than a referendum. They determine not simply
who gets published or what gets read, but *who reads*, and how" (3; emphasis
added).[7] Anthologizers, then, not only leave out writers, but they also inherently leave out or change certain readers when they exclude particular writers, pieces, or genres. This exclusion is inherent to every anthology regardless
of the particular politics or agendas of any given anthologizer.

In contrast to this ontology of exclusion, anthologies also function as
significant sites of inclusion and recuperation. Multi-author anthologies
often serve to rescue certain authors from oblivion, as well as to imprint a
different trend, mode, or (sub)genre in the literary field. The same is true for
"selected works" that recuperate previously ignored pieces; even the literary find of recondite or buried material is often the justification for a new
series of edited works, reassessing an author's stance in terms of literary innovation. An anthology's or an edition's most radical potential rests in the
possibilities it allows for providing different coverage from the anthologies
or editions that preceded it. Including previously ignored or forgotten writers
in a new anthology or choosing different texts to represent an author in a
new edition have the potential to create new canons in specialized fields; to
alter how, when, and/or if a particular author is studied at all; and to change
the canon—the limited number of texts by a limited number of writers that
professors and professionals in the fields of literary and cultural studies deem
a well-read or well-trained individual should know.

In Poe's case, at least from the twentieth century onward, these potentialities revolve more around the type of Poe that an anthologizer or editor
hopes to emphasize rather than on his complete exclusion from or inclusion
in the canon. However, decisions to include what have become viewed as
Poe's "minor" or "atypical" texts (his comic or satiric pieces, for example) do
have canonical consequences in Poe studies, in how Poe is read or taken seriously (or not) in the academy, and in how Poe is understood by the reading
public and media consumers at large (most often as a writer of horror and/
or detective stories). Indeed, we could argue that the seriousness with which
Poe's mediators—from Rufus W. Griswold to Charles Baudelaire, and from
Thomas O. Mabbott to Jorge Luis Borges—have treated Poe's "darker" or
"heavier" texts (whether that treatment demonstrates itself in the commentary surrounding these works and/or via the exclusion of works that do not
match these texts in tone or content) clearly demonstrates the anthology's
power to shape an author's reputation. Across almost every tradition that

Anthologizing Poe covers, the simultaneous inclusion and/or praise for Poe's dark works and exclusion and/or belittling of his lighter corpus has remained intact for 170 years. In short, anthologies, editions, or collections that emphasize what we might call the "other" Poe still have a canon to challenge and a long-running tradition (both academic and popular) to confront when making a case for Poe's lesser-known works.

Apart from the space that anthologies allow for recovery or recuperation, anthologies—for better and for worse—also recontextualize, creating new relations between the materials included. The inevitable blending of textual and editorial procedures that occurs whenever texts are put together (and more blatantly when the responsibility falls on an agent other than the author) challenges, as T. S. Eliot once feared, an idea of "significant unity" of the writer's work (4). However, this mixture can and should be studied for the richness of its "contexture," a felicitous term coined by Fraistat for "a larger whole fabricated from integral parts" (4).[8] There are cases in which the very integrity of the parts is challenged, particularly in textbook anthologies that use excerpts. One extreme example exists in the popular French pocket readers, analyzed in this collection's chapter 13, "Startling Restitutions, Significant Partialities," which announced the author *par lui même* (by himself), while in fact presenting an intricate narrative that was culled by someone else from excerpts of that author's work and a mix of critical and historical documents. The interweaving of text and paratext in editions under a particular light—an author, a theme, a period, a trend—is one of the elements that concur with the dichotomy between integration and disunity in what we broadly call an anthology.

The framing and order within an anthology—especially when, as previously suggested, its editor's aims differ from the author's—put forth a genealogy of reading along a new interpretative context. Anne Ferry, studying the forces that submit the individual poem to different readings when grouped in an anthology, stresses that "[t]he anthologist as author of the book supplants the author of the poem, in choosing how it should be presented, with interpretative consequences that . . . can give a different direction to the experience of reading a poem than if it were read elsewhere" (2). We suggest that Ferry's argument applies to other short texts—tales, sketches, and essays—that are published alongside various other pieces (whether in the groupings made by the author in an original collection or by the anthologizer in a later publication). In Poe's case, nearly all of his works go through this type of contextual shift because he only published one novel and one lengthy prose poem during his lifetime. Our contemporary reading experience of Poe, unless we are hunting down first editions or reading them online, is always affected by the surrounding texts (whether in Poe editions or in anthologies that place him alongside other authors) in a way outside of or foreign to what Poe could have planned, and *Anthologizing Poe* seeks both to map and to analyze these differences.

Perceiving and receiving this type of combined literary object entails three operations described in the title of a study by René Audet—"To Relate, to Read, to Separate." Audet sees these cognitive processes as increasingly intertwined in postmodern and contemporary times, revealing the ascendency of "a poetics of diffraction," with portions that are either aggregated by more or less loose common elements, or orchestrated as layers favoring "representational complexity" (44). Although Audet's piece envisages "the [story] collection," applicable to volumes organized by the author of the assembled texts, or at least under his or her supervision or blessing, the narrative of (dis)aggregation that he enunciates seems portable to our book's broader scope of text types—anthologies, collections, editions—that take texts from their original homes and place them in new contexts.

The anthology compensates for the disunity it causes when pulling texts from their original contexts by offering a greater picture of the collective—a picture that favors distinctive American resonances since it propitiates the metaphor of "quilting" pieces together, particularly in the case of the short-story anthology, as compellingly argued by Kasia Boddy (147). In her "Variety in Unity, Unity in Variety: The Liminal Space of the American Short-Story Anthology," Boddy claims for anthologies of multiple authors, much as Rólf Lundén or J. Gerald Kennedy have done for the short story cycle, an expression of the composite communities and the confederate organization of the United States. Boddy also highlights a unique characteristic of anthologies in the strictest sense, which is the paratextual framing we have already foregrounded—things like section titles, introductions, and headnotes—for which she borrows from Gérard Genette the term "thresholds of interpretation" (148). This is likely a prominent feature in the institutionalizing role performed by anthologies, including the making of the literary canon and the production of national and regional traditions.[9]

The quilt that is the U.S. literary canon certainly contains both stitches and blocks from Poe's literary fabric, and we would argue that significant patterns in this patchwork come from Poe's cloth; but, how do these pieces change when viewed alongside the surrounding pieces? We could ask the same question of how Poe's texts change in the smaller quilts that are each anthology or edition in which his works appear. How does the reading of a Poe text differ when that text is bookended by the works of other writers (Hawthorne and Phoebe Cary in the current Heath, John Greenleaf

Whittier and Abraham Lincoln in the current Norton, or the lighthearted poems or stories of long-forgotten authors in the early 1840s releases of *The Gift*), and how much of that difference depends on the specific writer him- or herself or on the particular work selected to represent that writer? What happens when Poe's poems are kept apart from his fiction (as in all of his own book-length publications) versus when they reside in the same volume (in, for example, Penguin's *The Portable Edgar Allan Poe*)? How do we see individual Poe works differently when they are placed with, or even cast as foundational to, specific genres? These questions matter, especially when reading an author who carefully crafted a unity of effect—in his second review of Nathaniel Hawthorne's *Twice-Told Tales* and in "The Philosophy of Composition"—that demonstrates fastidious concern with word, sentence, and textual organization and that favors mathematical calculation and order over inspiration or communion with the muse. In short, *Anthologizing Poe* examines how the shifts in effect, due to the changes of the textual surroundings in various forms of the anthology, influence Poe's individual works and his varying reputations.

Anthologizing Poe

We have divided *Anthologizing Poe* into four sections based on Poe's differing relationships with anthologies and editions in both time and space. Our first section contains three chapters that reveal how Poe himself attempted to anthologize his works and/or his literary relationships. In the leadoff chapter, Jana Argersinger sees Poe's whimsical fashion of selecting and framing his peers (in "The Literati of New York City" and "The Living Writers of America") as "an attempt to establish the authorial self at the center of an anthological web of people and texts that stays unsteady— . . . because it is roiling with affective crossfire" (28), while in the second chapter, Harry Lee Poe argues that Poe conceived his works in an anthological way following a system of scansion similar to what he advocates in "The Rationale of Verse." In the third chapter, Alexandra Urakova examines a book format cherished by both publishers and consumers during Poe's life—the gift book—to shed light on how particular factors such as "dress (the cover, binding, title) and society (the company of its poems, stories, and plates)" (64) influence Poe's story "Eleonora" in *The Gift* of 1842.

This first section emphasizes how the work of anthologies puts subjectivities and affinities into play, with combinatory strategies that favor exchange of feelings and stir audiences toward particular moods. The practice of assembling texts and/or literary relationships becomes, in this light, an agency of the "cultural politics of emotion"—to use the words of Sara Ahmed's impacting title, which has boosted the recent equation of rhetoric, performance, and affect theory.[10] Poe was concerned about the company he kept, both in the literal and literary senses, and these initial chapters demonstrate a marked effort on his part to control how his works and his person were seen and interpreted both on an individual level and among groups of peers.

The second section of our volume addresses the creation of a Poe canon through the work of his major editors from the 1850s through the present (in both the United States and the United Kingdom) and Poe's ever-present but shifting place in the canon of American literature. Poe is a particularly fitting subject for this section's focus on both editions and anthologies for several reasons examined by the authors of these five chapters, not the least of which is Poe's purported request that Rufus W. Griswold, a rival editor and a pioneer of national poetry anthologies in the United States, serve as his literary executor. The double facet of Poe's editor/collector and critic/anthologizer of American literature was followed by other important literary figures, such as Edmund Clarence Stedman and Floyd Stovall in the United States and Jorge Luis Borges in Argentina, which helps us make the case for "anthologizing" in a broad sense that comprises not only compilations of multiple authors, but also "single author collections" (Mujica 210) and even complete editions. How the latter were constituted in the formative years of Poe scholarship is addressed by Jeffrey Savoye's meticulous account of the preparation of notable early editions by Griswold, J. H. Ingram, E. C. Stedman and G. E. Woodberry, and J. A. Harrison. The twentieth century, according to Travis Montgomery's chapter, favors more specialized endeavors, as well as attention to more private documents and supplementary sources—Killis Campbell and Floyd Stovall for the poetry, John Ward Ostrom for the correspondence, Thomas Ollive Mabbott for variants of poems and tales, Burton R. Pollin for the longer narratives—along with the popular consecration of the Library of America, divided by G. R. Thompson and Patrick F. Quinn.

Poe's reputation in the United States also fluctuated according to international praise in languages other than English (which we will return to in section four) and the different estimations of various members of the literati in the United Kingdom, who also went to great lengths to establish Poe's body of work and construct his multifaceted image in anthologies and collections. Starting in 1874–1875 with John H. Ingram's attempt to rescue Poe's status from what he deemed to be the editorial bias of Griswold, Bonnie McMullen takes us through collected and selected Poe editions in the United Kingdom, considering also the impact of anthologies in the poetics shared by communities of affinities until the Second World War. In the subsequent chapter,

J. Gerald Kennedy provides a valuable insider's look into one of Penguin's most circulated formats of representative dissemination of a particular author, the "portable." Kennedy offers a remarkable "think aloud" rationale for his mapping of Poe, very much aware that "[e]very single-author anthology produces a certain version of the writer by selection and exclusion, based on available texts, calculations of essential material, and copyright constraints" (135).

Our book moves from single-author to multi-author anthologies, and its second section ends with the most influential type, encompassing literary entertainment, information, and education: the "textbook anthology." Referencing Joseph Csicsila's previous work in survey anthologies of American literature, Scott Peeples corroborates the impression that Poe's fiction in the later part of the twentieth century became more valued than his poetry, but he also demonstrates a remarkable consistency between the choices over the last ninety years, indicating an overlap between the academic and the popular Poe.

The third section of *Anthologizing Poe* analyzes Poe's presence in (and, sometimes, his founding influence on) various types of genre anthologies. Stephen Rachman focuses on Poe's works that have been included or referenced in publications that endorsed a nascent "scientific" approach to storywriting in the late nineteenth century, and particularly the dissemination of speculative and science fiction in the twentieth century, very much connected with the "hothouse culture" of pulps in the United States (173). Rachman also enunciates the "anthology-function" that mostly informs the rationale of our entire third section: to "represent crucial generic elements or innovations" (167). John Gruesser's chapter demonstrates how Poe's consensual status as the father of detective fiction, in its modern guise, is likewise greatly indebted to the critics and editors who have ranked him as such in anthologies and collections. Gruesser argues that the eventual "recognition of Poe as a major writer with a profound and sustained influence abroad and at home coincided with and contributed to the coalescing of detection into a discrete literary genre" (194). This particular genre is also significant in our book's fourth section because Poe's detective tales have formed a sturdy foundation upon which his global reputation has been built since Charles Baudelaire's French translations of Poe in the 1850s.

Michelle Hansen's chapter continues our third section by offering an original interpretation of Poe's reputation as a "horror" author through her analysis of a significant multimedia lens: the thirteen audiobooks that constitute *Doug Bradley's Spinechillers* audio anthology. Produced between 2010 and 2016, this collection is emblematic of the audiobook revolution, and Hansen's interpretive work proves that the anthological force in literature is likewise capable of revolutionizing itself by adopting new formats and an intersemiotic approach to literary dissemination. The fact that these horror audiobooks pervasively showcased not only Poe's tales but his poems demonstrates that "genre," conceived as a literary mode (science fiction, satire, horror, the fantastic), crisscrosses the traditional literary genres, basically defined in terms of shape and utterance (lyric, drama, narrative). However, the evaluation of Poe's poetry, which has been much disputed and negotiated transnationally, deserves and receives an exclusive chapter in our volume. Philip Phillips considers how multi-author anthologies have appraised Poe in "the canonical pantheon of American poetry" (233), revealing "not only the changing literary tastes of different generations of editors and readers, but also the ways in which the inclusion or exclusion of his poetry affected his status as a poet" (222).

With the fourth section of *Anthologizing Poe*, we turn outward to translated literary anthologies and editions and to the contextualization of their significance in negotiating national and universal claims of literary merit and cultural attribution/appropriation. Translators and anthologizers share much in common—they both make decisions about which authors deserve further representation; they include certain materials and exclude others; they offer philological criticism; and they make connections between writers, between literary movements, between literary traditions (both national and regional), and between individual texts. As we have already cited in our opening paragraphs, both anthologizers and translators "are image makers" (Lefevere 7).

Many translators simultaneously play the double role of anthologizing/editing and translating, and one particular translator-anthologizer of Poe looms large in Poe's global reputation and in this fourth section. Charles Baudelaire, arguably still Poe's most influential collector-critic and translator, can also be pointed to as one who recognized, at a very early date, Poe's penchant for the ratiocinative and the fantastic. This estimation not only affected Poe's French reception, but it also influenced how Poe was seen in several other national and regional literary traditions, including the Spanish and Argentine traditions covered in the fourth section of our volume.

Margarida Vale de Gato opens this last section with a chapter that not only analyzes how Baudelaire inaugurated a model of restoring the "real" Poe, seen from the point of view of a learned and distanced congenial mind, but also explores how the American author was parceled in different "selves" according to different anthology formats in the French literary field. These range from multi-author volumes dedicated to the "fantastic" to single-author poetry selections and the aforementioned pocket editions that blend criticism and supporting extracts of works and documents as well as illustrations. In a chapter that converses both with Vale de Gato's piece and with McMullen's entry in our second section, Christopher Rollason offers further analysis on what he calls the "quality popular" editions (277) of Poe in the United Kingdom during the twentieth century, comparing them with their French counterparts. This juxtaposition sheds light upon the anthological practices of two major publishers that have shaped the European market of literature, Penguin and Gallimard.

Fernando González-Moreno and Margarita Rigal-Aragón's chapter is unique in our volume, in two senses. First, they offer an "interpretative tool of narration" of the images that have accompanied Spanish Poe anthologies since 1887, "demonstrat[ing] how Spanish artists render their visual understanding of Poe's works" (293), and thus offering a complementary account of how anthologies work with the languages of different media. Second, in a national literary tradition whose long-term embrace of Poe has been heavily determined by the work of Baudelaire, González-Moreno and Rigal-Aragón's chapter explores a lineage of image-making in Spain that might be regarded as straying autonomously from the French reception. Emron Esplin's chapter also examines a Spanish-speaking literary tradition in which Poe's reputation has been mediated through Baudelaire. Esplin shows how both lesser-known (Carlos Olivera and Armando Bazán) and internationally renowned (Jorge Luis Borges and Julio Cortázar) anthologizers, editors, and translators of Poe's fiction in Argentina have demonstrated a century-long proclivity for Poe's tales of terror, ratiocination, and the supernatural. Finally, our volume concludes with a non-Western exploration of the anthologizing process as the prominent Japanese Poe scholar, Takayuki Tatsumi, examines various Poe editions and anthologies in twentieth- and twenty-first-century Japan. Tatsumi, himself a Poe translator and a Poe anthologizer, frames his narrative autobiographically and takes his reader on a dual journey—the journey of Poe's literature in Japan and the journey of a Poe anthologizer from his childhood readings of Poe, to his graduate studies about Poe, and to his eventual participation in both the academic and publishing industries as a curator or creator of Poe for a Japanese reading audience.

Edited volumes, just like the broader umbrella of anthologies under which they rest, can never be all-encompassing, even of their specific subject matter. The editors—as anthologizers themselves—include and exclude material, invite some scholars and not others, have their invitations both accepted and rejected, and help their participants hone their topics and their coverage. In short, an edited volume is also a mini-canon for its subject, and it inherently limits the very conversations it hopes to nurture. This bind can be particularly problematic in a study on anthologies. In the introduction to *Translation in Anthologies and Collections*, Seruya and her colleagues suggest that a "study of anthologies is strongly advised—if it is not the best possible means—to understand the interplay between the dynamics and relationality principles as they meet in given corpora" (12).

Recognizing our own limits, we would have preferred to cover many more traditions than circumstances have allowed, to offer an even broader picture of the "transnational" perspective offered in our title. We also wish that we could have forayed into other avenues of research in anthologies. For instance, we originally hoped to examine how Poe shifts and changes in crossover literature—especially juvenile adaptations—a feature addressed only in Takayuki Tatsumi's contribution; we had also planned to include a study of celebration anthologies or collections of homage, especially those where a host of invited writers is called to reimagine the predecessor's work. It was our aim with *Anthologizing Poe*, after having co-edited *Translated Poe*, to both broaden the research in matters of perception and reception related to Poe and to continue to work in liminal spaces where single-author studies can fertilize interdisciplinary research. We are aware, and gladly so, that much terrain remains left to mine, and we hope that other scholars will carry this work to adjacent grounds.

Like any other anthology, ours, despite its structure, invites any and all disaggregated readings, as well as the combination and circulation of topics and subtopics between individual chapters. For instance, there are editors—such as Griswold, Stedman, and Baudelaire—who appear at length in more than one chapter, and the advances of Poe in science fiction and in the detective genre emerge in contributions outside of the two chapters especially devoted to these subjects. The chapters on audiobooks and illustrations create a space in which to debate the reach of anthologies beyond written language, and the juxtaposition of chapters focusing on American and British traditions with the non-Anglophone chapters leaves room for conversations about the similar or disparate structuring or grouping of Poe's works in these traditions. We invite our readers to leaf through the volume and build their own narrative of reading, to create their own anthology from ours. We hope that this book will trigger discussions on the concept of the anthology (single-author edition or collection, miscellany, multi-author anthology, genre collection, translated edition, or translated anthology), including further suggestions on how to integrate its study within other fields of research. Whether focusing on an author or a group of texts, the crossroads of investigation in anthology studies are multiple: the canon, genre theory, transnationalism, reception and translation studies, affect theory, or other combinations of literary and cultural studies. We also hope, in the end, to inspire further study of Poe's texts and their contexts—the ways he has been packaged, framed, constructed, and conveyed in both literary and academic markets across the world.

Notes

1. J. Gerald Kennedy and Scott Peeples open their introduction to *The Oxford Handbook of Edgar Allan Poe* with a similar claim about Poe's visibility, although they limit their scope of comparison to Poe's nineteenth-century peers (1). For us, this judgment about the depth and breadth of Poe's global impact is less an argument and more a fact; we make a similar statement in our introduction to *Translated Poe* (xi), and Emron Esplin substantiates the claim in the opening paragraphs of "Poe and His Global Advocates" (597–98) in Kennedy and Peeple's aforementioned handbook. Poe's influence on specific literary traditions (for example, the French or the Spanish traditions) has been examined seriously for several decades, but one of the first books to show Poe as a truly global author was Lois Davis Vines's 1999 edited volume, *Poe Abroad: Influence, Reputation, Affinities*. That collection has been a key text for us while working on both *Translated Poe* and *Anthologizing Poe*, and it has inspired scores of other scholars to write on Poe's connections with various writers and traditions across the globe.

2. Di Leo's 2004 edited volume, and the 2000 double issue of *symplokē* out of which the edited volume emerged, serve as early foundational texts in the field of anthology studies.

3. With the exceptions of Fraistat and Golding, each of these scholar's works on anthologies and/or editions has been published from 2000 onward.

4. It was the turn of attention to the fluctuations of Poe's ranking and appearance in early American poetry anthologies as studied in Golding's 1984 article, "A History of American Poetry Anthologies," that lingered in Margarida Vale de Gato's mind when she decided to contribute to the series *The Anthology in Portugal*. Her preliminary study on Poe's editorial designs (and desires), followed by the examination of the successive arrangements in Portuguese anthologies over a century, led to the unveiling of the agendas and positions in the literary market of important mediators such as the Portuguese poets Fernando Pessoa and Jorge de Sena. This article also helped to shape, for our editorial team, the idea of where to go next with the study of Poe and the concept of the anthology.

5. The question of number is often blurred when discussing a "collection" across linguistic boundaries. In English, the term usually refers to a single volume while in the romance languages a *colección* (Spanish), *coleção* (Portuguese), *collezione* (Italian), *colectie* (Romanian), or *collection* (French) most often designates an editorial line or series.

6. The interpretative framework, critical viewpoint, and agendas of anthologies can be motivated by various causes and purposes, basically enumerated by Patricia Odber de Baubeta in the multivolume project, *The Anthology in Portugal*: "[An anthology's] selection could be made for any number of reasons: in order to convey a particular *message* (moral, religious, sentimental, ideological), to illustrate a *theme* (see, for example, all the Christmas anthologies that have been published in Portugal over the years), or to exemplify a particular mode of expression, a *literary school or artistic trend*, to allow the anthologist to *share his or her favourite* poems or stories with the reading public, to present readers with what are purportedly *the best or most beautiful* lyrics, the most moving or even the most terrifying short stories, or allow *a publishing house to foreground its authors*" (34; emphasis added).

7. By the same token, Theo Hermans uses the phrase "prejudice of perception" to refer to the translator's interference with the original, and it could likewise be said of editors that they "construct or produce their originals," and sometimes even "invent" them (95).

8. In the entry devoted to "Anthologies of Translation" in the first edition of *The Routledge Encyclopedia of Translation Studies*, Armin Paul Frank makes a similar point: "The arrangement, the configuration, creates a meaning and value greater than the sum of meanings and values of the individual items taken in isolation, and translation anthologies are important manifestations of this phenomenon" (13).

9. In this respect, also, anthologies arguably hold a more central place in the United States than in any other culture. Since the early nineteenth century, their double function of "historicizing" and inspiring (Golding, *From Outlaw to Classic* 6) a characteristically American repository has singularly placed them as a sort of frontier or crossroads, embodying representativeness and mobility, individual ingenuity, and democratic inclusion (Lockard and Sandell 229).

10. We are indebted to Aleix Tura Vecino, who has shared with us his insights and bibliography from his PhD research on the short-story anthology, and whose paper—"Affect and the Women-Only Short Story Anthology," presented in Lisbon at the 2018 Conference of the Society for the Short Story in English—inspired us to further explore the link between the anthology and affect theory.

Works Cited

Ahmed, Sara. *The Cultural Politics of Emotion*. Routledge, 2013.

Audet, René. "To Relate, to Read, to Separate: A Poetics of the Collection and A Poetics of Diffraction." *Cycles, Recueils, Macrotexts: The Short Story Collection in Theory and Practice*, special issue of *Interférences littéraires/Literaire interferenties*, edited by Elke d'Hoker and Bart Van den Bossche, vol. 12, February 2014, pp. 35–45.

Boddy, Kasia. "Variety in Unity, Unity in Variety: The Liminal Space of the American Short-Story Anthology." *Liminality and the Short Story: Boundary Crossings in American, Canadian, and British Writing*, edited by Jochen Achilles and Ina Bergmann, Routledge, 2014, pp. 145–56.

Csicsila, Joseph. *Canons by Consensus: Critical Trends and American Literature Anthologies.* U of Alabama P, 2004.

Di Leo, Jeffrey R. "Analyzing Anthologies." *On Anthologies: Politics and Pedagogy,* edited by Di Leo, U of Nebraska P, 2004, pp. 1–27.

———. *Anthologies.* Special issue of *symplokē,* vol. 8, nos. 1–2, 2000.

———, editor. *On Anthologies: Politics and Pedagogy.* U of Nebraska P, 2004.

Esplin, Emron. "Poe and His Global Advocates." *The Oxford Handbook of Edgar Allan Poe,* edited by J. Gerald Kennedy and Scott Peeples, Oxford UP, 2019, pp. 599–617.

Esplin, Emron, and Margarida Vale de Gato. "Introduction: Poe in/and Translation." *Translated Poe,* edited by Esplin and Vale de Gato, Lehigh UP, 2014, pp. xi–xxi, 329–33.

Essman, Helga, and Armin Paul Frank. "Translation Anthologies: An Invitation to the Curious and a Case Study." *Target,* vol. 3, no. 1, 1991, pp. 65–96.

Ferry, Anne. *Tradition and the Individual Poem: An Inquiry into Anthologies.* Stanford UP, 2001.

Frank, Armin Paul. "Anthologies of Translation." *Routledge Encyclopedia of Translation Studies,* edited by Mona Baker, Routledge, 1998, pp. 13–14.

Fraistat, Neil. *The Poem and the Book: Interpreting Collections of Romantic Poetry.* U of North Carolina P, 1985.

Golding, Alan C. *From Outlaw to Classic: Canons in American Poetry.* U of Wisconsin P, 1995.

———. "A History of American Poetry Anthologies." *Canons,* edited by Robert von Hallberg, U of Chicago P, 1984, pp. 279–307.

Hermans, Theo. *Translation in Systems. Descriptive and System-Oriented Approaches Explained.* St. Jerome Publishing, 1999.

Kennedy, J. Gerald. "From Anderson's Winesburg to Carver's Cathedral: The Short Story Sequence and the Semblance of Community." *Modern American Short Story Sequences,* edited by Kennedy, Cambridge UP, 1995, pp. 194–215.

Kennedy, J. Gerald, and Scott Peeples. "Introduction: The Unfolding Investigation of Edgar Poe." *The Oxford Handbook of Edgar Allan Poe,* edited by Kennedy and Peeples, Oxford UP, 2019, pp. 1–17.

Kilcup, Karen L. "The Poetry and Prose of Recovery Work." *On Anthologies: Politics and Pedagogy,* edited by Jeffrey R. Di Leo, U of Nebraska P, 2004, pp. 112–38.

Lauter, Paul. "Taking Anthologies Seriously." *Pedagogy, Canon, Context: Toward a Redefinition of Ethnic American Literary Studies,* special issue of *MELUS,* vol. 29, nos. 3–4, 2004, pp. 19–39. doi:10.2307/4141840.

Lefevere, André. *Translating Literature: Practice and Theory in a Comparative Literature Context.* MLA, 1992.

Lockard, Joe, and Jillian Sandell. "National Narratives and the Politics of Inclusion: Historicizing American Literature Anthologies." *Pedagogy: Critical Approaches to Teaching Literature, Language, Composition, and Culture,* vol. 8, no. 2, 2008, pp. 227–54.

Lundén, Rolf. *The United Stories of America: Studies in the Short Story Composite.* Rodopi, 1999.

Mujica, Barbara. "Teaching Literature: Canon, Controversy, and the Literary Anthology." *Hispania*, vol. 8, no. 2, 1997, pp. 203–15.

Odber de Baubeta, Patricia Anne. *The Anthology in Portugal: A New Approach to the History of Portuguese Literature in the Twentieth Century.* Peter Lang, 2007.

Price, Leah. *The Anthology and the Rise of the Novel: From Richardson to George Eliot.* Cambridge UP, 2000.

Seruya, Teresa, Lieven D'hulst, Alexandra Assis Rosa, and Maria Lin Moniz, editors. *Translation in Anthologies and Collections (19th and 20th Centuries).* John Benjamins, 2013.

Vale de Gato, Margarida. "100 Years and Something of Poe in Portuguese Anthologies." *The Anthology in Portugal*, vol. 2, edited by Patricia Odber de Baubeta, Margarida Vale de Gato, and Maria de Lurdes Sampaio, Peter Lang, 2013, pp. 153–219.

Vecino, Aleix T. "Affect and the Women-Only Short Story Anthology." Beyond History: The Radiance of the Short Story—15th International Conference of the Short Story in English, 27 June 2018, Faculdade de Letras, U of Lisboa. Panel Presentation.

Vines, Lois Davis, editor. *Poe Abroad: Influence, Reputation, Affinities.* U of Iowa P, 1999.

PART I

DECIDING WHO BELONGS AND WHERE THEY FIT: (PROTO) ANTHOLOGIES OF THE 1840s

CHAPTER ONE

~

Anthology, Relational Aesthetics, and the (Dis)unity of Affect

Poe Collects People and Griswold Frames Poe

Jana L. Argersinger

Words from Edgar Allan Poe, relative to Margaret Fuller:

> The supposition that the book of an author is a thing apart from the author's self, is, I think, ill-founded. . . . [Miss Fuller's] personal character and her printed book are merely one and the same thing. We get access to her soul as directly from the one as from the other. . . . Her acts are bookish, and her books are less thoughts than acts.

This excerpt comes from Poe's literary and personal profile of the writer, published in "The Literati of New York City," his 1846 anthology of forty-one such profiles serialized in *Godey's Lady's Book*. As J. Gerald Kennedy notes in his article "Inventing the Literati," the Fuller that Poe pictures here is an avatar of the author whom Barthes and Foucault will pronounce dead to literary criticism some 120 years later (26; cf. 13–14). I would argue that she can also stand, with caveats, for the author who has nevertheless persisted, to be recovered in recent years as a legitimate subject for study.[1] And I propose extending this renewed recognition beyond the author *in propria persona* to the author in human relation. Poe, like his Fuller, is not "a thing apart" from his text; nor are he and his text "a thing apart" from the human others around him.

That interpersonality manifests itself in form, what I want to present as a relational aesthetics—by taking up literary anthology as a genre in point that virtually requires us to account for its structures of human connection. The impulse to construct canons of authors together with their writings—to judge, select, relate—that commonly informs this genre propels the anthological projects, including "The Literati," of both Poe and his contemporaneous rival Rufus W. Griswold. They make for an odd couple, these two, in their fractious relations during life and after Poe's death: the legacy of Poe's affectively messy attempts to collect the literati and establish himself as arbiter of literary worth will run up against Griswold's destructive fixation on his departed competitor, which makes itself felt in the contours of his own ambitious anthologies. Aesthetic relation, a living web of intertextuality and interpersonality, can extend both within and between anthologies and their creators.

Such an interpersonal approach to literary work finds broad warrant in "relationship science"—which a 2017 report in the *Annual Review of Psychology* describes as a discipline with "growing coherence and influence . . . on myriad scholarly fields" in both soft and hard sciences (Finkel et al. 383), including, among others, attachment theory, affect theory, and interpersonal neurobiology. "Matters of belonging," to quote two theorists of affect—matters of integration and dis-integration, to echo the founder of interpersonal neurobiology—run through them all (Seigworth and Gregg 8; Siegel): belonging, being in secure relation, it seems increasingly clear, is a core need of human nature. As the 2017 report points out, "poets, novelists, and philosophers have long recognized the centrality of relationships to human existence" (383), while scientists have lagged behind. But as relationship science comes along, we can harvest its insights to further grow our own understanding of humanistic thinkers and creators. In interdisciplinarian E. O. Wilson's terms, this is a vital act of consilience. In literary scholar Clark Davis's view, it promotes a "hermeneutics of respect" for the author as a human communicant aspiring to relate.[2]

Matters of Belonging and
Poe's "The Literati of New York City"

Those familiar with Poe's biography, both personal and vocational, know how fraught it often was with painful "matters of belonging." A significant through line in his life's story, if not the only one, shows him beset by alcoholism, poverty, and professional estrangement, bereft of loved ones early and often, and destined to die at age forty in mysterious circumstances, uncomforted by close friends or family. What "The Literati of New York City" manifests in anthology form, I would suggest, is this: the relational imperative under stress. "The Literati," densely peopled as it is, makes conspicuous the effect that the urge to relate, in all its complicated individual expressions, can have on the shape of a text. In this case, a proprietary will—Poe's—tries to constellate a crowd of literary individuals (and intended readers, many of whom are the self-same literary individuals) into relation with himself and with each other. We know the high stakes of this enterprise for him: it is one in a linked series of attempts to construct an American literary canon.[3] But the literati, it turns out, can be difficult to collect and organize. Readers don't always take well to direction. And the anthologizer's own relational dispositions, his complex affective drives—toward love, friendship, antagonism, community, jealousy, power, creative accomplishment, recognition, affluence—prove just as hard to order. In other words, both self and others sometimes resist integration, the *sine qua non* of human systems, as interpersonal neurobiology would have it.

Poe *was*, in celebrated ways, a master of design—pleasurably intent on manipulating readers and, by his own account, on holding them in narrative thrall through well-crafted "unity of effect," to name one key aesthetic principle that he applies most explicitly to poems and tales ("Philosophy of Composition" 164).[4] An anthology is, of course, a different kind of text than a poem or a tale, but the genre by its nature offers the potential for masterminding: the anthologizer might step into the role of literary potentate, shaping a canon for the culture-minded public according to his own vision and judgment—which, in the case of Poe, has to do with American literary nationalism, in tension at times with literary globalism.[5] Contemporaneous critic E. P. Whipple finds a dark version of this potential realized in Poe's earlier "Autography" series, calling him out as a high-handed pretender to "absolute power" (112). In "The Literati of New York City," however, Poe is curiously at pains to disavow design, to abjure some of that formal authority commonly considered proper to the anthologizer—insisting at such a pitch as to give one pause. This series, Poe asserts in his subtitle and preface to "The Literati," simply offers "in brief" some "unbiased" and "honest opinions at random respecting [the literati's] autorial [sic] merits, with occasional words of personality" (May 194)—and "the length of each article," he suggests in later unpublished notes, is not meant to be "taken as the measure of the author's importance" ("Living Writers" 2). Following no "precise order or arrangement" in his notices of both male and female writers, most of whom he purports to know well, Poe conveys not only his own views but those of "conversational society" in the "literary circles" to which he claims special entrée, exposing in print what had been shared in private ("The Literati," May 194). "The Literati" will be something of a jumble, he implies, and this purported jumble is an aesthetic effect worth studying as such.

What strikes me about Poe's claims here, along with the content and structure of the profiles themselves, is the extent to which they entangle matters of literary form with matters of relationship and feeling. "The Literati of New York City," in fact, seems at the point of bursting with affect, putting under pressure Poe's aim of building an elite, cohesive "republic of letters" ("Prospectus of the Penn")—with all the gravitas such an undertaking may require. It does appear likely that the practical need for income entered into the hash of motives behind, for example, the decision by Poe himself and/or by *Godey's* editors to let fly the famously scathing wit he wielded as a literary reviewer in order to whip up controversy for the sake of sales (Weiner 16–17; Cassuto).[6] Some readers (perhaps profiled literati among them) obliged, responding with outrage to the emotional manipulation of their allegiances; and, according to the editors, sales did soar. A statement from the editors on the second installment of "Literati" sounds its own notes of relational anxiety and defiance:

> We have received several letters from New York, anonymous and from *personal friends*, requesting us to be careful what we allow Mr. Poe to say of the New York authors, many of whom are our *personal friends*. We reply to one and all, that we have nothing to do but publish Mr. Poe's opinions, *not our own*. . . . We are not to be intimidated by a threat of the loss of *friends*, or turned from our purpose by honeyed words. . . . The May edition was exhausted before the first of May. . . . ("Editors' Table"; some emphasis added)

But I suspect this reader response did not sit entirely well with Poe, impoverished though he was. There was certainly delight for him in wielding the reviewer's tomahawk;[7] and there would have been satisfaction in provoking scandal at will. But securing authority over a band of American literary honorables he himself had assembled? That would require a consistently measured critique that commanded the respect both of those honorables and of discerning readers. Such insightful criticism does appear, but in tension with, often jostling against, vividly personal attacks, plaudits, expressions of pique or jealousy, and stirrings of attraction.

We can see these impulses mixing it up in the aesthetic spaces of Poe's profiles, which typically begin with a digest of the subject's professional life and an appraisal of his or her work and then conclude with what Poe's subtitle has termed "words of personality," divining character and attitude from manner and appearance. Of N. P. Willis—tale-writer, poet, editor, and friend—Poe begins by saying, "Whatever may be thought of [his] talents . . . he has made a good deal of noise in the world—at least for an American"

("The Literati," May 196). "His success," however, "is to be attributed one-third to his mental ability and two-thirds to his physical temperament" (196). "Unseen Spirits," a poem of Willis's that Poe includes, is graced with "true *imagination*," even if the "whole *finale* is feeble" (198). Willis is a "remarkably well-looking man," though "neither his nose nor his forehead can be defended," and "the latter would puzzle phrenology" (199). Two other notices exemplify the often-remarked tendency in Poe's literary criticism to boost women of the pen, to seriously critique and praise more often than bury them—a tendency less conspicuous in his treatment of men.[8] Margaret Fuller, whose "Literati" profile is one of the longest and most intellectually engaged, emerges as a writer of "high genius." Fuller's *Woman in the Nineteenth Century* is brilliant, and while Poe shares its conclusions only in part, the dissent is generally rendered with respect. She does bear the taint, alas, of transcendentalism, and her "ignorance of grammar" is a little hard to forgive (August 72–73). Frances Sargent Osgood—successful poet, author, and partner in public literary flirtation—warrants Poe's close critical attention and effusive applause, couched at times in the language of seduction: "I feel tempted to copy some seven or eight of the later poems, but the deep interest of my subject has already led me too far" (September 128). Writer Charles Fenno Hoffman gives occasion for lambasting Rufus Griswold for "indiscriminate . . . approbation" of Hoffman in his ambitious 1842 *Poets and Poetry of America* (October 157–58). And Richard Adams Locke, editor of the popular newspaper that put the famous "Moon Hoax" over on readers, holds pride of place at the conclusion of "The Literati" (October 159–62)—a suggestive choice for a proudly designing author who claims not to be a designing anthologizer.

Finally, embedded in the anthology's profile of poet Fitz-Greene Halleck is an entertaining exercise in canon-building—an anthological *mise en abyme* whose language jumps, in rapid turns, between the overbearing and the unassuming.

> Our principal poets are, perhaps, most frequently named in this order—Bryant, Halleck, Dana, Sprague, Longfellow, Willis, and so on. . . . The accuracy of the arrangement as above made may, indeed, be questioned. For my own part, I should have it thus—Longfellow, Bryant, Halleck, Willis, Sprague, Dana; and . . . there are three or four comparatively unknown writers whom I would place in the series between Bryant and Halleck. . . . Two dozen at least might find room between Sprague and Dana—this latter, I fear, owing a very large portion of his reputation to his *quondam* editorial connection with "The North American Review." One or two poets now in my minds [sic] eye I should have

no hesitation in posting above even Mr. Longfellow—still not intending this as very extravagant praise. (July 13)

This explicitly judgmental act of ranking fellow writers—the flaunting, if sometimes coy, display of power over such luminaries as Dana and Longfellow (Poe's *bête noire*)—stands in tension with the casual act of aggregation that, Poe insists, brought forth "The Literati" series as a whole. It is a small outbreak of order driven at least in part by animus, pride, and jealous ambition. Here, affect maps briefly into a relatively disciplined hierarchy, notably all male, that is subject to the movements of Poe's will—a hierarchy that is yet contained within something close to affective chaos.

It is not that other anthologizers of Poe's time were necessarily paragons of disinterestedness. Their projects often betray the signs of vexed ego, however veiled or downplayed or earnestly disavowed. Humble-braggers are hardly scarce among editorial practitioners of anthology, a genre prone to tense imbalances, to the collector's wavering between self-directed ambition on the one hand and responsibility toward those collected on the other. The preface to the first volume of John Keese's *Poets of America* (1840), for example, laments American literature's obscurity—"We have left our pearls unstrung"—and declares, semi-humbly, that "the design of the present volume, is in some degree, to repair the deficiency" (10). Who is more important here, the pearl-stringer or the pearls to be strung? Manifesting other forms of partiality, Griswold, though sometimes given to touting the impersonality of his literary judgments, uses anthological means to puff friends and eventually to bloody the reputation of the dead Poe himself. As this chapter's second section explores in greater depth, Griswold's 1850 edition of Poe's works includes the notoriously venomous "Memoir of the Author" (much expanded from the earlier obituary he published under the name "Ludwig"), to which the many subsequent editions of his *Poets and Poetry of America* and his post-1850 editions of *The Prose Writers of America* refer.[9]

Poe engages in conduct similar to Griswold's. But, he wears a distinct form of interestedness in extraordinarily—even excruciatingly—plain sight, despite his own claim to objectivity in the "Literati" preface. The collection in *Godey's* displays, for all to see, not the rounded results of a careful vetting, but the messy and sometimes savage process of vetting itself—a strikingly personalized, fundamentally relational, and affect-charged choice. And it is a formal choice, I would argue, that gives rise to its own purportedly unregulated form. Does Poe admit into "The Literati of New York City" only those he considers canonically fit? No. He admits some he means to disqualify, sharpening his critical knives for the job—in order to cause a commotion, yes, but also to make a case for his cultural authority and to create a web of relationship to his liking. We see him planning his republic of letters by marking undesirables for exile—and more of them are marked than not. The citizenry of Poe's republic promises to be a small, select group, and that is part of the ambition—but we are left to wonder how lonely it will be.

This question of finding the circumference of relation best suited to one's aims and desires expresses itself in the geography of Poe's successive efforts, from the mid-1830s through 1848, to design a canon. Poe's two "Autography" series, one in the *Southern Literary Messenger* (1836) and an expanded version in *Graham's* (1841–1842), analyze the handwriting of cultural notables from New England, New York, Philadelphia, the Deep South, and, in the second series, the frontier; "The Literati of New York City" dramatically tightens its focus to what Poe now considers the literary heart and "fair representa[tive]" of all America (May 195). "The Living Writers of America" (1846–1847), Poe's unfinished critical history (alternatively titled "Literary America"), then laments the lack of "centralization," which in his opinion "gives birth to a peculiar [regional] *cliquism*" (1, full front). And last, an 1848 prospectus for Poe's never-realized literary magazine, the *Stylus*, establishes a center much smaller than a city: to succeed, Poe asserts, such a magazine must be informed by "*individuality*," "continuity," and "a marked certainty of purpose," and these qualities are "attainable only where one mind alone has at least the general control." Here, the master designer or, in Whipple's less admiring sobriquet, "literary dictator" (111) makes himself heard.

In this expansion and contraction lies a pattern of interpersonal flux that maps onto Poe's shifting ideas of U.S. literary identity (as well as his own regional identity). A literary theory of affect that is germane to the key question of scale involves "critical discourses of the emotions" that have "progressively left behind the interiorized self or subjectivity" to "unfold regimes of expressivity tied" to "diffusions of feeling," "often including atmospheres of sociality, crowd behaviors, contagions of feeling" (Seigworth and Gregg 8). I am interested in networks of individual communicants, like Poe and those he represents in "The Literati," that lie partway along the sliding scale of relation—between the "interiorized self" (Poe's "one mind alone . . . in general control") and broad "atmospheres of sociality" (a circumference expanding to the point of impersonality)—and how they manifest themselves in aesthetics. It may be that stretching too far afield makes the network of literati uncomfortably diffuse, bringing it too close to facelessness, for a literary self so achingly and at the same time so discordantly alive to relational experience. But "one mind alone" makes little allowance for communion—falling short of what Daniel Siegel (founder of interpersonal neurobiology) has recently defined, on the basis of interdisciplinary research, as healthy "mind": the embodied brain and relations to the other, all composed into a dynamic integrated system (*Developing Mind*, esp. 1–10). Within the framework of interpersonal neurobiology (IPNB) and psychology's attachment theory, prominent among related fields, the need for relations that are securely reciprocal or integrated runs deep in human beings, and the ways in which that need finds healthy, sustainable fulfillment—or becomes to some degree blocked, distorted, misdirected—have to be understood as fundamental to any system, whether within or among individuals in social, in political, or, as I suggest here, in literary form.

The vitality of such systems within and beyond the so-called "individual" mind, as suggested by IPNB, depends on flexibility—on the capacity to shift and grow over time by incorporating new elements, respecting their differences, and at the same time maintaining the network's meaning as a coherent, integrated system. In IPNB, the mathematical concept of "maximal complexity" becomes Siegel's representation of the greatest number of parts that can integrate into any smoothly working aggregate, whether of mind, of close relational circles, or of larger communities (*Pocket Guide* 16-3 through 16-5); as one luminous analogy, Siegel offers a chorus in harmonious and at the same time manifold ensemble, comprising individual voices and sections (*Developing Mind* 347). On the other hand, an unintegrated system, one that is "not linking its differentiated parts, . . . not moving to maximize complexity, . . . moves either toward chaos or rigidity" (*Pocket Guide* 16-4).[10] This model of relationality tends to de-center and is by nature scalable—into social, political, and economic groups of various sizes, for instance—in partial contrast to attachment theory, which concentrates on the imperative of secure relationship between two individuals, provoking the question of whether and how such necessary security can live within necessary flux on expanding interpersonal scales.[11]

In literary consilience with these findings, Paul Lauter observes that "an anthology . . . is like a culture itself, a work always in progress"—an unsteady state perpetually challenged by "issues of inclusiveness and value," and in tandem with these, I would stress, by issues of scale (29).[12] Under such lights, one way to understand Poe's literati project is to see it as an idiosyncratic failure of integration, an attempt to establish the authorial self at the center of an anthological web of people and texts that stays unsteady—not because it is growing and incorporating and proceeding toward maximal complexity, but because it is roiling with affective crossfire. It moves, not toward the coherence of Siegel's harmonious chorus, but toward chaos—a jumble. Poe, in other words, is being quintessentially human in his enterprise, seeking interpersonal grace even as he reaches for the egotistical sublime[13]—grappling along the way with peculiarities of temperament, personal and historical circumstance, and generic constraint.

On one page of the manuscript of "The Living Writers of America," Poe sketches a simple but telling image: a large circle, and next to it the phrase "Circular battle of authors." In this moment of reflection and planning, later in life and career than he knows, Poe envisions a potential community of letters turned in on itself at the edge of mutual destruction. His "Literati" project strains for the symmetry of completion, for the authority he seems to believe completion will bring. But neither the center nor the circumference is inclined to hold.

Matters of Fixation: Poe According to Griswold and Osgood

Just two months after Poe's death in October 1849, Frances Osgood—his friend, sometime partner in literary courtship, and herself one of his collected literati—reminisces in a brighter tone about his canonical project:

> One morning, towards the close of [Poe's] residence in this city . . . I found him just completing his series of papers entitled "The Literati of New-York." "See," said he, displaying, in laughing triumph, several little rolls of narrow paper, (he always wrote thus for the press,) "I am going to show you, by the difference of length in these, the different degrees of estimation in which I hold all you literary people. In each of these, one of you is rolled up and fully discussed. Come, Virginia, help me!" And one by one they unfolded them. At last they [came] to one which seemed interminable. Virginia laughingly ran to one corner of the room with one end, and her husband to the opposite with the other. "And whose lengthened sweetness long drawn out is that?" said I. "Hear her!" he cried, "just as if her little vain heart didn't tell her it's herself!" ("Reminiscences" 118; Pollin, "Frances Sargent Osgood" 31–32)

The genesis story of Poe's collection of people had belonged to Poe, and now it escapes his hands: Osgood rewrites it, putting lighthearted, affectionate—if not indisputably fictional—words in his mouth. She rewrites, strikingly, one of the very points about which he was most emphatically explicit: that length does not matter. (Her profile is indeed one of the longest.)

This passage, in fact, excerpts a longer memorial by Osgood that demonstrates, in its movement through webs of rhetoric, publication, and reprinting,[14] how relational aesthetics can work not only within but among anthologies and other texts, disrespecting the boundaries between them and challenging the concept of singular proprietary authorship—as the genre of edited anthology itself does by virtue of inherent authorial instability. In the memorial's patterns of migration, Rufus Griswold, mutual acquaintance of Osgood and Poe—and Poe's competitor in the business of curating the American literati—is the prime mover, the dominant figure in what could be called a "circular battle of anthologizers." And the system is informed by repetition and rigidity, one sign in IPNB of dis-integration, of homogenization as opposed to the relative chaos of Poe's anthologies.

Osgood's piece first appeared anonymously, under the header "Written for *Saroni's Musical Times*," as "Reminiscences of Edgar A. Poe" in the December 8, 1849, issue of Herrman Saroni's periodical. In September 1850, the piece resurfaced almost unchanged in the front matter to volume 3 of Griswold's *The Works of the Late Edgar Allan Poe* (first edition)—spliced in, with Osgood's name unveiled, toward the end of the editor's much longer and darker "Memoir of the Author" (xxxvi–xxxviii). According to this "Memoir," which posts the "Ludwig" Poe at the gateway to a collection of his own critical works ("The Literati" dominant among them), the author was a misanthropic genius consumed by vulgar ambition who "walked the streets, in madness or melancholy": "He believed in nobody, and cared for nobody. . . . He became, and was an Ishmaelite" (xxxviii, xxxix). All of this, Griswold asserts, makes itself felt in Poe's writing—brilliant though the editor allows much of that writing to be (xxxvii).

For fourteen decades, the 1850 printing of Osgood's memorial of Poe within Griswold's memoir was assumed to be the first, so effectively did Griswold set about his several acts of coverture. He neglects to acknowledge the *Saroni's* publication, and then goes so far as to contrive a sentimental scene in which Osgood explicitly promises to compose her account especially for his anthology.[15] In Griswold's telling, Osgood had from her invalid bed offered "Reminiscences" as counterbalance or supplement to his "harsher" estimations, which she nonetheless considered, he says, "perfectly just" when it came to Poe's "relations with men." With women, she declared, Poe "was different" ("Memoir" xxxvi). Griswold folds this difference, Osgood's text, into "Memoir of the Author" and calls it proof of impartiality, inoculating himself against criticism of his intemperate attacks on Poe. But an odor of fraud lies about his frame story.

In 1990, Burton Pollin would announce that he had uncovered the original publication, presenting in a journal article the text itself along with evidence that Griswold and Poe as well as Osgood were familiar with *Saroni's*, possibly with Herrman Saroni himself, and tracing out as far as possible "a tangled set of interrelationships" among people and texts (34). Like biographer Kenneth Silverman, Pollin sees in the complex disaffections between

Griswold and Poe an element of rivalry over Osgood, but his study of "Reminiscences" admits the possibility of a third admirer (Silverman 280, 342; Pollin, "Frances Sargent Osgood" 28–30). If Osgood and Saroni were also more than acquaintances, Griswold's handling of her text's "prehistory" would achieve at least two things: the blunt erasure of one competitor, Saroni, altogether; and the posthumous overthrow of another, Poe, accomplished by situating Osgood as his own closer intimate. All the while, Griswold elevates himself as the superior maker of canons.

Conjuring a primal scene for "Reminiscences of Edgar A. Poe" to displace the original setting is a neat—a relationally insidious—rhetorical ploy that makes the most of what lies conveniently at hand: Osgood's language. Griswold's narrative moves directly from the scene between Griswold and Osgood into the memorial itself: "You ask me, my friend, to write for you my reminiscences of Edgar Poe," says Osgood. "For you, who knew and understood my affectionate interest in him, and my frank acknowledgment of that interest to all who had a claim upon my confidence, for you, I will willingly do so" ("Memoir" xxxvi). For you, for you, for you, my friend: the pulse of Osgood's prose bespeaks a tender confidence, a close attachment, and Griswold has intercepted it—substituting himself in the new frame story as antecedent for those second-person references. (Although the person addressed in the unframed *Saroni's* printing stays unspecified, the periodical's editor is the implicit antecedent.) Griswold has engulfed Osgood's kindlier account, including her revision of Poe's "Literati" story, creating a re-revision by inventing a new context and redirecting the story's internal referents. Her version of the story will remain half-occluded in Griswold's memoir for almost a century and a half.

Appropriate and repeat—this emerges as a broad Griswoldian strategy. Having made Osgood's irresistible rhetoric of repetition his own, Griswold multiplies and capitalizes on it in a plexus of numerous editions and reprintings of his *Works of the Late Edgar Allan Poe* (the standard edition for twenty-five years), as well as an intersecting network of references to "Memoir of the Author" and the pseudonymous "Ludwig" obituary in Griswold's multi-author anthologies. Again and again from 1850 to 1871, relentlessly, his "Memoir" appears in *Works* with Osgood's memorial embedded. In the front matter to volume 3 of the first edition, it follows a preface in which Griswold defends his October 1849 obituary (adducing letters from Poe to himself, some questionable in authenticity, to show an amicable relationship).[16] Poe's essay "The Poetic Principle" comes next, and after that "The Literati of New-York City," which Griswold, two pages before Osgood's piece, has swept aside along with Poe's literary criticism generally: "A volume might be filled with passages to show that [Poe's] criticisms were guided by no sense of duty, and that his opinions were so variable and so liable to be influenced by unworthy considerations as to be really of no value whatever" (xxxiv)—this, at the head of the very volume that contains one of Poe's most ambitious and concerted critical efforts. Griswold's imagined collection of damning examples tries to void, in advance, the actual collection that follows, Poe's fullest published realization of his "republic of letters."[17]

In the 1853 and subsequent editions of *Works*, Griswold places his memoir at the head of volume 1. And repeatedly, near-obsessively, in headnotes to Poe selections, Griswold's other often-reprinted anthologies (*The Poets and Poetry of America* and *The Prose Writers of America*) perpetuate the nightmarish Poe by referring back to that memoir and the obituary that preceded it. The circles of recursion are everywhere. The defensive preface to the volume 3 "Memoir" in Griswold's first edition had pointed to a piece by N. P. Willis printed at the head of volume 1: several paragraphs from Griswold's obituary "having been quoted by . . . Willis, in his Notice of Mr. Poe, were as part of that Notice unavoidably reprinted in the volume of the deceased author's Tales" (v). Passive voice notwithstanding, however, Griswold himself had solicited the reprinting. Similarly, to pre-empt dissent, he appropriates voices and opinions. In the preface, he presumes to say of the "Ludwig" notice, "As every one who knew its subject readily perceived, [it] was a very kind article" (v). And this "kind article" had presumptuously announced at the outset: "[The news of Poe's death] will startle many, but few will be grieved by it. The poet was well known . . . but he had few or no friends" (2). Griswold, in his campaign against Poe, proves to be a master of coopted pronouns, ventriloquisms, and self-referential loops: a textual self *en abyme* abetted by the conventions of anthology that moves, not toward maximal complexity, not toward chaos, but toward rigidity—a Griswoldian "unity of effect."

This mighty will to power, more determined and ultimately more effective than Poe's, finds expression in the anthological vehicle both men chose for their highest canon-making ambitions. And Poe himself has become powerless against the assault, dropped in death from the "circular battle of anthologizers." He had his posthumous defenders, certainly, but Griswold would long prevail. In light of my premise that authors are not "things apart" from their texts or from each other, it is shocking that Griswold used his rhetorical platform to execute a radical program of literary-social exile, severing Poe in posthumous reputation from the republic of letters and the company of humankind he sought to collect in "The Literati." Given what we are learning in consilient areas of research on human relationality and its imperatives, this may be the cruelest cut.

It is by no means, however, as if Poe honorably stayed his own critical "tomahawk" when it came to this rival—*The Poets and Poetry of America* is, in his partly self-concerned private and public judgments, both the "best collection" yet of the American poets and a "most outrageous humbug."[18] And it is not as if Poe's days never saw acclaim or the pleasure of society. Neither is it that Griswold's strategies of dominance secured unbroken influence and well-being—his last home was a small solitary room "decorated with portraits of himself, Fanny Osgood, and Poe" (Silverman 441). Partial by necessity, my brief study claims only space and time enough to explore one nexus in a much larger story of literary and human connectedness.

In his much-circulated "Memoir of the Author," Griswold opens the door to Osgood's portrayal of "social qualities" in Poe that she finds "beautiful" (xxxvi), and then he shuts it again with a dark rebuttal: the portrait of a man unworthy of literary authority, who "despise[d] a world which galled his self-conceit"—the memoir's last word (xxxix). By contrast, the creation tale Osgood tells about "The Literati" is poignant with the warmth of belonging that often eluded her friend in both personal and professional life; and as we now know, it first came into print when he was barely cold in his grave. Elsewhere in her reminiscence, Osgood sounds an unshaded celebratory note of human intercourse: "It was in his conversations and his letters, far more than in his published poetry and prose writings, that the genius of Poe was most gloriously revealed" (xxxviii). While I hope there is more of the truth in Osgood's account than in Griswold's, we cannot know just how closely either—or any—account, including Poe's own jumble, hews to lived reality. But that is fundamental to my point about anthology and relation.

As I have argued throughout this chapter, relational aesthetics assumes a singular relevance for the anthology, a genre constituted in motive interpersonality. Studying this interweave of affect and form in such collections as Poe's and Griswold's can turn us toward a respectful approach to authors that privileges neither biography nor text (nor indeed cultural and historical context) one above the other, that does not revive an idea of the isolate genius, or presume to find the farthest boundaries of complex human artists, their creations, and the intricate webs in which they live.

Notes

1. In one turn on the new author studies, which I source to Clark Davis and his book on Hawthorne's shyness (and through him to Emmanuel Levinas and Stanley Cavell, among other ethics theorists), we are enjoined to respect the hidden *and* the

public (or better, the farther *and* the nearer) faces of the author—that is, both the private self that lives partly in unknowable stretches beyond our reach as readers and the human interlocutor who can be—and ethically *must* be—recognized as agent in her or his own writing.

2. As Charles Gillispie's review of Wilson's book-length treatment of consilience puts it: "The goal . . . is to achieve progressive unification of all strands of knowledge in service to the indefinite betterment of the human condition" (280). Davis adopts the phrase "a hermeneutics of respect" from Robbins (28).

3. For invaluable work on this genealogy, see Kennedy's in-depth study as well as Hayes's chapter in *Poe and the Printed Word*. According to Kennedy, "various efforts to construct an idea of the literary nation and to install himself as a critical kingpin—by naming the country's principal literati, by promoting a quality periodical to feature U.S. authors exclusively, and by compiling materials for an American literary history—comprise an illuminating yet largely unappreciated dimension of Poe's achievement" (13).

4. Also see Poe's "Tale-Writing—Nathaniel Hawthorne," esp. 254; reprinted in Thompson, *Essays and Reviews*, 577–88.

5. In "The Living Writers of America," as Kennedy puts it, Poe "insisted that 'there should be *no* nationality' in our writing, which should rather aim for global appeal" ("Inventing" 27); also see https://www.eapoe.org/works/misc/livingw.htm.

6. In Sandra Tomc's illuminating account of Poe's tactics as reviewer and critic, marketplace motives course through not only "networks of cultural friendliness" but also "networks of hatred," their productive complement, among literary practitioners of his time (560).

7. Poe was known in some literary circles as the "tomahawk man" (Pollin, *Poe, Creator* 8–13).

8. See, for example, Eliza Richards's nuanced analysis of how Poe treated female poets (esp. 36–41). Matters of gender in "The Literati" and in Griswold's anthological framing of Poe (for example, his appropriation of Frances Osgood's "Reminiscences") call out for attention beyond what this essay can encompass.

9. See Silverman's chapter on the turbulent Poe-Griswold relationship, which includes details of Griswold's private and professional life—among them the magnitude of success attained by *The Poets and Poetry of America* (211–19). Jeffrey A. Savoye of the Edgar Allan Poe Society of Baltimore also addresses the Poe-Griswold relationship in helpful detail at https://www.eapoe.org/geninfo/poegrisw.htm.

10. In the related philosophical discipline of assemblage theory, as articulated in the work of Manuel DeLanda, relational fluidity takes the form of people, environments, ideas, and things (which can include texts) connected in assemblages that in turn can nest within and intersect with other assemblages, whose still-differentiated elements in some cases "disarticulate" and "rearticulate" into new assemblages—all processes that DeLanda typically describes in complex functional terms rather than Siegel's evaluative and more human-focused terms of mental well-being. Like interpersonal neurobiology, DeLanda's version of assemblage theory (derived from Gilles

Deleuze and Félix Guattari) moves both inherently and deliberately toward interdisciplinarity and consilience.

11. See Holmes for an overview of attachment theory, from its origins in John Bowlby's work on the child-caregiver bond through recent work that explores the adult-adult relationship. Also see Siegel's treatment of evolving attachment theory within the integrative framework of interpersonal neurobiology (*Pocket Guide* 20-1 through 20-12).

12. Similarly, Lawall describes anthology as "a theoretically interesting form whose potential for opening up discourse has yet to be sufficiently explored"—by which Lawall refers, in part, to the "web of communicative relationships" manifest in the genre and its audience (47). Ways to understand such potential and the barriers it faces may lie in intersections between theories of literary anthology, interpersonal neurobiology, and assemblage—among ideas of systemic openness.

13. For the term "egotistical sublime," see John Keats's letter to Richard Woodhouse, October 27, 1818.

14. See Meredith McGill on editorial and authorial proprietorship in mid-nineteenth-century America's culture of reprinting.

15. In "Frances Sargent Osgood and *Saroni's Musical Times*," Pollin asserts that Griswold almost certainly knew of the prior publication (32).

16. Pollin parses out an alternate scenario in which Griswold is less a villain—based on a letter Griswold attributed to Osgood, now extant only in unverified transcription, that seems to corroborate his claim to the first printing of "Reminiscences." On balance, however, the evidence against Griswold—including contradictory dates in his accounts, combined with what we know of his character and his practices (which demonstrably included forgery), and indications of a friendly acquaintance, at least, between Osgood and Saroni—seems for Pollin to weigh strongly in favor of *Saroni's* (32–33). Arthur Hobson Quinn makes a convincing case that Griswold, in his preface, altered and even invented letters from Poe to himself (668–71).

17. See Savoye's essay in this volume on Griswold's presentation (perhaps influenced by Poe) of "The Literati" in his edition. "By listing the reviews under the names of the authors," Savoye pertinently observes, "Poe—or Griswold—has, intentionally or unintentionally, made the focus more about the people and less about the works being evaluated" (80).

18. These remarks appear, respectively, in a review commissioned by Griswold, a mixed one as it turned out, that appeared in *Graham's Magazine*, June 1842 (*The Complete* 11: 124–26); and an 1842 letter to Joseph Snodgrass (*The Letters* 1: 341).

Works Cited

Cassuto, Leonard. Headnote to selections from "The Literati of New York City." *Edgar Allan Poe: Literary Theory and Criticism*, Dover, 1999.

Davis, Clark. *Hawthorne's Shyness: Ethics, Politics, and the Question of Engagement.* Johns Hopkins UP, 2005.

DeLanda, Manuel. Introduction. *Assemblage Theory*, by DeLanda, Edinburgh UP, 2016, pp. 1–8.

———. *A New Philosophy of Society: Assemblage Theory and Social Complexity*. Continuum, 2006.

"Editors' Table." *Godey's Lady's Book*, June 1846, p. 288. Edgar Allan Poe Society of Baltimore. https://www.eapoe.org/works/misc/litratb2.htm.

Finkel, Eli, Jeffry Simpson, and Paul Eastwick. "The Psychology of Close Relationships: Fourteen Core Principles." *Annual Review of Psychology*, vol. 68, 2017, pp. 383–411.

Gillispie, Charles C. "E. O. Wilson's *Consilience*: A Noble, Unifying Vision, Grandly Expressed." *American Scientist*, vol. 86, no. 3, 1998, pp. 280–83.

Griswold, Rufus Wilmot. (Ludwig). "Death of Edgar Allan Poe." *New York Tribune*, 9 October 1849, p. 2.

———. "Edgar A. Poe." *The Poets and Poetry of America*, edited by Griswold, 16th ed., Parry and McMillan, 1855, pp. 469–70.

———. "Edgar A. Poe." *The Prose Writers of America*, edited by Griswold, 4th ed., Hart, 1851, pp. 523–24.

———. "Memoir of the Author." *The Works of the Late Edgar Allan Poe*, edited by Griswold, vol. 3, Redfield, 1850, pp. vii–xxxix.

Hayes, Kevin. "The Road to *Literary America*." *Poe and the Printed Word*, by Hayes, Cambridge UP, 2000, pp. 98–111.

Holmes, Jeremy. *John Bowlby and Attachment Theory*. 2nd ed., Routledge, 2014.

Keats, John. *Selected Letters of John Keats*, edited by Grant Scott, revised ed., Harvard UP, 2002.

Keese, John. Preface. *The Poets of America: Illustrated by One of Her Painters*, vol. 1, Colman, 1840, pp. 9–12.

Kennedy, J. Gerald. "Inventing the Literati: Poe's Remapping of Antebellum Print Culture." *Poe and the Remapping of Antebellum Print Culture*, edited by J. Gerald Kennedy and Jerome McGann, Louisiana State UP, 2012, pp. 13–36.

Lauter, Paul. "Taking Anthologies Seriously." *Melus*, vol. 8, nos. 3–4, 2004, pp. 19–39.

Lawall, Sarah. "Anthologizing 'World Literature.'" *On Anthologies: Politics and Pedagogy*, edited by Jeffrey Di Leo, U of Nebraska P, 2004, pp. 47–89.

McGill, Meredith. *American Literature and the Culture of Reprinting, 1834–1853*. U of Pennsylvania P, 2002.

[Osgood, F. S.]. "Reminiscences of Edgar A. Poe." *Saroni's Musical Times*, 8 December 1849, pp. 118–19. Edgar Allan Poe Society of Baltimore, https://www.eapoe.org/papers/misc1827/fso18491.htm.

Poe, Edgar Allan. *The Complete Works of Edgar Allan Poe*, vol. 11. Edited by James Harrison, Thomas Y. Crowell, 1902.

———. *Edgar Allan Poe: Essays and Reviews*. Edited by G. R. Thompson, Library of America, 1984.

———. *The Letters of Edgar Allan Poe*. 3rd ed., edited by John Ward Ostrom, Burton R. Pollin, and Jeffrey Savoye, Gordian P, 2008. 2 vols.

———. "The Literati of New York City. Some Honest Opinions at Random Respecting their Autorial Merits, with Occasional Words of Personality." *Godey's Lady's Book*, May–October 1846. Edgar Allan Poe Society of Baltimore. https://www.eapoe.org/works/info/pmlny.htm.

———. "The Living Writers of America. Some Honest Opinions about their Literary Merits, with Occasional Words of Personality." 1846–1847, MA 624, Morgan Library New York, Edgar Allan Poe Society of Baltimore. https://www.eapoe.org/works/misc/livingw.htm.

———. "The Philosophy of Composition." *Graham's Magazine*, April 1846, pp. 163–67. Reprinted in Thompson, *Essays and Reviews*, pp. 13–25.

———. "Prospectus of the Penn Magazine." Broadside, 1 January 1841, Edgar Allan Poe Society of Baltimore. https://www.eapoe.org/works/misc/prosp004.htm.

———. "Prospectus of the Stylus." Broadside, April 1848, Edgar Allan Poe Society of Baltimore. https://www.eapoe.org/works/misc/prosp013.htm.

———. "Tale-Writing—Nathaniel Hawthorne." *Godey's Lady's Book*, November 1847, pp. 252–56. Reprinted in Thompson, *Essays and Reviews*, pp. 577–88.

Pollin, Burton R. "Frances Sargent Osgood and *Saroni's Musical Times*: Documents Linking Poe, Osgood, and Griswold." *Poe Studies*, vol. 23, 1990, pp. 27–36.

———. *Poe, Creator of Words*. Nicholas T. Smith, 1980.

Quinn, Arthur Hobson. *Edgar Allan Poe: A Critical Biography*. Appleton-Century, 1942.

Richards, Eliza. *Gender and the Poetics of Reception in Poe's Circle*. Cambridge UP, 2004.

Robbins, Jill. *Altered Reading: Levinas and Literature*. U of Chicago P, 1999.

Savoye, Jeffrey A. "Selecting for Posterity: Poe's Early Editors and the Battle for a Definitive Collection." *Anthologizing Poe: Editions, Translations, and (Trans)National Canons*, edited by Emron Esplin and Margarida Vale de Gato, Lehigh UP, 2020, pp. 75–98.

Seigworth, Gregory, and Melissa Gregg. "An Inventory of Shivers." *The Affect Theory Reader*, edited by Gregg and Seigworth, Duke UP, 2010, pp. 1–27.

Siegel, Daniel. *The Developing Mind, Second Edition: How Relationships and the Brain Interact to Shape Who We Are*. Guilford Press, 2012.

———. *Pocket Guide to Interpersonal Neurobiology: An Integrative Handbook of the Mind*. Norton, 2012.

Silverman, Kenneth. *Edgar A. Poe: Mournful and Never-ending Remembrance*. HarperPerennial, 1992.

Tomc, Sandra. "Edgar Allan Poe and His Enemies." *The Oxford Handbook of Edgar Allan Poe*, edited by J. Gerald Kennedy and Scott Peeples, Oxford UP, 2019, pp. 559–75.

Weiner, Bruce. *The Most Noble of Professions: Poe and the Poverty of Authorship.* Enoch Pratt Free Library, the Edgar Allan Poe Society, and the Library of the University of Baltimore, 1987.

[Whipple, E. P.]. "Mr. Edgar A. Poe's 'Chapter on Autography.'" *Boston Notion,* 18 December 1841. Quoted in Gerald E. Gerber, "E. P. Whipple Attacks Poe: A New Review," *American Literature,* vol. 53, 1981, pp. 110–13.

Wilson, Edward O. "Consilience among the Great Branches of Learning." *Science in Culture,* special issue of *Daedalus,* vol. 127, no. 1, 1998, pp. 131–49.

———. *Consilience: The Unity of Knowledge.* Vintage Books, 1998.

CHAPTER TWO

~

Poe as Anthologizer of Himself

Harry Lee Poe

During his lifetime, Edgar Allan Poe published four collections of poetry and three collections of short stories between 1827 and 1845. While Poe sought to earn his living by editing and writing for magazines and newspapers, he knew that his reputation and his fortune would be enhanced by the prestige and notoriety that came with the publication of a collection of his works. He did not have the usual criteria for selection that would normally govern an anthologist's decision about which of an author's works to include in an anthology because he never wanted to publish merely a selection of his stories. Instead, he always tried to interest publishers in producing his complete works. This study will demonstrate how Poe's conceptions of "unity of effect" and of variation in styles governed his anthological decisions, based mostly on the kinds of stories he decided to write and the order in which he would present them in his published and his hypothetical collections.

Most of all, Poe hoped to make his reputation as a great poet; however, fame did not accompany his first three volumes of poetry: *Tamerlane* (1827), *Al Aaraaf* (1829), and *Poems* (1831). In 1831, Poe changed his strategy. He began writing short stories in addition to poetry, and he submitted five short stories to a competition sponsored by the *Saturday Courier* in Philadelphia. He did not win the competition, but within a year, the *Courier* published all five stories. "Metzengerstein," his first published story, appeared in the January 14, 1832, issue (Thomas and Jackson 125). Shortly afterward came "The Duc de L'Omelette" on March 3, which was reprinted within the month in the *Minerva* of Baltimore and the *Literary Gazette* of Albany (126). The third story published was "A Tale of Jerusalem" on June 9 (127). On November 10, the *Saturday Courier* published "A Decided Loss," now known as "Loss of Breath," and on December 1, the same weekly published "The Bargain Lost," later revised as "Bon-Bon" (128). What these five stories have in common is that they are nothing alike, which demonstrates that from the very beginning of his fiction writing, Poe strived for variety in the kinds of tales he wrote.

We do not know the specific order in which Poe wrote his tales, though we know a general order. We know the publication date of his tales, so we know the general period in which they were written. We do not know, however, if "Metzengerstein" was written before "The Duc de L'Omelette," even though it was published first. If we are to discern a plan or strategy to the publication of his tales, we might do so by comparing the tales to see what kind of tales Poe chose to write.

In a letter to Philip Cooke on August 9, 1846, Poe explained the approach he had taken to writing his tales, always as pieces of a collective whole:

> In writing these Tales one by one, at long intervals, I have kept the book-unity always in mind—that is, each has been composed with reference to its effect as part of *a whole*. In this view, one of my chief aims has been the widest diversity of subject, thought, & especially *tone* & manner of handling. Were all my tales now before me in a large volume and as the composition of another—the merit which would principally arrest my attention would be the wide *diversity and variety*. You will be surprised to hear me say that (omitting one or two of my first efforts) I do not consider any one of my stories *better* than another. There is a vast variety of kinds and, in degree of value, these kinds vary—but each tale is equally good *of its kind*. The loftiest kind is that of the highest imagination—and, for this reason only, "Ligeia" may be called my *best* tale. (Ostrom et al. 1: 595–96)

One of the problems in describing the kinds of stories Poe was writing and how they fit together in a unified collection is that the kinds of stories went by different names, and even Poe was not consistent in how he referred to them. The common term "gothic tale," which so troubled Poe and which he avoided, is an example of an imprecise term that was more jargon and fad among literary people. To complicate matters even more, Poe's creativity led him to write types of stories that did not previously exist.[1] Poe described his first seventeen tales as "of a bizarre and generally whimsical character," and neither term provides a clear description (163). Poe once claimed that his literary criticism fell into two categories—he wrote "funny" criticism, of which

"Flaccus" is an example, and he wrote "serious" criticism, of which *Barnaby Rudge* is an example (487). In much the same way, Poe's stories tended to be "funny" or "serious." As we shall see, Poe's stories usually fell into these two categories throughout his writing career, though each of these classifications could take many shapes.[2]

Rather than define his stories in terms of genre or structure, Poe tended to define his stories in terms of their effect on the reader. A review from 1839 remarked, "We laughed at Mr. Poe's humorous sketch of 'The Man that was used up,' a tale of the late Kickaboo campaigns" (*New York Times* 2). His comic stories caused people to laugh; his serious stories did not. Poe was far too creative to limit himself to the constrictions of genre. He could write science fiction as comedy or horror. He could write horror as comedy. He might include a humorous episode for comic relief in a story that does not make the reader laugh, but that does not mean that Poe was not dead serious. He created variety and diversity by mingling elements of different kinds of stories.[3]

Poe's funny or comic stories included parody, farce, and romantic comedy, though he seems to have been particularly fond of satires, with a preference for the slapstick and the employment of outrageous names. These satires dealt with aspects of society that offended Poe greatly: pseudo-intellectual posturing, literary pretensions, quack scholarship, mob gullibility, and the corruption of vanity. His serious stories included crime, detective fiction, horror, suspense, science fiction, and romance. For his serious stories, Poe had the problem of appealing to the popular audience (for he wanted his stories to sell) without lowering his standards. Thus, his subject matter might come from the popular taste for blood and gore, but his manner of dealing with his subject left the blood and gore to the imagination of his readers. When he submitted "Berenice" to Thomas W. White for inclusion in the *Southern Literary Messenger* in 1835, White feared that the story would offend his readers. Poe defended the story on the grounds that this was precisely the kind of story that the public wanted, but he went on to explain the characteristics of the kind of tale he aimed to write in this vein: "the ludicrous heightened into the grotesque: the fearful coloured into the horrible: the witty exaggerated into the burlesque: the singular wrought out into the strange and mystical" (Ostrom et al. 1: 84). The story has the desired effect of lingering in the mind of the reader. It suggests blood and gore, but the horror itself lies within the imagination of the reader. This technique characterized Poe's serious tales throughout his career.

Poe had no control over the order of publication of his earliest stories, and he did not necessarily have a plan for the order in which he wrote different kinds of tales. For a collection of his stories presented to the public, however, the "unity of effect" in relation to the order of presentation in the whole collection became of paramount importance.[4] In addition to the unity of effect, Poe prized variety and originality. We see this variety in the first five short stories that Poe wrote and submitted to the *Saturday Courier*'s short story competition. We also see that the order of publication is not the order of presentation that Poe followed when he finally published his first collection of tales.

The first tale published in the *Saturday Courier*, "Metzengerstein," opened Poe to the charge of mere imitation of the German gothic tales so popular at the time. Poe set the tale in Hungary at an indeterminate time period and announced with the first word that it was a horror story. He reprinted the tale in the *Southern Literary Messenger* in January 1836 and included it in *Tales of the Grotesque and Arabesque* in 1840, where it appeared in the second volume as his twenty-first selection. In his plans for *Phantasy-Pieces*, Poe placed it as his twentieth selection with a new name—"The Horse-Shade." It is conspicuously absent from Poe's *Broadway Journal*, in which he reprinted almost all of his tales, perhaps because it reminded him of the criticism leveled against him as a writer of German gothic stories.

The second story, "The Duc de L'Omelette" (originally published as "The Duke de L'Omelette") contrasts dramatically with "Metzengerstein" in tone, mood, and subject matter. This comic tale involves a French duke who drops dead of shock upon being served ortolan without paper ornaments. Poe presented the punch line in French, leaving his less-educated audience to wonder what just happened. This story appeared as the sixth selection in volume 1 of *Tales of the Grotesque and Arabesque*, but Poe proposed moving it to his thirtieth selection in the never-published *Phantasy-Pieces*. Poe republished this story in the *Broadway Journal* on October 11, 1845.

For the third *Saturday Courier* story, "A Tale of Jerusalem," Poe turned to antiquity and the Roman conquest of Palestine for his setting, writing a story in which the Romans' prejudice against Jews not eating pork is turned against them. The story appeared in volume 2 as the eighteenth selection of *Tales of the Grotesque and Arabesque*, and as the twenty-ninth selection in *Phantasy-Pieces* with the revised name, "A Pig Tale." Poe printed this story in his *Broadway Journal* on September 20, 1845.

Poe changed the title of the third tale, "A Decided Loss," to "Loss of Breath" when he significantly expanded and reprinted it in the *Southern Literary Messenger* in September 1835. This farcical piece set in the United States was intended as a satire on "the extravagancies of Blackwood" (Ostrom et al. 1: 125). Poe placed this tale in volume 2 of *Tales of the Grotesque and Arabesque* as his twentieth selection, while it was slated to be twenty-fifth in *Phantasy-Pieces*. The story appeared in the *Broadway Journal* on January 3, 1846.

Venice was the original setting for "The Bargain Lost," the last *Saturday Courier* tale, published on December 1, 1832, but when Poe revised it for the *Southern Literary Messenger* in August 1835, he changed the setting to Paris and the title to "Bon-Bon." It is a story that once more resorts to gastronomy to expose the failings of "great" philosophers. This story made the first volume of *Tales of the Grotesque and Arabesque* as the eighth selection, and it was listed as the fourteenth selection for *Phantasy-Pieces*. Poe republished the story in the *Broadway Journal* on April 19, 1845.

Of these first five stories, only "Metzengerstein" can be described in any way as German gothic. Three ("The Duc de L'Omelette," "Loss of Breath," and "Bon-Bon") are comic tales. "A Tale of Jerusalem" comes close to being a morality tale as the Romans play a joke on the Jews, who turn the tables and drop the hog on their heads. Thus, Poe wrote three funny and two serious stories to submit to the *Saturday Courier* competition.

In June 1833, the *Baltimore Saturday Visiter* announced a literary competition with a 25 dollar prize for best poetry and a 50 dollar prize for best fiction (Thomas and Jackson 129). In May, a month before the announcement of the *Visiter* competition, Poe had offered a collection of his tales without success to the editors of the *New-England Magazine* as *Eleven Tales of the Arabesque*, which suggests that Poe had always conceived of his tales as a unified collection to be experienced as a whole (Ostrom et al. 1: 77). Poe submitted "The Coliseum" in the poetry category together with five, and possibly six, stories in the fiction category (Thomas and Jackson 133).[5] He lost the poetry competition, but he won the fiction competition with his tale "MS. Found in a Bottle," a dark story with supernatural elements set in the South Seas, which was published on October 19, 1833 (133). The five remaining stories that Poe had submitted to the *Saturday Visiter* competition began to appear in the *Southern Literary Messenger* with the publication of "Berenice," a dark psychological tale set in Europe, in the March 1835 issue (149). "Morella," a dark tale with occult elements, appeared in the April issue followed by "Lion-izing," a comic satire set in England, in May. "Hans Phaall—A Tale," a comic science fiction story set in Holland, came out in June. "The Visionary—A Tale" (later known as "The Assignation"), a dark love story set in Venice, was published in July (151, 155, 159–60, 163–64). Poe had now accumulated a collection of eleven short stories, and with them, he pursued a plan to publish a collection of stories to be called *Tales of the Folio Club*.[6] Thus, Poe added four serious tales and two funny tales to his collected works, for a total of six serious and five humorous tales. We should also note that

Poe set nine of his first eleven stories in different places and times ranging from ancient Rome to the Moon. He discovered that time and place could suggest a mood that his readers' imaginations would supply.

Tales of the Folio Club

In order to provide a structure that would create a sense of unity among the diverse tales included in the collection, Poe conceived of a group of writers, known as the Folio Club, who took turns reading their works at a monthly meeting. The stories in the planned volume *Tales of the Folio Club* are the stories told by each member of the fictional club.[7] Chaucer used a similar device to provide a sense of unity to *The Canterbury Tales*. William Gilmore Simms used the same device in his collection, *Southward, Ho!* Except for the manuscript draft of a prologue, we know little of how Poe intended to interweave this framing device with the tales proper, or of the extent to which the book could count as a "short story sequence" or something other than a "miscellaneous collection" (Kennedy vii). On the one hand, the range of tales planned for inclusion, from eleven to seventeen, is diverse and apparently discontinuous from story to story. On the other hand, the sequence of different storytellers for the tales makes for an anthology of narrators engaged in a mock experiment. Margarida Vale de Gato has gone as far as suggesting that their incongruous names and descriptions in the surviving preface poise them as "nonsense" precursors, emphasizing the "novelty" (226) of the "settled intention to abolish Literature, subvert the press, and overturn the Government of Nouns and Pronouns" (Poe, *Poetry and Tales* 131).

The project had a thwarted editorial history. A week after publishing Poe's prize-winning story, the *Visiter* announced that Poe intended to publish a collection of his short stories with the title *The Folio Club*. The announcement went further and declared that Poe's winning story had not been his best; the tales comprising *The Folio Club* were even better! The announcement explained: "They are all characterized by a raciness, originality of thought and brilliancy of conception which are rarely to be met with in the writings of our most favored American authors" (qtd. in Thomas and Jackson 134). On November 2, however, the paper announced that Poe had decided not to publish *Tales of the Folio Club* by subscription and that he planned to publish with a firm in Philadelphia (135).

Poe's efforts to publish *Tales of the Folio Club* illustrate something often overlooked about his personality. While the myth of Poe presents a gloomy, dark, pessimistic soul, the young writer who continually pitched *Tales of the Folio Club* was the eternal optimist, not unlike Wilkins Micawber of *David*

Copperfield. Once told finally by Carey & Lea and by Harper Brothers that nei-ther publisher would publish his book, and for the same basic reasons, Poe went back to both of them again. Though his letters to them have not survived, the responses from the publishers give us some idea of how he kept his foot in the door. His approach appears to have been to ask about the location of his manuscript. It would be a perfectly reasonable question, but it allowed him to press them one more time with another way to think about publishing his col-lection. When Poe made this final effort with Harper Brothers, the publisher replied on June 19, 1836, that American readers simply had no interest in "detached tales and pieces" (qtd. in Thomas and Jackson 212). The American literary market did not yet have a niche for a collection of short stories.

Poe's difficulty in finding a publisher for a collection of short fiction was not unique at the time. Arthur Hobson Quinn pointed out that Nathaniel Hawthorne was having a similar problem with his efforts to publish *Twice Told Tales*. When *Twice Told Tales* finally came out in 1837, it made its way into print because Hawthorne's friend Horatio Bridges paid $250 to have it printed. Henry Wadsworth Longfellow, a friend of Hawthorne from school days, gave the collection of tales a favorable review in the *North American Review*. As Quinn observed, Poe had no such friends with ready cash (252). Such matters never dampened Poe's optimism about his work, nor his pursuit of new editorial and publishing plans.

On September 2, 1836, Poe began anew with an approach to Harrison Hall, a Philadelphia publisher. Hall had written to T. W. White about the possibility of the *Messenger* reviewing two books his firm had published, a Latin grammar and *Sketches of History, Life, and Manners in the West* by Hall's brother James. Poe replied to the letter for White and commiserated with Hall over an unfavorable review in the *North American Review* with an as-surance that he would write a notice of the books for the September issue of the *Messenger* (Ostrom et al. 1: 104).[8] Having established a tone of goodwill, Poe proceeded to pitch *Tales of the Folio Club* to Hall. In this letter, Poe laid out the full scheme he had in mind for his collection of tales:

> At different times there has appeared in the *Messenger* a series of Tales, by myself—in all seventeen. They are of a bizarre and generally whimsical charac-ter, and were originally written to illustrate a large work "On the Imaginative Faculties." I have prepared them for republication, in book form, in the follow-ing manner. I imagine a company of 17 persons who call themselves the Folio Club. They meet once a month at the house of one of the members, and, at a late dinner, each member reads aloud a short prose tale of his own composition. The votes are taken in regard to the merits of each tale. The author of the

worst tale, for the month, forfeits the dinner & wine at the next meeting. The author of the best, is President at the next meeting. The seventeen tales which appeared in the Messr are supposed to be narrated by the seventeen members at one of these monthly meetings. As soon as each tale is read—the other 16 members criticize it in turn—and these criticisms are intended as a burlesque upon criticism generally. The author of the tale adjudged to be the worst demurs from the general judgment, seizes the seventeen M.SS upon the table, and, rushing from the house, determines to appeal, by printing the whole, from the decision of the Club, to that of the public. The critical remarks, *which have never been published*, will make about ¼ of the whole—the whole will form a volume of about 300 close pages. oct (1: 162–63).

Most wonderful of all, Poe claimed to be making the first offer of the manuscript to Hall! From a technical point of view, Poe was not lying, for his previous offers to publishers involved a book containing only eleven tales, and by the time he wrote to Hall, the collection had grown to seventeen. Because the tales comprising three-quarters of the book had already been published, Poe said that he expected no compensation other than several free copies of the published book, but nothing came of this overture. The larger work, "On the Imaginative Faculties," appears to be an invention that would only be followed up if the proposal was accepted. However, to combine intellectual speculation with imagination would make for quite an innovative anthology of short stories, with criticism interweaving with fiction. Both the subject— the several types of imagination and how they were orchestrated by the intellect—and the method—deconstructing an imaginative piece—deeply interested Poe until his death. He must have seen how this collection of tales could provide an opportunity to develop literary theory and criticism, just as "The Raven" would do when he wrote "The Philosophy of Composition."

Poe's last attempt to publish *Tales of the Folio Club* appears to have been with the English publishing firm of Saunders and Otley. As in all the previous exchanges with publishers, Poe had a go-between, this time in the person of Edward W. Johnston, who communicated through T. W. White. The complications of a trans-Atlantic arrangement proved too complicated, and the project to publish *Tales of the Folio Club* was abandoned when Poe left the *Southern Literary Messenger* to seek his fortune in New York.

Tales of the Grotesque and Arabesque

By September 1839, Poe informed Joseph Evans Snodgrass, a partner with Nathan Brooks for the magazine *American Museum*, that he had plans to publish a collection of his tales (Thomas and Jackson 269). Poe's literary output had outgrown the parameters of the *Tales of the Folio Club*, and he dropped its artificial organizational structure. In that same month, Poe contracted with Lea & Blanchard to publish *Tales of the Grotesque and Arabesque* in two volumes with a projected print run of 1750 copies. The publishers declined to pay Poe, but agreed to provide him with a few copies "for distribution among your friends" (qtd. in Thomas and Jackson 272). The title for the volume appears to come from Sir Walter Scott's definition of the kinds of tales Poe had written: "the tales of the arabesque are the product of an intense imaginative effort and the tales of the grotesque tend toward satire or burlesque" (qtd. in Loewentheil 41). Poe regarded his arabesque and his phantasy-pieces as his more serious tales (*Tales of the Grotesque* 1: 5). Lea & Blanchard published *Tales of the Grotesque and Arabesque* on December 4, 1839, in time for the Christmas trade. Poe finally had a collection of his stories in print. The two-volume collection included twenty-five tales that Poe had written over the previous six years, all of which had appeared in magazines or newspapers.

The title for this volume has prompted prolonged discussion of how to define an "arabesque" and a "grotesque" piece of literature. The problem is compounded because these terms belong to the visual arts rather than to literature. Arabesque refers to Islamic-inspired art, noted for its geometric and mathematical design. Grotesque refers to the distorted medieval sculpture represented by gargoyles. Poe uses arabesque in "The Philosophy of Furniture" as a visual term to describe the appearance of furniture (*Poetry and Tales* 384, 387). Some scholars attempt to draw a distinction between the two classes of story that Poe purported to write.[9] Arthur Hobson Quinn paraphrased Sir Walter Scott's distinction by explaining that "the Arabesques are the product of powerful imagination and the Grotesques have a burlesque or satirical quality" (289). The original title for the *Tales of the Folio Club* collection, however, was *Eleven Tales of the Arabesque*, suggesting that Poe considered all of his tales to be arabesque—characterized by their intricate and mathematical design—whether comic or serious and, consequently, that all his tales involved a degree of exaggerated distortion termed grotesque.

The arrangement of the tales in the collection appears to be based on the principle of poetic symmetry that was so dear to Poe's heart. In "The Rationale of Verse," Poe discussed at length the principle in poetry of long and short stresses and their alternation. He insisted that the alternations need not be regular so long as they were of equal proportion (*Essays and Reviews* 30–31). The arrangement of his tales in a generally equal proportion of alternating comic and serious stories fits his conviction that people take pleasure and enjoyment in the perception of equality, which embraces the concepts of "similarity, proportion, identity, repetition, and adaptation or fitness" (33).

Because Poe's principal concern in poetry and fiction was with creating an effect on his audience, we can think of his tales in terms of the desired effect. The serious tale tends to produce an effect of long duration, while the comic tale has an effect of short duration. By alternating the arrangement of tales between serious and comic, Poe created poetic "feet" in the overall arrangement of his tales.

Thirteen of the tales are comic, and twelve are serious. Poe placed six serious stories in each volume. Volume 1 contained eight comic tales, and volume 2 contained five comic tales. He began volume 1 with a serious tale and volume 2 with a comic tale. He set half of the stories in the first volume in Britain, perhaps with the view to finding a London publisher. As became his custom when republishing his stories and his poetry, Poe made extensive revisions to the tales he included in this collection, and he changed some of the titles.

Volume 1 included fourteen tales. Poe alternated serious and comic tales until the end of the volume, where he placed three comic tales together. Seen another way, Poe arranged the tales of volume 1 as a series of six trochee feet (long, short) followed by a single pyrrhic foot (short, short). He created another interesting pattern in the arrangement of the stories in this volume based on the length of the stories. In the first volume, the fourteen stories seem to be organized in seven couples. In the first three couples, the first story is longer than the second. In the next two couples, Poe reverses the pattern with the first story shorter than the second. For the last two pairs, the stories are of approximately equal length. Thus, Poe ameliorates what might have been a monotonous pattern with a variation that maintains the equality.

While some scholars who focus on a few of Poe's stories tend to think of Poe's tales as all set "Out of SPACE—Out of TIME," Poe normally set his stories in specific locations that played to the stereotypes that the reader brought to the story. Setting contributes to effect. He saved an enormous amount of space and verbiage by allowing the prejudices of the reader to set the tone by association with place during a period when U.S. cities were experiencing a bustle of immigration, and anti-immigrant feelings ran high.[10] Thus, the variety of locations for the stories correlates with Poe's desire to experiment with different kinds of stories and their potential for having varied effects.

Here, the tales are listed in the order they appear in *Tales of the Grotesque and Arabesque* with their order of original publication in parentheses, followed by their identification as serious or comic, their setting, and their length:

1. "Morella" (9): serious/no location/10 pp.
2. "Lionizing" (10): comic/England/8 pp.
3. "William Wilson" (23): serious/England/32 pp.
4. "The Man That Was Used Up" (21): comic/United States/16 pp.
5. "The Fall of the House of Usher" (22): serious/England/30 pp.
6. "The Duc de L'Omelette" (2): comic/France and Hell/6 pp.
7. "MS. Found in a Bottle" (6): serious/South Seas/16 pp.
8. "Bon-Bon" (originally "The Bargain Lost") (5): comic/Paris/26 pp.
9. "Shadow" (13): serious/Ptolemais/4 pp.
10. "The Devil in the Belfry" (20): comic/Germany/14 pp.
11. "Ligeia" (17): serious/England/22 pp.
12. "King Pest" (originally "King Pest the First") (12): comic/London/ 20 pp.
13. "The Signora Zenobia" (originally "The Psyche Zenobia") (18): comic/Philadelphia and Edinburgh/16 pp.
14. "The Scythe of Time" (19): comic/Edina [Edinburgh]/15 pp.

Volume 2 included eleven tales. This time, Poe reversed the order of his first volume and began with a comic tale. He also altered the regular pattern of alternating comic and serious stories at the middle of the volume by placing two comic stories together, followed by two serious stories, then one comic story, followed by two serious stories. Seen another way, Poe gives two iambic feet, followed by one pyrrhic, followed by another iambus, and ending with the single caesura, "a perfect foot—the most important in all verse—and consists of a single *long* syllable" (*Essay and Reviews* 31). Again, Poe reinforced the effect of his "feet" by varying the length of the stories:

15. "Epimanes" (14): comic/Syria/14 pp.
16. "Siope" (16): serious/Africa/6 pp.
17. "Hans Phaall" (originally "Hans Phaall—A Tale") (11): comic/Holland and the Moon/72 pp.
18. "A Tale of Jerusalem" (3): serious/Jerusalem/8 pp.
19. "Von Jung" (originally "Von Jung, the Mystific") (15): comic/Hungary and Germany/18 pp.
20. "Loss of Breath" (originally "A Decided Loss") (4): comic/United States/28 pp.

21. "Metzengerstein" (1): serious/Hungary/16 pp.
22. "Berenice" (8): serious/Europe/16 pp.
23. "Why the Little Frenchman Wears His Hand in a Sling" (25): comic/London/10 pp.
24. "The Visionary" (7): serious/Venice/20 pp.
25. "The Conversation of Eiros and Charmion" (24): serious/Heaven/10 pp.

The variation in comic and serious selections in the second volume may be because of Poe's conviction that some variation was necessary to avoid monotony just as long as the equality was preserved, but Poe also had a practical problem that required some variation—he had more comic stories than serious stories. We should also note the wide variety of settings Poe used in creating a mood that would accomplish his desired effect.

In his preface, Poe suggested that the twenty-five stories comprising the collection had been written with a view toward their eventual publication in a single volume that would reflect the "unity of design" he had intended (*Tales of the Grotesque* 1: 5). Rather than a collection of independent and unrelated tales, this collection represented "the results of matured purpose and very careful elaboration" that Poe wanted his readers to see as a whole (6). He also defended himself against the dismissive characterization by some critics that his tales were merely derivative of German gothicism, as he had complained to Snodgrass. Instead of a dependence on German gothicism, Poe argued, "If in many of my productions terror has been the thesis, I maintain that terror is not of Germany, but of the soul,—that I have deduced this terror only from its legitimate sources, and urged it only to its legitimate results" (6). The charge of Germanism had particularly irked Poe, who had written to Snodgrass that the inclusion of Washington Irving among the other literary figures who agreed to write "blurbs" for the collection would "afford me a complete triumph over those little critics who would endeavor to put me down by raising the hue & cry of *exaggeration* in style, of *Germanism* & such twaddle" (qtd. in Thomas and Jackson 275–76).

Phantasy-Pieces

By August 1841, Poe had completed eight new tales not included in *Tales of the Grotesque and Arabesque*, and he decided it was time to issue a revised edition that would include the new works (Ostrom et al. 1: 301–2). In reply to his proposal to Lea & Blanchard, however, the publishers informed him that the edition had not done as well as he assumed, and that they preferred not to proceed with any new publishing projects with Poe (Thomas and Jackson 338).

By June 1842, Poe had left *Graham's Magazine* and had in mind a new collection of his tales, to be published in three volumes as *Phantasy-Pieces*. The proposed collection would include an additional thirteen tales that he had completed since the publication of *Tales of the Grotesque and Arabesque* two years earlier (Thomas and Jackson 370). Poe prepared a mock title page for the projected collection, which he may have carried with him to New York to help promote the idea when calling on prospective publishers (Quinn 337–38).[11] His proposed collection had a new arrangement and ordering of tales that reflected the significance of some of his newer stories. If our proposal for the poetical arrangement of stories in *Tales of the Grotesque and Arabesque* is true, then we might expect to find a similar approach in Poe's proposed order of tales in *Phantasy-Pieces*. In fact, that is exactly what we find.

Poe's revised plan for a two-volume collection included thirty-six tales. The collection included twenty serious stories and sixteen comic tales. The first sixteen tales alternate between serious and comic in a regular trochee (long, short) pattern. These first sixteen tales probably formed volume 1. The next twenty tales follow a more complicated pattern, probably because this time, Poe had more serious tales than comic. Beginning with the seventeenth tale, the order comprises four tales in two iambic feet (short, long or comic, serious), followed by one trochee (long, short or serious, comic), and ending with one spondee (long, long or serious, serious). Poe then repeats this same pattern for the next eight stories. He concludes by presenting the final four tales in one pyrrhic foot (short, short or comic, comic) and one spondee (long, long or serious, serious). The stories are presented below in the order Poe suggested. Earlier titles are given in brackets, followed by the order of stories from *Tales of the Grotesque and Arabesque* given in parentheses, and their identification as comic or serious:

1. "The Murders in the Rue Morgue": serious
2. "The Man That Was Used Up" (1: 4): comic
3. "A Descent into the Maelström": serious
4. "Lionizing" (2: 2): comic
5. "The Colloquy of Monos and Una": serious
6. "The Business Man": comic
7. "The Mask of the Red Death": serious
8. "Never Bet Your Head": comic
9. "Eleonora": serious
10. "A Succession of Sundays": comic

11. "The Man of the Crowd": serious
~~"The Pit and the Pendulum"~~
12. "King Pest" ["King Pest the First"] (1: 12): comic
13. "Shadow—A Parable" (1: 9): serious
14. "Bon-Bon" ["The Bargain Lost"] (1: 8): comic
15. "Life in Death": serious
16. "The Unparalleled Adventure of One Hans Pfaall" ["Hans Phaall,"—A Tale"] (2: 17): comic

The probable break between volume 1 and volume 2 comes here.

17. "The Homocameleopard" ["Epimanes," "Four Beasts in One: The Homo-cameleopard"] (2: 15): comic
18. "Manuscript Found in a Bottle" [MS. Found in a Bottle] (1: 7): serious
19. "Mystification" ["Von Jung," "Von Jung, the Mystific"] (2: 19): comic
20. "The Horse-Shade" ["Metzengerstein"?] (2: 21): serious
21. "The Assignation" ["The Visionary," "The Visionary—A Tale"] (2: 24): serious
22. "Why the Little Frenchman Wears his Hand in a Sling" (2: 23): comic
23. "The Teeth" ["Berenice"?] (2: 22): serious
24. "Silence—A Fable" ["Siope"] (2: 16): serious
25. "Loss of Breath" ["A Decided Loss"] (2: 20): comic
26. "The Island of the Fay": serious
27. "The Devil in the Belfry" (1: 10): comic
28. "Morella" (1: 1): serious
29. "A Pig Tale" ["A Tale of Jerusalem"?] (2: 18): serious
~~"The Mystery of Marie Rogêt"~~
30. "The Duc de L'Omelette" ["The Duke de L'Omelette"] (1: 6): comic
31. "Ligeia" (1: 11): serious
32. "The Fall of the House of Usher" (1: 5): serious
33. "How to Write a Blackwood Article" ["The Psyche Zenobia," "The Signora Zenobia"] (1: 13): comic
34. "A Predicament" ["The Scythe of Time"] (1: 14): comic
35. "William Wilson" (1: 3): serious
36. "The Conversation of Eiros and Charmion" (2: 25): serious

In his search for a publisher, Poe called on J. and H. G. Langley, who published the *Democratic Review* in New York, as well as Robert Hamilton, who published the *Ladies' Companion* (Thomas and Jackson 371). Though he had no success with this venture, both magazines published several of his pieces over the next few years. After the initial rejection by the New York publishers, Poe dropped plans for *Phantasy-Pieces* and turned his attention once more to another of his dreams—his own magazine.

The Prose Romances

In July 1843, William Graham—whose brother, George Graham, owned *Graham's Magazine*, a periodical with which Poe kept collaborating—published a cheap pamphlet containing two of Poe's tales as the initial effort to develop a series of cheap volumes for the popular market. It was priced at 12½ cents and bore the title, *The Prose Romances of Edgar A. Poe*, as the first number in the Uniform Serial Edition (Quinn 399). It is uncertain whether the Uniform Serial Edition was a scheme of William Graham or of Poe. It is also unclear whether it was Graham or Poe who bore the cost of publication. It is not even clear whether Graham or Poe selected the tales for the pamphlet, but the selection suggests Poe's concern to demonstrate his versatility. The slim volume contains Poe's first mystery story, "The Murders in the Rue Morgue," and one of his well-received satires, "The Man That Was Used Up" (*Nevermore* 48–49).[12] These are the first two stories that Poe listed in *Phantasy-Pieces*.

The little publication received favorable notice in several journals and newspapers, but the venture must not have done well enough financially to warrant a continuation of the Uniform Serial Edition to a second number. Today, it is one of the most valuable volumes of fiction ever published in the United States. A. S. W. Rosenbach once remarked of it, "If I am found dead with a book in my pocket, I hope it will be the first edition of 'The Murders in the Rue Morgue'" (qtd. in Dalby 54).

Tales (1845)

Following the astonishing success of "The Raven," Wiley and Putnam agreed to publish a collection of Poe's short stories (Thomas and Jackson 513).[13] Poe's *Tales* was published on June 25, 1845, in New York (540). Rather than an expansion of *Tales of the Grotesque and Arabesque*, it was comprised almost entirely of tales that had not been included in the earlier collection. The only duplications were "Lionizing," "The Fall of the House of Usher," and "The Conversation of Eiros and Charmion." In addition to these three earlier tales, the new volume included nine tales that Poe had written since the appearance of the first collection: "The Gold-Bug," "The Black Cat," "Mesmeric Revelation," "A Descent into the Maelström," "The Colloquy of Monos and Una," "The Murders in the Rue Morgue," "The Mystery of Marie Rogêt," "The Purloined Letter," and "The Man of the Crowd" (listed in the table of contents as "The Man in the Crowd"). Though this volume took advantage of the sudden interest in Poe generated by "The Raven," Poe had little involvement in the project. He did not even select the tales for inclusion. That task fell to Evert Duyckinck, who thus became the first editor of a single-author anthology of Poe. Poe had written a preface for all of his earlier books except *Al Aaraaf*, which included a poem at the beginning of his "Miscellaneous Poems" titled "Preface," but for *Tales* he did not contribute a preface. This omission further suggests the extent to which he had no hand in the production of *Tales*. On the other hand, Poe made a number of revisions to these tales from their earlier printings. For the most part, the revised versions of the tales included in *Tales* have become the standard texts (Quinn 466).

In a letter to George W. Eveleth, Poe briefly remarked that the tales in the Wiley and Putnam volume did not represent his best tales, nor did they fairly represent his work (Ostrom et al. 1: 601). He explained in a letter to Philip P. Cooke that the unevenness of the collection was due to Duyckinck's love of Poe's tales of ratiocination, which led him to focus on analytical tales almost exclusively (595). In an uncharacteristically modest moment, Poe allowed that he had demonstrated no great "ingenuity of unravelling a web which you yourself (the author) have woven for the express purpose of unravelling" (595). Though Poe was understandably proud of the invention of his detective stories, he wanted all collections of his tales to demonstrate his ability to address "the widest diversity of subject, thought, & especially *tone* & manner of handling" (596). Poe considered "Ligeia" to be his best tale because it represented his highest imagination, but Duyckinck had failed to include it.

Poe was conscious of the fact that his earlier works included in *Tales of the Grotesque and Arabesque* were mere prelude to what he accomplished after 1840. Had he died in 1840, he would be ranked with his literary friends John Pendleton Kennedy, N. P. Willis, and William Gilmore Simms as writers of merit who deserve to be studied in graduate seminars on American literature in the first half of the nineteenth century. After 1840, he became a great writer on the world stage as he worked deliberately at creating original pieces. His works of science fiction are absent from *Tales*. Also missing are his more sophisticated comic tales. In "A Succession of Sundays," Poe wrote a story that is, at the same time, a comedy, a love story, and a science fiction story. With "The Balloon Hoax," Poe combined the adventure story with science fiction. "Eleonora" combines the love story with metaphysical terror. For Poe, who up until this time had always arranged his stories to contrast the comic and the serious, the Duyckinck selection—which only included one comic tale—must have seemed disastrous for one who wanted to be known for his mastery of a wide range of story types. Duyckinck unwittingly established the tradition of typecasting Poe.

What pleased Poe most about the complete corpus of his tales was their rich diversity and variety, which he had managed to master; Duyckinck's collection failed to reflect this accomplishment, which had preoccupied his tale writing since he began writing tales (Ostrom et al. 1: 596). In the opinion of Lee Biondi, the prominent twentieth-century rare book dealer, *Tales* was a better collection than *Tales of the Grotesque and Arabesque* precisely because it did not include a broad representation of Poe's comic pieces (34). Poe's earlier comic pieces often tended to a form of satire that almost always dates itself by its treatment of matters in a particular time period. Poe's earlier humor also tended toward the sarcastic. Neither of these factors need have harmed Poe's reputation as a humorist, however, since Mark Twain followed the same course. In spite of his disappointment at the narrow nature of stories included in *Tales*, Poe did not publish his discontent widely.

In terms of the history of American literature, this volume is of paramount importance. Ellery Queen described *Tales* as "the first important book of detective stories, the first and the greatest, the cornerstone of cornerstones in any readers' or collectors' guide, the highspot of highspots" (qtd. in Kopley 53). A. S. W. Rosenbach, the Philadelphia rare book dealer, called it "the greatest volume of short stories ever to appear from the hand of man" (53).

Poe never realized his dream of a complete collection of his short stories after the publication of *Tales of the Grotesque and Arabesque*. The publication of *Tales* in 1845 only provides a supplement of sorts to the earlier collection, and it only includes "selected" pieces instead of a full collection of all stories written by Poe after *Tales of the Grotesque and Arabesque*. Ironically, with the exception of *Prose Romances*, we do not have an example of how Poe might have made editorial decisions about which of his works to include in an anthology. Poe wanted to publish everything, largely because he conceived of his tales as a totality that demonstrated his versatility across the wide spectrum of the kinds of stories that people tell. It would be left to his greatest literary enemy, Rufus Griswold, to publish a more comprehensive edition of Poe's tales in the year following Poe's death.

On the other hand, even as *Tales* went to press, Poe busied himself publishing a serialized anthology of his works in the pages of his *Broadway Journal*. Before the journal went bankrupt, he published an enormous number of his tales and poems, which required him to make the anthologist's decisions about which story to print with others, and in what order, between January 3, 1845 and January 3, 1846. An examination of Poe's choices of what to print and when to print it in the *Broadway Journal* lies outside the scope of this study, but it is interesting to note a few matters. Poe republished "Lionizing" as "Some Passages in the Life of a Lion" on March 15, 1845. He republished "Berenice" on April 5, and he followed it with "Bon-Bon" on April 19, 1845. For the most part, however, Poe re-used stories that he wrote after the publication of *Tales of the Grotesque and Arabesque*. Notable for their absence, however, are Poe's five detective stories, four of which had appeared in the 1845 *Tales*. Apart from the absence of his mysteries, the tales published in the *Broadway Journal* provide the most comprehensive example of the variety of Poe's stories, for they include science fiction, romantic comedy, horror, terror, satire, and the supernatural.

In terms of the arrangement of his stories within a collection, this examination suggests that Poe's ideas about symmetry, equality, and patterns that create an effect lie at the heart of his conception of his unified body of work. While some writers might have in mind a political or social theory that they care to advance, Poe aimed at a conception of order that belonged to his understanding of beauty. This arrangement of his works also suggests that the ideas he advanced in "The Philosophy of Composition" formed a philosophy that he took seriously and that would play such a significant part in his magnum opus, *Eureka*.

Notes

1. In *Evermore: Edgar Allan Poe and the Mystery of the Universe* (24–27), I identified sixty-eight stories that I categorized as humor and satire (24), science fiction (11), mystery and crime (10), supernatural horror (10), natural horror (8), and beauty (5). This division does not even include adventure, tragedy, and love story. The problem, of course, with any attempt to categorize the stories like this is that each tale belongs to at least two categories, and sometimes three or four. For a discussion of Poe's efforts at combination, see Margarida Vale de Gato (161–71).

2. Scholars have long debated whether Poe's serious stories were really serious, or simply well-veiled satires. On the other hand, we may safely say that Poe was deadly serious about all his satires. We can see that even the most serious tale might be broken by light moments, often involving confusion, but these moments do not make the tale comic. Dennis Eddings (155–56) provides a brief review of several of the more significant aspects of this debate, including treatments of Clark Griffith, David Halliburton, Stephen Mooney, Robert Regan, and G. R. Thompson.

3. Benjamin F. Fisher has argued that, in spite of Poe's reputation for horror, he "may have composed in the comic vein" (50).

4. Poe discussed the concept of effect in relation to poetry and prose in several places, including "The Philosophy of Composition," "The Poetic Principle," his second review of Hawthorne's *Twice-Told Tales*, and "The Philosophy of Furniture." See Poe, *Essays and Reviews*, 13, 71, 572, 583; and Poe, *Poetry and Tales*, 382–87. Poe also explored this idea of the unity of effect throughout *Eureka*, in which he sought to identify the cause of the universe in terms of the present effect.

5. In publishing their decision in the *Visiter* on October 12, 1833, the judges indicated that Poe had submitted six tales.

6. Arthur Hobson Quinn gave his account of the stories to be included in the various proposals for this volume in the appendix of his definitive biography of Poe (745–46).

7. Jeffrey Savoye has suggested that this fictional group took inspiration from the Delphian Club, a literary group that had been active in Baltimore until 1825 (104).

8. John Ostrom suggested that Hall's *Sketches* might have been a volume by Basil Hall (104).

9. In "Poe in Europe: Recent German Criticism," Roger Forclaz has discussed approaches to the relationship between the arabesque and the grotesque, with special attention to the work of Bernd Gunther (49–55).

10. For example, Rufus Griswold insinuated himself into public notice by his participation in the anti-Catholic movement in Philadelphia, bolstered by his fictitious clerical credentials.

11. Poe made several changes to the handwritten sample title page and table of contents. Where he had indicated three volumes, Poe struck through three and replaced it with two. In the table of contents he struck through "The Pit and the Pendulum" and "The Mystery of Marie Rogêt," probably because they had not yet been published in a magazine, and Poe would have wanted the additional revenue. See Quinn, 337–38.

12. Susan Tane's collection catalog, *Quoth the Raven*, published in conjunction with her Poe exhibition at Cornell, includes bibliographic and publication details about this rare volume along with a full-page photograph. For an image of the title page, see Quinn 398.

13. In a letter to James Russell Lowell on March 8, 1845, C. F. Briggs, who edited the *Broadway Journal* with Poe, mentioned the news.

Works Cited

Biondi, Lee. "Collecting Edgar Allan Poe." *Firsts: The Book Collector's Magazine*, vol. 8, no. 10, 1998, pp. 30–51.

Dalby, Richard. "Edgar Allan Poe." *Book and Magazine Collector*, no. 44, 1987, pp. 50–58.

Eddings, Dennis W. *The Naiad Voice: Essays on Poe's Satiric Hoaxing*. Associated Faculty Press, 1983.

Fisher, Benjamin F. *The Cambridge Introduction to Edgar Allan Poe*. Cambridge UP, 2008.

Forclaz, Roger. "Poe in Europe: Recent German Criticism." *Poe Studies*, vol. 11, no. 3, December 1978, pp. 49–55.

Kennedy, J. Gerald. "Introduction: The American Short Story Sequence." *Modern American Short Story Sequences: Composite Fictions and Fictive Communities*, edited by Kennedy, Cambridge UP, 1995, pp. vii–xv.

[Kopely, Richard]. *Quoth the Raven: Selections from the Susan Jaffe Tane Collection Exhibited to Celebrate the 75th Anniversary of the Edgar Allan Poe Museum in Richmond, Virginia*. The Poe Museum, 1997.

Loewentheil, Stephan. *The Poe Catalogue: A Descriptive Catalogue of the Stephan Loewentheil Collection of Edgar Allan Poe Material*. The 19th Century Shop, 1992.

Nevermore: The Edgar Allan Poe Collection of Susan Jaffe Tane. Cornell University Library, 2006.

New York Times and Commercial Intelligencer, 4 Aug 1839, p. 2.

Ostrom, John Ward, Burton R. Pollin, and Jeffrey A. Savoye, editors. *The Collected Letters of Edgar Allan Poe*. Gordian Press, 2008. 2 vols.

Poe, Edgar Allan. *Essays and Reviews*. The Library of America, 1984.

———. *Poetry and Tales*. The Library of America, 1984.

———. *Tales of the Grotesque and Arabesque*. 2 vols. Lea and Blanchard, 1840.

———. *Tales*. Wiley & Putnam, 1845.

Poe, Harry Lee. *Evermore: Edgar Allan Poe and the Mystery of the Universe*. Baylor UP, 2012.

Quinn, Arthur Hobson. *Edgar Allan Poe: A Critical Biography*. D. Appleton-Century Company, 1941.

Savoye, Jeffrey A. "Poe and Baltimore: Crossroads and Redemption," *Poe and Place*, edited by Philip Edward Phillips, Palgrave Macmillan, 2018, pp. 97–122.

Thomas, Dwight, and David Jackson. *The Poe Log*. G. K. Hall & Co., 1987.

Vale de Gato, Margarida. "100 Years and Something of Poe in Portuguese Anthologies." *The Anthology in Portugal*, by Patricia Odber de Baubeta, Margarida Vale de Gato, and Maria de Lurdes Sampaio, vol. 2, Peter Lang, 2013, pp. 153–219.

CHAPTER THREE

The "Flower-Gemmed" Story

Gift Book Tradition and Poe's "Eleonora"

Alexandra Urakova

In the 1840s, the gift book occupied an intermediary position between miscellaneous collections and the literary anthologies that were coming into fashion during the latter part of Poe's career. The nineteenth-century gift book, or literary annual, was not an anthology in the typical sense. This unique type of collection, however, was important for Edgar Allan Poe and the dissemination of his work during his lifetime. The fact that gift books appear to come so close to anthologies and sometimes overlap with them evokes terminological confusion. To clarify this matter, I will briefly discuss gift books, their peculiar status in the antebellum literary market, and, especially, their relation to the genre of anthology. I will then turn to Poe and his gift book publications, focusing particularly on the publication of "Eleonora" in *The Gift, a Christmas and New Year Present* for 1842.

The gift book vogue came to the United States from Great Britain in the 1820s and declined in the wake of the Civil War. Gift books were collections of poetry and prose bound together as holiday gifts, usually sold during the Christmas season. Stephen Nissenbaum calls them "the *very first* commercial products of any sort that were manufactured specifically, and solely, for the purpose of being given away by the purchaser" (143). Gift books' share in Christmas circulation and exchange, indeed, distinguished them from other antebellum printed matter. They were, in the first place, objects of luxury suitable for gift-giving—elegant volumes decorated with engravings and printed on fine paper; bound in silk, morocco, velvet, or leather; and often miniature in size.[1] Some of them came with gilt or varnished covers, card-board slipcases tied by a ribbon, or marble endpapers. Gift books commonly contained presentation plates, sometimes hand-colored, where the giver was supposed to leave a dedication and thus personalize the gift in the act of bestowal. Telling titles, such as "Souvenir," "The Token," "The Leaflets of Memory," "Forget-me-not," "The Diadem," "The Pearl," "The Jewel," and "The Gift" underlined the gift books' sentimental status of souvenir or memento and contributed to their "gem-like presentation," in the words of Cindy Dickinson (55). As Frederick F. Faxon neatly summarizes, "in bind-ing, contents, illustrations, and name these interesting 'butterfly books' were easily distinguished from the common run" (xv).

In light of recent interest in book history, material culture history, and gender studies, gift books have not escaped critical attention. Scholars, however, have not come to an accord about whether gift books should be considered anthologies or not. Some call gift books, either British or Ameri-can, "lavishly illustrated anthologies of poetry and prose" (Hawkins 103), "anthologies, 'cabinets' of poetry and romance" (Lehuu 80), or "expensive, lavishly bound, flowery-titled anthologies that are still collected as binding specimens" (Blocker et al. 380). Others, instead, insist on distinguishing them from anthologies. Mary Louise Kete, for example, writes: "Gift books, newspapers, and magazines all share aspects of the anthology in that they are collections, but the new anthologies, pioneered by Rufus Griswold in 1842 with the publication of his *Poets and Poetry of America*, offered readers collections sorted by broad rubrics that apparently appealed strongly to the readers" (30). In her reading, Kete juxtaposes anthologies with newspapers, magazines, and gift books, recasting gift books as periodicals. Barbara Onslow proposes to differentiate between gift books and annuals, merging the former with anthologies against periodical editions: "The distinguishing feature is that the gift books and anthologies are not periodicals, though several an-nual titles only survived for a couple of years" (79). While such differences did exist within the field of gift books—some volumes came out annually, while others happened to be published only once—the terms "gift book" (or "souvenir," or "keepsake") and "annual" were usually interchangeable. Peri-odicity, largely a measure of the gift book's commercial success, was unlikely to be the defining generic factor.

The dividing line between anthologies and gift books—"Romantic mis-cellanies" (Piper 123)—lies rather in the way their editors selected and organized their contents. By definition, an anthology is the opposite of a miscellany. As Barbara Mujica suggests, "the very format of an anthology prompts canon formation, for while a miscellany invites short, disconnected readings, an anthology invites prolonged study. Anthologies convey the notion of evolution (the succession of literary movements) and hierarchy (the recognition of masterpieces)" (203). In the case of gift books, we are mostly speaking of randomly chosen, miscellaneous publications. Some American gift books pirated poetry and prose from English gift books and periodicals. Others, of higher quality and stand, paid fees to American contributors or awarded prizes for publication; "the payment naturally varied with the reputation of the writer" (Thompson 22). Many editors used their personal connections, and often received literary pieces as gifts from friends.

A typical gift book volume would include one or two seasonal (Christmas or holiday-related) publications or stories and poems about gift-giving, gifts, tokens, or gems, usually sentimental in character. However, a belief that gift books were anthologies of sentimental poetry or fiction is a widespread mistake, even if sentimental genres commonly prevailed. "The Pit and the Pendulum," a torture chamber narrative and one of the darkest of Poe's tales, for instance, came out in *The Gift* for 1843 alongside mourning poetry and happy-ending love stories. This is but one example of how gift book compilers miscellaneously blended works belonging to very different trends and styles. Less miscellaneous in character were gift books with a particular focus on one main theme or audience—anti-slavery, temperance, religious, masonic, or anti-immigrant gift books; bridal and mourning books; and juvenile annuals (Thompson 16–17; Jackson). Yet, as in the case of periodicals, the selection process was contingent on the editorial necessity to fill in the volume and produce it in time for the season, usually in October. While anthologies "represent a repackaging of primary sources" (Di Leo 9), gift books published both reprints and original works.

As Margarida Vale de Gato has argued while further developing Mujica's statement, "the sense that the whole is greater than the sum of its parts is largely contrived through book binding; if we think that the miscellany can be bound as well, we must on the other hand admit that there is a sense of continuity that it lacks" (52). Gift books, indeed, lacked the "sense of continuity" that distinguish anthologies as collections. At the same time, "the sense that the whole is greater than the sum of its parts," in the case of gift books, was not contrived through book binding alone. Unlike periodicals, the annual was a *keepsake*, a book to bestow, to keep, and to cherish in its integrity. Everything—from the title and opulent cover to the self-advertising interpolations "inscribed within the literary matter itself" (Nissenbaum 144)—worked toward the whole. In this respect, Barbara Korte's definition of anthology, "a *mixtum compositum* whose assembled parts have entered a new relationship, have been woven together to move a new textual whole"

(18), may be neatly applied to gift books. This "new textual whole" included not only texts but also, importantly, what Gérard Genette calls peritexts: "book format, cover, title-page, page layout, type-setting and other features of book morphology" (qtd. in Korte 20). The gift book, a "token of affection" or a "messenger of love," had unambiguous sentimental value: "displayed in recipients' homes, gift books served to remind viewers and readers that someone close by felt the sentiments expressed in their pages" (Stevenson 340). It was also an ornament lying upon the parlor table and "awaiting a re-examination in an idle hour" (Thompson 2).

Many gift books shared with anthologies the ambitious interest in promoting national literature and art. Griswold, in his famous *Poets and Poetry of America*, claims to "exhibit the *progress* and *condition* of Poetry in the United States" (v; emphasis added). The publisher's advertisement for the 1842 *Gift*, for example, similarly boasts: "The present volume of 'The Gift' is in every respect an American work. The contributions are by American authors,—the illustrations by American artists; and the publishers believe that it will be found fully equal, if not superior to any that have preceded it." (np). Although *The Gift*'s editor does not pursue "evolution and hierarchy," as Griswold does, he nevertheless emphasizes the gift book's role in the dissemination of national literature.

Antebellum anthologies, in their turn, often patterned themselves on gift books. Writing about Victorian poetic anthologies, Korte observes: "As a precious institution of culture, many anthologies on the Victorian book market were offered in costly editions of high material value to equal their cultural value: these editions had expensive bindings, were published in larger formats and with illustrations. These were books suitable for display in the drawing room, as a gift for special occasions, or as a school prize" (27).

The same is true for the United States. According to Susan Belasco, besides educational purposes, Griswold was "developing anthologies . . . for use as gift books" (187). The 1842 edition of *The Poets and Poetry of America*, "a handsome book of 468 pages" (187), with its red-colored cover and gilded engraving, looked like a gift book. Griswold's anthology of female poets published in the same year has a "gift book" title: *Gems from American Female Poets*.[2]

Many gift book titles, in a similar manner to anthologies, advertised their "select(ed)ness" (Korte 2). Indeed, gem- or jewel-related titles of gift books fulfilled a double purpose: they served as signs of luxury, referring to actual gifts of jewelry, while at the same time implying the literary brilliance of the selected poetry and prose. In some cases, titles and formats are so misleading that it becomes a difficult task to distinguish a gift book from an anthology. Ralph Thompson attributes the 1840 *Gems of American Poetry by Distinguished Authors* published in New York by Charles Fenno Hoffman to gift books; in fact, it was a re-edition of the 1837 *The New York Book of Poetry* (143). Yet, when we open the volume, we will find poems arranged in alphabetical order. The mention of "distinguished authors" in the title, on the other hand, signals the recognition of masterpieces rather than miscellaneous choice.

"Select(ed)ness" may be found in gift book floral titles as well, such as, for example, numerous *Garlands* and *Bouquets*. Flowers in the titles—"Forget-me-not," "The Violet," "Flowers of Loveliness," "Flora's Gem," "Hyacinth," "Honeysuckle," "Mayflower," "Rose," "Rose Bud"—offer another promising cross-cut between gift books and anthologies. Di Leo notes that "[i]n Greek, anthology, or a bouquet means a collection of poems" (2); the earliest anthology known, by Meleager, was called the *Garland*. Korte argues that "[a]n anthology, in its basic understanding, is a collection of *picked* flowers, of *selected* texts" (2), and she ties the Latin meaning of the word back to the Greek: "from Greek anthos = flower and legeín = to gather," anthology is translated as florilegium (2). Florilegia, anthologies of flower language and flower-related poems, belonged to another antebellum genre, kin to gift books. Thompson speaks of a special thematic subgenre of annuals, "illustrated volumes dealing with flowers and flower language": "there were at least fifty such, appropriately named 'Flora's Album,' 'Flora's Dial,' 'Flora's Interpreter,' 'Floral Keepsake,' 'Poetry of Flowers,' or 'Flower Garden'" (17). Even when speaking of general gift books, we can say that the bouquet was one of the basic metaphors; albeit randomly gathered and arranged, gift books were still bouquets, with every flower and leaf making up the whole.

I would like to conclude this brief survey by saying that gift books were *miscellaneous anthologies* of a sort, even if this seems to be a contradiction in terms. Though there is certainly an important difference in the way gift books and anthologies selected and presented their literary matter, and although gift books had their own distinctive features and morphology, the borderline between the two is often blurred. Moreover, gift books invite us to think of anthologizing in a broad sense—as flower-gathering or gem-mining—and highlight its kinship to gift-giving. A gift usually comes in a nice package or a giftwrap, and "(re)packaging" literary texts into a new whole or composite was one of the ways to make a memorable gift out of literary texts and plates, inspiring the recipient to keep them among treasured belongings. It was also a way to challenge and compete with the transience of the periodical world that pervaded the antebellum literary market.

It does not seem counterintuitive to suggest that gift book publications, to a larger or lesser extent, interacted with their material framework: on the one hand, they were pieces randomly brought together under the same cover, yet on the other, synecdochically related to the gift book as a whole.[3] As Poe wrote to Isaac Lea in 1829, in reply to the invitation to publish in *The Atlantic Souvenir*: "I know nothing which would give me greater pleasure than to see any of my productions in so becoming a dress and in such good society as *The Souvenir* would ensure them" ("Poe to Carey" 40). As is evident from Poe's polite and "diplomatic" response (Shinn 180), there are two factors that determine a gift book publication: a dress (the cover, binding, title) and society (the company of its poems, stories, plates and, perhaps implicitly, the distinguished audience of the gift books themselves). Though Poe did not send anything to *The Atlantic Souvenir* at that time, he published a number of his important works in gift books later in his career. His five stories—"MS. Found in a Bottle," "The Pit and the Pendulum," "William Wilson," "Eleonora," and "The Purloined Letter"—each appeared in *The Gift*. One of the "most ambitious undertaking[s]" of the Carey and Hart publishing house "in the gift book field" (Thompson 74), this annual was known for its high-quality plates and literary matter; its contributors included Irving, Emerson, Longfellow, Willis, Kirkland, Stowe, Sedgwick, Sigourney, and Child. Poe also wrote "The Morning on the Wissahiccon" for *The Opal*, another gift book with a good reputation, and he published pieces in regional and minor volumes: *The Baltimore Book*, *The Missionary Memorial*, and *The Mayflower*.

In the only existing survey of Poe's collaboration with gift books, Kathryn Shinn claims that "his gift book publications seem to go against the very nature of the gift book, as his publications represent some of the most psychological, innovative, and important literature of the time" (186). She also argues that Poe "was detached from the usual content of gift books" (185). While Poe's works certainly stood out from the common run, to say that they were "detached" or even "[went] against the nature of the gift book" is a serious oversimplification. Rather, we can speak of different forms or levels of engagement. For example, "William Wilson" is the result of an exchange that took place between two writers: Washington Irving, who gave a gift of the plot in his essay, "The Unpublished Drama of Lord Byron" (*The Gift* for 1836), and Poe, who "returned" the gift in the form of "William Wilson" (*The Gift* for 1840).[4] "The Purloined Letter" appeared in the volume of *The Gift* side by side with two tales about stolen/fatal letters. As I have argued, the tale "inverts the exemplary plot-model of *The Gift*" while "the purloined letter in the story strikingly resembles a gift book turned inside out" ("'The Purloined Letter' in the Gift Book" 346). In "The (Gift) Book That Keeps on Giving," Gila Ashtor pushes my claim further by showing the tale's counter-action not only with the stories, but also with the neighboring poetical pieces and plates (59–65).

Finally, we can speak of the texts that seem congenial with the gift book framework, such as Poe's pastorals: "The Morning on the Wissahiccon" and "Eleonora." For the remainder of the chapter, I will focus on the latter tale that saw light in *The Gift* for 1842. I will demonstrate that "Eleonora" was engaged in a dialogue with the volume's poems contributed by female authors; that it retained its distinctive and recognizably Poesque features regardless of that dialogue; and that the story may be seen as a model gift book publication, not in spite of but due to its singular and peculiar style.

Dismissed by Poe himself as "a good subject spoiled by hurry in the handling" (Fisher 180), "Eleonora" seems rather marginal in his heritage and, to my knowledge, has not received much scholarly attention in recent years.[5] Yet, of the five tales Poe published in *The Gift*, "a story of happiness lost and regained, and a favorite of romantic readers" (Mabbott 2: 635), it seems most suitable for the gift book audience. The plot's combination of the death of the beloved with the death of a childlike maiden was among the most popular gift book poetic subjects. The description of death and mourning in "Eleonora" contained no horror element, unlike many other Poe stories. The hint at spiritual reunion of the lovers at the end of the tale was likely to find sympathy in the "average" gift book reader seeking sentimental reconciliation with death, even though the story makes no use of religious reconciliation rhetoric.

The pastoral element of "Eleonora" in *The Gift* becomes visible in its idyllic setting in the Multi-Colored Valley gemmed with buttercups, daisies, violets, and asphodels. Flowers perform an allegorical function in the tale, standing respectively for health, passion, and death. When Eleonora dies, "the tints of the green carpet faded, and one by one the ruby-red asphodels withered away" (160). The tale implies that Eleonora, compared to the lily of the valley (157), herself faded like a flower. Thomas Ollive Mabbott names a story about a fairy mourning over a dead flower as one of the sources for "Eleonora" (2: 636); in "A Fairy Tale," published by Miss Mercer in *The Southern Literary Messenger* for January 1836, a fairy that lives in "one of the loveliest valleys upon the face of the earth" (77) grieves over the death of her favorite lily. Even spring does not bring her peace: "She wished no longer for Spring. She wished never again to fix her heart upon the perishing flowers of the Earth" (78). Finally, she dies to find "a home utterly free from the chilling shadows of mortality" and enjoys flowers growing "in glorious and imperishable beauty" (78).

Whether through mere coincidence or through Eliza Leslie's purposeful editorial design, the 1842 volume has a handful of poems with a popular motif of fading or dying flowers. The book opens with Lydia Sigourney's "Autumn and the Garden," an elegy on the death of flowers. Sigourney's contribution was a follow-up on a long-standing tradition—one could think of Bryant's famous "Death of Flowers" from 1832, later anthologized in *The Poets and Poetry of America*—poems on this subject were favorites in gift books. Sigourney mournfully addresses her flowers killed by "the fierce frost-king" (17). Among them are "brave Chrysanthenium," "fair and graceful Poppy," "poor Sweet-Pea," "dear lonely Violet," "flowering Bean," "yellow Marigold," and a few others (17–19). The flowers, dear, sweet friends, described as "sickening, pale, and dead," have conspicuous anthropomorphic features: for example, "the pure life-blood" runs curdling to the heart of the Chrysanthenium (17). Sigourney's metaphoric language builds on the fading flower as a common emblem of human fate. The poem's tone is at once melancholic and concilia-tory: the final stanzas contain a promise that the flowers will return in their "glorious pomp" in spring; they are "ambassadors to show / The truth of those eternal worlds / Which on God's pages glow" (19). In the same volume, Mary Ann Brown's "Glimpses of Heaven" expresses a very similar idea. It is the glimpse of heaven "when the death of some pale violet, blowing / Alone in autumn, through the heart doth bring, For one rapt moment, a bright current flowing / With all the light and radiancy [sic] of spring" (82).

Both Sigourney and Brown value spring primarily as a glimpse or promise of eternal life. The ambiguous, neo-Platonic finale of Poe's "Eleonora" in *The Gift* can be read in a similar vein. The narrator finds himself in a strange city where he meets a woman whose "radiant loveliness . . . bewildered and intoxicated [his] brain" (161). Although the city blotted his memories of the Valley of Many-Colored Grass, and even though Ermengarde replaced Eleonora, the tale suggests that the "ethereal" and "seraph" Ermengarde is an earthly counterpart of his spiritual, heavenly union with his lost beloved:

> I wedded, nor dreaded the curse I had invoked, and its bitterness was not vis-ited upon me. And in the silence of the night there came once again through my lattice the soft sighs which had forsaken me, and they modelled themselves into sweet voice, saying—"Sleep in peace!"; for the spirit of Love reigneth and ruleth; and in taking to thy passionate heart her who is Ermengarde, thou art absolved, for reasons which shall be made known to thee in Heaven, of thy vows unto Eleonora. (162)

Another feature that makes Poe's "Eleonora" consonant with gift book publications is its use of the flower language that *The Gift*'s readers had no trouble understanding. White daisies at the beginning of the tale stand for

Eleonora's innocence (Shoberl 55) and the narrator's childish love for her; one of the meanings of violets—constancy or faithfulness (Cortambert 41)— gives extra emphasis to the reincarnation interpretation of the tale's finale. Lily of the valley means the return of happiness (Shoberl 89), another hint at the tale's denouement. In *The Gift*, "Eleonora" is immediately followed by Frances Osgood's "A Wreath of Riddles," a playful poem-puzzle about a lover "wreathing" a "fair and fragrant" wreath for his beloved (163). Each flower is oddly paraphrased, and the receiver has to guess the botanic name of each.

While not as odd and whimsical as Osgood's, Poe's flower language in "Eleonora," however, was likely to puzzle the reader. Why would he make asphodels symbols of love and passion instead of more traditional roses? Asphodel means "My regrets follow you to the grave" (Cortambert 283; Shoberl 295). Louise Cortambert states that "[i]n ancient times, the Asphodel was planted near tombs, and it was thought that beyond the Acheron the shades of the deceased wandered in a vast field of Asphodels, and drank the oblivious waters of Lethe" (283). Perhaps Poe meant to suggest that the love of Pyrros and Eleonora had a shade of death upon it from the very beginning, or that they were seeking oblivion from mortality in the Multi-Colored Valley. Regardless, we have come to the point where the flower language is no longer transparent.

Since "Eleonora" is not the only Poe tale that mentions asphodels—they figure in "Berenice" and another Poe pastoral, "The Island of the Fay"—we may suspect that Poe preferred the musicality and peculiarity of the word itself. It might also be an allusion to his poem, "The Valley of Unrest," since this valley, the Valley Nis, is a direct poetic antipode of the Multi-Colored Valley. In the poem, the sun grows paler when falling "on the quiet Asphodel" that grows side by side with "uneasy violets" lying like "the human eye" (192). This makes us wonder whether Poe used "asphodel" as a poetic signature, a self-referential sign. In "Eleonora," asphodels are also paired with "uneasy" violets: "one by one asphodels withered away, and there sprang up in place of them, ten by ten, dark eye-like violets that quivered uneasily" (160). Poe's anthropomorphic trope "eye-like" is somehow more disturbing than the blood of the dying Chrysanthenium in Sigourney's poem; it evokes a feeling of inquietude and anxiety that is at odds with the sentimental reconciliation with mortality suggested in the tale and makes the flower's meaning—"faithfulness"—sound uncanny. Jerome McGann's words about Poe's poetry are also true for the poeticized language of "Eleonora": "Poe's poetry is unusual because it marks itself as such: a mournful and never-ending remembrance, haunted in inter-text" (148).

In "Eleonora," Poe offers his own florilegium in miniature that is at once recognizable and distinct. For his purposes, he changes the color of asphodels; in "Eleonora," they are "red, transformed by the power of love," in Mabbott's words (2: 647 n13). Unlike their pale, deadly counterparts, ruby-colored asphodels seem to match perfectly with their new meaning and fit in the landscape, enkindled by love and with red and gold colors prevailing, that Poe fashions in the "literary-annual" style, to paraphrase Fisher (183).

> And life arose in our paths; for the tall flamingo, hitherto unseen, with all gay glowing birds, flaunted his scarlet plumage before us. The golden and silver fish haunted the river, out of the bosom of which issued, little by little, a murmur that swelled, at length, into a lulling melody more divine than that of the harp of Æolus—sweeter than all save the voice of Eleonora. And now, too, a voluminous cloud, which we had long watched in the regions of Hesper, floated out thence, all gorgeous in crimson and gold, and settling in peace above us, sank, day by day, lower and lower, until its edges rested upon the tops of the mountains, turning all their dimness into magnificence, and shutting us up, as if forever, within a magic prison-house of grandeur and of glory. ("Eleanora," *The Gift* 157)

In this dense, poetic fragment, Poe uses a handful of shared clichés. Compare, for example, the fragment from "Early Death," a poem by Miss Miles published in the same volume, also describing the innocent spring-time of a young girl's life before her premature death: "She loved the merry spring-time, / Its gay and sunny hours, / The glad song of its bright birds, / Its wealth of buds and flowers; / The gushing of its fountains, / Its sunset's lingering ray, / And the golden cloud that floated / So silently away!" (170).

The parallels between both fragments are worth highlighting: "gay hours" and "bright birds" versus "gay glowing birds"; "the gushing of the fountains" versus "a murmur" of the river; the floating "golden cloud" versus the cloud "all gorgeous in crimson and glowing." The cloud in "Eleonora" will also float away, but after Eleonora's death. However, in Poe's story, the same apparently hieratic pastoral clichés have something troubling about them. Poe's metaphoric language seems excessive compared to that of Miles. Poe's birds are not just bright—they are glowing. The river is not just "gushing" or "murmuring"; its murmur is a "lulling melody more divine than that of the harp of Æolu—sweeter than all save the voice of Eleonora." The cloud is not simply golden, but "all gorgeous in crimson and gold." Poe's description suggests a poetic intensification of reality that makes it at once surreal and conspicuously ornamental. In "Eleonora," everything, indeed, is redundant:

the green grass is "thick, short, perfectly even, and vanilla-perfumed" (156) while flowers are "strange," "brilliant," and "star-shaped" (157).

The style of "Eleonora" is different from that of the neighboring pieces that are written in a considerably more moderate and balanced manner. Poe's tropes also lack a generalizing, and therefore reconciling, cathartic effect of traditional emblematizing as widely used by his fellow poets, such as Lydia Sigourney. My point is not that Poe's style is superior to that of *The Gift's* female poets discussed above. Rather, I argue that he draws on the contemporary language of sentimental poetry and yet, at the same time, purloins and transforms this language, placing his signature on it and marking it as Poesque.

In a similar vein, it is tempting to suggest that the tale's exuberant style mimics the excessive ornamentality of gift books as a genre. The volume of *The Gift* in which "Eleonora" was published, for example, is a fine piece of artwork, bound in gilt-decorated full calf with gilt-edge pages, the title-page vignette representing a beautiful female head, and decorated with seven exquisite plates. Reviewers usually discussed the "dress" of gift books in detail. Some, like Poe, praised their handsome bindings and elegant engravings while others, for example, Park Benjamin, a contemporary critic, expressed contempt for their lavish and gaudy looks.

"Eleonora" relates to *The Gift* thematically through the flower and flower language motif that was endowed with extra symbolic meaning in the gift book pages. But more significantly, it assumes a similar gem-like quality due to its language, dense with metaphors, similes, descriptions, and other stylistic adornments—replicas of the gift book's ornaments. The story's stylistic exaggerations, almost verging on bad taste, bring us to the limits of the gift book's own ornamental character and test its potential. Or, to use Poe's own favorite phrase, in "Eleonora" he "out-herods Herod."[6]

My reading of "Eleonora" in *The Gift* is an example of one possible way we may re-read and reconsider Poe in gift books, and how gift books may be used for studying and teaching Poe. We may further inquire, following up on Eliza Richards's seminal study on the subject, the extent of Poe's indebtedness to contemporary female poets or to sentimental poetry and fiction in general. We may examine if and how editorial arrangements and a specific gift book genre influenced contemporary perception of his tales. We may ask how far Poe's engagement in material and book culture went, and how aware he was of the contextual and paratextual framework that gift books offered. In the case of "Eleonora," its gift book publication appears to intensify and justify certain properties of the tale's manner and style that otherwise may seem trivial and clichéd or, instead, too peculiar and extravagant.

The "Eleonora" example also returns us to the metaphor of flower picking or bouquet arrangement that may describe the specific anthologizing practices we encounter in gift books. While the tale's inclusion in a gift book and its thematic echoes with the neighboring poems are coincidental, arbitrary, and perhaps even unintentional, together these pieces make up the whole of a sort, bound together by the power of association. *The Gift*'s flower pieces, including Poe's "Eleonora," literalize the book's ornamental, festive arrangement, adding a unifying aesthetic dimension to the otherwise miscellaneous collection.

Notes

1. Leon Jackson relates the antebellum gift book vogue with "a revolution in political thought, specifically the displacement of republican ideology by modern liberalism, that made it possible for middle class Americans to think, for the first time, of luxurious objects as desirable, rather than as dangerous or corrupting" (np).

2. The term "gem" was often used in the titles of annuals—e.g., *Gems of the Season*, *Gems of the Western World*, and *Gems from the Sacred Mine*.

3. See more on this in my essay on Hawthorne's tale in *The Token* ("Hawthorne's Gifts," 590).

4. I discuss this subject briefly in "'The Purloined Letter' in the Gift Book: Reading Poe in a Contemporary Context" (339–40).

5. Classic studies of "Eleonora" emphasized its allegorical character, numerous literary allusions, and explicit biographical context. It is often read as a story belonging to the subgenre of Poe's tales with "the death of the beautiful woman" motif. See, for example, Baskett, Benton, Dayan (210–23), and Fisher (178–88).

6. Poe uses this Shakespearean phrase in "Metzengerstein," "William Wilson," and "The Masque of the Red Death."

Works Cited

Ashtor, Gila. "The Gift (Book) That Keeps on Giving: Poe's 'The Purloined Letter,' Rereading, Reprinting, and Detective Fiction." *Poe Studies*, vol. 45, no. 1, 2012, pp. 55–77.

Baskett, Sam S. "A Damsel with a Dulcimer: An Interpretation of Poe's 'Eleonora.'" *Modern Language Notes*, vol. 73, no. 5, 1958, pp. 332–38.

Belasco, Susan. "Walt Whitman and the Poetry Marketplace of Antebellum America." *Leaves of Grass: The Sesquicentennial Essays*, edited by Susan Belasco, Ed Folsom, and Kenneth M. Price, U of Nebraska P, 2007, pp. 179–98.

Benton, Richard P. "Platonic Allegory in Poe's 'Eleonora.'" *Nineteenth Century Fiction*, vol. 22, no. 3, 1967, pp. 293–97.

Blocker, Jack S., Jr., David M. Fahey, and Ian R. Tyrell, editors. *Alcohol and Temperance in Modern History.* ABC-CLIO, 2003.

Brown, Mary Ann. "Glimpses of Heaven." *The Gift: A Christmas and New Year's Present.* Carey and Hart, 1842 (1841), pp. 81–82.

Cortambert, Louise, translator. *The Language of Flowers with Illustrative Poetry.* Saunders and Outley, 1835.

Dayan, Joan. *Fables of Mind: An Inquiry into Poe's Fiction.* Oxford UP, 1987.

Dickinson, Cindy. "Creating a World of Books, Friends, and Flowers: Gift Books and Inscriptions, 1825–60." *Winterthur Portfolio,* vol. 31, no. 1, 1996, pp. 53–66.

Di Leo, Jeffrey R., editor. *On Anthologies: Politics and Pedagogy.* U of Nebraska P, 2004.

Faxon, Frederick F. *Literary Annuals and Gift Books: A Bibliography 1823–1903.* Private Library Association, reprinted edition 1973.

Fisher, Benjamin Franklin. "'Eleonora': Poe and Madness." *Poe and His Times: The Artist and His Milieu,* edited by Fisher, Edgar Allan Poe Society, 1990, pp. 178–88.

The Gift: A Christmas and New Year's Present. Carey and Hart, 1843 (1842).

Griswold, Rufus W., editor. *The Poets and Poetry of America, with an Historical Introduction.* Carey and Hart, 1842.

Hawkins, Ann R. *Teaching Bibliography, Textual Criticism, and Book History.* Routledge, 2015.

Jackson, Leon. "The Gift, the Book, and the Gift Book: The Biography of an Antebellum Commodity." Gift Economy and the US Antebellum Market, 6 June 2016, Budapest, Central European U. Workshop Presentation.

Kete, Mary Louise. "The Reception of Nineteenth-Century American Poetry." *The Cambridge Companion to Nineteenth-Century American Poetry,* edited by Kerry Larson, Cambridge UP, 2011, pp. 15–36.

Korte, Barbara. "Flowers for the Picking: Anthologies of Poetry in (British) Literary and Cultural Studies." *Anthologies of British Poetry: Critical Perspectives from Literary and Cultural Studies,* edited by Barbara Korte, Ralf Schneider, and Stefanie Lethbridge, Rodopi, 2000, pp. 1–41.

Lehuu, Isabelle. *Carnival on the Page: Popular Print Media in Antebellum America.* U of North Carolina P, 2000.

Mabbott, Thomas Ollive, editor. *The Collected Works of Edgar Allan Poe.* Harvard UP, 1969 and 1978, 3 vols.

———. "Eleonora." *The Collected Works of Edgar Allan Poe,* vol. 2, Harvard UP, 1978, pp. 635–47.

Mercer, Miss. "Fairy Tale." *Southern Literary Messenger,* vol. 2, no 2, 1836, pp. 77–78.

McGann, Jerome. *The Poet Edgar Allan Poe: Alien Angel.* Harvard UP, 2014.

Miles, Miss M. "Early Death." *The Gift: A Christmas and New Year's Present.* Carey and Hart, 1842 (1841), pp. 170–72.

Mujica, Barbara. "Teaching Literature: Canon, Controversy, and the Literary Anthology." *Hispania,* vol. 80, no 2, 1997, pp. 203–15.

Nissenbaum, Stephen. *The Battle for Christmas: A Cultural History of America's Most Cherished Holiday*. Vintage Books, 1997.

Onslow, Barbara. "Gendered Productions: Annuals and Gift Books." *Journalism and the Periodical Press in Nineteenth-Century Britain*, edited by Joanne Shattock, Cambridge UP, 2017, pp. 66–84.

Osgood, F[rances]. S[argent]. "A Wreath of Riddles." *The Gift: A Christmas and New Year's Present*. Carey and Hart, 1842 (1841), pp. 163–64.

Piper, Andrew. *Dreaming in Books: The Making of the Bibliographic Imagination in the Romantic Age*. U of Chicago P, 2009.

Poe, Edgar Allan. "Eleonora." *The Gift: A Christmas and New Year's Present*. Carey and Hart, 1842 (1841), pp. 154–63.

———. "Poe to Carey, Lea, and Carey," July 28, 1829. *The Collected Letters of Edgar Allan Poe*, edited by John Ward Ostrom, Burton R. Pollin, and Jeffrey A. Savoye, vol. 1, Gordian, 2008, p. 40.

———. "The Valley of the Unrest." *The Complete Works of Edgar Allan Poe*, edited by Thomas Ollive Mabbott, vol. 1, 1969, pp. 189–96.

Richards, Eliza. *Gender and the Poetics of Reception in Poe's Circle*. Cambridge UP, 2004.

Shinn, Kathryn K. "Gift Books." *Edgar Allan Poe in Context*, edited by Kevin J. Hayes, Cambridge UP, 2013, pp.179–87.

Shoberl, Frederic. *The Language of Flowers with Illustrative Poetry*. Lea & Blanchard, 1848.

Sigourney, [Lydia]. "Autumn and the Garden." *The Gift: A Christmas and New Year's Present*. Carey and Hart, 1842 (1841), pp. 154–63.

Stevenson, Louise. "Home, Books and Reading." *A History of the Book in America*, edited by Scott E. Kasper, Jeffrey D. Groves, Stephen W. Nissenbaum, and Michael Winship, vol. 3, U of North Carolina P, 2007, pp. 319–30.

Thompson, Ralph. *American Literary Annuals and Gift Books, 1825–1865*. The H. W. Wilson Company, 1936.

Vale de Gato, Margarida. "The Collaborative Anthology in the Literary Translation Course." *The Interpreter and Translator Trainer*, vol. 9, no 1, 2015, pp. 50–62.

Urakova, Alexandra. "Hawthorne's Gifts: Re-reading 'Alice Doane's Appeal' and 'The Great Carbuncle' in *The Token*." *New England Quarterly*, vol. 88, no 4, 2015, pp. 587–613.

———. "'The Purloined Letter' in the Gift Book: Reading Poe in a Contemporary Context." *Nineteenth-Century Literature*, vol. 64, no 3, 2009, pp. 323–46.

PART II

ASSEMBLING POE IN ENGLISH: EDITORS, EDITIONS, AND THE COLLEGE ANTHOLOGY

CHAPTER FOUR

~

Selecting for Posterity

Poe's Early Editors and the Battle for a Definitive Collection

Jeffrey A. Savoye

The idea of a complete edition of Edgar Allan Poe's writings seems tantalizingly possible, and yet it has consistently resisted fruition. Poe died young, his literary career spanning only about twenty-four years, beginning a little before the publication of *Tamerlane and Other Poems* in 1827 and ending with his death in 1849. He wrote approximately ninety-seven poems, sixty-seven short stories, and two novels.[1] In addition, there are pieces that are difficult to place in terms of genre, such as *Eureka*, "Autography," "Marginalia," a number of essays, many notable reviews, criticisms, and miscellaneous items. Considerable problems arise as one delves further into the editorial and unsigned material. Did Poe write the review of Cooper's *Mercedes of Castile* or Ainsworth's *The Tower of London* from *Graham's Magazine* (respectively January and March 1841), or are they indeed too early for his connection to that magazine?[2] Can he be called the author in any meaningful sense of either of the cut-and-paste series, "A Chapter on Science and Art" or "A Chapter on Field Sports and Manly Pastimes" from *Burton's Gentleman's Magazine*? Which of the short unsigned items in the *New York Mirror* for 1844–1845 are by Poe, and which are by Willis, or someone else unknown? Should an edition strive to include as much of Poe's criticism as possible, or just the longest and most significant items? In printing the criticism, must Poe's frequently long quotations from the works being reviewed also be retained? If the quotations are removed, how much of Poe's text should be adjusted to cover the omissions? Should a complete collection of Poe's poems include such dubious items as "A Monody on Doctor Olmstead" and "Epigram on Wall Street," as T. O. Mabbott did in 1969?[3] Even for the tales there are complications to the idea of being truly complete, mostly due to Poe's penchant for modifying and reprinting his texts. Is "The Domain of Arnheim" a fully new story, or a heavy revision of "The Landscape Garden"?[4] In printing "Berenice" or "The Oval Portrait," which of the versions authorized by Poe should be presented? If one favors later versions, what about the paragraphs Poe himself omitted from these two tales? Must an editor present a variorum edition to be complete? Most importantly, will more than a handful of readers really care?[5]

In the decades following Poe's death, a series of editors tackled the ever-shifting challenge of selecting and presenting a collection of Poe's works that balanced intellectual, artistic, and commercial interests, preserving what seemed to them to be Poe's best or most representative writings while also appealing to readers they hoped would buy and appreciate the resulting volumes. Although each generation of scholars generally built on the work of its predecessors, the evolution of editions was not always directly linear. Seeking to leave their own imprint on Poe's legacy, or to borrow for themselves a little of Poe's enduring fame, these editors enjoyed the relatively rare luxury of being able to revisit what was largely the same material over and over. Sometimes they were able to capitalize on recent discoveries or on an evolving audience for increasingly elaborate production values or academic apparatus. The key to the demand for a new crop of these editions, however, has always rested primarily in the popularity inherent in Poe's writings themselves and on the strangely symbiotic relationship between interest in Poe's writings and the emulsion of uncertain fact, gossip, and myth-making that forms Poe's personal biography. Accordingly, the public marketplace for Poe has always blended intellectual and more vulgar attentions. For the present study, I will evaluate the following notable early editions of Poe's collected works, those prepared by R. W. Griswold (*The Works of the Late Edgar Allan Poe*, in four volumes, 1850–1856), J. H. Ingram (*The Works of Edgar Allan Poe*, in four volumes, 1874–1875, 1876, and 1884), E. C. Stedman and G. E. Woodberry (*The Works of Edgar Allan Poe*, in ten volumes, 1894–1895), and J. A. Harrison (*The Complete Works of Edgar Allan Poe*, in seventeen volumes, 1902). These editions represent the formative period of scholarly attempts at publishing a comprehensive collection of Poe's writings.[6]

During his lifetime, Poe frequently appealed to publishers for a more extensive collection of his writings, but in these efforts he was consistently frustrated.[7] It would not be until after his death that an edition combining the poetry, fiction, essays, and criticism would become a reality. Even then the edition was issued in fits and starts, first with two volumes early in 1850, then a third later in 1850 and, finally, in 1856, the addition of a fourth volume.

This edition could certainly be argued as having been a commercial as well as a literary success as it remained in print, with nearly annual reissues, for more than twenty years, and because it was the basis for several later editions.[8]

Perhaps ironically, the 1850–1856 collection, ostensibly published not only as a literary memorial to Poe but also for the financial benefit of Poe's impoverished mother-in-law, Maria Clemm, was edited by his literary nemesis, Rufus Wilmot Griswold. The resulting edition has often been attacked, mostly due to Griswold's despicable memoir of Poe (first published in the third volume) and the suspicions it understandably casts over the entire collection. Even today, however, it stands as a very good basic collection, including all of Poe's most important writings and often incorporating Poe's final revisions, not otherwise available. Of particular interest is a statement made in the brief preface of the fourth volume: "The publisher has now finished the complete collection of the WORKS OF EDGAR A. POE, originally contemplated. The series of volumes, of which this is the fourth, embraces, it is believed, everything written by him which he himself would have wished thus to preserve" (4: v).[9] Here we are confronted with what certainly seems like a contradiction—a "complete collection" and yet "everything written by him *which he himself would have wished thus to preserve*." The obvious implication is that Poe wrote other things not included in the collection, which, by definition, cannot truly be called "complete" and, if a selection has been made, it must necessarily be a subjective evaluation by the editor and not the author himself. Although only one of the editions covered by this survey actually uses the word "complete" in its title, all proudly make some claim of completeness. Some were limited by access to material and others by editorial preferences. Admitted or not, all were also restricted by practical matters of what publishers would print and what readers were thought likely to buy.

Following confirmation of Poe's death on October 9, 1849, his mother-in-law, Mrs. Clemm, was understandably wracked by implacable grief and a desperate sense of financial survival. Encouraged by her friend, Mrs. Sarah Anna Lewis, she approached Griswold with the hope that he would "act as his [Poe's] literary Executor, and superintend the publication of his works" (1: iii).[10] Thus, while Griswold is not specifically listed on the title page as editor, his role is made clear. In assigning this challenge, Mrs. Clemm made freely available to Griswold a daunting archive that had been accumulated by Poe himself, including manuscripts, copies of printed works with Poe's own corrections, and letters that Poe had kept from various correspondents. In addition, Griswold actively sought out manuscripts of Poe's lectures and whatever material could be donated by the field of editors and literary folk who had dealt with Poe's writings in a professional capacity and who felt moved to comply with the public appeals of preparing the edition for the noble cause of benefitting Poe's beloved and bereft "Muddy" (the affectionate and well-known nickname Poe used for Mrs. Clemm).

Having secured what he considered adequate legal authority, and sufficient material to proceed, Griswold sought a publisher willing to undertake the expense, and with some interest in the charitable aspects of the project.[11] He found a suitable candidate in Justus Starr Redfield, a New York bookseller and minor publisher, established in 1841. Although he has some slight fame as the publisher of several works by William Gilmore Simms, it is for the Poe edition that Redfield is chiefly remembered (see Raymond). Griswold was clearly in a hurry to execute his assigned task, presumably to take advantage of the currency of public sentiment in the light of Poe's recent death and to have the books available for the lucrative Christmas market. These intentions were necessarily delayed by practical considerations, with the first two volumes (featuring tales and poetry) being issued in January 1850, while Griswold continued to labor on the volume of criticism and miscellanies. Perhaps in part as a result of this haste, the arrangement of material is somewhat careless, beyond the basic division of tales, poems, and criticism plus miscellaneous items. As Poe's designated literary executor—by Mrs. Clemm if not actually by Poe himself—Griswold had access to a unique set of materials, most of which appears to have been destroyed in the process of typesetting, and others of which later spent many years in hiding as treasures of various private collectors.[12]

In the first volume, Griswold presented thirty-one of Poe's short stories, including the eight or nine tales, such as "The Cask of Amontillado" and "The Fall of the House of Usher," that are still among Poe's best-known writings. No obvious rationale is apparent in the order, other than the fact that a number of related tales are grouped together. Following the 1845 *Tales*, which had been selected and edited by E. A. Duyckinck, Griswold puts the three Dupin stories one after the other, in order of composition, and also the cosmological dialogues of "The Colloquy of Monos and Una" and "The Conversation of Eiros and Charmion." Extending this idea, he groups together Poe's four woman-centered tales, "Berenice," "Eleonora," "Ligeia," and "Morella." He also arranges "The Domain of Arnheim" and "Landor's Cottage" in sequence ("Landor's Cottage" being "a pendant to the Domain of Arnheim"), and he puts back-to-back "Mesmeric Revelation" and "The Facts in the Case of M. Valdemar" as two tales involving mesmerism. Not all of the stories that might be deemed similar are forced into such a considered order, with "The Tell-Tale Heart" being nestled somewhat incongruously between "The Assignation" and "The Domain of Arnheim," isolated by the pleasant daydream of "The Island of the Fay" from a distinct block of such horror stories as "The Black Cat," "The Cask of Amontillado," and "The Masque of the Red Death." In the overall sequence, it does not appear that Griswold has followed any instructions directly from Poe. As Poe made clear in his letter of August 9, 1846, to Philip P. Cooke:

> In writing these Tales one by one, at long intervals, I have kept the book-unity always in mind—that is, each has been composed with reference to its effect as part of a whole. In this view, one of my chief aims has been the widest diversity of subject, thought, & especially tone & manner of handling. Were all my tales now before me in a large volume and as the composition of another—the merit which would principally arrest my attention would be the wide diversity and variety. (Ostrom et al. 1: 595–96)

His own handwritten table of contents for the proposed but never published *Phantasy-Pieces* (about 1842) seems to embody this same idea, with Poe spreading out tales with similar themes or moods, intentionally emphasizing the differences rather than sustaining a given effect across more than a single tale.[13]

In the second volume, rather than simply continuing with the remaining tales, Griswold began with forty-two poems, twenty-nine from the 1845 *The Raven and Other Poems* and thirteen additional poems. A few of these poems had been published in the 1829 *Al Aaraaf, Tamerlane and Minor Poems*, but were not used in 1845. Mostly, the new poems had been written since 1845, such as "Ulalume," "Eldorado," "For Annie," "The Bells," and "Annabel Lee." Following the poems, the prose-poem *Eureka*, and the two essays on poetry—"The Rationale of Verse" and "The Philosophy of Composition—Griswold resumed with another twenty-three tales, which, considering their position at the end of the second volume, were presumably considered by Griswold as lesser works.[14]

The third volume has generally been the most controversial, featuring Poe's frequently pointed criticisms and the long, miscellaneous collection of "Marginalia," which often touched on critical matters (especially in the form printed by Griswold). The criticism expands the idea of "The Literati of New York City" to "The Literati" in general, incorporating material from the 1846 series with longer versions from Poe's unfinished manuscript for his proposed "Literary America," supplemented with excerpts and full reviews on a variety of mostly American and British authors. How much of the final product is the result of Poe's intentions, and how much was influenced by

Griswold, is almost impossible to say. We know from a December 15, 1846, letter to George W. Eveleth that Poe had planned a book "on American Letters in general" (Ostrom et al. 1: 602), recycling earlier reviews, and it seems likely that Poe had accumulated one or more stacks of his own reviews for this purpose. Unfortunately, by listing the reviews under the names of the authors, Poe—or Griswold—has, intentionally or unintentionally, made the focus more about the people and less about the works being evaluated. Given the overlapping nature of much of this material, Griswold was particularly concerned about eliminating duplication, and the delay in publication presumably demonstrates the degree of effort necessary for editing and arranging the remaining selections into a useable form.[15] The most drastic changes were made to the "Marginalia," which reduced Poe's original 291 entries to 201, but added another 25 short items culled from various criticisms.

The three-volume set was reprinted in 1852, with no changes other than the imprint date on the title page. The 1853 edition incorporated a number of alterations, mostly reallocating material so that Griswold's preface and memoir joined the other introductory essays by Lowell and Willis in volume 1. By 1856, Griswold had been persuaded to assemble a fourth volume, featuring Poe's only finished novel, *The Narrative of Arthur Gordon Pym*, with some of what he had considered Poe's least meritorious tales (primarily humorous works), essays, and criticism to fill out the pages. Griswold died in 1857, and there were no further changes of note made to the set until late in 1860, when it moved from the hands of publisher J. S. Redfield to W. J. Widdleton. The new publisher made some effort to correct a number of typographical errors that had mostly appeared in 1855, presumably as a result of damage to the original stereoplates. Under Widdleton's devoted attention, the set was printed annually until Mrs. Clemm's death in 1871, at which time it was discontinued, although Widdleton continued to issue separate editions of Poe's poems and two "series" of the prose tales.[16]

This break in publication may have been seen as an invitation to John Henry Ingram, a British civil servant, industrious part-time author, and devoted Poe fan, to create a new edition of Poe's works. As an outgrowth of his series of biographical articles about Poe, Ingram sought to supplant the Griswold edition, at least in England. He first made known his plans in a letter of February 3, 1874, to Mrs. S. H. Whitman: "I want to edit all his works not reprinted in England and prefix *the* life," adding that he was being forced to rush his efforts as "it is necessary *to be before* Mr. Stoddard & Messers. Routledge, to be sure of success" (qtd. in Miller 16). In the same letter, he further noted that "If Routledges' [sic] bring out a collection with Mr. Stoddard's information, I fear that I shall not succeed in getting another publisher to take my edition out unless I have something *very different* to say & give. My real wish is to clear Poe's fame but to succeed I must, as you well know, come before the world with something fresh, clear, and attractive" (16). The volumes would initially be published one at a time, presumably for financial considerations as well as to have at least part of the set available for purchase as holiday gifts. The first volume was advertised as early as October 16, 1874, and it was ready for sale by November.

In his preface to the edition, Ingram states:

> In presenting to the public this collection—the first complete one—of Edgar Allan Poe's works, a few prefatory words are necessary. A considerable portion of the contents of these volumes, it may be pointed out, has escaped the notice of previous editors; and no pains have been spared to insure the accuracy of the whole by collating the various editions published during the author's lifetime,—including, in several instances, copies that received his personal supervision and correction,—in order to avoid the numerous errata which disfigure previous collections, both American and British (1: v).

In these bold claims, Ingram is clearly more interested in asserting the merits of his edition than in serving any cause of accuracy. While he did expend considerable effort in seeking out Poe's original printings, he had nothing like the access to manuscript material that Griswold had enjoyed, and he was forced by necessity to rely heavily on those earlier volumes, in terms of content and presentation, in making his own edition. Indeed, Ingram noted in a March 10, 1874, letter to George W. Eveleth: "I shall be glad to purchase any paper or publication containing anything not included in the 4 vol. collection of his works," specifying that his own copy was printed by "Widdleton, 1864" (qtd. in Brown 429).[17]

Whatever might have been his grand intentions, Ingram ended up mostly using Griswold's texts, with some additional editing. Although he was perhaps simply bragging, Ingram's edition of 1874–1875 did include a few important additions and restored a good deal of the text from Poe's original reviews, especially in "Longfellow's Ballad." More significantly, he rearranged material in a more cohesive manner, although consistently with a conscious adherence to Griswold's edition. Ingram's volume 1 has the same contents, in terms of Poe's writings, as Griswold's volume 1, only slightly rearranged. Ingram presents the same thirty-one tales, but he moves "The Gold-Bug" from the second tale to the first. (By putting "The Gold-Bug" first, Ingram may be following the 1845 *Tales*, which also starts with "The Gold-Bug.") "The Thousand-and-Second Tale of Scheherazade" is moved several tales further down the list. The three Dupin stories are moved as a block to the end of the entries.[18]

For volume 2, Ingram continued to shuffle things around, primarily reuniting the tales Griswold had scattered across volumes 2 and 4. Ingram takes *Pym*, from Griswold's fourth volume, and puts that first. He follows that long work with the same twenty-three tales as Griswold's second volume, omitting only "The Philosophy of Furniture" (more properly moved to the sequence of essays elsewhere), supplemented by the twelve tales from volume 4, omitting only "The Landscape Garden" (presumably because he felt it duplicated "The Domain of Arnheim"). In doing so, he retains Griswold's original sequencing of these tales.

For his third volume, Ingram presented the poems with no additional texts, although he greatly altered the order of items, presumably reflecting his own sense of their importance. Following the 1845 edition, Ingram more formally divides them into mature poems and poems written in youth, although he does not precisely follow the same selection or sequence of items in these sections. ("Israfel," for example, which appears in the main section of poems in *The Raven and Other Poems*, is relegated by Ingram to the poems of youth.) Ingram alters a number of titles, but technically adds only one poem, "To Helen" ("Helen thy beauty is to me . . ."), which in Griswold's edition appeared only in the reprint of Lowell's article on Poe. Ingram does not include the Lowell article, and thus places the poem more prominently among its brethren. Like Griswold, he follows the poems with *Eureka* and then essays, which he expanded by bringing "The Philosophy of Furniture," "Maelzel's Chess-Player," "Letter to B——," and "Magazine Writing—Peter Snook" from other volumes and by adding "Cryptography" (reprinting the first of Poe's essays on secret writing, taken from *Graham's Magazine* of 1841). He then repeated "Fifty Suggestions" (from Griswold's volume 3), and made a new compilation of "Marginalia," further supplemented by his own selection of "Pinakidia" (originally published in the *Southern Literary Messenger* in 1836), "Some Secrets of the Magazine Prison-House," and "Anastatic Printing" (both from the *Broadway Journal* of 1845). In making his own selection of "Marginalia," Ingram includes all but nine of the items from Griswold's edition, restoring a mere dozen from the original first two installments of forty-three items in the *United States Magazine and Democratic Review* of 1844, and another four items from a later installment of 1846 in the same periodical, plus three more from the final installments in the *Southern Literary Messenger* of 1849. To the main selection, Ingram appends an "addenda" with ten short items culled from reviews in *Graham's Magazine* of 1841 and the *Broadway Journal* of 1845. In his zeal to add new material, Ingram mistakenly includes an excerpt from an unsigned review of Lord Bolingbroke from *Graham's* July 1841 issue, which is not by Poe.[19]

Volume 4 was devoted entirely to criticism, beginning with the newly resurrected "Autography" series of 1841–1842.[20] In selecting and arranging the criticism, Ingram made extensive and complicated changes, revealing not only sensitivity in serving what he saw as Poe's literary reputation, but also particular awareness of his immediate audience of British readers. He added, for example, Poe's review of Thomas Hood's "Prose and Verse" and moved reviews of seven British authors to the front of the list.[21] The entries for "The Literati of New York City," mostly featuring obscure American writers who were even more obscure in 1874, were moved to the end of the main section, and several were dropped entirely (such as Elizabeth Bogart and James Lawson). The exceedingly bitter Thomas Dunn Brown entry was restored to the originally published version of Thomas Dunn English.[22] Reviews of *Arabia Petraea*, *The Quacks of Helicon*, and *Astoria* were taken from Griswold's volume 4. The review of *The Book of Gems*, edited by S. C. Hall, was added under the new title, "Old English Poetry," a title that would be retained in numerous reprints. He also renamed a number of other reviews, and removed the review of "Mr. Longfellow and Other Plagiarists." Ingram retains the review of Mrs. Osgood (from the *Southern Literary Messenger*), but he moves it out of the section on "The Literati" (and does not restore the "Literati" article on Mrs. Osgood). For the entry on Hawthorne, Ingram retained Griswold's text (itself reprinted from *Godey's Lady's Book*), but he reversed the order of the two sections. Ingram retitles "Mr. Griswold and the Poets" as merely "The Poets and Poetry of America," and he omits the portion about the *Female Poets of America*. He also reverted the title of the review of E. P. Whipple to "Critics and Criticism." In making these changes, Ingram may have felt that he was undoing Griswold's editorial meddling.

In addition to his own editorial efforts, Ingram's primary innovation was the creation of a general subject index, which includes material in the memoir and in the various Poe texts. (For example, the page range containing the tale "Some Words with a Mummy" is cited under an entry for "Egypt, ancient, arts and sciences in.") In a similar vein, Ingram not only made his own selection of items for "Marginalia," but he also assigned short titles to each item and arranged them alphabetically by these titles, essentially functioning as a secondary subject index.[23]

In discussing the Ingram edition, it is necessary to also consider two other distinct but related printings, both of which reflect Ingram's editorial hand: the resurrected Widdleton edition (four volumes, 1876), and the Nimmo edition of *Tales and Poems of Edgar Allan Poe* (four volumes, 1884). When

Widdleton resumed publication of the Griswold set, the publisher replaced Griswold's memoir with Ingram's and added several of the more significant items collected by Ingram, but otherwise essentially retained Griswold's texts, allowing the printer to continue to use the stereoplates already on hand and to accept the cost of new type only for wholly new material that Ingram had added to his edition. One other item added to the 1876 Widdleton set was the poem "Alone." Although it has long been accepted under that assigned title as canonical, the attribution was somewhat controversial at the time, and Ingram himself was never quite able to accept it.[24] The Nimmo edition is chiefly notable for adding Poe's second but never completed novel, "The Journal of Julius Rodman," which Ingram had discovered in 1876, and for which he had printed brief excerpts in the November 3, 1877, issue of the London *Mirror of Literature*. A second feature of some interest may be the introduction of categorization of the tales, a practice that would be more extensively followed by Stedman and Woodberry and some modern editions, such as Stuart and Susan Levine's *The Short Fiction of Edgar Allan Poe: An Annotated Edition*.[25]

Nearly two decades later, the Stedman and Woodberry edition inverted the previous pattern of editors in search of a publisher. Herbert Stuart Stone and Hannibal Ingalls Kimball, Jr. had both attended Harvard College, graduating in 1894. While still undergraduates, they had formed the publishing house of Stone and Kimball, in January 1893, with an intended emphasis on important and, above all, beautifully produced books. Moving their base of operations to Chicago after graduation, the firm would move to New York in January 1896 and dissolve in 1897 (see Creek and also Kramer). On December 29, 1893, Stone wrote to Edmund Clarence Stedman, soliciting the eminent poet and critic to serve as editor for a proposed edition of Poe's works, at that time envisioned as eight volumes, with illustrations by Aubrey Beardsley and Elihu Vedder (Scholnick 264). The set was to be a demonstration of what the new publisher could offer to an educated readership as well as a kind of personal memorial to Poe. Stedman, although he had long been interested in Poe, was reluctant to start another demanding editorial effort, but he agreed on the condition that the entire text would be newly edited, and that George Edward Woodberry would serve as his co-editor. By January 10, 1894, the terms were agreed upon, and the editors began their labors (265). By the time it was finally realized, the set would run ten volumes. Beardsley had only provided four illustrations, and he was replaced by Albert Edward Sterner, a well-known American illustrator for such popular magazines as *Harper's*, *Century*, and *Scribner's*. It would indeed be a beautiful edition, available in cloth and a more deluxe vellum, both decorated with art-nouveau poppies, subtly invoking the idea of De Quincey's "Confessions of an Opium Eater" and the hallucinatory nature of some of Poe's more fantastic writings.

Extending Ingram's notion of categorizing the tales, Stedman and Woodberry arranged Poe's stories across five volumes under the somewhat poetic groupings of "Romances of Death" (further divided as "Overture," "Terrestrial," "Celestial," and "Finale"), "Old-World Romances," "Tales of Conscience," "Tales of Natural Beauty," "Tales of Pseudo-Science," "Tales of Ratiocination," "Tales of Illusion," "Extravagance and Caprice," and "Tales of Adventure and Exploration." The editors categorized the essays "The Poetic Principle," "The Philosophy of Composition," and "The Rationale of Verse" as Literary Criticism (putting them at the head of the first volume of criticism). For the tales in volume 1, Stedman and Woodberry added locations beneath the title, almost as a subtitle, such as Rome for "The Cask of Amontillado" and Northern Italy for "The Masque of the Red Death." For the poems, they put first the handful of poems that Poe marked for changes in his personal copy of *The Raven and Other Poems*, roughly following the 1845 order, but with more substantial items leading the group.

Stedman and Woodberry even more heavily restructured the "Marginalia," adopting Ingram's idea of entry titles (although not his actual titles) and going even further to combine entries under a related topic. The entries dedicated to a given author are mostly presented in sequence (i.e., Foque, Bulwer, Dickens, etc.). As they get closer to the end, the topics are more and more miscellaneous in nature and tend to represent single items from the original series. We end up with two sections that are both called "Art." The editors included Poe's "Letter to B——" but removed it from the status of an essay proper, as it had enjoyed in previous editions, and buried it instead in the notes to the poems. From Ingram's various additions, the pair retain several but omit the "Pinakidia." In giving the text of "Anastatic Printing," Stedman and Woodberry comment in a note: "This is an example of a few similar articles, such as 'Street Paving' in the same journal, which are not reprinted, as they are of ephemeral nature" (9: 317).

The chief innovations of the Stedman and Woodberry edition are the long, thoughtful introductory essays for the various divisions of Poe's writings, the variorum texts for the poems, and an overall scholarly attitude toward the whole production, with editorial policies well considered and applied. It is also the first edition to implement the numerous manuscript changes Poe made in the J. L. Graham copy of *Tales* and *The Raven and Other Poems*, and in the Hurst-Wakeman copy of *Eureka*.

All of Poe's earliest editors apparently felt quite free to impose their own preferences in terms of spelling and punctuation. An initial turning point, in terms of historical fidelity, may have begun in 1884 with the so-called "second edition" of *Tamerlane and Other Poems*, edited by Richard Herne Shepherd. Ingram, who had discovered what was then thought to be the unique copy of the original edition in the collection of the British Museum, published his findings in *Belgravia* (June 1876), with full texts of the "suppressed" poems, including "The Happiest Day" and "Evening Star," which had not been seen in print since they were included in the original pamphlet of 1827. In so doing, Ingram, as he had done previously for Poe's works, modified spellings and punctuation, presumably in what he saw as his proper role as editor. Shepherd reprinted the texts with an almost pedantic fidelity to the originals, retaining Poe's punctuation, spellings, and quaint use of contractions, such as "tho'" for "though" and "th'" for "the." Stedman and Woodberry continued to apply their own editorial preferences in 1894–1895, but the discussion had presumably already begun, and a new set of Poe's works, published in 1902, would be the first to at least claim more faithful adherence to the historical texts.

The origins of this new edition, credited primarily to James Albert Harrison, are the murkiest, and they require a certain amount of conjecture. It appears that the idea began when Harrison, a professor of English and Romance Languages at the University of Virginia, was "engaged in collecting material for filling the Poe Alcove in the new Rotunda Library" ("New Glimpses" 2158). The alcove project was itself inspired by long-standing interest in Poe by the students of the university. Although Poe had not actually finished his studies at the institution, it is clear from contemporary articles in the *University of Virginia Magazine* that he was considered by later generations of students to be a kind of honorary graduate, perhaps as much for his reputedly wild ways as for his literary reputation.[26] The Poe Memorial Association was formed by a group of students on April 13, 1897, with the vague notion of dedicating as a kind of shrine the room Poe had inhabited while a student, and as part of the plans for a commemoration to Poe's memory on the fiftieth anniversary of his death. As Harrison sought out not only the well-known editions but also the early copies of such magazines as *Graham's* and the *Southern Literary Messenger* from the library shelves, he would have been faced with the difficulties of attempting to determine which of the unsigned reviews in these magazines were by Poe. In so doing, he must have been greatly impressed by the number of items not represented in any of these editions, and the opportunity of expanding the known works of Poe seems to have set his mind on a new edition. In his preface to the published form of the dedication ceremonies, dated May

1, 1901, Charles W. Kent states that "Our distinguished Secretary, Professor James A. Harrison, is now engaged upon a Critical Edition of Poe's works. This edition, with its peculiar merits and its scholarly accuracy in all details, will, it is hoped, leave so little to be done hereafter that it will be recognized at once as the final critical edition" (6).[27]

Harrison was assisted in his labors by Charles William Kent, another member of the faculty, and Robert Armistead Stewart, a graduate student who earned his PhD during the course of working on the edition and whose doctoral dissertation, a study of the textual changes in Poe's works, was used as notes for the edition.[28] Above all, it seems that Harrison and his colleagues wanted to reclaim Poe as a Southern writer whose reputation had spread around the world. Harrison included all of the works that had already been printed in earlier editions, but he returned them, more or less, to the form in which they had originally been published. "The Literati of New York City," for example, was no longer integrated with the criticism, but restored to a full entry in its own right. Similarly, Harrison's "Marginalia" follows the original order of publication, although inadvertently omitting two installments (*Democratic Review*, July 1846, and *Graham's Magazine*, March 1848). Most significantly, the criticism was expanded to occupy six of the seventeen volumes, even omitting many of the quotations Poe provided to illustrate his points. In so doing, Harrison included a large amount of material that was not previously available to scholars, arranged chronologically by the original date of publication rather than by the author being evaluated. So expansive was his selection that it became the primary subject of both praise and attack.[29]

Thomas Y. Crowell Company was an established and experienced publisher, but not an especially respectable one. It had been chiefly a reprint house of inexpensive books, particularly of poetry, but in printing the Harrison edition the company did so with enthusiasm and style (DeLowry-Fryman). The set was issued in two sizes, a large paper edition and a cabinet-sized edition, the latter being designated the Virginia Edition (as a pun on the name of Poe's beloved wife and the state he considered his home). Both sets used the same type and pagination, with the large paper edition simply affording wider margins. Both sets were available in elegantly decorated cloth and leather, and they were judiciously illustrated. In addition to genuinely striving for something approximating completeness, the chief innovations of the Harrison edition are the extension of a variorum text to the tales, the most substantial biography that had been included, and especially the volume of letters, for the first time accumulating Poe's correspondence in its own right and not merely as excerpts.

Now the stage was fully set, and the battle scene played out before the public. The Griswold edition had more or less been subsumed by the Ingram set, although these volumes carried forward a good deal of Griswold's labors (eschewing the infamous memoir). Ingram's editions, both the British and American sets with their somewhat divergent texts, continued to be printed by various publishers and in various forms until about 1901. Thereafter, they continued to survive in several alternate forms.[30] The Harrison edition was reprinted several times in 1902, both as a full set and as separate volumes of the biography, letters, poems and essays, presumably reflecting a reasonable demand for owning, if not necessarily for actually reading, the extended works. The publishing house of Fred De Fau produced a set of all seventeen volumes, but bound in the form of eleven volumes, which was not only slightly cheaper but may also suggest that the number of volumes was seen as a bit cumbersome. With Stone and Kimball having gone under in 1897, the Stedman and Woodberry set was slightly corrected by the editors and given new life in 1903 by the Colonial Company, with the clearly defiant designation of "The Definitive Edition." There was even an attempt at surpassing the Harrison in its apparent size with a special edition of the Stedman and Woodberry set in which each volume was split in half, with its own title page, so that it became the same contents presented in a deluxe binding in twenty volumes. Charles Scribner issued the ten-volume set again, in very handsome form, in 1914 and 1927, with minor updates to the bibliography.[31]

By the time of his death in 1916, Ingram, in spite of his continued claims of relevance, had passed into obscurity, a source for a new generation of biographers and scholars but no longer the most prominent authority on Poe. Although still valued by collectors, and sufficient for most general readers, his confusingly varied collections could not quite compete with the more carefully prepared and stable editions. The Stedman and Woodberry sets generally gave way to Harrison as the standard reference for scholarly articles, particularly in regard to the criticism, but both editions have been pushed aside in regard to the tales and poems by more modern editions, such as the heavily annotated set originally planned and edited by Thomas Ollive Mabbott and continued by Burton R. Pollin. Even for the criticism, the far more convenient one-volume collection for the Library of America, edited by G. R. Thompson, is likely to be used.

Yet, no truly complete edition of Poe's works has ever been put into print, and perhaps never will be. We cannot be sure what Griswold, Ingram, Stedman and Woodberry, or Harrison might have thought of items that were brought to light only after these editors had passed on, such as Poe's "Doings of Gotham" series, written for the *Columbia Spy* in 1844 (first discovered and published in 1929 by Jacob Spannuth and T. O. Mabbott), or the miscellaneous anonymous articles that Poe wrote for *Alexander's Weekly Messenger* in 1839 and 1840 (first discovered and published in 1942 by Clarence Brigham). Perhaps only Harrison would have argued for their inclusion, and yet would anyone today argue that they should simply be ignored? Collections aimed at a broad popular audience of readers need not worry much about such extended material, unless for the purpose of differentiating from the legion of competing editions. They can confidently print and reprint the same handful of stories and poems that have always formed the core interest in Poe's writings.

Having documented the history of these editions, what can we say about their significance? The Griswold edition was never intended to be a work of profound scholarship, for which standards scarcely existed in 1850. The value of this early four-volume set is the fact that it preserved more than a dozen versions of texts with Poe's final changes, versions that might otherwise be totally lost to us. Ingram removed the blemish of the disgraceful "Memoir," replacing Griswold's heavy-handed smearing of Poe's reputation with a more favorable account of Poe's life and, arguably, an equally heavy-handed whitewashing. Ingram also restored several substantial works to the public canon of Poe's writings, emphasizing that Poe was much more than merely the author of sensational horror stories and melancholy poetry. Most notably, these added articles show Poe's interest in cryptography and technological progress, and they reveal the demoralizing frustrations of working in what Poe called "The Magazine Prison-House." The kind of serious critical attention that Poe sought for American literary scholarship began its infancy in the generation after his death, finding its early stumbling steps in the pages of such magazines as *Harper's Monthly*, the *Atlantic Monthly*, and—slightly later—*Scribner's Monthly*. Interrupted somewhat by the Civil War, scholarly attention to American literature rose toward maturity at the same time that Poe's own reputation was being redeemed from the slanders of Griswold and the moralizing optimists who did not wish to admit what Poe saw hiding just under the thin veneer of civilization.

In 1887, Albert H. Smyth wrote an article declaring that "in the splendid progress of English criticism in the last twenty years America has not participated" and encouraging "the extension of the English curriculum to include the genesis and brief history of American authorship" (240). Almost as a response to this charge appeared the landmark eleven-volume *Library of American Literature*, produced in 1889–1890 and edited by E. C. Stedman and Ellen Mackay Hutchinson. When, only a few years later, H. S. Stone and H. I. Kimball, two former students with their newly minted degrees from

Harvard, proposed that the first substantial project of their high-minded publishing firm would be a lavish multivolume edition of Poe's works, they were,
in part, inspired by Smyth's patriotic clarion call. Stedman and Woodberry
were respectable poets and literary critics, with reputations that lent further
credibility to the project. It was clear that Poe's legacy had not only survived
but risen in estimation, such that it was deemed worthy of careful study,
scholarly attention, and expensive production values. Harrison emphasized
Poe as a hardworking critic, and he made readily accessible a host of Poe
material from rare sources. His accomplishment is somewhat complicated by
the fact that some of his unsigned selections are no longer considered to be
the work of Poe (see Hull and also Dameron). The popular reading audience
mostly remained happy with the handful of stories and poems that immediately come to mind when one thinks of Poe, but generations of scholars were
inspired to make use of the expanded material and to tackle anew the question of a full bibliography, adding and removing items from the Poe canon.

One of these scholars was Thomas Ollive Mabbott, whose volumes of
Poe's *Poems* (1969) and *Tales and Sketches* (1978) in his three-volume set
are still standard editions for texts and annotations. In his cautious respect
for Griswold's editorial efforts, Mabbott is clearly aligned intellectually with
Stedman and Woodberry, but in his strong desire to collect every scrap of
writing that could reasonably be attributed to Poe, he is also a disciple of
Ingram and Harrison. Indeed, it was in the ample margins of his own copy of
Harrison's edition that Mabbott began to write his notes, with some inten-
tional resemblance to Poe's own careful print-like hand.[32] As his plans mate-
rialized, over the course of forty years these notes were eventually transferred
to index cards, expanded on full sheets of yellow ruled paper, and finally
rendered in the form we know today. This process of accumulating and refining, building on the efforts of those who have come before, encapsulates the
evolutionary tendency of scholarship. Whether or not they are consciously
aware of the fact, all scholars who labor in the field of Poe, and all devoted
fans of his writings, are forever indebted to these early editors for ferreting
out and illuminating increasingly obscure points, and most importantly, for
preserving and refining Poe's texts for future generations to appreciate and
enjoy.

Notes

1. A specific count becomes complicated by various factors. Does one, for example, classify "The Island of the Fay" as a story? Does one count both "Imitation"
of 1827 and "A Dream within a Dream" of 1849 as separate poems? The two novels

were *The Narrative of Arthur Gordon Pym*, first published in 1838, and "The Journal of Julius Rodman," started in 1840 in serialized form in *Burton's Gentleman's Magazine* but never completed beyond the first six installments following Poe's abrupt severance from that periodical.

2. Both reviews were first collected by Harrison in 1902. As an example of the challenges involved in conjectural cases for attribution, some detail is warranted. Harrison does not expressly state his reasoning, but the basis for inclusion may be deduced from his biography of Poe, which quotes William E. Burton as telling George R. Graham that his "young editor [Poe] is to be taken care of" (*Complete Works* 1: 163), thus presuming that Poe was on Graham's staff from the inception of the new magazine. Harrison does not give the source of this quote, but it is almost certainly taken from a comment by Albert H. Smyth, giving the identical statement and apparently relying on information from Graham himself, as Graham was still alive until 1894 and Smyth's comments suggest direct personal contact (*Philadelphia Magazines* 217). In his 1941 doctoral dissertation on the Poe canon, William Doyle Hull argued against these attributions on stylistic grounds (303–4 and 319–21). On February 9, 1966, Thomas Ollive Mabbott wrote a letter to Eric Carlson, listing these reviews as among those he considered erroneously collected by Harrison (Dameron 56). The most serious of Harrison's attribution errors may be his inclusion of the favorable review of the strongly pro-slavery books by Paulding and Drayton, from the *Southern Literary Messenger* of April 1836, a review now known to have been written by Beverley Tucker (see Ridgely).

3. A minor warning to scholars may be made here, as the latter of these slight poems is now known not to be by Poe (Brandoli 58–63), and the case in favor of the former is certainly very shaky.

4. Griswold begins the tradition of printing both tales.

5. These questions are necessarily rhetorical because answers would vary depending on practical circumstances and personal preferences.

6. The full text of all of these historical editions may be found online at https://www.eapoe.org, under the section on Poe's collected writings. I have not extended my reach to the numerous separate editions of the poems and tales, most of which were culled from the larger collections, and I have specifically omitted the 1884 edition printed by A. C. Armstrong in six- and eight-volume sets, sometimes misleadingly referred to as the Stoddard edition. This 1884 edition is merely the continuation of the 1876 Widdleton edition, with the material spread out and with some illustrations. In this edition, Ingram's memoir has been replaced by one written by Richard H. Stoddard, but there is no indication that Stoddard newly edited the material beyond the addition of a few notes. Both of the Stoddard sets have the same content, with one requiring more volumes as it is printed on heavier paper.

7. For examples of such letters, see Poe's draft to C. Anthon, about late October, 1844 (Ostrom et al. 1: 470–71); Poe to E. A. Duyckinck, January 8, 1846 (550–51); and Poe to G. W. Eveleth, December 15, 1846 (600).

8. According to James Cephas Derby, "The sale reached about fifteen hundred sets every year" (587). The validity of the claim cannot be verified, and it must be admitted that Derby makes a number of errors in other statements, such as the idea that the copyright was initially paid to Poe himself when Poe was already deceased.

9. The preface, which speaks favorably of Poe's humorous stories, was probably not written by Griswold. The idea that the edition was always intended to include four volumes is contradicted by the existence of a letter written by Griswold to John R. Thompson on February 19, 1850, documenting that he was then "preparing . . . the third and concluding volume of his [Poe's] works" (Whitty and Rindfleisch 54–56). A letter from Mrs. Lewis to Griswold, dated November 9, 1849, had unsuccessfully encouraged Griswold to publish *Pym*, saying "I think that a collection of Mr. Poe's Tales will be incomplete without it" (Bayless 283–84, n24).

10. See "To the Reader," appearing at the front of the volume 1, signed by Maria Clemm, but probably written by, or at least with the assistance of, Griswold. The contract, somewhat dubiously assigning to Griswold the rights to Poe's works for the sake of publishing the edition, is dated October 15, 1849 and signed by Mrs. Clemm and Sylvanus D. Lewis, a lawyer and Mrs. Lewis's husband.

11. The document granting power of attorney is in the Gimble Collection of the Philadelphia Free Public Library. The text is most readily available as given by Quinn (754). Griswold's efforts were somewhat complicated by the fact that although he had a signed contract with Mrs. Clemm as "the sole owner and lawful possessor of the writings and Literary Remains of the late Edgar A. Poe," Poe's sister, Rosalie, actually had a stronger legal claim. After some difficulty between these two self-interested parties, with the generally cooperative intervention of John R. Thompson as legal representative for Rosalie, the matter was apparently settled in some amicable fashion that is not clearly known (Savoye 15–42).

12. We know that Griswold had Poe's heavily annotated copy of *Tales of the Grotesque and Arabesque* (1840), for which Poe had created a new table of contents and title page, proposing the revised and expanded collection to be called *Phantasy-Pieces*. The now-lost second volume provided Griswold's texts for "Hans Phaall" and "Metzengerstein." Griswold also had Poe's own double-bound copy of *Tales* and *The Raven and Other Poems*, with numerous changes in Poe's hand. Griswold implemented a few of the more significant changes to the volume of poems, but none of those for the tales. In addition, a close study of Griswold's texts strongly suggests that he had a copy of the *Broadway Journal* of 1845 in which Poe had made many small changes to the items reprinted there, a copy that has never been traced and is presumed lost. The only clearly unauthentic material appears in the "Preface to the Memoir," where several of the letters by Poe are now known to be forgeries by Griswold.

13. "The Murders in the Rue Morgue," for example, appears at the top of the list, and is separated from "The Mystery of Marie Rogêt" by twenty-nine tales. The full page of contents is reproduced by Mabbott (*Tales*, following 2: 474). See Harry Lee Poe's chapter in this volume for more on Poe's organizing logic for *Phantasy-Pieces*.

14. "To Helen," beginning "Helen, thy beauty is to me," was included in J. R. Lowell's introductory essay, and thus not repeated among the poems proper. Griswold also initially included "The Poetic Principle" in volume 3, primarily because it had not been printed during Poe's lifetime, and he had been unable to get his hands on Poe's manuscript until about March or April of 1850. Griswold never saw Poe's first little collection of poems, *Tamerlane and Other Poems*, and thus necessarily omitted a few items appearing there but not subsequently reprinted. The ephemeral pamphlet had been crudely printed in 1827, acknowledging the author only as "a Bostonian," and Poe had not retained a copy. (Poe wrote to J. R. Lowell on July 2, 1844: "I have been so negligent as not to preserve copies of any of my volumes of poems," for which, see Ostrom et al. 1: 450.) So completely had it vanished by 1850 that Griswold, in revising his 1849 obituary of Poe as the longer and more detailed "Memoir of the Author," eliminated the 1827 date, possibly originally given because it had been cited by Lowell in his own 1845 article on Poe, and mentions only the 1829 *Al Aaraaf, Tamerlane and Minor Poems* as Poe's first publication.

15. Griswold makes a number of significant comments on his editorial role for the volumes in a letter of February 19, 1850, to J. R. Thompson. In regard to volumes 1 and 2, Griswold notes that he "contented myself with collecting and arranging the materials, and superintending the press—which you may be sure was not a very slight labor" (Whitty and Rindfleisch 54). About volume 3, then still in preparation, Griswold says "The new volume will cost me more trouble than the others" (Whitty and Rindfleisch 55).

16. For the Griswold set, across the two main publishers, J. S. Redfield and W. J. Widdleton, editions are known with the following imprint dates on the title pages: 1850, 1852, 1853, 1855, 1856, 1857, 1858, 1859, 1860, 1861, 1863, 1864, 1865, 1866, 1867, 1868, 1869, 1870, and 1871. A set of the Widdleton printing, with no imprint date, matches the earlier style of binding and may be from 1862. Jeanette L. Gilder, a near contemporary of Widdleton, has left us an interesting comment: "A number of years ago, when I was young in the business, there was a Broadway publisher who may be said to have been a one-author publisher. This was the late W. J. Widdleton, who published the works of Edgar Allan Poe to the exclusion of all but two or three books of other writers, which he put on his list because he liked them, rather than because they were among the best 'sellers'" (Gilder 382). Because so many editions were printed in essentially the same format, it is not uncommon to encounter sets that mix volumes from different years, sometimes with the bookplate or inscription of an early owner and date in all four volumes, indicating that they were originally assembled in this form. Widdleton began to issue Poe's *Prose Tales* in two "series" (volumes) in 1867. Redfield began to issue various one-volume editions of Poe's *Poems* in 1859. Widdleton reissued these editions, with numerous alterations in the format and choice of memoir until the demise of the publisher in 1882, with sufficient frequency and variety as to suggest that they were the most popular portion of Poe's works.

17. An example of one item that Ingram eagerly sought but did not find was "The Elk," which Poe had published under the name "Morning on the Wissahiccon" in *The Opal* for 1844 (1843). Ingram was aware of "The Elk" from a footnote in Lowell's article on Poe as it was printed in *Graham's Magazine* in 1845, but apparently did not realize that he was searching for it under the wrong name. Woodberry tentatively identified the item in 1885 and mentioned it in his biography of Poe (*Edgar Allan Poe* 187). It was first collected by Stedman and Woodberry.

18. Ingram did not have the set of the *Broadway Journal* with Poe's minor changes in three tales until Mrs. S. H. Whitman sent it to him on March 27, 1874. He comments on having received and "looked through" the volumes in a letter to Whitman of April 28, 1874 (Miller 132). (The Nimmo edition was the first to incorporate these changes, although Ingram appears to have already corrected editorially the spelling of Hinnom in "Morella.") For "The Oval Portrait," Ingram restores the motto and first paragraph from *Graham's*, but otherwise retains Griswold's text.

19. In a letter to William Landor (H. B. Wallace), July 17, 1841, Poe writes, "You have seen, I believe, the July no: of Mag. Among the critical notices is one on Bolingbroke, the only notice not written by myself" (Ostrom et al. 1: 296).

20. Ingram was aware of "Autography" because it was reprinted in 1853 in the New York *Illustrated News* (see Ingram to Whitman, April 28, 1874, in Miller 133).

21. Ingram's text is from the *Broadway Journal* of August 9, 1845, excerpted and cobbled together with additional reviews in the subsequent issues of August 23 and 30, 1845.

22. Ingram was presumably unaware of the surviving manuscript of this item and may have suspected Griswold of tampering with the text.

23. In some cases, this attempt at arrangement is a little clumsy, as "International Copyright" is listed with the "C" entries, and both "Definition of Art" and "Machinery of Art" are listed with the "A" entries. Ingram also makes small changes to the text of his entries. For example, in "Marginalia XXXVI," Ingram omits the list of names Poe gives for good conversationalists, presumably as being too obscure to be important to his readers

24. The poem first appeared publicly in September 1875 in the form of a facsimile in *Scribner's Monthly*, but with some unfortunate and unacknowledged modifications, including the title, which were apparently made by E. L. Didier, the discoverer, and continued to cast unnecessary concerns over its authenticity. Ingram finally collected the poem in his 1888 single-volume edition of the poetry (114), but he did so among the "doubtful" items, along with several poems that are now known to have been written by A. M. Ide, Jr. (which Ingram had originally—and mistakenly—thought might be a Poe pseudonym).

25. An advertisement of the Nimmo edition appeared on November 22, 1884 in the *Athenaeum* (647), quoting several reviews, with a particular emphasis on the new arrangement. The *Saturday Review*, for example, is cited as saying, "Further, it should be stated that in the new edition the works are, for the first time, intelligibly classified." The *Daily Telegraph* is similarly quoted: "The volumes before us are un-

questionably the fullest and the best arranged edition of Poe's writings as yet given to the world. In fact, it is the only one in which any serious attempt is made to classify the prose tales, those of Imagination being assigned to one volume, and those of Humour to another; the Miscellaneous Stories and Poems filling the third and fourth."

26. William Wertenbaker noted, in 1868, while he was still the librarian at the university, "Mr. Poe's works are more in demand and more read than those of any other author, American or foreign, now in the Library" (117).

27. So thoroughly connected to these events was the creation of the edition that Hamilton Mabie's "Poe's Place in American Literature," which had been the principle address at the ceremonies, appeared prominently in the second volume, the first volume having been Harrison's biography of Poe.

28. Stewart's PhD was granted on June 12, 1901. A one-volume selection of *Poems and Tales of Edgar Allan Poe* (Richmond: B. F. Johnson Publishing, 1911) gives Robert Armistead Stewart as the editor, noting him as "Editor of the Revised Edition of the Virginia Poe (Harrison) and Associate Professor in Richmond College."

29. A review of the Harrison edition in *The Nation* (December 4, 1902) is particularly relevant. Although it is unsigned, the author is clearly none other than Woodberry, mingling attacks on Harrison's work with defenses of previous editors: "They have greatly increased the bulk of the section, partly by including reviews hitherto thought too valueless to be revived, and partly by printing the earlier forms of later critical writing in addition to the latter. . . . The truth is, that the editor's prejudice against Griswold has led him to reject Poe's own late and mature revision of his major critical writings in favor of these early, scattered, and fragmentary forms in which they appeared in the magazines in their original helter-skelter production" (Woodberry, "New Editions" 445). He also decries the use of historical spellings and punctuation as "a facsimile method of editing" (445). In a letter dated March 9, 1909, and written, in French, to the editor of *Mercure de France* in Paris, Ingram complains that a commentator in that journal had recently spoken favorably about the Harrison edition, with Ingram lamenting "But it is not complete nor satisfactory. My edition of 1874 and that of Chicago of 1895, in ten volumes, are better" (Ingram collection, University of Virginia, item 424, original typed letter, my own translation). Ingram essentially proceeds to argue, as he often did, that everyone had basically stolen his work and stripped him of the credit.

30. The four-volume set was printed again in 1913, by the same publisher (A. & C. Black), but without Ingram's preface or memoir of Poe. After the death of William James Widdleton in 1882, the rights for the American set fell into the hands of A. C. Armstrong, and later G. Putnam and Sons. Armstrong replaced Ingram's memoir but basically retained Ingram's updated American edition, spread out among six and eight volumes, and eventually ten volumes, which became the standard number of volumes for the majority of "complete" sets issued in various special editions, with introductory material by Edwin Markham, Nathan Haskins Dole, and Charles F. Richardson. (Of these scholars, only Richardson seems to have actually reconsidered the content and texts of the edition, ultimately making only a few relatively minor

changes.) Another line of editions focused on the tales, poems, and a selection of the essays, mostly in six volumes printed without date but generally assumed to be about 1886. Traces can still be found in the Raven Edition issued by Collier in 1903 and again in 1904. Although it was already devoid of Ingram's name, it retains a few notes on the poems that are clearly taken from his edition of the *Complete Poems*.

31. AMS Press reprinted both the Harrison and the Stedman and Woodberry sets in 1965, and they reprinted the Harrison set again in 1979 (with a new introduction by Floyd Stovall).

32. Mabbott's copy of the Harrison edition is currently held in the Mabbott Collection at the University of Iowa.

Works Cited

Bayless, Joy. *Rufus Wilmot Griswold: Poe's Literary Executor*. Vanderbilt UP, 1943.

Brandoli, Enrico. "'Epigram for Wall Street': Who Did It? Who?" *Edgar Allan Poe Review*, vol. 12, no. 2, 2011, pp. 58–63.

Brigham, Clarence S. "Edgar Allan Poe's Contributions to *Alexander's Weekly Messenger*." *Publications of the American Antiquarian Society*, vol. 52, no. 1, 1942, pp. 45–125.

Brown, William H. "The Green Table." *Southern Magazine*, vol. 15, 1874, pp. 428–32.

Creek, Alma Burner. "Stone and Kimball." *Dictionary of Literary Biography*, vol. 49, Gale Research, 1986, pp. 440–43.

Dameron, J. Lasley. "Thomas Ollive Mabbott on the Canon of Poe's Reviews." *Poe Studies*, vol. 5, no. 2, 1972, p. 56.

DeLowry-Fryman, Linda. "Thomas Y. Crowell and Company." *Dictionary of Literary Biography*, vol. 49, Gale Research, 1986, pp. 107–8.

Derby, James Cephas. *Fifty Years among Authors, Books and Publishers*. G. W. Carleton, 1885.

Gilder, Jeanette L. "The Lounger." *Putnam's Monthly*, vol. 3, no. 3, 1907, pp. 371–85.

Harrison, James Albert. "New Glimpses of Poe (I)." *The Independent*, vol. 52, no. 2701, 6 September 1900, pp. 2158–61.

Hull, William Doyle. *A Canon of the Critical Works of Edgar Allan Poe*. 1941. U. of Virginia, PhD dissertation. Edgar Allan Poe Society of Baltimore, https://www.eapoe.org/papers/misc1921/hullw00c.htm.

Ingram, John Henry, "The Journal of Julius Rodman: A Newly-Discovered Work by the Late Edgar A. Poe," *Mirror of Literature* (London), vol. 1, no. 1, November 3, 1877, pp. 9–10.

Kent, Charles W. *The Unveiling of the Bust of Edgar Allan Poe in the Library of the University of Virginia, October the Seventh, 1899*. J. P. Bell Co., 1901.

Kramer, Sidney. *A History of Stone and Kimball and Herbert S. Stone & Co. With a Bibliography of Their Publications, 1893–1905*. U of Chicago P, 1940.

Miller, John Carl, editor. *Poe's Helen Remembers*. UP of Virginia, 1979.

Ostrom, John W., Burton R. Pollin, and Jeffrey A. Savoye, editors. *The Collected Letters of Edgar Allan Poe*. Gordian Press, 2008. 2 vols.

Poe, Edgar Allan. *The Collected Works of Edgar Allan Poe*. Edited by Thomas Ollive Mabbott. Belknap Press of Harvard UP, 1969 and 1978. 3 vols.

——. *The Complete Poetical Works and Essays on Poetry of Edgar Allan Poe*. Edited by J. H. Ingram, Frederick Warne & Co., 1888.

——. *The Complete Works of Edgar Allan Poe*. Edited by J. A. Harrison, T. Y. Crowell, 1902. 17 vols.

——. *The Raven and Other Poems*. Wiley & Putnam, 1845.

——. *The Short Fiction of Edgar Allan Poe: An Annotated Edition*. Edited by Stuart Levine and Susan Levine, Bobbs-Merrill, 1976.

——. *Tales*. Wiley & Putnam, 1845.

——. *The Tales and Poems of Edgar Allan Poe*. Edited by J. H. Ingram, John C. Nimmo, 1884. 4 vols.

——. *The Works of Edgar Allan Poe*. Edited by J. H. Ingram, A. and C. Black, 1874–1875. 4 vols.

——. *The Works of Edgar Allan Poe*. Edited by J. H. Ingram, W. J. Widdleton, 1876. 4 vols.

——. *The Works of Edgar Allan Poe*. Edited by E. C. Stedman and G. E. Woodberry, Stone & Kimball, 1894–1895. 10 vols.

——. *The Works of the Late Edgar Allan Poe*. Edited by R. W. Griswold, J. S. Redfield, 1850–1856. 4 vols.

Quinn, Arthur Hobson. *Edgar Allan Poe: A Critical Biography*, D. Appleton-Century, 1941.

Raymond, David W. "J. S. Redfield." *Dictionary of Literary Biography*, vol. 49, Gale Research, 1986, 385–87.

Ridgely, Joseph V. "The Authorship of the 'Paulding-Drayton Review.'" *PSA Newsletter*, vol. 20, no. 2, 1992, pp. 1–3, 6.

Savoye, Jeffrey A. "Two Biographical Digressions: Poe's Wandering Trunk and Dr. Carter's Mysterious Sword Cane." *Edgar Allan Poe Review*, vol. 5, no. 2, 2004, pp. 15–42.

Scholnick, Robert J., "In Defense of Beauty: Stedman and the Recognition of Poe in America, 1880–1910." *Poe and His Times: The Artist and His Milieu*, edited by Benjamin Franklin Fisher IV, The Edgar Allan Poe Society of Baltimore, 1990, pp. 256–69.

Smyth, Albert H., "American Literature in the Class-room." *Transactions and Proceedings of the Modern Language Association*, vol. 3, 1888, 238–44.

——. *The Philadelphia Magazines and Their Contributors*. Lindsay, 1892.

Spannuth, Jacob E., and Thomas Ollive Mabbott, editors. *Doings of Gotham: Poe's Contributions to the Columbia Spy*. Jacob E. Spannuth, 1929.

Wertenbaker, William. "Edgar A. Poe." *Virginia University Magazine*, vol. 7, nos. 2–3, 1868, pp. 114–17.

Whitty, James H., and James H. Rindfleisch. *The Genius and Character of Edgar Allan Poe*. Privately printed, 1929.

Woodberry, George Edward. *Edgar Allan Poe*. Houghton Mifflin and Company, 1885.

———. "New Editions of Poe," *The Nation* 75, December 1902, pp. 445–47.

~

CHAPTER FIVE

The Scholars' Poe(s)

Landmark Editions of the Twentieth Century

Travis Montgomery

Throughout the twentieth century, the primary task of Poe editors was updating the work of James A. Harrison, who had carried on the labors of his nineteenth-century predecessors. Seven specialists who took up that task were Killis Campbell, John W. Ostrom, Floyd Stovall, Thomas Ollive Mabbott, Burton R. Pollin, Patrick F. Quinn, and G. R. Thompson, and their editions contained generally reliable texts of Poe's writings, texts based on careful study of available sources. Yet none of these scholars produced a single, complete edition that included *all* the writing known to be Poe's. The volumes that they published, which differed markedly from popular anthologies, did, however, bear some similarities to compilations of that order. In a way, the editions of Campbell and others gave readers portraits of Poe, images reflecting the knowledge and interests of the editors, and those representations corresponded in part to the figures of Poe presented in anthologies such as the Dover Thrift Edition of *Tales of Terror and Detection*, in which two Poes—the horror author and the detective writer—are the focal points. The perspectival limits that such collections imposed allowed readers to see particular qualities of Poe's work in relief while other matters faded into the background. A similar filtering characterized the Campbell, Ostrom, Stovall, Mabbott, Pollin, Quinn, and Thompson editions, and those volumes as well as the circumstances of their publication have shaped interpretive practice, creating various Poes whom readers know today.

Campbell's Poe: Disciple of the British Romantics

Among the first scholars to pick up Harrison's mantle was Killis Campbell, who published *The Poems of Edgar Allan Poe* in 1917. Adding some uncollected verse to the Poe canon, Campbell made significant editorial progress, pointing out a number of Harrison's misattributions and providing more inclusive lists of variants—lists that Campbell, unlike Harrison, placed prominently beneath his texts. Especially significant were Campbell's detailed notes about Poe's sources and the lengthy introduction, in which the editor provided a chronicle of the poet's life, outlined the influence of British writers on Poe's style and imagination, commented on the poet's obsessive revision, and addressed the critical controversy surrounding Poe's place in the literary canon. These supplemental materials constituted the majority of the pages in the Campbell volume—of the 332 pages marked with Arabic numerals, only 145 contained poetic texts. For C. Alphonso Smith, the annotations and introductory matter were the impressive work of a scholar "fearlessly and consistently interpretive" (173), and George Sherburn praised Campbell's "astonishingly illuminating account of Poe's indebtedness to other poets" (56). That account did not, however, receive similar accolades from Earl L. Bradsher, who disliked what he considered the excessive annotation of the editor. Moreover, Bradsher claimed that "Campbell's parallels and sources" occasionally "fail[ed] to carry conviction in spite of Poe's reputation as a borrower" (243).

That surfeit of notes, however, offered insight into Campbell's conception of Poe, whom the editor portrayed as a disciple of the British romantics. In his introductory chapter, Campbell identified Byron, Moore, Coleridge, Shelley, Wordsworth, and Keats as poetic models for Poe, who, especially in his early works, imitated his literary forebears. Campbell's notes, which documented allusions and references to these writers, reinforced the notion that the verse works of Poe were best understood as products of the romantic movement, especially its English strain.[1] For Campbell, that poetic tradition was clearly the predominant imaginative stimulus for Poe, who "was but little influenced by the American poets" (lii). Linking Poe to respected authors such as Byron helped Campbell defend the author of "The Raven" against critics who judged Poe a mediocre talent. To be sure, the editorial introduction suggested that Poe's early attempts to emulate romantic giants evinced artistic earnestness, a commitment to the pursuit of literary excellence.[2] Thus, Campbell helped readers understand the young poet's ambitions. Emphasizing British influences on Poe had, however, some problematic results. With that editorial move, Campbell drew attention to the poet's imitative tendencies, and even though the editor celebrated the mature Poe's "extraordinary originality and individuality" (lvii), Campbell's exhaustive presentation of allusions to and borrowings from other poets did not stress the singular qualities of Poe's verse-making. Despite that limitation, "[t]he appearance of [the Campbell] volume" was, as Sherburn claimed, "an important event in the annals of Poe criticism" (56), an event through which Campbell urged critics to take Poe the poet seriously.[3]

Ostrom's Poe: Aspiring Bourgeois

Whereas the verse writings of Poe preoccupied Campbell, the author's correspondence received the editorial attentions of John W. Ostrom, whose *Letters of Edgar Allan Poe* appeared in 1948. Featuring 339 letters, most of which were complete texts, the Ostrom edition contained over twice the number of Poe letters that appeared in the seventeenth volume of the Harrison set, a book including not only epistolary writings of Poe but also several letters from the author's correspondents as well as posthumous communications about Poe. Unlike Harrison, Ostrom reproduced only Poe's missives, and Ostrom's reliance on available "original autograph letters, facsimiles, [and] photostats" marked an improvement on Harrison's practice (1: vii). To illustrate, the forgeries of Rufus Wilmot Griswold, who had "resorted to almost every trick of dishonest editing in order to blacken the name of a dead man, including omissions from and distortions of Poe's correspondence" (Cunliffe 249), are notably absent from the texts featured in the Ostrom edition. Some of those forgeries appeared, however, in the Harrison volume, which came out long before the true extent of Griswold's editorial treachery was known.[4] Throughout the second half of the twentieth century, Ostrom updated the collection with supplements published in academic journals and a second edition issued by Gordian Press in 1966.[5]

Ostrom's labors advanced the effort to see Poe the man through the fog of myth. Focusing on the letters alone helped Ostrom dispel some of that fog. Separated from the tales and poems populated with unhinged narrators and speakers that many readers treated as portraits of Poe, the letters gave a fresh perspective on the writer. In these texts, Poe was stripped of the Byronic accoutrements with which many readers had equipped him. No dark, satanic genius, the Poe revealed in his correspondence was the *"littérateur,"* as the writer called himself in an 1849 letter to Frederick W. Thomas, an epistle in which Poe declared "Literature . . . the most noble of professions" (2: 427). Documenting what James Southall Wilson called "the vicissitudes of [Poe's] fortunes" (xx), the letters offered insight into his difficult relationships with colleagues and employers. Supplementing such pictures of Poe at work were images of the writer among friends and family. An author pursuing financial security and domestic tranquility, "the epistolary Poe"—to borrow a phrase from Thomas Bonner, Jr.—was, in short, surprisingly bourgeois in his aspirations.[6] This figure resembled the Poe conjured up by biographer Arthur Hobson Quinn, who had presented in 1941 what he considered "the real Edgar Poe," an "industrious, honorable gentleman," a "warm friend and courteous host," and above all, an uncompromising "artist" (694). Like Quinn's work on the biographical front, the Ostrom edition held inestimable value for Poe scholars trying to recover what was, if not the real Poe, then a vision of the writer truer to life than the scamp of Griswoldian imagination.[7]

Stovall's Poe: Singular Poet

The year 1965 marked another important event in Poe studies: the publication of *The Poems of Edgar Allan Poe*, a volume edited by Floyd Stovall, who had been a student of Killis Campbell. Building on scholarly discoveries since 1917, Stovall supplied updated lists of textual variants, and that information appeared at the back of Stovall's edition instead of within footnotes, which Campbell had employed to document such material. Other departures from Campbell were the omission of some lyrics attributed to Poe, and the inclusion of a corrected text of *Politian* featuring material from a typescript supplied by Thomas Ollive Mabbott (Stovall, *Poems* viii).

Comparing Stovall's edition with Campbell's, some scholars found the former wanting. I. M. Walker asserted that the *Politian* supplement was "the only significant uncollected material" provided by Stovall (214). Stovall's reliance on his predecessor also caught the attention of James Schroeter. According to Schroeter, Stovall often printed "the same basic texts as Campbell" (84), who generally opted for versions from the 1845 edition of *The Raven and Other Poems* while incorporating changes that Poe made in his personal copy, "but at times [Stovall employed] an earlier or later version" (84), leaving himself "open to the charge of being arbitrary" in copy-text selections (85). The paucity of annotations in the Stovall volume was another problem. Whereas Campbell's notes were profuse, filled with references to literary sources and Poe biography, Stovall supplied only publication histories and textual variants. For this reason, some scholars insisted that Campbell's edition remained essential for the study of Poe's poetry.[8]

Nevertheless, the enduring value of the Stovall volume had little to do with its texts and annotations; the book was most important for the vision of Poe that it conveyed. According to Stovall, Poe was primarily a gifted poet whose unique lyrical productions were underappreciated. Observing that "Poe's tales are thought to be his best work" (*Poems* xxxii), Stovall considered the nineteenth-century author's criticism and verse just as important as the fiction, arguing that many of Poe's poems and essays exhibited "originality," which Stovall deemed "Poe's greatest single literary virtue" (xxxvii). The verse productions merited, as Stovall indicated, additional praise: "It is possible that [Poe] made his most enduring contribution to literature in the creation of a few unforgettable poems" (xxxvii). The physical appearance of the Stovall edition registered that idea. Large as a display volume for a coffee table, this book, with its blue cloth cover that featured Poe's signature in gold lettering, was "a pleasing sample of the bookmaker's art" (Schroeter 84).[9] The contents were equally impressive. Printed on fine paper, the italicized texts of Poe's poems, which Donald Weeks thought "precious" (471), appeared in black ink under blue titles. Relegating the variant lists to an appendix, Stovall presented the poems without the clutter of apparatus. All of these aesthetic decisions had a purpose. The poems, with their colored titles and large italicized fonts, stood isolate like art objects in a museum, and housed in a lovely binding, these pieces seemed literary touchstones, works worthy of the respect that Stovall paid them.

Significantly, the Stovall volume appeared while the critical rehabilitation of Poe's verse was underway. A milestone in this process was the 1959 publication of a Poe volume edited by Richard Wilbur for the Laurel Library Series. Two decades earlier, the influential critic Yvor Winters had judged Poe "a bad writer accidentally and temporarily popular" (93) and "an excited sentimentalist" (104), but dismissive appraisals of this kind left Wilbur cold. The close readings featured in his introduction to the Laurel edition suggested that Poe's poetry deserved serious scrutiny, and although Wilbur had reservations about the life-denying attributes of Poe's imagination, he nevertheless declared that "[t]here has never been a grander conception of poetry" than Poe's (39). Similarly convinced that Poe's poems and the ideas animating them were valuable, Stovall put out an edition embodying that value, carrying on the reassessment project in *Edgar Poe the Poet*, a collection of critical essays in which Stovall placed Poe in the august company of Coleridge and offered analyses of individual poems. Such revaluation of Poe's verse continued into the twenty-first century, which saw the publication of Jerome McGann's *The Poet Edgar Allan Poe: Alien Angel*. Although he rejected the notion that Poe was a quintessential romantic, McGann took the poetry of Poe seriously, arguing that Poe, a writer with a creative self-consciousness atypical of the earnest age in which he lived, was the equal of Algernon Charles Swinburne and Stéphane Mallarmé, poets whose "theoretical writings" sustained their "poetic practice" (6). An artist of that caliber bore few similarities to the pitiful hack imagined by Winters, and although McGann and Stovall advanced different interpretations of the poet, they shared the assumption that the careful study of Poe's poetic work was rewarding.[10]

Mabbott's Poe: Reviser

The most significant of Harrison's and Campbell's successors was Thomas Ollive Mabbott, a professor, numismatist, and woodblock collector, whose scholarly precision and deep learning were evident in *The Collected Works of Edgar Allan Poe*, a project conducted under the aegis of Harvard University Press. Published in 1969, the initial volume of the series, which bore the subtitle *Poems*, was more comprehensive than Campbell's or Stovall's. Mabbott enlarged the canon of Poe's poetry, declaring some former attributions authentic works of Poe and adding previously uncollected poems, including juvenilia, which did not appear in the Campbell edition. For copy-texts, Mabbott relied on versions that he believed best reflected "the latest intentions of the author" (1: xix), and the editor accounted for more variants than did his predecessors. For pieces that Poe revised extensively, such as "Tamerlane," Mabbott "print[ed] two or more complete versions" instead of simply listing variants from the copy-texts (Robbins 247). Another divergence from previous editions was the inclusion of annotations that evinced Mabbott's mastery of Poe scholarship unavailable to Campbell. The *Poems* volume contained some errors, such as an incorrect manuscript date of "Eulalie," a mistake that Jeffrey Savoye has recently identified in "Dating 'Eulalie,'" but imperfections of this kind notwithstanding, Mabbott's edition of Poe's verse superseded Campbell's.[11]

While this edition was in press, Mabbott died, leaving his widow Maureen to supervise publication of the next two volumes of the *Collected Works of Edgar Allan Poe*, and these books, which contained the tales and sketches of Poe, appeared in 1978. With the assistance of Eleanor Kewer, an editor at Harvard University Press, and Patricia Edwards Clyne, Maureen Cobb Mabbott carefully reviewed the deceased editor's typescripts and "t[ook] care of the variants," to modify her phrase (*Poe Scholar* 30). As she observed, these variants were of crucial importance to Thomas Ollive Mabbott, who wanted readers to see "not only the copy-text but also all the authorized variants from it" (30). In the Mabbott edition, variants appeared on the same pages as the texts, not at the end of the book, the place where Harrison put the textual notes for each volume of tales in his edition. To show the extent of Poe's revisions, Mabbott printed different versions of tales that Poe effectively rewrote, such as "A Decided Loss," a story transformed into "Loss of Breath." Canon expansion was another feature of the edition, and the works Mabbott added were "nine definitely new pieces," one of which was "The Light-House," a tale that Poe left incomplete (2: xxvii). Eight of these pieces were sketches such as "Instinct vs. Reason" and "Theatrical Rats," and although Joseph J. Moldenhauer noted that scholars might dispute the authorship of that material, he acknowledged that Mabbott was "right to risk erring on the side of inclusiveness rather than the contrary" (45).

Mabbott's selection of copy-texts also differed from Harrison's. Choosing texts that reflected what he considered "the latest intentions of the author," Mabbott often relied on Griswold's edition of Poe's works, the merits of which Harrison had questioned. For critics familiar with the "Ludwig" obituary and Griswold's general rottenness, that practice must have seemed peculiar, but Mabbott defended it, insisting that Griswold, whom Poe did, after all, name as his literary executor, performed his editorial duties well.[12] According to Mabbott, "Careful study of the variants [revealed] that Griswold had for some tales obviously superior readings, improvements that must have come from Poe" (2: xxviii). Reviewing those variants while preparing her late husband's editions for publication, Maureen Cobb Mabbott drew the same conclusion about the Griswold texts, which some critics had wrongly declared "full of typographical errors" (*Poe Scholar* 31). The Mabbott policy on copy-texts was not, however, without controversy. Thomas Philbrick rejected that approach entirely, and in a review of the *Tales and Sketches* volumes, he wrote, "Instead of choosing the text closest to the author's hand, Mabbott and his successors have in most instances chosen, from the texts with which Poe may have had anything at all to do, the one that lies farthest from the author's manuscript" (403). Philbrick dismissed Mabbott's claim "that Griswold [probably] had clippings with revisions in Poe's hand," materials now lost (2: xxviii).[13] Moldenhauer was equally critical of Mabbott's editorial procedure, declaring that "Mabbott's principles of copy-text choice are the direct inverse of those being used today by most, if not all, scholarly editions of American authors" prepared according to the system established by W. W. Greg and Fredson Bowers (43). Nevertheless, the Mabbott edition of Poe's tales and sketches became an essential resource for Poe scholars.[14]

In these books, readers found a portrait of Poe the reviser, a craftsman who "constantly revised his stories, sometimes rewriting them completely" (2: xxv). Similar textual tinkering characterized the poetic expression as well, and Poe's revising proclivity was, of course, something that critics had long recognized. For example, R. A. Stewart, who prepared the textual notes for Harrison's 1902 Virginia edition, attested to the "careful and repeated revision" to which Poe "subjected" his tales (299).[15] What made Mabbott different from his predecessors was the emphasis he put on Poe's revisions, which Mabbott highlighted by placing the variants and texts in proximity. This procedure marked a clear break from previous Poe editions, with the notable exception of the Campbell volume, and not all critics appreciated the change. For example, William A. O'Brien complained about the "cumbersome apparatus on almost every page" (1106). Nevertheless, Mabbott's method had its merits, the most important of which was making readers aware of the fluidity that characterized the texts of Poe, a writer who shaped and reshaped his work while perfecting his craft and responding to marketplace realities that encouraged the repackaging or rebranding of literary commodities. Focusing attention on Poe's revisions, Mabbott pointed critics toward fields of inquiry that proved fruitful, as Benjamin F. Fisher's investigation of the ways that Poe enhanced the Gothic effects of his prose has demonstrated.[16]

Pollin's Poe: Reader

Mabbott did not complete an edition of Poe's long narratives, but Burton R. Pollin published such a volume in 1981. *Imaginary Voyages*, the first installment in a series titled *Collected Writings of Edgar Allan Poe*, contained texts and variants for *The Narrative of Arthur Gordon Pym* and "The Unparalleled Adventure of One Hans Pfaall" as well as a corrected text of "The Journal of Julius Rodman," an unfinished work that Poe had published serially in successive issues of *Burton's Gentleman's Magazine*. Each text was, in Pollin's estimation, "as close as possible to the form that Poe conceived and wished known" (*Collected Writings* 1: xvii), and lists of variants helped readers study the textual evolutions of the three narratives. Of particular interest were Pollin's exhaustive notes, in which the editor identified Poe's sources and provided explanatory material. These notes filled approximately 40 percent of the volume's pages, and for Harold Beaver, the wealth of information contained therein was a testament to Pollin's "monumental" achievement, which would "stand as proof of contemporary scholarship well into the next century" (914).

The circumstances under which *Imaginary Voyages* saw print probably had other important consequences for Poe studies, especially for *Pym* criticism. In 1968, Mabbott's death interrupted the production of a complete scholarly edition of Poe's writings, and Pollin's edition of *Pym* did not appear until 1981. In the interim, controversy swirled around *Pym*, a book with racial themes that elicited powerful responses. Eight years before Mabbott died,

Sidney Kaplan, following the lead of Harry Levin, deemed *Pym* "an al-legorical and didactic damning of" people of African descent, whom Poe's Tsalalians supposedly represented (xxiii). That interpretation gathered steam over the following decades, and many readers assumed that the dark-skinned islanders described in the second half of *Pym* symbolized black men and women on Southern plantations. Filled with references to Benjamin Morrell's *A Narrative of Four Voyages* and other accounts of South Seas ex-ploration, Pollin's notes on *Pym* pointed to other readings. Comparing the descriptions of the Tsalalians with the accounts of Pacific Islanders in Poe's probable sources, many of which Pollin identified and quoted, critics such as Paul Lyons and Terence Whalen have suggested that portrayals of the na-tives whom Pym met on the island of Tsalal mirror depictions of the peoples of the South Seas in books that were familiar to many of Poe's antebellum readers.[17] Pollin was not, of course, the first person to recognize Poe's reliance on texts written by mariners such as Morrell, but Pollin helped readers better understand the *extent* of that reliance, which indicated Poe's interest in the South Seas region, an object of American imperial desire. Had Pollin's notes on *Pym* been available before 1981, critical responses to *Pym* might have fol-lowed a different interpretive path. Instead of focusing on the Tsalal episode and reading it as a parable about domestic slavery, critics working before the 1980s might have emphasized the ways that the entire book exposed the colonial ambitions of the United States.[18]

Thorough annotation also marked the following three volumes that Pollin prepared. Published in 1985, the first of these books was devoted to what the editor called Poe's "brevities," sets "of brief essay-notes" featuring "comments on books, people, contemporary events and topics of mood and reminiscence" (2: v). Among these collections were the "Pinakidia" and the "Marginalia," which Poe published in literary journals. Pollin presented texts more reliable than Harrison's, but a mark against the *Brevities* volume was, as Benjamin F. Fisher noted, "the flawed apparatus" characterized by irregular abbreviation and acronym usage (Review 284). Editorial infelicities of that order did not, however, diminish the value of Pollin's notes. Most of these annotations were longer than the texts glossed; however, the information that Pollin gave was of great use to scholars interested in the books that shaped Poe's writing, works such as John Milton's *Paradise Lost*, Matthew Parker's writings on the Psalms, Isaac Disraeli's *Curiosities of Literature*, and Jacob Bryant's *A New System: or, An Analysis of Ancient Mythology*—to name only four sources identified by Pollin.

The year after the *Brevities* volume appeared, Pollin brought out an edi-tion of Poe's writings from the *Broadway Journal* with a companion text containing extensive notes.[19] These 1986 publications differed significantly from the *Imaginary Voyages* and *Brevities* volumes, the most notable change being Pollin's use of facsimile texts for the *Broadway Journal* material. As Patrick F. Quinn observed, this puzzling "departure from standard editorial practice" produced "an outsized volume" (Review 463). Other matters bothered John E. Reilly, who identified "numerous inaccuracies in the keying of notes to text" (3) and considered "Pollin's failure to draw up from his notes some sort of table or list identifying the three dozen or so items in *The Broadway Journal* which he adds, deletes, challenges, or confirms as belonging to the canon of Poe's criticism" a real problem (4). Such editorial errors and peculiarities suggested that Pollin believed his primary purpose was identifying and commenting on Poe's sources, not preparing texts of Poe's works.

Pollin continued that practice in the next installment of *Collected Writings*, an edition of Poe material from the *Southern Literary Messenger*. Joseph V. Ridgely assisted with this volume, which appeared in 1998 and contained a number of critical reviews and essays written by Poe during his tenure as editorial assistant at the Richmond journal. For the *Southern Literary Messenger* volume, Pollin and Ridgely made peculiar formatting decisions, which included the presentation of altered facsimile texts. Such editorial idiosyncrasies aside, the Pollin/Ridgely volume offered readers valuable insights into Poe's life as a magazinist. In his review of that work, Terence Whalen claimed, "The image of Poe that emerge[d] from this volume [bore] less resemblance to the unrestrained romantic genius than to the workaday commercial writer" (425). The *Brevities* and *Broadway Journal* editions that Pollin had prepared served a similar purpose, helping readers see Poe as a literary professional engaged in the consumption and production of texts, not a lone wanderer caught up in otherworldly reveries.

Pollin offered yet another picture of Poe, who was, as Whalen suggested, a more complex writer than the sour-faced *poète maudit* who graced many anthology covers, and all the volumes in Pollin's edition showcased Poe the reader. That figure appeared in the notes documenting "Poe's sources and influences," which were, as Jeffrey Savoye has remarked, "abiding interests" of Pollin ("Burton R. Pollin" 163). The print materials cited included an array of writings from antebellum periodicals, narratives of travel and exploration, and forgotten novels—a textual stockpile with contents of bewildering variety. What Pollin displayed here was not so much his own learning as Poe's deep familiarity with the print culture of Jacksonian America. The Poe who read widely was not a tortured soul preoccupied with personal demons; troubled he was, but the trials of producing work that would be read consumed his creative energies.[20] Poe the professional writer, who read to understand his audience and its expectations, was the man Pollin brought to the fore. This Poe has been the subject of a great deal of important scholarship produced over the last three decades, examples of which include Whalen's *Edgar Allan Poe and the Masses*, Kevin J. Hayes's *Poe and the Printed Word*, and *Poe and the Remapping of Antebellum Print Culture*—a collection of essays edited by J. Gerald Kennedy and Jerome McGann.

Poe in the Library of America Editions

While Pollin was at work on the volumes for his *Collected Writings* set, the Library of America issued two collections of Poe's writings in 1984. Patrick F. Quinn prepared the *Poetry & Tales* volume, which included "all of Poe's poems except those of doubtful attribution and those surviving in fragmentary form" (*Poetry & Tales* 1370), and he consulted Mabbott's and Stovall's editions of Poe's verse while selecting copy-texts. Poe's fiction, in which category Quinn placed the voyage narratives, appeared complete in texts that were, in many cases, based on Mabbott's or the *Broadway Journal* versions with Poe's handwritten revisions. A key addition was a carefully edited text of Poe's *Eureka*, the previously unpublished work of Roland W. Nelson. All of these texts appeared in a single volume comprising over 1300 pages, with so many Poe texts crammed together that Quinn left little room for apparatus or annotations. Printed sans variants, the Quinn edition did not draw attention to the revising work that preoccupied Poe, and the omission disappointed Pollin, who also found fault with what he considered "a kind of metaphysical ambiguity" in the handling of errors, some of which Quinn attributed to Poe and others to typesetters without setting forth a rationale for distinguishing the two sorts of mistakes ("Poe Editions" 31).

The other Library of America volume was *Essays & Reviews*, which G. R. Thompson edited. While preparing texts, Thompson opted for "[t]he first appearance of each title . . . unless the piece was subsequently rewritten and expanded or reprinted as part of a later, more extensive article" (1482). The Thompson edition was not complete, but the volume contained some important critical pieces such as "The Literati of New York City" that were outside Pollin's editorial scope. Another significant feature of the Thompson volume was the omission of the infamous Paulding-Drayton review, which Harrison had misattributed to Poe.[21] This essay, which was a laudatory response to two pro-slavery books, had often been presented as evidence of Poe's deep commitment to slavery. Some scholars, notably Whalen, have, however, challenged the notion that Poe was an ardent defender of the peculiar institution. Pollin and Ridgely similarly omitted the Paulding-Drayton review from their edition of Poe's *Southern Literary Messenger* writings, but that volume appeared over a decade after Thompson's collection. In a review, Pollin praised Thompson for including an impressive "variety of material" ("Poe Editions" 29). The *Essays* volume was, however, incomplete. Furthermore, although Thompson omitted a number of Poe pieces, he included a "call for a New York city library" from 1845 that Pollin insisted was not the work of Poe (30). In addition, Pollin took issue with the thinness of the annotations, the majority of which were "merely translations of foreign phrases" in Poe's prose (31). Selective annotation was also a feature of the *Poetry & Tales* volume, and whatever its limitations, such streamlining had some positive effects. Comprehensive but not complete, the Quinn and Thompson additions were affordable and portable—perfect for classroom use. These features made the Library of America volumes ideal vehicles for conveying to the widest audience the *range* of Poe's literary output, the knowledge of which helped readers place Poe in his professional milieu.[22]

Presenting different portraits of Poe, the editors Campbell, Ostrom, Stovall, Mabbott, Pollin, Quinn, and Thompson helped readers focus on particular facets of the writer's life and work, with positive and negative effects. To the extent that each portrait brought out attributes of Poe obscured or overlooked in popular biographical works and critical writings, the focusing power of the portraits was salutary, correcting misconceptions of Poe the man and/or illuminating his artistry, but in some ways each portrait, which highlighted a particular trait of Poe, operated as an interpretive blinder, hiding from view other aspects of the writer's creative existence. Taken together, those editorial portraits afforded, however, an expansive view of Poe, and the contributions of Campbell, Ostrom, Stovall, Mabbott, Pollin, Quinn, and Thompson still influence responses to Poe and his writings. The Library of America volumes remain in print, and the paper editions of Mabbott and Pollin live anew on the Edgar Allan Poe Society of Baltimore website, where they appear in digitized versions prepared by Jeffrey Savoye, whose appended corrections and annotations keep those editions in step with recent critical developments. Time will tell what effects these works will have on the study of Poe as critics continue to explore the different Poes that scholars—even editors—have envisioned, and academic editions of Poe's writings published in the twenty-first century will surely offer additional objects for critical scrutiny.[23]

Notes

1. Romantic poets dominate the list of Poe's influences that appears on pages xliv–liii of Campbell's introduction.

2. In his introduction, Campbell did, of course, survey the "wide difference of opinion" on "the worth of Poe's poems" (liv), suggesting that inaccurate biographies of the poet shaped negative reactions. According to Campbell, the anti-Poe set was probably "influenced in their judgments by what they knew—or believed themselves to know—about the irregularities of Poe's life and character" (lxiv).

3. In 1911, J. H. Whitty published his edition of Poe's poetry. Campbell's volume appeared only six years later, superseding Whitty's. For this reason, a section devoted to the Whitty edition does not appear in this essay.

4. Arthur Hobson Quinn played an important role in that revelation. Commenting on Quinn's famous biography of Poe, Shawn Rosenheim pronounced the biographer's detailed record of "many of Griswold's forgeries" an important scholarly achievement, through which Quinn challenged Griswold's "slanders with a rather charming moral clarity" (xv).

5. For bibliographic information about Ostrom's supplements, see *Collected Letters of Edgar Allan Poe* (2: 970). 2008 saw the publication of *The Collected Letters of Edgar Allan Poe*, which Jeffrey Savoye prepared with Burton R. Pollin. In this two-volume set, Savoye and Pollin provide texts for 422 letters—53 more than Ostrom had documented in *The Letters of Edgar Allan Poe* and its supplements (1: xxiii). Those additions notwithstanding, Savoye and Pollin declare their work a continuation of Ostrom's, naming their predecessor a co-editor.

6. In *The Epistolary Poe*, Bonner argues that Poe's "missives reveal a [writer] of many selves" (1) and bear witness to "the complexity of his private and public lives" (13).

7. In a review of the 1948 Ostrom set, Carroll D. Laverty draws a similar conclusion, linking Ostrom's work and Quinn's: "*The Letters of Edgar Allan Poe* is . . . the most important book in Poe scholarship since Professor Arthur Hobson Quinn's biography, published in 1941, and is indispensable to a thorough understanding of the great writer" (246). According to Laverty, Ostrom's edition presents "a more comprehensive picture of Poe the man than was possible heretofore" (247).

8. See, for example, the judgment of Walker: "[S]cholars will still have need of Campbell. Not only are his notes a mine of information, but in some respects his edition is more complete than" Stovall's (215).

9. Henry A. Pochmann also admired Stovall's presentation, calling the "page of text . . . a thing of beauty" (247).

10. The author thanks Kent Ljungquist for recommending the addition of a Stovall section to this chapter.

11. J. Albert Robbins offers a balanced assessment of the *Poems* volume: "This is not the ultimate, the perfect edition of the poems, but it is of great importance and will continue to be so for a long time" (247).

12. See George Graham's remarks on the matter. According to Graham, an employer of Poe during the Philadelphia years, "it may be said . . . that Mr. Poe himself deputed him [Griswold] to act as his literary executor, and that he must have felt some confidence in his ability at least—if not in his integrity—to perform the functions imposed with discretion and honor" (qtd. in Arthur Hobson Quinn 662).

13. To some extent, Patrick F. Quinn agrees with Mabbott, claiming that "evidence from collation of texts suggests that Griswold used copy revised by Poe" (*Poetry & Tales* 1371).

14. Mabbott's edition is the only collection of Poe's writings that *both* of the major Poe journals, *The Edgar Allan Poe Review* and *Poe Studies*, list as acceptable for citation in submissions.

15. See also Campbell, who deemed "the multifarious revisions made by the poet in republishing his verses . . . a matter of extreme importance for the understanding of his art" (v).

16. See the following essays by Fisher: "Poe's 'Metzengerstein': Not a Hoax," "To 'The Assignation' from 'The Visionary' and Poe's Decade of Revising," and "To 'The Assignation' from 'The Visionary' (Part Two): The Revisions and Related Matters." These articles appeared before 1978, the publication year for the *Tales & Sketches* volumes of *Collected Works*, but *after* Harvard University Press issued the 1969 *Poems* volume, in which Mabbott had already stressed the importance of Poe's revisions.

17. See Lyons's "Opening Accounts in the South Seas: Poe's *Pym* and American Pacific Orientalism," and chapter 6 of Whalen's *Edgar Allan Poe and the Masses*.

18. Those ambitions have not, of course, escaped critical notice. To illustrate, the following three books—all of which appeared after 1981, the year that the *Imaginary Voyages* volume saw print—contain commentary on *Pym* in its imperial contexts: Dana D. Nelson's *The Word in Black and White: Reading 'Race' in American Literature, 1638–1867*, Malini Johar Schueller's *U.S. Orientalisms: Race, Nation, and Gender in Literature, 1790–1890*, and Paul Giles's *Antipodean America: Australasia and the Constitution of U.S. Literature*.

19. The texts of the *Broadway Journal* writings fill volume three of the *Collected Writings*, and the contents of the fourth volume are Pollin's notes on those writings.

20. In an 1835 letter to Thomas W. White, his employer at the *Southern Literary Messenger*, Poe famously declared "To be appreciated you must be *read* . . . ." (Ostrom et al. 1: 85).

21. Building on the work of William Doyle Hull, Joseph V. Ridgely argued that Nathaniel Beverley Tucker, not Poe, penned the Paulding-Drayton review, an 1836 essay about two pro-slavery works that critics such as Bernard Rosenthal thought reflective of Poe's own attitudes toward race and slavery. Terrence Whalen shed additional light on the authorship controversy, identifying passages in the Paulding-Drayton review that featured language and ideas found elsewhere in Tucker's works. See Ridgely's "The Authorship of the 'Paulding-Drayton Review'" and chapter 5 of Whalen's *Edgar Allan Poe and the Masses*. Combined with Ridgely's comments on Poe's correspondence with Tucker, Whalen's rhetorical analysis of the Paulding-

Drayton review indicates that the review is probably not the work of Poe. At any rate, "no one will have an easy time refuting Terry Whalen," as Leland S. Person has acknowledged (10).

22. The Quinn and Thompson volumes are more inclusive than the mid-century collection *The Portable Poe*, in which Philip Van Doren Stern dwells on Poe the terror writer, subjecting the poetry and prose to hackneyed biographical readings. J. Gerald Kennedy's *The Portable Edgar Allan Poe* represents a recent effort to combine portability and comprehensiveness in one book, and Kennedy takes pains to place Poe's imaginative work in its historical context. Kennedy discusses his work on this edition in chapter 7 of this volume—*Anthologizing Poe*.

23. Two recently published editions are *Eureka* and *Critical Theory: The Major Documents*, both prepared by Stuart and Susan Levine.

Works Cited

Beaver, Harold. Review of *Collected Writings of Edgar Allan Poe*, vol. 1, edited by Burton R. Pollin. *Modern Language Review*, vol. 79, no. 4, 1984, pp. 912–14.

Bonner, Thomas, Jr. *The Epistolary Poe*. Edgar Allan Poe Society of Baltimore and the Library of the University of Baltimore, 2001.

Bradsher, Earl L. Review of *The Poems of Edgar Allan Poe*, edited by Killis Campbell, *Sewanee Review*, vol. 26, no. 2, 1918, pp. 241–44.

Campbell, Killis, editor. *The Poems of Edgar Allan Poe*. 1917, Russell & Russell, 1962.

Cunliffe, Marcus. Review of *The Letters of Edgar Allan Poe*, edited by John W. Ostrom. *The Modern Language Review*, vol. 45, no. 2, 1950, pp. 249–50.

Fisher, Benjamin F. "Poe's 'Metzengerstein': Not a Hoax." *American Literature*, vol. 42, no. 4, 1971, pp. 487–94.

———. Review of *Collected Writings of Edgar Allan Poe*, vol. 2, edited by Burton R. Pollin. *American Literature*, vol. 58, no. 2, 1986, pp. 284–86.

———. "To 'The Assignation' from 'The Visionary' and Poe's Decade of Revising." *Library Chronicle*, vol. 39, no. 2, 1973, pp. 89–105.

———. "To 'The Assignation' from 'The Visionary' (Part Two): The Revisions and Related Matters." *Library Chronicle*, vol. 40, no. 2, 1976, pp. 221–51.

Giles, Paul. *Antipodean America: Australasia and the Constitution of U.S. Literature*. Oxford UP, 2013.

Hayes, Kevin J. *Poe and the Printed Word*. Cambridge UP, 2000.

Kaplan, Sidney. Introduction. *The Narrative of Arthur Gordon Pym*, by Edgar Allan Poe, Hill and Wang, 1960, pp. vii–xxv.

Kennedy, J. Gerald, editor. *The Portable Edgar Allan Poe*. Penguin, 2006.

Kennedy, J. Gerald, and Jerome McGann, editors. *Poe and the Remapping of Antebellum Print Culture*. Louisiana State UP, 2012.

Laverty, Carroll D. Review of *The Letters of Edgar Allan Poe*, edited by John W. Ostrom. *American Literature*, vol. 21, no. 2, 1949, pp. 246–48.

Levine, Stuart, and Susan F. Levine, editors. *Critical Theory: The Major Documents.* By Edgar Allan Poe, Illinois UP, 2009.

———. *Eureka.* By Edgar Allan Poe, Illinois UP, 2004.

Lyons, Paul. "Opening Accounts in the South Seas: Poe's *Pym* and American Pacific Orientalism." *ESQ: A Journal of the American Renaissance,* vol. 42, no. 4, 1996, pp. 291–326.

Mabbott, Maureen Cobb. *Mabbott as Poe Scholar: The Early Years.* The Enoch Pratt Free Library, the Edgar Allan Poe Society, and the Library of the University of Baltimore, 1980.

Mabbott, Thomas Ollive, editor. *The Collected Works of Edgar Allan Poe,* vol. 1, Harvard UP, 1969.

Mabbott, Thomas Ollive, Eleanor D. Kewer, and Maureen C. Mabbott, editors. *The Collected Works of Edgar Allan Poe,* vols. 2 and 3, Harvard UP, 1978.

McGann, Jerome. *The Poet Edgar Allan Poe: Alien Angel.* Harvard UP, 2014.

Moldenhauer, Joseph J. "Mabbott's Poe and the Question of Copy-Text." *Poe Studies,* vol. 11, no. 2, 1978, pp. 41–46.

Nelson, Dana D. *The Word in Black and White: Reading 'Race' in American Literature, 1638–1867.* Oxford UP, 1992.

O'Brien, William A. Review of *Collected Works of Edgar Allan Poe,* edited by Thomas Ollive Mabbott et al., vols. 2 and 3. *Modern Language Notes,* vol. 93, no. 5, 1978, pp. 1104–6.

Ostrom, John W., editor. *The Letters of Edgar Allan Poe.* Harvard UP, 1948. 2 vols.

Ostrom, John W., Burton R. Pollin, and Jeffrey A. Savoye, editors. *The Collected Letters of Edgar Allan Poe.* Gordian Press, 2008. 2 vols.

Person, Leland S. Review of Whalen's *Edgar Allan Poe and the Masses: The Political Economy of Literature in Antebellum America.* PSA *Newsletter,* vol. 28, no. 1, 2000, pp. 9–10.

Philbrick, Thomas. Review of *Collected Works of Edgar Allan Poe,* edited by Thomas Ollive Mabbott et al., vols. 2 and 3. *Nineteenth-Century Fiction,* vol. 33, no. 3, 1978, pp. 403–5.

Pochmann, Henry A. Review of *The Poems of Edgar Allan Poe,* edited by Floyd Stovall, *American Literature,* vol. 38, no. 2, 1966, pp. 247–48.

Pollin, Burton R. "The Poe Editions of the Library of America." *Poe Studies,* vol. 18, no. 2, 1985, pp. 29–32.

———, editor. *Collected Writings of Edgar Allan Poe,* vol. 1. Twayne, 1981.

———. *Collected Writings of Edgar Allan Poe,* vols. 2–4. Gordian Press, 1985–1986.

Pollin, Burton R., and Joseph V. Ridgely, editors. *Collected Writings of Edgar Allan Poe,* vol. 5, Gordian Press, 1998.

Quinn, Arthur Hobson. *Edgar Allan Poe: A Critical Biography.* D. Appleton-Century Co., 1941.

Quinn, Patrick F. Review of *Collected Writings of Edgar Allan Poe,* vols. 3 and 4, edited by Burton J. [sic] Pollin. *American Literature,* vol. 59, no. 3, 1987, pp. 463–64.

———, editor. *Poetry & Tales.* By Edgar Allan Poe, Library of America, 1984.

Reilly, John E. Review of *Collected Writings of Edgar Allan Poe*, vols. 3 and 4, edited by Burton R. Pollin. *PSA Newsletter*, vol. 15, no. 1, 1987, pp. 3–4.

Ridgely, Joseph V. "The Authorship of the 'Paulding-Drayton Review.'" *PSA Newsletter*, vol. 20, no. 2, 1992, pp. 1–3, 6.

Robbins, J. Albert. Review of *Collected Works of Edgar Allan Poe*, vol. 1, edited by Thomas Ollive Mabbott. *American Literature*, vol. 42, no. 2, 1970, pp. 246–47.

Rosenheim, Shawn. Foreword. *Edgar Allan Poe: A Critical Biography*, by Arthur Hobson Quinn, Johns Hopkins UP, 1998, pp. xi–xvii.

Savoye, Jeffrey. "Burton R. Pollin (1916–2009)." *Edgar Allan Poe Review*, vol. 10, no. 2, 2009, pp. 161–64.

———. "Dating 'Eulalie': A Reevaluation of Poe's Manuscripts." *Edgar Allan Poe Review*, vol. 18, no. 1, 2017, pp. 1–14.

Schroeter, James. Review of *The Poems of Edgar Allan Poe*, edited by Floyd Stovall, *Modern Philology*, vol. 65, no. 1, 1967, pp. 84–86.

Schueller, Malini Johar. *U.S. Orientalisms: Race, Nation, and Gender in Literature, 1790–1890*. Michigan UP, 1998.

Sherburn, George. Review of *The Poems of Edgar Allen* [sic] *Poe*, edited by Killis Campbell, *Modern Philology*, vol. 16, no. 1, 1918, p. 56.

Smith, C. Alphonso. Review of *The Poems of Edgar Allan Poe*, edited by Killis Campbell, *Modern Language Notes*, vol. 33, no. 3, 1918, pp. 172–75.

Smith, Philip, and Alan Weissman, editors. *Tales of Terror and Detection*. By Edgar Allan Poe, Dover, 1995.

Stern, Philip Van Doren. *The Portable Poe*. Viking, 1945.

Stewart, R. A. "Introduction to the Notes." *The Complete Works of Edgar Allan Poe*, edited by James A. Harrison, vol. 2, 1902. AMS Press, 1965, pp. 299–306.

Stovall, Floyd. *Edgar Poe the Poet*. Virginia UP, 1969.

———, editor. *The Poems of Edgar Allan Poe*. Virginia UP, 1965.

Thompson, G. R., editor. *Essays & Reviews*. By Edgar Allan Poe, Library of America, 1984.

Walker, I. M. Review of *The Poems of Edgar Allan Poe*, edited by Floyd Stovall, *Modern Language Review*, vol. 63, no. 1, 1968, pp. 214–15.

Weeks, Donald. Review of *Poems* by Edgar Allan Poe, edited by Floyd Stovall, *Journal of Aesthetics and Art Criticism*, vol. 25, no. 4, 1967, p. 471.

Whalen, Terence. *Edgar Allan Poe and the Masses: The Political Economy of Literature in Antebellum America*. Princeton UP, 1999.

———. Review of *Collected Writings of Edgar Allan Poe*, vol. 5, edited by Burton Pollin and Joseph V. Ridgely. *American Literature*, vol. 72, no. 2, 2000, pp. 425–26.

Wilbur, Richard, editor. *Poe*. Dell, 1959.

Wilson, James Southall. Introduction. *The Letters of Edgar Allan Poe*, edited by John W. Ostrom, vol. 1, Harvard, 1948, pp. xvii–xxi.

Winters, Yvor. *Maule's Curse: Seven Studies in the History of American Obscurantism*. New Directions, 1938.

CHAPTER SIX

~

Poe Anthologies
and Editions in Britain

1852–1914

Bonnie Shannon McMullen

Few writers have experienced the range of responses from reverence to re-
vilement that Edgar Allan Poe has received in Britain. These responses were
both created by and reflected in the collections of Poe's writings published in
Britain following his death in 1849. Poe was, by temperament and necessity,
a writer who demonstrated a many-faceted talent. Poe's first publishers in
Britain were well advised to present him as a writer who excelled in modes
already familiar and popular with the public. *Blackwood's Magazine* had
both catered to and helped to create a readership for certain genres of short
fiction, including adventure, horror, and scientific speculation. Poe, by his
own testimony, read and was influenced by these stories, which he absorbed
with intense attention as a boy, and their effects can be seen in much of his
work. Sea literature was another popular genre in Britain, unsurprisingly in
a seafaring, imperialist nation. Thus, as Benjamin F. Fisher has pointed out,
the British reading public's introduction to Poe came, initially, through *The
Narrative of Arthur Gordon Pym* (52).

Poe's poetry, on the other hand, was indebted to the English romantics—
particularly the late romantics, including Keats, Shelley, and Byron—and
was taken up by editors who sought an audience among readers of these
poets. From the beginning, it is possible to discern a division in the treatment of Poe's prose and poetry, the former presented as a kind of popular
entertainment, often churned out in cheap editions, and the latter meticu-
lously edited and expensively packaged for serious readers seeking something
beyond momentary diversion. Thus, in the early years of Poe's writings in

Britain, he appeared as a kind of double personality—a mass entertainer in prose, a prophet of truth in poetry. There is little evidence that many early readers ever tried to bridge the divide.

This chapter will discuss the history of Poe anthologies and editions in Britain from the earliest volume of stories in 1852 to an edition of Poe's essays and criticism in 1914. No steady growth of appreciation can be discerned: some early editors such as Ingram and Hannay treated Poe's poems with great reverence, while a few later editors regarded the stories and their author with near contempt. Gradually, however, toward the end of the nineteenth century, the nature of British publishing changed. Formerly the province of printers and booksellers, as the twentieth century approached, the publishing industry was increasingly run by upper-middle-class, educated people. With this change came an increasing respect for Poe's versatility and pre-eminence in all the genres he practiced. By 1914, Poe's position in Britain as a serious writer was secure.

The Beginning: A Writer for Many Tastes

British publisher Henry Vizetelly, perhaps counting on an appetite already whetted by American collections of Poe's tales and poems that appeared in Britain in the mid-1840s, brought out *Tales of Mystery, Imagination, and Humour, and Poems* in 1852. Selling for one shilling, with an ornate cover in red with a gold foliate design, it was illustrated with twenty-six unattributed wood engravings.[1] Part of a series titled "Readable Books," the prospectus describes its aim: Works will be distinguished by "a certain vivacity of style or subject, suitable alike to the family circle, and the solitary student—to the idler suffering from *ennui*, and the man weary with work—to the sedentary stayer at home, and the more mercurial traveller on river, road, and rail." The last part of this statement is, perhaps, the most interesting. A national rail network in Britain was established in the 1840s, only a few years before Vizetelly's Poe, and he was one of the first, after Routledge, to exploit this new marketing opportunity. Short fiction might be deemed particularly suitable for train journeys, and stations were rewarding marketplaces for booksellers, as airports are today.

Vizetelly's preface, however, might have caused a purchaser misgivings. It states that the publisher "might have begun with a better work, but this was ready to hand, and . . . the work has been overlooked by the buccaneers of the book trade—those gentry who treat the public to three separate editions of every work they see cried up on the other side of the Atlantic, no matter how dull it may be, and, in their predatory haste, occasionally fail to respect the legal copyrights of others " (vii). The publisher then cautiously assures the reader "that but few of the works he has in preparation are importations from the American market," implying that American fare needed to be doled out sparingly (viii). The contents include the memoir by Rufus W. Griswold, followed by several tales and poems. All of the Dupin tales appear, along with "A Descent into the Maelström," "The Premature Burial," "Some Words with a Mummy," "The Facts in the Case of M. Valdemar" (here entitled "The Startling Effects of Mesmerism on a Dying Man"), and "The Gold-Bug", carrying the title "The Gold-Beetle." Apart from the license taken with Poe's titles in the latter two stories, the particular substitution of "beetle" for "bug" in Poe's tale of cryptography and treasure-hunting suggests a failure to recognize the *double entendre* of "gold-bug" as both the beetle itself and as gold fever.[2] The eleven poems included, leading with "The Raven," suggest that they were chosen for their sonority and romantic evocativeness. The note of apology for presenting Poe ("the publisher might have begun with a better work") and the whiff of anti-Americanism in the assurance that there will not be many more American books in the series are features that surfaced in a number of subsequent Poe anthologies, most notably in the Haweis edition of 1886. Vizetelly was bowing to an attitude of cultural imperialism at the height of the British Empire that required a semi-apology for a writer from a former British colony. Also, he probably feared—with jus-tification—that with the rise of High Victorian morality and a turn toward didacticism in literature, Poe would not be to everyone's taste.

In that same year, *Tales and Sketches to which is added The Raven, A Poem* appeared. Part of Routledge's "New Cheap Series," this anthology contained a wider range of stories, including some less frequently anthologized pieces such as "The Philosophy of Furniture" and "The Sphinx," but only one Dupin story, "The Murders in the Rue Morgue." The decisions to concen-trate on the tales and to include only one poem, the popular "Raven," with its strong narrative drive, suggest that this volume was aimed at a slightly wider audience in search of entertainment. A larger selection of poems was included in *Poe's Tales of Mystery and Imagination; and Poems*, also published in 1852 by Clarke, Beeton, and Co.

Vizetelly's apologetic diffidence was not universal. During the following year, 1853, the Scottish novelist James Hannay published *The Poetical Works of Edgar Allan Poe* with a dedication to Dante Gabriel Rossetti. This impres-sive volume, published by Addey, was illustrated by E. H. Wehnert, F. W. Hulme, James Godwin, and Harrison Weir. E. H. Wehnert, an English artist of German parentage who had been educated in Germany, was a painter best known for his book illustrations, including illustrations for Grimms' fairy tales. His frontispiece for the volume, showing Pre-Raphaelite influence, depicts the grieving lover, with the dead Lenore and angels floating overhead. Hulme's illustrations, such as the one for "The Coliseum," are less emotionally evocative. Godwin, essentially romantic, provides an illustration for "Lenore" more in the spirit of Wehnert's frontispiece, showing ethereal figures flying away with the dead woman. Weir, known as an animal artist, favoring cats, illustrates "The Bells" with two figures in a sleigh pulled by a prancing horse. Wehnert and Godwin both attempt to convey the emotional force of Poe's poems, while Hulme's coliseum fails to connect with the poem, and Weir's sleigh could be the design for a Christmas card. The contrast between Wehnert and Godwin on one hand and Hulme and Weir on the other shows the difference between illustrators who attempted to capture the spirit of Poe, as they understood it, and those who merely seized on the first idea that the works suggested.

Hannay's "Notice" of the "Life and Genius" strikes a respectful note. He observes "with a great deal of pleasure" the spread of literature by "our American kinsmen" (xv)—an admiration for American culture most notable for its absence among English editors. Hannay suggests that after the arrival of American writers whose tone, thought, and style reflect an English influence, Britain is now encountering American authors "who are really national—in the sense that American apples are national," and he continues, "An Englishman ought to require no apology from one who introduces an American Poet to him" (xvi). Hannay repeats many of Griswold's errors, such as Poe's place and date of birth, but using a simile seldom applied to Poe, he describes his entry to the world "as naked as a cherub" (xviii). Continuing the analogies with nature suggested by "American apples," he states that Poe's "verse is all as pure as wild flowers" (xx). Wildness is natural and wholesome; if Poe was sometimes too wild, so are hundreds of others, "but this one wrote 'To Helen'" (xxi). Of the poems in general, Hannay asserts, "If his circle is a narrow, it is a magic one" (xxxlv). This account, in spite of some inaccuracies and a tendency to overcorrect Griswold's negative portrait of Poe by leaning too far the other way, is refreshing for its admonition to focus on the work, to see Poe for his genius and not his human failings. Hannay, as a Scot, implicitly finds an affinity between Poe and a Scottish literary tradition, distinct from the larger English canon. Hannay's *Poe* went through a number of editions, but despite his efforts to rehabilitate Poe's reputation, later anthologies, such as *Edgar Allan Poe's Poetical Works*—published in Edinburgh by Alexander Hislop and Co. in 1869—continued to preface the poems with Griswold's memoir.

Reassessment in the 1870s

Champions of Poe, such as Algernon Charles Swinburne, who praised Poe's "one pure note of original song" in *Under the Microscope* in 1872, introduced a new perspective (418). In 1873, *The Works of Edgar Allan Poe, including the choicest of his Critical Essays, now first published in this country, with a study of his life and writings, from the French of C. Baudelaire* was published by John Camden Hotten. It is divided into the following sections: Miscellaneous Poems, Poems Written in Youth, Tales of Mystery and Imagination, Humorous Tales and Sketches, and Critical Essays. The French reading of Poe posed a challenge to British insularity and helped to bring about a reassessment of his work.

The most comprehensive edition of Poe's work in Britain was John H. Ingram's four-volume *Works of Edgar Allan Poe*, published in 1874 and 1875 in Edinburgh by Adam and Charles Black. Ingram asserts in his preface that "no pains have been spared to insure the accuracy of the whole . . . in order to avoid the numerous *errata* which disfigure previous collections" (v). Like most of Poe's later editors, Ingram begins his volume with a long biographical memoir in which he explicitly sets out to rescue Poe's reputation from the calumnies generated by Griswold. In addition, he attempts a balanced view of a complex figure, and although later researchers have found errors and omissions, the memoir is informative and fair. In spite of Ingram's reverence for Poe's writing, however, the volumes lack any critical appraisal or major editorial additions or replacements, as demonstrated by Jeffrey Savoye in chapter 4 of this book. The poems, tales, and criticism are left to speak for themselves and, in its textual accuracy, this edition was the best available in Britain at that time. Ingram had his critics, and in 1884 Richard Herne Shepherd used his preface to *Tamerlane and Other Poems* to protest against Ingram's alleged "moral right of monopoly over" that work (ii).

At the opposite end of the spectrum were publishers who exploited Poe's sensationalism with cheap fare for the masses. C. H. Ross's Penny Library was one such example, producing in 1875 several of the more arresting stories in pamphlet form as *Tales*, with a lurid cover illustration of a hand with blood dripping from its fingertips. With no regard for Poe's titles, the publisher includes, among seven tales, "The Murder [sic] in the Rue Morgue," "The Stolen Letter," "Mesmerizing a Dying Man," and "The Story of the Black Cat. " The back cover announces, "most extraordinary stories by that weird genius, Edgar Allan Poe," followed by comments excerpted from newspapers. "Good wholesome penny works" is the unexpected verdict of the *Daily Chronicle* while the *Hull Bellman* avers, "This is cheap literature indeed."

Toward an Aesthetic Appreciation and a Victorian Backlash

Appealing to a better-educated audience was *The Poems of Edgar Allan Poe, with an essay on his poetry*, edited by the Scottish writer Andrew Lang in 1881. Lang's note on the text explains that "original copies of Poe's poetical works are very rare in England" and none of "the booksellers who deal in such curiosities" could supply him (vii). Therefore, for "The Raven and Other Poems," he has used the Wiley and Putnam edition of 1846, while, for the later poems, he has used the Redfield edition published in New York in 1850.

Lang sensibly asserts that "The life of Edgar Allan Poe . . . little concerns readers of his poetry" (xiii). Poe's "theory and practice" were, he argues, "the result of reaction" to the idea that poetry should "teach morality" (xiii). Poe was in revolt against those who thought poets "should dignify industrialism, and indite paens, perhaps, to sewing machines and patent electric lights" (xiii). By contrast, Poe's province was the beauty and music of the written word. Lang, who is best known as a collector of fairy tales, ends his introduction with a fable that summarizes his view of Poe's poetic qualities:

> Some foolish old legend tells of a musician who surpassed all his rivals. His strains were unearthly sad, and ravished the ears of those who listened with a strange melancholy. Yet his viol had but a single string, and the framework was fashioned out of a dead woman's breast-bone. Poe's verse—the parallel is much in his own taste—resembles that player's minstrelsy. It is morbidly sweet and mournful, and all touched on that single string, which thrills to a dead and immortal affection. (xxvi)

Lang's fable calls attention to a number of Poe's salient characteristics, as well as the critical precepts expounded in "The Philosophy of Composition." The reference to "rivals" recalls Poe's competitiveness. "*Sadness,*" Poe wrote, was the "highest manifestation" of beauty (484). "Unearthly sad" conveys the quality of Poe's melancholy, "the most legitimate of all the poetical tones," with constant evocations of the immaterial in the poems (484). The "single string" chimes with Poe's theory that "the death . . . of a beautiful woman is . . . the most poetical topic in the world" (486). Finally, the analogy with a harpist reminds us of the importance of music to Poe's theory and practice. In "The Poetic Principle," Poe wrote "in the union of Poetry with music . . . we shall find the widest field for the Poetic development" (Lang 506). While Lang's appreciation of Poe has much to commend it, exhibiting great sympathy between author and editor, it fails to account for the range of Poe's work. Could this idealized figure have written "The Tell-Tale Heart"?

In 1886, as part of Walter Scott's "Canterbury Poets" series, *The Poetical Works of Edgar Allan Poe* appeared, edited by the former miner and self-taught poet, Joseph Skipsey. Skipsey can barely restrain his enthusiasm for Poe, whose best poems, he declares, "are among the finest things that ever sprang from the depths of the human soul" (27). He interprets "poetical works" in its broadest sense, and the volume includes "The Poetic Principle" and four tales. According to Skipsey, "Ligeia," "The Assignation," and other tales contain "all the harmonic organic completeness and aerial beauty of fine poems" (27). This volume has the merit of seeing the unity of Poe's work, as opposed to the divided way in which many earlier editors had treated it.

Routledge's World Library Edition of *Tales of Mystery and Imagination* of 1886 marks a different approach. It was part of a series of fifty-two books a year, selling at threepence a volume for a paperback and sixpence for a cloth cover, and it was marketed to a wide readership, the publisher's stated aim being "[t]o make the price of each volume so low that none need borrow it, everyone being tempted to buy it, and nobody to steal it!" (1). Lest anyone fear that Poe was too highbrow for inclusion in such a cheap series, the publisher continues, "There is no greater mistake than to try to write and publish down to the people. Give the people something to work up to" (1). As if to illustrate this high-minded didacticism, the volume has a cover design by Walter Crane depicting an angel blowing a trumpet held in his right hand, while the other hand holds aloft an open book.

The introduction by the Rev. Hugh Reginald Haweis strikes a very different note. Haweis hosted George Eliot in his London home at least once and later became the father-in-law of Mina Loy, but he exhibits limited literary sensibilities. Nor does this clergyman display much in the way of Christian charity toward his subject, failing to see what later critics have identified as a Christian worldview underlying Poe's writing. Poe favored "the grotesque and lawless," Haweis insists, and this tendency "was fostered by his early training, or want of training" (5). Raised in America, Poe, it seems, never had a chance, as "[t]he extreme indulgence with which Americans bring up their children fostered his worst faults" (6). In this view, America in general and the Allans in particular failed Poe, but the severest discipline might not have redeemed him, as "[i]t is more than likely that he imbibed some taint of disease from his parents" (5). Poe's mother, Haweis avers, "had more beauty than brains" (6). Although Haweis cannot completely ignore the testimony of Poe's teachers and others that he had an aptitude for learning, even Poe's school records show that "he learned in the wrong way" (7). Then Poe compounded these disadvantages by marrying a girl "as weak of will . . . as himself" (9). This badly brought up, ill-educated writer, genetically compromised to boot, was "morbid to the finger-tips" (10). A genius, Haweis grudgingly admits, but "his genius gleams and quivers like the phosphorescent light that plays over a bed of corruption" (11). Considering its prejudice against the United States in general and against Poe's natural and foster families in particular, the essay can be seen as an apotheosis of the anti-Americanism that shadows the Vizetelly edition, magnified many times over, and expressed in terms that even Poe, at his most vitriolic, would have hesitated to use. Haweis, in his day, had a high profile as a preacher, writer, and public speaker, and his opinions, supported in most cases by no evidence whatsoever, probably earned more credence than they deserve. In addition, they did a disservice to Poe the writer as well as the man by directing readers' attention away from the work to focus on the allegedly morally and mentally corrupt author and the disordered culture that produced this literary anomaly.

Such an introduction, it must be admitted, could pique the curiosity of a certain kind of reader, and perhaps that was the hope of the series editor. However, the reader would have to look hard for the "bed of corruption" in the particular selection of Poe texts that Haweis offers. Only one tale, "The Black Cat," concerns crime and degeneracy, while the other five include a comic hoax, "Hans Pfaall"; a tale of mystery and code-breaking, "The Gold-Bug"; two tales of terror, "The Pit and the Pendulum" and "A Descent into the Maelström"; and a poetic fantasy, "The Island of the Fay." This lineup seems timid—and possibly disappointing—given the squalid moral decay promised by the preface; on the other hand, the range of stories includes several of Poe's most memorable works and shows a number of different facets of Poe's talent. In spite of Haweis's introductory judgments, the volume itself provides a well-rounded selection for any reader coming to Poe's fiction for the first time.

Ernest Rhys: In Praise of Short Fiction

It is seldom possible to identify with assurance who bought and read any particular Poe anthology or what impact such a reading experience might have had. However, in 1889 a Poe collection appeared which, because of its editor's influence, probably had far-reaching reverberations. Walter Scott publishers, as part of its "Camelot" series, published *The Fall of the House of Usher and Other Tales and Prose Writings of Edgar Poe: Selected and edited, with an introduction*, by Ernest Rhys. Rhys, an aspiring writer himself, later made a significant contribution to the availability of good literature by establishing Dent's thousand-titled Everyman Library. The introduction applauds the rise of "the shorter tale," a development to be celebrated "seeing to what insane results the long novel is apt to lead us." Poe's tales should be read "anew for their admirable example in the art of fiction" (v), a contrast with Skipsey, who looked at the tales as an alternative kind of poetry. Rhys quoted Baudelaire's assessment of Poe's genius approvingly, but took issue with editors who include Poe's reviews, which Rhys finds of little interest. He was possibly the first to highlight the importance to Poe's development of "short tales of effect" in *"Blackwood's Magazine* in its palmy days" (xxii). Rhys called *Eureka* "a futile, if suggestive, farrago of science and philosophy," a turning from Poe's "natural ways of expression" caused by a "brain weakened by long excess and suffering" (xxiv).

The nonchronological arrangement of the tales reflects "some general idea of preserving their correspondence to [Poe's] life" (v). The "more sensational" tales, accessible in earlier anthologies, are excluded, the volume being intended "to satisfy the interest created by his poems" (xxviii). Roughly half of the sixteen selections are infrequently anthologized poetical and reflective tales, such as "Eleanora," "The Domain of Arnheim," "Landor's Cottage," "Shadow—A Parable," and "The Colloquy of Monos and Una." Rhys continued Skipsey's initiative in taking Poe's prose tales as seriously as his poetry, not as populist entertainment, as many cheaper anthologies had done. His praise for "the shorter tale" reflects a reaction against the triple-decker Victorian novel. It is also an invitation to consider the question, "What constitutes excellence in fiction?" For Poe, it was not length. Like many editors, Rhys had blind spots; he failed to appreciate the acuteness of Poe's criticism, and *Eureka* defeated him.

This anthology appeared in the context of Rhys's role as the founder in 1890, with W. B. Yeats, of the Rhymers Club—a group that included Ernest Dowson, Arthur Symons, and Oscar Wilde, who shared their work and published anthologies of their poetry. Several, including Wilde, were already admirers of Poe, and all, in the mood and technicalities of their work, reflected his writing. They could be considered a kind of cultural exchange center, receiving and transmitting the work of Poe both directly through their own writing and indirectly, particularly in their activity as journalists promoting French enthusiasm for Poe and translating these writers for an Anglophone public. Arthur Symons's essay on symbolism in *The Yellow Book* was later expanded and published as *The Symbolist Movement in Literature* in 1895, a work that implicitly incorporated many of Poe's ideas and was a seminal influence on the practice and criticism of literary modernism. The Rhymers Club created ripples far beyond its time and place, and haunting echoes of Poe, as channeled through Dowson, in particular, can be found in twentieth-century American drama, fiction, film, and popular song.

Fiction for the Middle Market

In 1890, Ward, Lock, & Co. published *Tales of Adventure, Mystery and Imagination* in their series, the "Minerva Library of Famous Books." The title is a concession to the series' concentration on books of travel and exploration. The editor, G. T. Bettany, author of a biography of Darwin and a study of Indian religion, noted in his introduction that "some of the stories are not at all suited for nervous people" and, for that reason, "a few have been left out owing to the subjects or the effects being too horrible" (ii). Nevertheless, this substantial book includes *Arthur Gordon Pym* and thirty-six tales such as the far-from-anodyne "The Cask of Amontillado." Lovers of adventure and mystery might not be overly sensitive, but publisher and editor apparently hoped, with the introduction if not the contents, to appeal to a more genteel reader. There was a large market for sentimental and morally uplifting works aimed at middle-class women with ample reading time. These potential readers were worth capturing.

Several further cheap editions of the tales appeared in the 1890s, catering to a trend of increasing interest in Poe's fiction. In 1893, a sixpence edition of *The Murders in the Rue Morgue and other Tales of Mystery* was published by Sampson Low, Marston & Co. Eleven frequently anthologized tales, including the three Dupin stories, appear in double columns of small print between cardboard covers. "The Murders in the Rue Morgue" and "The Gold-Bug" are illustrated with line drawings by an anonymous artist. The words "murders" and "mystery" in the title, as well as the low price and a print size for young eyes, are clues to the intended market.

The first decade of the twentieth century saw the appearance of a number of Poe anthologies and editions. One, more interesting for its ninety-seven illustrations by Heath Robinson than for its by then familiar content, was *Poems of Edgar Allan Poe*, published by George W. Bell & Sons in 1900. Now best remembered as an artist of comically overcomplicated machinery and gadgets, Robinson's early style is reminiscent of the Pre-Raphaelites and Aubrey Beardsley, highly elaborate with a strong sense of line. His illustration for "Al Aaraaf" shows a woman in white robes standing in a field of flowers, rising stem-like from the center with her hair billowing upwards like an exotic blossom. Behind her are white onion-domed buildings. The introduction by H. Noel Williams states that Poe's domain is "so peculiarly his own . . . that he will [n]ever have to encounter anything approaching serious rivalry" (xxxii). The same could be said for Robinson.

Grant Richards and C. Arthur Pearson brought out *Tales of Mystery and Imagination* in 1902 and 1905 respectively, the former as part of the "World's

Classics" series. The two shilling Pearson edition, by the founder of the mass circulation *Daily Express*, was melodramatically illustrated by A. D. McCormick. The content of these editions was the same as that of nineteenth-century editions with the same title, and their appearance at this point suggests the continuing appetite for Poe's stories among members of the relatively unsophisticated but increasingly literate general public.

In 1906, Edward Hutton edited *Poems of Edgar Allan Poe* as part of the "King's Classics" series under the general editorship of Shakespeare scholar Israel Gollancz, uncle of Victor who later founded the publishing house. Hutton's introduction to this edition of the complete poems exhibits discomfort with Poe's poetry, stating that "it seems as though he has sung . . . a song of death in a voice disembodied to a tune from a music hall" (xlii). He warns that "No one would ever go to his work for consolation or encouragement" (xlviii)—probably true, but hardly a winning sales pitch. Still, he concludes, Poe's achievement is remarkable, considering his birth "in that almost barbarian land which . . . was without a literature, or a tradition, or any time-honoured expression in art" (xliv). Hutton's assessment of Poe seems dated, given the recognition his work was by then receiving from other editors and critics. The volume contains notes on the textual sources and, unlike most earlier editions of the poems, an index of first lines.

In 1907, Cassell's National Library published *Edgar Allan Poe's Tales: A Selection*, edited by the writer and campaigner for penal reform, Tighe Hopkins. Intended for the general reader, the seven popular tales include two Dupin stories and "The Gold-Bug." In his introduction, Hopkins railed against the "rogue" Griswold, who "made money out of lies" (1), another approach that seems dated, since by this time Griswold's calumnies had been refuted by previous editors and biographers.

An Offer of "Significant Experience"

Stories by Edgar Allan Poe, edited by Arthur Ransome in 1908, was the third volume in T. C. and E. C. Jack's "The World's Story Tellers" series. Ransome, who in 1910 was to write a critical study of Poe, was later famous as a children's writer but had earlier led a bohemian life in London and Russia, becoming personally acquainted with Lenin and Trotsky, whose secretary he married. Ransome's introduction is a welcome antidote to Haweis's essay of 1886. Like Rhys, Ransome treats Poe the storywriter with the same respect formerly afforded to Poe the poet by editors such as Hannay and Lang. He notes a connection between Poe's description of choosing an effect and the method used by William Godwin in *Caleb Williams*, a connection probably borrowed from "The Philosophy of Composition." There, Poe refers to Godwin as having allegedly written *Caleb Williams* backwards. As Paul Valéry was later to do, Ransome placed Poe in even more eminent company, comparing him to Leonardo da Vinci.[3] Both were men "whose works were the result of the energetic fusing of an emotional personality into moulds designed by reason" (xvii). Like Leonardo's, "Poe's work depends . . . on his power of retaining the poetry, the energy of his material, after submitting it to his constructive science, and then, when the moulds have been made, of bringing it out red-hot and fluid, as if in the primal vitality of its conception" (xvii). These are stories for the connoisseur, Ransome implies, which

> can only be fully enjoyed by those who come to them with the reverence and careful taste it is proper to bring to a glass of priceless wine. . . . They are the key to strange knowledge of ourselves, and . . . we find . . . that we have waited for them . . . . Like old melody, like elaborate and beautiful dancing, like artificial light, like the sight of poison or any other concentrated power, they are among the significant experiences that are open to humanity. (xxi)

Ransome is writing at a time when faith in Christianity was receding, while an interest in psychology grew rapidly. (Freud's *Interpretation of Dreams*, for example, had been published eight years earlier, in 1900.) Ransome borrows the language of religion, "reverence," but applies it to sensual and aesthetic experience which, in its intensity, can enhance our apprehension of life, but also, like poison, be dangerous. The selection of only seven stories concentrates on those with the greatest psychological interest such as "The Tell-Tale Heart" and "William Wilson," both featuring protagonists lacking self-knowledge, and two Dupin stories.

Something for Everyone

In 1909, Routledge published, as part of "The Muses' Library" series, *The Poems of Edgar Allan Poe*, with a sketch by John H. Ingram, catering to those who wanted to build a home library of hardcover volumes without exorbitant expense. "The Muses' Library" was clearly intended for purchasers who valued books primarily for their textual content. Since the *Poetical Works* edited by James Hannay in 1853, there had been few publications illustrated by serious artists, but in 1909 Sidgwick & Jackson published *Selected Tales of Mystery* as one of its first imprints, illustrated in color by Byam Shaw. The sixteen stories include nearly all of Poe's most popular pieces. Shaw, who spent his early years in India and later trained under the Pre-Raphaelites, demonstrates an almost orientalist approach to Poe. The cover shows a spiral with floating human and animal parts—skeletal hands, feet, a bat wing. In most cases, the dramatic turning point in each story is chosen. The illustration for "The Fall of the House of Usher" is captioned "Madman! I tell you that she now stands without the door!" A red-haired Usher, in a long dressing gown, sits with his back to the viewer, clutching his head. The narrator, rising, grabs with both hands a table holding an open book. Usher's hair color is repeated in the arabesque carpet pattern; the narrator's greenish skin tone matches the curtain behind him. Shaw has captured, not the climax of the story, but its moment of greatest suspense and dramatic intensity. The illustration exudes energy and movement. For "Ligeia," Shaw has chosen the text, "[t]he thing that was enshrouded advanced boldly and palpably into the middle of the apartment." Here, a tall enshrouded woman with dark hair to her knees walks across a fantastically figured carpet from an elaborately carved and canopied bed. The coloring is entirely red and orange apart from the white shroud. Again, Shaw has captured the tale's dramatic turning point, before the narrator, or reader, realizes that the figure is Ligeia. Shaw, in these and other theatrical illustrations, shows evidence of a careful reading of the tales, as well as respect for their detail. Although arguably garish by today's taste, these illustrations evocatively suggest the spirit of these works.

In 1912 Hodder & Stoughton produced a similarly lavishly illustrated edition of *The Bells and other Poems*, part of its series of gift books and, now, a collector's item. A publisher specializing in religious titles, Hodder & Stoughton censored fiction for its moral content. Nevertheless, the editors apparently deemed Poe's poems appropriately uplifting. This quarto volume of forty-six poems contains twenty-eight color plates by Edmund Dulac, as well as intricate ink drawings which serve as headpieces. The work of the French-born Dulac is often loosely described as "orientalist," a popular style for the fairy tales and children's books he mainly illustrated. The cover is a gold-embossed pattern of bells, and the color plates are of interest in their own right. In his illustration for "The Raven," Dulac shows the narrator (whose features are disconcertingly like Poe's) in a posture of despair opposite an oval portrait of Lenore. The bust of Pallas is in the upper right corner of the picture, and the raven is mostly out of the frame. Like several illustrators before him, Dulac concentrates on the despair of the narrator, rather than on the more obvious subject of the talking bird. In fact, the near invisibility of the raven could suggest that it exists only as a projection of the narrator's troubled mind. "The Conqueror Worm" is illustrated by a pile of half-clothed corpses on the left side of the picture, with a black curtain about to descend. Unlike some earlier illustrators, Dulac's images offer an original reading of Poe's works, never shrinking from the morbid implications of some of the poems.

The last Poe anthology in Britain before the First World War, *Essays and Stories,* was published in London by G. Bell & Sons, a publisher with an interest in the betterment of the public. The volume was edited by Hardress O'Grady, Fifth Viscount Guillamore in the County of Limerick. O'Grady had written extensively on English composition and phonetics, and the thirteen pieces include a high proportion of Poe's critical writings and the "Marginalia," but few of Poe's popular stories. In his introduction, O'Grady states that Poe's "finished pieces not less than his random musings show a mind under complete control of the will, a settled purpose, a definite progress towards a predetermined object." (viii). Although earlier editors, such as Ransome, had praised Poe's technical command, O'Grady's assessment marks another step away from the romantic mad genius myth toward an emerging view of Poe the professional writer, in confident control of his craft.

O'Grady's edition was sixty-sixth of ninety-six titles in Bohn's "Popular Library" series. Bohn's reprint business had reduced the average price of all books, causing *The Spectator* to note on April 4, 1914, that "Mssrs. Bell have now reduced the price to the nimble shilling" (575). Starting with Vizetelly's "Readable Books," Poe's writing often appeared as part of a publisher's series. Routledge followed with its "New Cheap Series." Ross's "Penny Library" was the extreme end of this marketing ploy. In 1886, Routledge continued its project of low-priced books, but with its "World Library Edition," suggested that cheapness was not incompatible with a cosmopolitan range of authors. Walter Scott's "Camelot" series suggested historical romanticism. Ward, Lock & Co.'s "Minerva Library of Famous Books" might have been designed to appeal to those who wished to round out their education, or at least hold their own in literary conversations, and Routledge's "New Universal Library" series and Grant Richards' "World's Classics" appealed to the same market. T. C. and E. C. Jack's "The World's Story Tellers" series implicitly places its authors in a narrative tradition as old as civilization. Routledge's "Muse's Library" series offered the aspirational edification at a reasonable price. For Routledge, Bell, and a few others, it was the publisher's stated aim to contribute to the general improvement of the public, although profit was always another consideration. That so many publishers included Poe anthologies in their series confirms the value of his work in business terms. The evolution of series' names from "Readable" or "Cheap" to "Famous," "Universal," "Classic," or "Library" suggests that from about the mid-1880s onward, publishers and editors had recognized Poe's place in a literary tradition of international importance.

Britain is a land of strong regional differences and diverse subcultures that are reflected in responses to Poe. Five of the six important editors of Poe in this period were "provincial." Two of the most sympathetic, James Hannay and Andrew Lang, were Scots, and many affinities can be found between Poe's forms and techniques and the Scottish literary tradition. Ernest Rhys, though London-born, was of Welsh parentage and spent much of his childhood in Carmarthen, giving him an outsider's perspective on English culture. Hardress O'Grady, an Irish aristocrat, again offered an approach to Poe that differed from conventional English responses, while Tighe Hopkins had Irish parents and spent his later years in Ireland. Arthur Ransome, although English, had his roots in Yorkshire, known for its independent spirit, and the Lake District, important in early Romanticism but far from the heart of Edwardian literary culture. The Northumbrian Skipsey was another outsider, regionally and socially. Only the Londoner John Ingram could challenge Hannay, Lang, Rhys, Ransome, and O'Grady in importance as an editor of an American writer who was himself an outsider by temperament and origin. It is also worth noting that a high proportion of Poe's British publishers and illustrators were either immigrants or children of immigrants. Thus "Poe in Britain" was a product of the blending of many national and international influences, the English being only one.

The volumes discussed here were chosen for their intrinsic importance or for their representative nature. Throughout the period, large numbers of anthologies aimed at the general public were published. These volumes, mainly of Poe's tales but many with a few poems, tended to concentrate on the more "popular" works, although this category is problematic, raising the question, "Popular with whom?" The repeated selection of particular stories and poems by publishers and editors did much to create the popularity of those pieces, since the public cannot show a preference for something they have not seen. At the same time, a smaller number of more comprehensive volumes were published, aimed at a more discriminating readership, usually with prefaces by other writers who argued for Poe's artistic importance. By the 1880s, editors began to promote a serious approach to the tales, regarding them as a form equal in importance to the poems, and by 1914 more of the critical writing was available in accessible form. In addition, toward the end of this period, Poe was presented in several sumptuous illustrated volumes with color plates. Notwithstanding the achievement of so many editors and publishers from 1852 to 1914, and a number of anthologies since then, in Britain today, Poe—although part of university American Studies courses—is little read by the general public. Regrettably, many have yet to find, through Poe, what Ransome called "the key to strange knowledge of ourselves" (xxi).

Notes

1. For about a hundred years, from 1814 to 1914, the average British income was £30 per annum. There were 20 shillings to a pound, making the average monthly income £2,6s. A book costing 1s would leave little change from an average day's wages. For further information on the engravings and illustrations in Poe publications in Britain, see Burton R. Pollin's *Images of Poe's Work: A Comprehensive Descriptive Catalogue of Illustrations* (111–25).

2. Later British anthologizers also tended to follow this practice of shifting "bug" to "beetle."

3. See Lois Davis Vines's "Paul Valéry and the Poe Legacy in France."

Works Cited

Bettany, G. T., editor. *Tales of Adventure, Mystery and Imagination*. By Edgar Allan Poe, Ward, Lock & Co., 1890.

Fisher, Benjamin F. "Poe in Great Britain." *Poe Abroad: Influence, Reputation, Affinities*, edited by Lois Davis Vines, U of Iowa P, 1999, pp. 52–61.

Hannay, James, editor. "Notice." *The Poetical Works of Edgar Allan Poe*, Addey, 1853.

Haweis, Hugh Reginald. *Tales of Mystery and Imagination*. By Edgar Allan Poe, Routledge, 1886.

Hopkins, Tighe, editor. Introduction. *Edgar Allan Poe's Tales: A Selection*, Cassell, 1907.

Hutton, Edward, editor. Introduction. *The Poems of Edgar Allan Poe*, Alexander Moreng Ltd. 1906.

Ingram, John H., editor. Preface. *The Works of Edgar Allan Poe*, Adam and Charles Black, 1874–1875. 4 vols.

Lang, Andrew, editor. *The Poems of Edgar Allan Poe, with an essay on his poetry*. Kegan Paul, Trench & Co., 1881.

O'Grady, Hardress, editor. *Essays and Stories*. By Edgar Allan Poe, G. Bell & Sons, 1914.

Poe, Edgar Allan. *The Bells and Other Poems*. Illustrated by Edmund Dulac, Hodder & Stoughton, 1912.

———. *Edgar Allan Poe's Poetical Works*. Alexander Hislop & Co., 1869.

———. *The Murders in the Rue Morgue and other Tales of Mystery*. Sampson Low, Marston & Co., 1893.

———. "The Philosophy of Composition." *The Fall of the House of Usher and Other Writings*, edited by David Galloway, Penguin, 1986, pp. 480–92.

———. *The Poems of Edgar Allan Poe*. Sketch by John H. Ingram, Routledge, 1909.

———. *Poe's Tales of Mystery and Imagination; and Poems*. Clarke, Beeton and Co., 1852.

———. *Selected Tales of Mystery*. Illustrated by Byam Shaw, Sidgwick and Jackson, 1909.

——. *Tales*. C. H. Ross's Penny Library. 1875.

——. *Tales of Mystery and Imagination*. Illustrated by A. D. McCormick, Arthur Pearson, 1905.

——. *Tales of Mystery and Imagination*. Grant Richards, 1902.

——. *Tales and Sketches to which is added The Raven, a Poem*, Routledge, 1852.

——. *The Works of Edgar Allan Poe, including the choicest of his Critical Essays, now first published in this country, with a study of his life and writings, from the French of C. Baudelaire*. John Camden Hotten, 1873.

Pollin, Burton. *Images of Poe's Works: A Comprehensive Descriptive Catalogue of Illustrations*. Greenwood Press, 1989.

Ransome, Arthur, editor. *Stories by Edgar Allan Poe*. T. C. and E. C. Jack, 1908.

Rhys, Ernest, editor. Introduction. *The Fall of the House of Usher and Other Tales and Prose Writings of Edgar Poe*, Walter Scott, 1889.

Shepherd, Richard Herne, editor. *Tamerlane and Other Poems*. By Edgar Allan Poe, George Redway, 1884.

Skipsey, Joseph, editor. Preface. *The Poetical Works of Edgar Allan Poe*, Walter Scott, 1886.

The Spectator, vol. 0, no. 4475, 4 April 1914, p. 575.

Swinburne, Algernon Charles. "Under the Microscope." *The Complete Works of Algernon Charles Swinburne, Prose Works, Vol. VI*, edited by Edmund Gosse and Thomas James Wise, William Heinemann Ltd., 1926.

Vines, Lois Davis. "Paul Valéry and the Poe Legacy in France." *Poe and Our Times: Influences and Affinities*, The Edgar Allan Poe Society, 1986, pp. 1–8.

Vizetelly, Henry, editor. Preface. *Tales of Mystery, Imagination and Humour, and Poems*. By Edgar Allan Poe, Vizetelly, 1852.

Williams, H. Noel. Introduction. *The Poems of Edgar Allan Poe*, illustrated by Heath Robinson, G. W. Bell & Sons, 1900.

~

CHAPTER SEVEN

Repatriating Poe

Revising the Penguin Portable

J. Gerald Kennedy

Anthologies represent many things, chief among them the publishing agenda of a press, the aim and expertise of an editor, and the durability of that cultural commodity Foucault called "the author"—at least for those particular anthologies built around a single author's works and often called editions or collections, rather than anthologies.[1] Such mass-market volumes bundle assorted texts for long-term profit, touting a writer (usually a dead one) as a reliable, recognizable brand. Marketing blurbs spotlight enticements, and cover art often conveys the new-and-improved aspect of the collection itself, its fresh packaging of a distinctive creativity. Every single-author anthology produces a certain version of the writer by selection and exclusion, based on available texts, calculations of essential material, and copyright constraints. Poe editions add an irony to any rethinking of the cultural work of single-author anthologies: the author who fought for literary property rights but never in his lifetime enjoyed national esteem or financial security has long after his death attained a profitable immortality.

These observations on single-author anthologies precede an account of my own involvement in this competitive and slightly ghoulish industry. In June 2003, the Americanist John Seelye, acting as a consultant to Penguin, contacted me about the possibility of editing a new version of the *Portable Edgar Allan Poe*. Seelye then recommended me to Penguin's executive editor, Michael Millman, who soon called to discuss an updated edition, noting the rare opportunity to introduce Poe to a vast global audience in an anthology likely to remain in print for a long time. Even though I was already

immersed in a demanding project—a broad-scale study of literary nationalism and cultural conflict in antebellum America—I could not resist the
invitation to renovate Penguin's Poe edition. The promise of modest, ongoing income offered another incentive. The Portable formula, introduced by
Viking but adopted by Penguin after their 1975 merger, was well established:
it implicitly promised to put the author (or the bulk of an author's literary
achievement) at the reader's disposal in a substantial but compact paperback
edition. The now-familiar format included not only representative primary
texts in several genres but also (as the Penguin author guidelines stipulated)
"letters, journals, and other minor works little known and not readily available to the general reader." The 1945 *Portable Poe*, then sitting on my book-
shelf, had appeared near the end of World War II.[2] Among the earliest titles
in the series, it had been prepared by Philip Van Doren Stern, a professional
editor and historical writer.

That edition still possesses merit as a volume of well-chosen texts. Stern
worked in the advertising world before moving into publishing with Pocket
Books, Alfred A. Knopf, and Simon & Schuster. During the war, he helped
to produce editions of selected books for U.S. troops overseas. Stern also
penned several well-regarded studies of U.S. Civil War history, beginning
with his 1940 book on John Wilkes Booth, *The Man Who Shot Lincoln*. He
followed that with a biography of Lincoln and then a study of Lincoln's
legacy in U.S. history. Stern later capitalized on the centennial of the Civil
War to publish a series of books highlighting the war's beginning, its ending,
everyday camp life, and extraordinary secret missions. He also wrote a biography of Robert E. Lee. A consummate wordsmith, Stern published two murder
mysteries and several collections of tales in the genres of science fiction and
fantasy, including *Travelers in Time* and *Strange Beasts & Unnatural Monsters*.
Stern's most enduring contribution to American popular culture, however,
was a wartime short story, "The Greatest Gift," transformed in 1946 into
the classic Frank Capra film, *It's a Wonderful Life*. Late in his career, Stern
penned youth biographies of Thoreau and Poe. He knew how to make a book
sound alluring and titled his surprisingly lifeless narrative of Poe's life *Edgar
Allan Poe, Visitor from the Night of Time*.

Stern's *Portable Poe* demonstrates both his knack for storytelling and fondness for occult material. His introduction begins: "There is a ghost haunting
America—a forlorn ghost who wanders at night through the older sections
of some of our Eastern seaboard cities" (xv). Stern actually locates separate
Poe ghosts in Boston, Providence, New York, Philadelphia, Baltimore,
Richmond, Charlottesville, and Sullivan's Island, South Carolina, conjuring a spectral horde. He presents Poe as "the great romantic," a writer who

converted his own nightmares into poems and tales entirely "divorced from reality" (xvii, xxxv). This claim begs the question of whether nightmares may be occasionally rooted in "reality," but no matter. Stern rightly notes Poe's attentiveness as a reviewer to "American books" and "current issues" but insists that his creative work had nothing to do with Jacksonian culture, arising instead from Poe's subconscious mind. Stern's account of Poe's career as a magazinist is accurate, but he returns to the romantic archetype of the tormented genius, insisting about Poe's last years that the "force that drove him to create also drove him mad" (xxxvii). The editor associates Poe with Hawthorne, Melville, Bierce, and Faulkner as writers who reveal that "the American mind is not all optimism and easy confidence" (xxxviii). Stern's vast understatement contains a point to which I shall return.

This first edition, however, ignores Poe's satirical tales as well as his penchant for hoaxing and parody. Stern's decision to begin the volume with a selection of twenty-five Poe letters underscores his argument that virtually all of the anthologized works are *about* Poe. He writes of the poems and tales that "In most of them, there are only two characters—Poe himself and the death-doomed or already dead mother-wife" (xxxvi). Such comments help to explain why so many naive readers still assume that *every* Poe protagonist is a stand-in for the author. The five categories into which Stern divides the tales reflect his view of Poe's chief preoccupations: "Fantasy," "Terror," "Death," "Revenge and Murder," and "Mystery and Ratiocination." These plausible distinctions nevertheless imply overlapping subjects and motifs. How, for example, could a tale of murder not end in death? Differentiating Poe's tales thematically, so that categories articulate sharp, meaningful distinctions, proves a daunting exercise—as I discovered many decades later.

For the *Portable Poe*, Stern chose twenty-three tales. Insofar as twenty-two of them also figure in my edition, his selections naturally strike me as sensible. His edition includes one tale, however, that I omitted, "The Mystery of Marie Rogêt." Stern thereby delivers the Dupin trilogy intact—but by reprinting the least effective of the detective tales, an inconclusive tale resulting from Poe's attempt to solve a real-life mystery (the New York death of Mary Rogers in 1841). Stern's most surprising omission—apart from his neglect of Poe's satires—is "The Imp of the Perverse," which (like "The Premature Burial") begins as an essay and evolves into a suspenseful narrative. "Imp" also elaborates a key idea in Poe, the central premise of "The Black Cat": that a spirit of perverseness lurks in every soul, pulling us toward self-ruin.

Between the tales and the poems, Stern inserted brief sections on "Articles" and "Criticism," representing Poe's journalism with "Maelzel's Chess-Player" and an excerpt from "A Few Words on Secret Writing." Stern suggestively introduces "Maelzel" as a precursor to the detective tale and ascribes Poe's interest in cryptography to his reverence for "reason and logic" (507). Though he concedes that the "Secret Writing" selection also illustrates Poe's need to flaunt his intellect, in neither case does Stern connect Poe's inclination to mystify the reading public with his hoaxes. (Not surprisingly, Stern's critical remarks on the tales of terror fail to identify "The Premature Burial" as a ruse.) His examples of Poe's criticism include "The Philosophy of Composition"; a portion of Poe's May 1842 Hawthorne review that advocates for a single, unifying effect in the prose tale; a part of "The Poetic Principle"; and the "Letter to B——," placed last by Stern although it represents Poe's early thinking about the Romantic poets and the demands of poetry.

Stern's examples of Poe's poetry include two prose-poems and twenty-four poems, among which one finds the standard favorites, such as "The Raven." A subsequent comparison of his selections with mine will clarify our differences. About the poems, Stern remarks that they were "few in number and extraordinarily limited in range," and in them Poe was "concerned almost exclusively with his inner self" (586), especially his preoccupations with love and death. Stern's recurrent suggestion of a purely autobiographical emphasis helps to explain why the New Critics warned students of the postwar years to avoid the "biographical fallacy."

The 1945 *Portable Poe* closes with a sampling of Poe's trenchant views on a variety of topics, taken from many unidentified sources, including several pieces later reprinted in Burton Pollin's edition of *The Brevities*. The "Opinions" revolve mostly around literary concerns—poetry, genius, imagination, logic, fancy, intuition, autobiography, plot, and the like. The last piece, an excerpt from *Eureka*, is the only selection identified with a specific source. His edition begins with a biographical chronology and ends with a brief bibliography, as do other Penguin Portable editions. For sixty years, this edition remained in print, offering students and general readers a broad sampling of Poe's writings, along with a melodramatic account of his life and Stern's insistence on an autobiographical basis for the poems and tales.

When I learned of the opportunity to prepare a revised edition of the *Portable Poe*, I had already been working in Poe studies for three decades, having joined the Poe Studies Association as a charter member at the MLA Convention in 1972. I therefore brought to the editorial work a grasp of major changes in Poe scholarship since 1945, which, when Stern published his anthology, consisted mainly of source studies, thematic readings, and Freudian interpretations. Subsequent waves of critical thinking had shaped my own work. The symbol and myth criticism of the mid-twentieth century formed part of my reading on Poe as a graduate student in the late 1960s and early 1970s. Two bold new books in 1973—G. R. Thompson's *Poe's Fiction: Romantic Irony in the Gothic Tales* and Daniel Hoffman's *Poe Poe Poe Poe Poe Poe Poe*—proved especially influential. But criticism also began to embrace structural and semiotic approaches arising from French theory, and in the mid-1970s nearly everyone was reading Jonathan Culler's *Structuralist Poetics*. During a Fulbright year in Paris in 1978–1979, I heard lectures by Jacques Derrida and Michel Foucault, and I attended a course at the Collège de France by Roland Barthes. That "seminar"—a meditation on death and the need to write—had a significant impact on my next book, *Poe, Death, and the Life of Writing* (1987). By the early 1990s, however, even deconstruction was passé, and criticism had been redefined by both New Historicism and cultural studies. Three important books of that decade, *The American Face of Edgar Allan Poe*, edited by Shawn Rosenheim and Stephen Rachman; Jonathan Elmer's *Reading at the Social Limit: Affect, Mass Culture, and Edgar Allan Poe*; and Terence Whalen's *Edgar Allan Poe and the Masses*, created a keen awareness of how Poe's work reflected the economic and sociopolitical conditions of antebellum America. My Baltimore memorial lecture of 1999, published as *The American Turn of Edgar Allan Poe* (2002), uncovered Poe's subversive response to the literary jingoism of the 1830s and 1840s. A similar interest in Poe's cultural and historical context motivated me to edit Oxford's *A Historical Guide to Edgar Allan Poe* and *Romancing the Shadow: Poe and Race*, the latter co-edited with Liliane Weissberg. It also inspired a broad, interdisciplinary project that culminated, many years later, in *Strange Nation: Literary Nationalism and Cultural Conflict in the Age of Poe*.

In fact, I had been working on the nationalism book for about three years when Penguin approached me about a new *Portable Poe*. I agreed to prepare the anthology because I wanted to counter the myths and misperceptions promulgated by Stern and others, especially the idea that Poe was oblivious to the American controversies of his day. I also wanted to challenge the view that his nervous fictional characters represented the author himself. Some of the best critical readings from the 1960s and 1970s, especially those by James Gargano, showed how Poe the sure-handed author created narrators who betrayed their own unreliability and instability. I wanted to dismantle persisting illusions and produce an edition better reflecting Poe's interests.

The guidelines for a Portable edition called for an introduction of five to ten thousand words, a chronology, texts and headnotes for each section, explanatory notes, and a bibliography. The projected volume length of 640 pages seemed vast, and initially I wanted to include *The Narrative of Arthur Gordon Pym* because the "Guidelines for Editors" stipulated that "one long and popularly recognized work should be included in its entirety." But in the end, I realized that too many indispensable shorter works had to be excluded to make room for *Pym*, and Penguin discouraged "fragments of longer works." I also recognized that the incongruities, excesses, improbabilities, stylistic shifts, and plagiarized passages that made *Pym* an interpretive funhouse for some critics might not enthrall general readers. In any event, I wished to showcase the short prose tales and illustrate their variety.

My book proposal explained changes in structure and content that I planned to incorporate. Rather than beginning with letters (as Stern did), I wanted to feature the prose tales first, in an expanded offering that would include several satirical tales showing Poe's response to American culture. Perhaps in a nod to theory and narrative deep structure, I divided the twenty-nine tales into five categories that, in my view, illustrated Poe's paradigmatic plots: "Predicaments," "Bereavements," "Antagonisms," "Mysteries," and "Grotesqueries." The inspiration for the first set came of course from Poe's own "How to Write a Blackwood Article," in which Mr. Blackwood advises an aspiring writer to get herself into a terrible predicament and then pay careful attention to her sensations. It was a formula Poe used for many riveting tales, whether his narrator was facing deadly pestilence, a vortex, premature burial, or a razor-sharp pendulum. The second section includes seven tales in which a narrator experiences the loss of a beloved woman, a sequence stretching from "The Assignation" to "The Oval Portrait" and including "Ligeia" and "The Fall of the House of Usher." The third group focuses on narratives that convert deadly hatreds into shocking acts of vengeance or cruelty, of which "William Wilson," "The Tell-Tale Heart," "The Black Cat," and "The Cask of Amontillado" provide the most brilliant examples. The fourth type, identified as "Mysteries," alternatively presents enigmas—unsolved crimes, undiscovered treasures, incomprehensible events, or inexplicable figures. The "ratiocinative" tales featuring C. Auguste Dupin clearly fall into this category. I also decided to leave a related tale, a quasi-parody of the detective story called "The Oblong Box," in the "Mysteries" section. To exemplify Poe's fondness for comic or ironic narratives—which Thompson estimated to comprise half of Poe's fictional output and which, as I mentioned above, Stern virtually ignored—I finally include a trio of "Grotesqueries": "The Man That Was Used Up," "The System of Doctor Tarr and Professor Fether," and "Some Words with a Mummy." With this category, I meant to signify satires hinging on monstrous revelations. In his satirical tales, Poe sometimes alludes mockingly to national attitudes and problems. If "The Man That Was Used Up" marks his most blatant American satire—lampooning Indian killers as bogus heroes—"Some Words with a Mummy" offers his most outrageous (and unexpected) assault on such American delusions as Anglo-Saxon "progress" and racial superiority.

Because my selection of twenty-nine tales exceeded by five those arrayed in Stern's edition, I reduced my selection of "Poems" to twenty-one. Stern's twenty-six had included two prose poems, "Silence—a Fable" and "Shadow—a Parable," which I judged obscure and expendable. He also chose four slim poems that I saw no need to reprint: "Stanzas," "The Happiest Day, The Happiest Hour," "The Coliseum," and "To ___," Poe's tribute to Marie Louise Shew. Rather surprisingly, Stern's selection of "Poems" excluded two important early poems, "Sonnet—To Science" and "Alone," and it omitted one of Poe's finest late poems, "Eldorado." If Poe's poems of youth sometimes reveal a derivative romantic self-consciousness, they also permit us to appreciate the great lyrics and haunting narrative verses for which Poe is most often remembered—"To Helen," "The City in the Sea," "Lenore," "Dream-Land," "The Raven," "Ulalume," "A Dream within a Dream," "The Bells," "For Annie," and "Annabel Lee." These works form the core of my poetic selections. Several other poems also figure in the anthology, including "Israfel" and the narrative poem "The Sleeper," which portrays a dead woman's slumber and, rather disconcertingly, entreats God or nature: "Soft may the worms about her creep!" (411). Poe had not yet imagined the gory "Conqueror Worm," the poem he later ascribed to Ligeia in that eponymous tale.

After the poetry, I arranged an assortment of Poe's letters, twenty-eight in all, stretching from 1827—when he was cutting ties with John Allan—to the tender note he sent to Mrs. Clemm less than three weeks before his death in 1849. Stern's selected correspondence, by comparison, reprints twenty-five letters, of which five are to Mrs. Clemm, all from Poe's last summer. The letters I collect offer a broader view of Poe's literary relations, and several reveal him in great difficulty, including his none-too-veiled suicide threat in the August 29, 1835, appeal to his aunt and Virginia; the angry letter severing his ties with William Burton on June 1, 1840; and his pathetic apology to Frederick W. Thomas and Jesse Dow from March 16, 1843, for his late drinking binge in Washington. Other letters to Thomas, Philip Pendleton Cooke, Thomas Holley Chivers, and George Eveleth provide valuable insights into Poe's literary values and judgments.

While Stern had interposed a short section on "Criticism" between the nonfictional "Articles" and his selection of "Poems," I follow the letters with a broader array of pieces illustrating Poe's "Critical Principles." This includes the four texts reprinted by Stern plus five other selections on "Unity of Effect," "Plot in Narrative," "The Design of Fiction," "The Effect of Rhyme," and "American Criticism," all excerpted from Poe's reviews or marginal commentaries. The "Unity of Effect" piece, drawn from an 1836 review of Dickens, suggests that Poe was honing in on the principle of "single effect" much earlier than his May 1842 review of Hawthorne's *Twice-Told Tales*. His 1841 review of Lambert Wilmer occasioned a diatribe on American cliques, coteries, and critical shams (like "puffing"). Here we find Poe lashing out at national self-congratulation, remarking sarcastically: "Our fine writers are legion. Our very atmosphere is redolent of genius; and we, the nation, are a huge, well-contented chameleon, grown pursy by inhaling it. We are *teretes et rotundi*—enwrapped in excellence" (567).

Stern's anthology omits Poe's cultural criticism, and his section on "Opinions," a series of sixteen short squibs, adheres to conventional literary questions and philosophical themes. My selection of nineteen "Observations" captures many of these same concerns but also represents Poe's trenchant remarks about "Literary Nationalism," "American Literary Independence," "National Literature and Imitation," "Magazine Literature in America," and "The Name of the Nation." These commentaries show Poe's engagement with the politics of nation-building and his insistence that literature should have a global appeal. Poe envisioned emerging American nationality as an independent cosmopolitanism—neither imitatively British nor crudely provincial. This is the Poe I wished to bring back into view: an oppositional figure, questioning the parochialism of native themes and even the "stupidity" (578) of certain American books. My inclusion of "Some Secrets of the Magazine Prison-House" makes accessible Poe's savage indictment of an American publishing system that exploited "poor-devil authors" (579). International copyright did not yet exist, and literary property rights signified little in a system of piracy and reprinting where, belatedly, publishers paid authors scanty sums—or nothing at all.

While including fictional satires of American culture and a handful of "Observations" showing his stubborn resistance to literary nationalism— even asserting that the name "America" properly belonged to the entire Western hemisphere—my effort to repatriate Poe, bringing him back into conversation with Jacksonian America, required editorial persistence. My introductory essay as well as section headnotes throughout the edition sporadically sound the long-missing note. The "Introduction," which underscores the paradoxes and contradictions of Poe's career, observes of his contrariety: "In an era of rampant optimism about his country's future, Poe lampooned democracy as mob rule and refuted 'human perfectibility' as well as the allied belief that civilization and progress culminated in the United States" (x). A later remark notes that he "attacked the 'misapplied patriotism' of nationalistic critics 'puffing' inferior books by American authors" (xvii). A mention of his collaboration with the Young America group calls attention to a burst of stories he penned in 1844: "Like 'The Gold-Bug,' most of the new tales portrayed American scenes. . . . Once indifferent to American subjects, he manifested a pragmatic shift in focus" (xxiii). A subsequent paragraph adds that Poe "privately mistrusted the expansionist agenda of Polk, and in a tale partly inspired by the election of 1844, he satirized the chief rationale for U.S. imperialism—belief in Anglo-Saxon cultural superiority—in 'Some Words with a Mummy'" (xxiii).

In the headnote preceding the "Tales," I supplement these comments by underscoring Poe's shift from predominantly European subjects in the early tales to what I called (in the Baltimore monograph) an "American turn": "By the early 1840s, literary nationalism had made American subjects and materials nearly obligatory, and beginning with 'The Gold-Bug,' set in South Carolina, Poe pragmatically shifted his fiction toward domestic scenes and situations. Yet he refused to rewrite history for the sake of American myth-making and argued defiantly that national literature was a contradiction in terms" (5). My editorial comments preceding the trio of "Grotesqueries" likewise highlight the specific national objects of Poe's derision—systematic extermination of Native tribes (in "The Man That Was Used Up"); slavery and its monstrosity (in "The System of Doctor Tarr and Professor Fether"); and vacuous claims of Anglo-Saxon superiority (in "Some Words with a Mummy"). The last paragraph of my headnote to "Observations" returns to the topic of Poe's concern for "the future of the nation" and "the fate of democracy itself" (575). The final sentence captures an overarching idea in the anthology: "If Poe sometimes conjured in fiction and poetry a fantastic place 'out of space—out of time,' he was nevertheless attuned to cultural politics and concerned that rabid nationalism was distorting American literature and criticism" (576).

But these scattered remarks, collected here to reveal a tacit editorial strategy, do not by any means reduce the author to a polemicist or portray his patriotic anti-nationalism as the dominant theme of his poetry and fiction. In its range of representation, my 2006 edition simply acknowledges the author's satirical side as well as his disdain for cultural backwardness. It permits readers to appreciate the fact that many subjects caught Poe's attention, including the public debates of Jacksonian America, as he devised works that typically transported readers to Old World scenes. If there is a predominant emphasis in my *Portable Poe* edition (and across the spectrum of Poe's works), it emerges near the end of the "Introduction," where I cite Sarah Helen Whitman's trenchant insight that Poe endeavored to "sound the very depths of the abyss" in works that captured "the unrest and faithlessness of the age" (xxix). Echoing my first book on Poe, I added that "as compellingly as any writer of his time, Poe intuited the spiritual void opening in an era dominated by a secular, scientific understanding of life and death" (xxix). In Poe's greatest poems and tales, his nervous or distracted narrators struggle to understand traumatic experiences. For instance, this anxiety drives the speaker's urgent interrogation of his visitor in "The Raven": "Is there—*is* there balm in Gilead?" he asks, and more desperately, "Tell this soul with sorrow laden if, within the distant Aidenn, / It shall clasp a sainted maiden whom the angels name Lenore" (425). Is there a heaven and an afterlife of the soul, he wants to know, as do many readers inhabiting a secular, skeptical postmodern world. Poe confronts the problem of unbelief in the face of death and loss, and there we discern the vast understatement of Stern's suggestion that "the American mind is not all confidence and easy optimism" (xxxviii).

By identifying this core of existential doubt, I meant to situate Poe in the vanguard of those writers and skeptics in Western culture who gave expression to what Mrs. Whitman called "unrest and faithlessness" (65). That is the idea that I hoped the cover art would suggest: a stunning image of Poe's head surrounded not by holy light but by a swirl of black thoughts. To this image I will return, but (as I argued in my Penguin book proposal), Poe's "strange fables of loss, revenge, cruelty, and madness" resonate with readers in the new millennium because they "brilliantly anticipate the radical uncertainty and deadly violence of our own time." And, in the aftermath of 9/11, I made a more immediate connection in the 2006 edition: "Caught up in a global war on terror, we . . . [recognize] more clearly than ever the author's uncanny insight into the long age of anxiety that began almost a century ago." I was thinking, I suppose, of the Great War as heralding an epoch of relentless slaughter, of weapons inflicting cataclysmic destruction, and of Poe's anticipation of a dark landscape where "Death looks gigantically down" (416).

However, this modern (or modernist) prescience in Poe also forms, it seems to me, an integral aspect of his American identity. For Poe had indeed resisted the national optimism of his age, even (or especially) when it was propounded by a philosopher like Emerson. He rejected the notion that his native land had been exempted from the tragedy of history or granted a perpetual innocence. But where, one must ask, does Poe actually say this? I would answer that his tragic vision informs most of his work, wherever love, disease, hatred, or perverseness lead to death.

Tragedy strikingly informs "The Haunted Palace," a poem Poe composed in Philadelphia in the early spring of 1839. Initially published in the April issue of the Baltimore *American Museum*, the six stanzas reappeared in September in "The Fall of the House of Usher" as the rhapsody of Roderick Usher. There, it resonates hauntingly (pun intended) with the downfall of a family and a house, evoking an ominous modulation from the music of "a lute's well-tunèd law" to a "discordant melody" (135). When Poe first conjured a dominion of happiness soon to be assailed by "evil things, in robes of sorrow" (135), he may already have had "Usher" in mind. But perhaps not. He may have been reflecting, just then, on another domain, perhaps a shining land once ruled by a heroic generation of enlightened gentlemen but now a veritable madhouse run by King Andrew Jackson, his surrogate Martin Van Buren, and the rioting masses who enforced mob rule. An economic depression, triggered by Jackson's bank policies, still gripped the land. The army was locked in a deadly, expensive war with the Seminoles—inspiring Poe's August 1839 satire, "The Man That Was Used Up."[3] Once the City of Brotherly Love, Philadelphia had lately been rocked by riots, outbursts of mob hatred for abolitionists and Irish Catholic immigrants. Sectional mistrust was deepening, and Theodore Weld's *American Slavery as It Is* inflamed both North and South in 1839 as no other book before *Uncle Tom's Cabin*. Of course we don't know that *any* of these issues specifically agitated Poe as he composed "The Haunted Palace." Perhaps the author was (as Stern would argue) merely giving form to his own nightmares. But awareness of Poe's cultural situation as an anti-Jacksonian in 1839 makes the transformation of Thought's palace into a madhouse populated by a "hideous throng" seem an apt Whig version of the national nightmare (135). Poe would insert a more explicit vision of American ruin in his futuristic "Mellonta Tauta" ten years later. But in 1839, on the cusp of writing "Usher" for *Burton's Gentleman's Magazine*, Poe may have endowed "The Haunted Palace" with veiled American significance.[4]

Elsewhere, in a very brief essay, I sketched some potential national implications of "Usher"—but without taking account of "The Haunted Palace."[5] The likely sequence of composition—the poem first, then the tale—makes the portentous allegory as likely to depict a decline from America's enlightenment origins, however, as to mirror the doom of Usher's mansion and family line. What I wish to underscore is not the *necessity* of reading national critique in Poe's stylized fantasies, but rather the *possibility* of discerning American undercurrents where they seem at first imperceptible. This is a guiding principle of the revised *Portable Poe*. The turn to cultural readings of Poe, which began around 1990, has already illuminated the American implications of such "European" works as "The Murders in the Rue Morgue" and "Hop-Frog." We now discern more clearly the anti-nationalist innuendo of "The Oblong Box" (where the *Independence* sinks) or "A Tale of the Ragged

Mountains" (as a fable of Native retaliation for U.S. incursions). In *Strange Nation*, I underscore a passing reference to John Randolph in "The Facts in the Case of M. Valdemar" to show Randolph's importance for Poe's opposition to jingoism and territorial expansion (388–91).

But, I would hasten to add that the power of "Valdemar" cannot be explained by the author's uneasiness with Manifest Destiny. Barthes was right; what Valdemar speaks is unspeakable: "Now—now—*I am dead.*" (77). His hideous transformation captures all the horror of a purely naturalistic death. Furthermore, we cannot fully appreciate Poe's crisis of unbelief without reading "Valdemar" against "Mesmeric Revelation," a visionary tale of the soul's survival and ultimate illumination (which, alas, I did not anthologize). Still, uncovering the trace of Poe's attention to antebellum controversies in the *Portable Poe* helps to situate his works in a thicker context and to complicate our understanding of the relationship between the author and his texts. For too long, before and after Stern's edition, Poe's life supplied a weak interpretive lens; now we have a plethora of suggestive critical approaches, including cultural historicism, to illuminate the subtleties of the poetry and fiction.

Poe's life retains, of course, an irresistible interest, and his visage has become the most recognizable among all American authors of the early nineteenth century, which leads me back to the cover art. When I was preparing to publish *Poe, Death, and the Life of Writing* in the mid-1980s, I discovered a surreal, black-and-white image with a nineteenth-century look—a man hovering over a tempestuous sea, asleep (or dead) in an easy chair, with a lighthouse in the background. The collage figured in a splendid volume by Max Ernst called *La Femme cent têtes*.[6] Seeking permission to use this image, I contacted Ernst's widow, painter Dorothea Tanning, who was still alive and well and painting in New York. Ms. Tanning, herself a onetime surrealist of prodigious talent, very generously granted permission to use the Ernst image without charge, but she also sent me a spectacular print of her own work, the aforementioned head of Poe titled "Poem." I told her how much I treasured that image and broached the possibility of using it for a book cover at some later date. She kindly agreed, and we kept in touch, intermittently, over the years. Sometime in the early 2000s, during a trip to Manhattan, I communicated with Ms. Tanning (then in her nineties), who invited me to her Greenwich Village apartment to see her extraordinary art collection, including many of her most famous paintings. A year or so later, when the opportunity to edit the edition for Penguin emerged, I proposed using Ms. Tanning's Poe print as the cover art, and there was an immediate agreement. Now her haunting image of the author glowers in perpetuity on the cover of my *Portable Poe*.

The editing of any anthology creates pedagogical opportunities but also requires intellectual labor, from selecting the right texts to editing, annotating, and introducing them. Then, there is the physical work of arranging texts in the correct order and proper format, with proofreading at every stage.[7] In the definitive Harvard edition of 1969 and 1978, Thomas Ollive Mabbott had established the proper copy texts for Poe's poems and tales (usually the latest version that reflected significant authorial revision). The Library of America edition by Patrick F. Quinn had followed and ratified Mabbott's selections. The texts themselves were naturally in the public domain; only the editorial notes, introductions, and other scholarly features remained proprietary. My preparation of the *Portable Poe* benefitted greatly from an agreement with Jeffrey Savoye, creator and curator of the eapoe.org website sponsored by the Edgar Allan Poe Society of Baltimore. For several years Savoye had been posting digital versions of every text Poe himself had composed. In return for use of his electronic versions of the standard copy texts of tales and poems, as well as for Poe's essays, reviews, and marginal comments, I proofread Savoye's texts and corrected some incidental errors remaining in his online electronic files. For the letters, I did the same thing, using Savoye's texts from the Ostrom edition (then being updated by Pollin and Savoye himself), but also securing permission from Gordian Press, which had bought rights to the letters from Harvard.

My headnotes for the various sections of the *Portable Poe*—as well as sub-sections of the tales—offer brief points of interest for curious readers. The textual notes are far less numerous and scholarly than those in the Mabbott edition; my aim was not to elucidate every possible influence, allusion, or obscurity, but to explain concisely any important reference that might well perplex a general reader. Rarely in the anthology do I provide more than a handful of notes for any text; among the tales, the most heavily annotated is "Some Words with a Mummy," which includes many antebellum topical references unfamiliar to readers in the twenty-first century. The bibliography identifies "First Editions of Poe's Works," then subsequent collected works and scholarly editions, then the standard edition of the letters, and, finally, two outdated bibliographic resources. Had I produced this edition a few years later, when I had a better understanding of digital scholarship, I would have identified reliable online resources as well. My bibliography continues with the principal biographies to date, with book-length critical studies, and then with a selection of critical essays. I now see many important books and articles that I omitted, such as Jonathan Elmer's *Reading at the Social Limit*. To be sure, every printed bibliography becomes outdated from the moment of its publication.

Many new scholarly resources, such as the *Oxford Handbook of Edgar Allan Poe*, which I co-edited with Scott Peeples, appear routinely in simultaneous print and electronic formats, the latter allowing ongoing revision and updating. Digital editions may indeed represent the future, or a part of it, for those who compile anthologies and single-author editions; such volumes (especially the heavy textbooks) will be read increasingly on lighter laptops, tablets, e-readers, or smartphones, with images, hyperlinks, and search capabilities built into the texts. Penguin seems unlikely to digitize the *Portable Poe* beyond e-book page images. The print edition has done well. Having brought Poe home, as it were, to the antebellum American culture in which he lived, worked, and wrote, I will content myself with knowing that the anthology continues to be read by new admirers of Poe around the world. Young people downloading the edition as an e-book are reading the most portable *Portable* yet available, and years from now, perhaps one of them will combine deep knowledge of Poe with editorial expertise and digital savvy to produce a fully functional, interactive *Portable* linked to a plethora of brilliant online resources.

Notes

1. I refer of course to Michel Foucault's famous 1969 essay, "What Is an Author?"

2. The cover of the 1945 edition reads *The Portable Poe*, the spine says *Poe: Tales and Poems*, and the title page says The Viking Portable Library *Edgar Allan Poe*.

3. I make the case for this connection in "Unwinnable Wars, Unspeakable Wounds: Locating 'The Man That Was Used Up.'"

4. Readers wishing for a more comprehensive treatment of Poe's resistance to literary nationalism might look at my 2016 study *Strange Nation*, which focuses on Poe extensively in the first and last chapters and briefly treats other Poe texts elsewhere.

5. That essay, "Terror: 'The Fall of the House of Usher' in *Burton's Gentleman's Magazine*," figured in an exhibition catalog and was compressed to fit a 2000-word limit.

6. The title incorporates a pun: *La Femme cent têtes* (the hundred-headed woman) likewise orally signifies a headless woman (*sans tête*).

7. With more than my usual compulsiveness, I tried to eliminate *all* typographical errors from the 2006 edition. But I did not succeed. In 2015, a professor using the anthology for a class at the University of Basel emailed me to ask whether the misspelling of Montresor on p. 214 (as "Montressor") had been deliberate on Poe's part and a hint of some hidden meaning. He nevertheless thanked me for the edition and reported that students were enjoying it.

Works Cited

Barthes, Roland. "Textual Analysis of a Tale by Edgar Poe." Translated by Donald G. Marshall, *Poe Studies*, vol. 10, 1977, pp. 1–12.

Elmer, Jonathan. *Reading at the Social Limit: Affect, Mass Culture, and Edgar Allan Poe*. Stanford UP, 1995.

Foucault, Michel. "What Is an Author?" 1969. *Textual Strategies: Perspectives in Post-Structuralist Criticism*, edited by Josué V. Harari, Cornell UP, 1979, pp. 141–60.

Gargano, James W. "The Distorted Perception of Poe's Comic Narrators." *Topic: A Journal of the Liberal Arts*, vol. 16, no. 30, 1976, pp. 23–34.

———. "Poe's 'Ligeia': Dream and Destruction." *College English*, vol. 23, no. 5, pp. 337–42.

———. "The Question of Poe's Narrators." *College English*, vol. 25, no. 3, 1963, pp. 177–81.

Hoffman, Daniel. *Poe, Poe, Poe, Poe, Poe, Poe, Poe*. Doubleday, 1972.

Kennedy, J. Gerald. "Introduction" and headnotes. *The Portable Edgar Allan Poe*, edited by Kennedy, Penguin, 2006, pp. ix–xx, 3–5, 573–76.

———. *Strange Nation: Literary Nationalism and Cultural Conflict in the Age of Poe*. Oxford UP, 2016.

———. "Terror: 'The Fall of the House of Usher' in *Burton's Gentleman's Magazine*." *Edgar Allan Poe in 20 Objects from the Susan Jaffe Tane Collection*, edited by Gabrielle Dean and Richard Kopley, Johns Hopkins Sheridan Libraries, 2016, pp. 58–63.

———. "Unwinnable Wars, Unspeakable Wounds: Locating 'The Man That Was Used Up.'" *Poe Studies*, vols. 39–40, 2008, pp. 77–89.

Kennedy, J. Gerald, and Scott Peeples, editors. *The Oxford Handbook of Edgar Allan Poe*. Oxford UP, 2019.

Poe, Edgar Allan. *The Collected Works of Edgar Allan Poe*. Edited by Thomas Ollive Mabbott, Belknap Press of Harvard UP, 1969 and 1978. 3 vols.

———. *Edgar Allan Poe*. Edited by Philip Van Doren Stern, Viking, 1945.

———. *The Portable Edgar Allan Poe*. Edited by J. Gerald Kennedy, Penguin, 2006.

Rosenheim, Shawn, and Stephen Rachman, editors. *The American Face of Edgar Allan Poe*. Johns Hopkins UP, 1995.

Thompson, G. R. *Poe's Fiction: Romantic Irony in the Gothic Tales*. U of Wisconsin P, 1973.

Whalen, Terence. *Edgar Allan Poe and the Masses: The Political Economy of Literature in Antebellum America*. Princeton UP, 1999.

Whitman, Sarah Helen. *Edgar Poe and His Critics*. Rudd & Carleton, 1860.

CHAPTER EIGHT

~

Textbook Poe

College American Literature Anthologies

Scott Peeples

A college student of the late 1950s, assigned James D. Hart and Clarence Gohdes's anthology, *America's Literature*, would have encountered a headnote beginning, "No other writer of American literature has been subjected to so many conflicting judgments as Edgar Allan Poe" (413). Or, had the professor chosen Scully Bradley's *The American Tradition in Literature*, that student would have been introduced to Poe with this opening sentence: "A century and more after his death, Poe is still among the most popular of American authors" (322). Both simple statements remain as true as they were in the 1950s and had been in the 1920s, when classroom anthologies of American literature became common: Poe has always elicited conflicting judgments, and he has always been popular. For about a century, American literature anthologies have repeated the first claim with some regularity while testifying to the second by consistently devoting ample space to his writing. His status among American authors might have been subject to debate in the late nineteenth century, but if we date the modern study of American literature from the advent of classroom American literature anthologies, Poe's place in the canon has always been secure. In this chapter, I discuss the historical shifts as well as the historical constants in the way Poe has been represented in college textbooks, drawing on a survey of forty representative anthologies from 1925 to 2017.

In his 2004 book, *Canons by Consensus*, Joseph Csicsila groups American literature anthologies into three periods: the historiographical (1917–1945), during which anthologists sought to reflect U.S. history, regional identity, and national character through literature; the New Critical (1946–1967), which privileged a cluster of literary values such as irony, ambiguity, and characters' inner conflict, while limiting attention to a small number of "major" authors; and the multicultural (post-1967), which emphasizes texts with social and political resonance and promotes a range of writers reflective of American ethnic and gender diversity. As Csicsila demonstrates, Poe thrived throughout all three generations of textbooks; he is "among not only the two dozen writers who have enjoyed relatively secure status among literary textbook editors but also a much more exclusive circle of pre-twentieth-century writers whose space apportionment in American literature anthologies has actually increased over the last eighty years" (36).

Csicsila's research indicates that while Poe's page count held steady or even increased, the balance between his poetry and fiction shifted—less poetry, more fiction—with the New Critical focus that predominated in the 1950s and 1960s. The logic underlying such a shift seems clear: while acknowledging Poe's conceptual influence on modern poetry via the symbolists, mid-century critics tended to regard the poems themselves as mechanical and limited in thematic range. On the other hand, close reading practices and Freudian vocabulary were helping to describe layers of textual ambiguity, psychic conflict, and paradox in the tales. My own survey of anthologies from 1925 to 2017—which overlaps with but does not duplicate Csicsila's—suggests that the shift toward fiction might not have been in full swing until the 1970s, though by the late 1940s some anthologists had indeed cut the number of poems and increased the number of stories. I examined eleven anthologies published between 1925 and 1945, and I found that they included an average of 17.2 poems and 5 stories, a median of 16 poems and 5 stories. I saw only a slight shift in the 1946–1966 period, where averages for the fourteen anthologies I included were 15.2 poems and 5.9 stories, a median of 14 poems and 5 stories. A more significant shift to a smaller selection of poems occurs after 1967, the third generation identified by Csicsila: an average of 9.93 poems with a median of 9, and an average of 5.7 stories with a median of 5. Somewhat surprisingly, then, among the books in my survey, the "typical" number of stories (5) remains constant over time, though the actual number ranges from three to thirteen (and the only anthologies with ten or more stories are published after 1960). Meanwhile, the number of poems certainly declines, and fairly sharply from the 1960s on. As for Poe's theoretical and critical essays, those numbers—both medians and means—hover between two and three across all periods, with a range of zero to six selections. The differences between my findings and Csicsila's are less significant than the big picture both surveys reveal: Poe has occupied roughly the same acreage throughout a century of anthologies, though his poems take up less of that ground over time.[1]

Regarding Poe texts that have tended to appear in college anthologies, the perennial favorites come as no surprise. "The Raven" and "To Helen" appeared in all forty of the anthologies that I charted for statistical purposes. "Sonnet—To Science," "Israfel," "The City in the Sea," "Ulalume," and "Annabel Lee" all appeared in thirty-five out of forty. "The Fall of the House of Usher" has the same status as "The Raven" and "To Helen" among Poe's stories, appearing in every anthology in my survey. "Ligeia" and "The Purloined Letter" are included in thirty-two out of forty; the only other tales that appear in at least half of the anthologies I examined are "The Cask of Amontillado" (22/40) and "The Masque of the Red Death" (20/40). The three critical/theoretical works that appear most frequently, by far, are the second review of Hawthorne's *Twice-Told Tales* (33), "The Philosophy of Composition" (29), and "The Poetic Principle" (19, frequently excerpted). These selections all tend to be dropped from the recent "concise" editions of the standard classroom anthologies. (And although "The Poetic Principle" became a less standard inclusion in the late twentieth century, it does appear, excerpted, in the current multivolume *Norton Anthology*.)

The "perennials" listed above exemplify the characteristics of Poe's writing that have attracted scholars and millions of fans: themes of obsession, mourning, self-torture, and the transcendent power of art; seemingly uncanny verbal sound effects; overt symbolism; and pervasive, multilayered irony. But as with any writer's oeuvre, over time some texts become more visible in academic study while others fade, and these trends are eventually reflected in college textbooks. In the case of Poe's poems, only nine or so would endure the slow winnowing process that began in the late 1940s. Because it has been synonymous with Poe since its first publication and is possibly the best-known American poem of all time, "The Raven" seems to be untouchable. "To Helen" not only features the famous couplet "To the glory that was Greece / And the grandeur that was Rome," but it also exemplifies Poe's romantic conception of idealized beauty while playing into discussions of his biography (since Poe identified a specific woman, Jane Stanard, as the poem's inspiration). "Sonnet—To Science" neatly opposes the world of art and imagination to the mundane world governed by time, providing a key to much of Poe's work. "Ulalume" foregrounds sonic atmosphere more effectively than any other of Poe's poems, pointing toward a discussion of Poe's influence on aestheticism.

On the other hand, "The Bells," which similarly tests the limits of sound as the poem's raison d'etre, rarely appears in American literature anthologies after about 1960, having been a standard inclusion through the mid-1950s. (Specifically, it appears in sixteen out of twenty of the anthologies surveyed through 1961 and only two of twenty after that date.) "The Bells" was particularly popular in the late nineteenth and early twentieth centuries—for instance, it was the title poem of a 1912 edition of Poe's poetry lavishly illustrated by Edmund Dulac—and would have seemed an odd omission from those early anthologies containing fifteen or twenty of Poe's poems. I suspect that by mid-century, though, anthologists following New Critical standards would have found "The Bells" simplistic in content and form, too painfully illustrative of the tendencies that led Emerson to dismiss Poe as "the jingle man," and it began to disappear from college syllabi despite its wide popularity, along with Whitman's "O Captain, My Captain!"[2] At least nine different pre-World War II anthologies included an excerpt from "Al Aaraaf," the song invoking Ligeia, beginning "'Neath blue-bell or streamer—", but, perhaps because editors became less comfortable with excerpts generally, that selection all but disappeared after the 1940s. "To One in Paradise" survived longer but became a rarity sometime after 1970, while "Annabel Lee" never fell out of favor. The one poem whose reputation, or classroom-readiness, seems to have strengthened after mid-century is "Sonnet—Silence," perhaps because it seems to require more explication than many of Poe's poems and potentially elicits discussion of the nature of the "two-fold *Silence*—sea and shore— / Body and Soul."

Turning to fiction, few Poe scholars would argue against "The Fall of the House of Usher" and "Ligeia" as stories that exemplify his theory of the subtle but unified, visceral effect; moreover, these stories are carefully crafted to evoke ambiguity regarding motivation, narrative reliability, and symbolic meaning. Which is to say, they teach well. The third standard selection among Poe's tales, "The Purloined Letter," is another model of craft, the cleverest of the three Dupin tales that provided the blueprint for the modern detective story. The more sensational "Murders in the Rue Morgue" has probably been more popular outside the classroom (having lent its title to at least three films and one Iron Maiden song), but the paradox of hiding an object in plain sight and the trope of the detective identifying closely with his criminal adversary make "The Purloined Letter" a more effective testament to Poe's originality and influence. Among scholars, its significance was heightened by the series of deconstructive essays originating with Jacques Lacan's 1956 psychoanalytic "Seminar on 'The Purloined Letter,'" but the tale was already well established in anthologies by that time. In my survey, only six of the forty anthologies included "Rue Morgue," none after 1950. Poe's other ratiocinative tales, "The Mystery of Marie Rogêt" and "The

Gold-Bug" (another popular title outside the classroom), are consistently absent from the anthologies. However, Poe's tale of unsolvable mystery, "The Man of the Crowd," began attracting more attention after Walter Benjamin's analysis of the text—as an example of nineteenth-century *flânerie*—was published in English and late-twentieth-century critics were drawn to Poe's surreal-Dickensian treatment of the modern city. "Crowd" was included in Perry Miller's 1962 *Major Writers of America* and has appeared sporadically ever since, notably in the most recent multivolume editions of the Norton and Heath anthologies.[3]

Generally, though, there have been few really meaningful trends in the inclusion of specific stories. It is hard to guess why "The Masque of the Red Death" was almost as standard a selection as "Ligeia" up until the 1950s but appears much less regularly from that time on (although it *is* included in the most recent [9th] edition of the multivolume *Norton Anthology*). Or why "The Cask of Amontillado," weighing in under three thousand words and thus taking little space, has always been a contender but never a reigning champ—for instance, it was dropped from the *Heath Anthology* in the 1990s, and has yet to return. "Eleonora," the most romantically reassuring of his tales of beautiful, dying women, made several appearances in the first half of the twentieth century but has been seen only rarely since then. "A Descent into the Maelström" and "William Wilson" have each appeared occasionally, but neither is included in the current crop of anthologies. Two other popular, heavily studied Poe texts, "The Black Cat" and "The Tell-Tale Heart," were anthologized off and on throughout the twentieth century, more frequently in recent decades; both can be found in the most recent (9th) Norton—shorter and multivolume editions—while "Heart" is in the most recent concise (2nd) and multivolume (7th) Heaths.

While some shifts—such as the removal of "The Bells" and the emergence of "The Man of the Crowd"—do follow broad trends in literary criticism, there seems to be little academic-cultural logic to most of these fluctuations: one might expect a story like "Hop-Frog," with its ambiguous commentary on slave insurrection, to gain traction in an era when questions of race, power, and history are all at the forefront of literary study, and yet—despite occasional appearances—this story is no more likely to appear in the anthologies of the 2010s than it was in the anthologies of the 1950s or 1960s. And how does one explain the persistence of "Israfel" and "The City in the Sea"—both fine, representative poems, in my view, but neither one a lightning rod for literary criticism over the past half-century, nor especially well known outside academic circles?

Similarly, the capsule biographies or headnotes introducing Poe are surprisingly consistent from decade to decade, even as they vary in detail and emphasis. As I suggested at the beginning of this chapter, the least controversial assertion one can make about Poe is that he has been controversial, or at least misunderstood. The claim made in the opening sentence of the 1961 McGraw-Hill *American Literature: A College Survey*, like the one from Hart and Gohdes, is typical: "No other major American author has created as much critical controversy as has Poe" (Brown and Flanagan 251). While the controversy usually concerns the merits of Poe's work, it frequently finds its roots in his personal image and character. In 1935's *Major American Writers*, Howard Mumford Jones and Ernest E. Leisy observe, "The greatest representative of the American romantic movement in point of influence and popularity, Poe has suffered from an enveloping mist of legend which he himself helped to create" (708). The editorial teams led by George McMichael from 1974 to 2011 agreed; for almost forty years, their headnote to Poe included some version of these sentences:

> To a world fascinated by the bizarre and the macabre, Poe has often seemed an embodiment of the satanic characters in his own fiction, the archetype of the neurotic genius. He left no diaries, had few intimate friends to set straight the details of his life, and the vivid derangements portrayed in his writings and the tales of his own depravities (many of which he told himself for their shock effect) created a false portrait not completely corrected to this day. (571)

This summary seems a bit exaggerated—for all the violence and perverseness in Poe's fiction, there is very little that is "satanic," and his self-representation rarely, if ever, accentuated depravity. The larger point McMichael et al. are making—that Poe, however creepy he may actually have been, was not as creepy as you think—has a way of perpetuating the myth it ostensibly debunks. They might have picked up that semi-debunking rhythm from Walter Blair, who in his 1947 Scott Foresman anthology wrote, "Probably more than any other American author, Edgar Allan Poe—as a personality—has appealed to popular imagination. Generally, people think of him as a figure who might have emerged from one of his stories or poems—mysterious, wild, abnormal. There are, to be sure, elements of strangeness in the life of this neurotic genius. But it is dangerous to guess that his tales were merely autobiographical exploitations of his weird way of living" (644). Here, too, the vagueness of "weird way of living" conjures up any number of possible antisocial or aberrant behaviors and suggests that they were a kind of lifestyle choice, even as Blair cautions against equating the "strangeness" of the tales with that of the author. Occasionally no such caution signs appear: Irving Howe opens his assessment of Poe in a 1970 anthology (McGraw-Hill's *The Literature of America: Nineteenth Century*) with the claim that "The story of Poe's life is ghastly enough to have been written by Poe himself" (136).

Howe is one of the few anthologist/editors whose headnotes disparage Poe more than they promote him. (In this case, the mixture of high praise and near condemnation might remind readers of some book reviews written by Poe himself.) Howe's comments on Poe's life are often overstated, though not technically inaccurate: following his break with John Allan, "For the rest of his life Poe was trapped between poverty and panic"; following Virginia's death, "The rest is disaster" (137). After quoting extensively from Yvor Winters's 1937 critique of Poe as an "American obscurantist," he concludes, "Remarkable figure that he was, Poe now can hardly be supposed one of our major poets" (140). His assessment of the stories is more favorable but still equivocal: "for all their melodramatic excess, gimcrack settings, and florid language, the best of Poe's stories are impressive" (140).

A much earlier assessment, in Robert Shafer's 1926 *American Literature*, forges a more direct link between a flawed character and defective, or at least limited, art. After praising Poe's genius—"a master of rhythm and melody and economical construction"—Shafer changes course:

> But, with all their mastery of technique for a few carefully chosen ends, Poe's tales and poems are remarkably lacking in human content, in human interest—so much so that their author has very curiously been regarded as a man working out of time and place, with no relation to his age or environment. This is a notion which cannot stand examination, but which, nevertheless, expresses the truth that Poe carries us into a non-human world of ghostly fancy. He was, indeed, really without character or moral integrity, and so was not interested in the drama of human existence. (523)

In what was already a familiar rhetorical move, Shafer debunks a Poe myth while reinforcing it through insinuation: Poe was not personally or professionally divorced from his environment, but he wrote as if he were because he was "without character." The headnote in Emory Elliott's *American Literature: A Prentice Hall Anthology* from 1990 balances a slightly less dim appraisal of Poe's personality with an enthusiastic assessment of his literary achievement. The writer (probably not Elliott but another member of a large editorial team) refers to Poe's "whining, self-dramatic, and condemnatory appeals for money" in his letters to John Allan, returns repeatedly to Poe's drinking as an explanation for his career setbacks, and attributes Poe's incorrect suspicion that Hawthorne plagiarized from him to an "evolving paranoia"

(762–63). None of those characterizations is fabricated, but the negative emphasis on Poe's personal failings is unusually strong. Yet, as is nearly always the case, Poe's accomplishments as a writer and critic are powerfully extolled. After all, it would seem hypocritical to devote significant space to Poe's writing while claiming that he does not deserve so much attention.

When anthologists criticize Poe's work, particularly in the 1920s and 30s, they describe it—his poetry especially—in terms similar to Shafer's: technically brilliant but without feeling or "human interest." While calling Poe a "great and original genius, and the supreme artist in American letters," Franklyn and Edward D. Snyder, in Macmillan's *Book of American Literature* (1927), also speculate that Poe's writing "has little significance so far as the fundamental problems of existence are concerned. One does not go to Poe for a 'criticism of life'" (1142). In a 1937 anthology, Harry R. Warfel's editorial team endorses Walt Whitman's view of Poe ("brilliant and dazzling, but with no heat"), adding that he avoided "the commoner themes and more human emotions to dwell, in subtle meters, upon his favorite subject, the death of a beautiful woman" (653). The editors of the 1936 *Oxford Anthology of American Literature* argue that "Poe's mind developed form to a point of stiffness and artificiality, and it is difficult to read Poe without an excessive awareness of structure" (Benet and Pearson 1604). Writing in 1935, Howard Mumford Jones and Ernest E. Leisy cast the same tendency in a more positive light; breaking with their usual practice, they provide variants to Poe's texts in their footnotes to demonstrate "Poe's development as a craftsman" (709). Indeed, this emphasis on Poe's technical prowess would continue to appear, though in more muted ways, into the twenty-first century.

Csicsila notes the New Criticism's influence in the ratio of tales to poems, but the New Critics' values also made their way into mid-century introductions to Poe's work. In Macmillan's *Masters of American Literature* (1949), Henry A. Pochmann and Gay Wilson Allen were among the first to single out Poe's opposition to didacticism as a significant contribution to literary history, praising "Poe's refusal to mix morality with aesthetics" and stating that he alone appreciated that "doctrine" while "no one else in the America of his day supported him in it" (513). In Sculley Bradley's *The American Tradition in Literature* (1956), Poe is said to have "influenced the course of creative writing and criticism by emphasizing the art that appeals simultaneously to reason and to emotion, and by insisting that the work of art is not a fragment of the author's life, nor an adjunct to some didactic purpose, but an object created in the cause of beauty—which he defined in its largest spiritual implications" (322). In Houghton Mifflin's 1959 *Masters of American Literature* (same title but different publishers and editorial team than the aforementioned Pochmann/Allen anthology), the editors make the connection explicit: Poe "anticipated the twentieth-century New Critics with his emphasis on textual analysis, and he challenged the moralistic aims of literature by proposing purely aesthetic considerations" (146). Clarence A. Brown and John T. Flanagan, editors of the 1961 *American Literature: A College Survey*, concur: "In his emphasis upon rationality, form, and unity, Poe was influential in the development of the analytical approach that is characteristic of the modern critical method" (253). Thus, Poe's formalism, which had been linked to a supposed lack of interest in the human condition in earlier assessments, by mid-century tended to be lauded as both a positive emphasis on craft and a modern avoidance and condemnation of didacticism.

Explicit endorsements of Poe's opposition to didacticism fade in the late twentieth century, but it is worth noting that significant shifts in the headnotes, like those in the tables of contents, were slow in coming—in fact, some multigenerational anthologies such as the McGraw-Hill *American Tradition in Literature* and the Macmillan (McMichael) *Anthology of American Literature* kept their Poe introductions virtually intact for decades, with only minor updating.[4] More recent headnotes are less likely to evaluate Poe's literary merit—the Heath and the Bedford anthologies, for instance, are almost entirely biographical. The most recent *Norton Anthology*, for which Robert Levine serves as general editor and editor of the volume covering 1820–1865, also avoids aesthetic pronouncements but does include two long paragraphs summarizing Poe's significance and influence. The Norton is also the only major anthology I have seen that addresses the vexing topic of race and slavery in Poe's writing, and it does so in an informed, even-handed manner. If there is an identifiable trend in the Poe introductions of the past thirty years or so, it is a greater emphasis on his professional life through the inclusion of specific information about the publishers and magazines he worked with. In general, the more recent introductions tend to be more responsible in their characterizations, more informative regarding his biography, and more cognizant of Poe's range as a writer, but (and this is probably for the best) less eager to go out on a limb in their assessment of Poe.

Meanwhile, if the introductions highlight Poe's exploration of various prose subgenres, the selections included in college American literature anthologies do not reflect that range. The multivolume Heath (7th ed.) and Norton (9th ed.) anthologies include "The Man of the Crowd," and the Norton includes the mesmeric tale "The Facts in the Case of M. Valdemar," but Poe's satires, burlesques, and landscape tales have yet to crack this market, despite the growing attention paid to works such as "The Man That Was Used Up" and "The Domain of Arnheim" in current scholarly conversations.

Excerpts from the cosmological treaties-as-prose-poem *Eureka* were fairly common in mid-century anthologies but, with the exception of Harcourt Brace's *Heritage of American Literature* in 1991, that work, often seen as a key to Poe's worldview and aesthetics, has been absent since the 1960s. Poe still gets his share of pages—the most recent multivolume *Norton Anthology* includes eight poems, ten stories, and two critical works—but the lineup deviates little from the one established over half a century ago, with gothicism and detective fiction prevailing.

In the internet age, teaching an author whose work is in the public domain makes the question of which texts are "in the book" arguably less relevant anyway. If I want to teach "Some Words with a Mummy" (and I do), the fact that it is not in the *Norton Anthology* is not much of an impediment, with every variant version of the story available on the invaluable Edgar Allan Poe Society of Baltimore website. Still, American literature anthologies, in print and electronic form, offer convenience and scholarly apparatus that few instructors are ready to give up, so the few that remain are still highly influential on how authors such as Poe are presented to students. Even though instructors can easily assign "Arnheim" or "Mummy," they are far less likely to, not only because of tight reading schedules but also because, for non-specialists, the anthology's table of contents still functions as a provisional canon to which most of us default when constructing a syllabus. Despite the deromanticizing work of biographical headnotes, the Poe of the American literature survey, circa 2020, is to a great extent the Poe celebrated in twentieth- and twenty-first-century popular culture: the author of "The Raven," "Annabel Lee," "The Fall of the House of Usher," and "The Tell-Tale Heart"—which should remind us how much correspondence there is between Poe's most popular work and his most academically valued work. More surprisingly, the Poe of the 2020 American lit survey looks a lot like the Poe of the 1927 American lit survey. The story of Poe's place in college anthologies has a number of odd twists and turns, but ultimately, for all the changes in emphasis and varieties of approaches to Poe in academic criticism over the last century, Textbook Poe has been remarkably consistent as well as resilient.

Notes

1. My survey of forty anthologies included five from the 1920s, six from the 1930s, three from the 1940s (World War II having interrupted the stream of anthology publications), five from the 1950s, seven from the 1960s, three from the 1970s, three from the 1980s, three from the 1990s, two from the 2000s, and three from the 2010s.

One reason recent decades are under-represented in number is that I included only two different editions of the Macmillan, Heath, and Norton anthologies, which tend to be lightly revised every few years. In each case, I included one full edition and one concise (or "shorter") edition. I reviewed and took notes on multiple editions of these and other earlier anthologies, but again, for the purpose of charting trends, I included no more than two editions of the same title. It is worth noting, too, that there were more anthologies on the market in the 1960s, whereas by the 2010s, as academic publishers consolidated or went out of business, the anthologies published by Norton, Heath, Pearson (a descendant of the old Macmillan), and Bedford (published by Macmillan and in its second edition as of this writing) controlled the market. Csicsila's bibliography of anthologies includes forty-four different titles and multiple editions of the most successful, such as the *Norton Anthology*, *The American Tradition in Literature*, and the Macmillan *Anthology of American Literature* (edited by George McMichael et al.). Counting each edition as a separate example, those three alone constituted twenty-four anthologies prior to 2000. Thus, while we examined similar lists of anthologies, we "crunched" different numbers. I would like to thank the staff of the Library of Congress's Collections Access, Loan, and Management Division for making this research possible.

2. Among the major literary figures who disparaged Poe's poetry for its gaudy sound effects and lack of intellectual sophistication were Aldous Huxley ("Vulgarity in Literature," 1930), Yvor Winters ("Edgar Allan Poe: A Crisis in the History of American Obscurantism," 1937), and, to a lesser degree, T. S. Eliot ("From Poe to Valéry," 1949). W. H. Auden damned "The Bells" with very faint praise in his introduction to the collection *Edgar Allan Poe: Selected Prose and Poetry* (1950): "'The Bells,' though much less interesting a conception than 'Ulalume,' is more successful because the subject is nothing but an excuse for onomatopoeic effects" (225). In *The Poet Edgar Allan Poe*, Jerome McGann argues that the polarized opinions regarding "The Bells" are an indication of its importance (174).

3. The inclusion of "The Man of the Crowd" can probably be attributed to Richard Wilbur. Wilbur, who wrote some of the most ambitious Poe criticism of the 1950s and 1960s, edited the Poe section of *Major Writers of America*, contributing a substantial introduction. Edward H. Davidson, who wrote a major study of Poe in 1957, was also on the editorial board.

4. The title and apparatus of *The American Tradition in Literature*, edited by Sculley Bradley and originally published in 1956 by W. W. Norton, was handed down to general editor George Perkins, then George and Barbara Perkins, who published with Random House and then McGraw-Hill. The twelfth edition of 2009 included essentially the same Poe introduction that appeared in 1956. *The Anthology of American Literature* edited by McMichael et al. changed publishers (from Macmillan to Prentice Hall to Longman) and made significant changes to its editorial team in the early 2000s but left its Poe introduction virtually intact from 1974 to 2011. *The Norton Anthology of American Literature* (1979–present) has revised and expanded its Poe introduction but has never completely revamped it. An exception to this general

rule, the Poe introduction in *The Heath Anthology of American Literature* (1989–present) received a complete rewrite when Meredith McGill replaced William Goldhurst as its author with the fourth edition in 2001.

Works Cited

Auden, W. H. "Introduction" (to *Edgar Allan Poe: Selected Prose and Poetry*). *The Recognition of Edgar Allan Poe*, edited by Eric W. Carlson, U of Michigan P, 1966, pp. 220–30.

Benjamin, Walter. "On Some Motifs in Baudelaire." *Selected Writings, Vol. 4: 1938–1940*, edited by Edmund Jephcott, Howard Eiland, and Michael W. Jennings, Harvard UP, 2003, pp. 313–55.

Csicsila, Joseph. *Canons by Consensus: Critical Trends and American Literature Anthologies*. U of Alabama P, 2004.

Eliot, T. S. "From Poe to Valéry." *The Recognition of Edgar Allan Poe*, edited by Eric W. Carlson, U of Michigan P, 1966, pp. 205–19.

Huxley, Aldous. "Vulgarity in Literature." *The Recognition of Edgar Allan Poe*, edited by Eric W. Carlson, U of Michigan P, 1966, pp. 160–67.

Lacan, Jacques. "Seminar on 'The Purloined Letter.'" Translated by Jeffrey Mehlman, *Yale French Studies*, vol. 48, 1972, pp. 39–72. Reprinted in *The Purloined Poe: Lacan, Derrida, and Psychoanalytic Reading*, edited by John P. Muller and William J. Richardson, Johns Hopkins UP, 1988, pp. 28–54.

Lauter, Paul, general editor. *The Heath Anthology of American Literature*. 7th ed., Cengage, 2014. 5 vols.

McGann, Jerome. *The Poet Edgar Allan Poe: Alien Angel*. Harvard UP, 2014.

McMichael, George, general editor. *Concise Anthology of American Literature*. 4th ed., Prentice Hall, 1998.

Poe, Edgar Allan. *The Bells and Other Poems*. Illustrated by Edmund Dulac, Hudder and Stoughton, 1912.

Winters, Yvor. "Edgar Allan Poe: A Crisis in the History of American Obscurantism." *The Recognition of Edgar Allan Poe*, edited by Eric W. Carlson, U of Michigan P, 1966, pp. 176–202.

Anthologies Surveyed (in Chronological Order)

Foerster, Norman, editor. *American Poetry and Prose: A Book of Readings, 1697–1916*. Houghton Mifflin, 1925.

Pattee, Fred Lewis, editor. *Century Readings for a Course in American Literature*. Century, 1926.

Shafer, Robert, editor. *American Literature*. Doubleday, Page, 1926.

Snyder, Franklyn, and Edward D. Snyder, editors. *A Book of American Literature*. Macmillan, 1927.

Quinn, Arthur Hobson, et al., editors. *The Literature of America: An Anthology of Prose and Verse*. Scribner's, 1929. 2 vols.

McDowell, Tremaine, editor. *The Romantic Triumph: American Literature from 1830 to 1860*. Macmillan, 1933.

Jones, Howard Mumford, and Ernest E. Leisy, editors. *Major American Writers*. Harcourt, Brace, 1935.

Hubbell, Jay B., editor. *American Life in Literature*. Harper & Brothers, 1936. 2 vols.

Warfel, Harry R., et al., editors. *The American Mind: Selections from the Literature of the United States*. American Book Co., 1937. 2 vols.

Benet, William Rose, and Norman Holmes Pearson, editors. *The Oxford Anthology of American Literature*. Oxford UP, 1938.

Ellis, Harold Milton, editor. *A College Book of American Literature*. American Book Co., 1939.

Blair, Walter, editor. *Literature of the United States, An Anthology and a History*. Scott-Foresman, 1946–1947. 2 vols.

Cargill, Oscar, general editor. *American Literature: A Period Anthology*. Macmillan, 1949. 4 vols.

Pochmann, Henry A., and Gay Wilson Allen, editors. *Masters of American Literature*. Macmillan, 1949. 2 vols.

Foerster, Norman, editor. *American Poetry and Prose*, shorter 3rd edition. Houghton Mifflin, 1952.

Hart, James D., and Clarence Gohdes, editors. *America's Literature*. Dryden Press, 1955.

Howard, Leon, Louis B. Wright, and Carl Bode, editors. *American Heritage: An Anthology and Interpretive Survey of Our Literature*. D. C. Heath, 1955.

Bradley, Sculley, editor. *The American Tradition in Literature*, shorter edition. Norton, 1956.

Edel, Leon, et al., editors. *Masters of American Literature*. Houghton Mifflin, 1959. 2 vols.

Brown, Clarence A., and John T. Flanagan, editors. *American Literature: A College Survey*. McGraw-Hill, 1961.

Miller, Perry, general editor. *Major Writers of America*. Harcourt, Brace & World, 1962.

Stern, Milton R., and Seymour L. Gross, editors. *American Literature Survey*. Viking, 1962. 4 vols.

Anderson, Charles Roberts, editor. *American Literary Masters*. Holt, Rinehart & Winston, 1965.

Bode, Carl, Leon Howard, and Louis B. Wright, editors. *American Literature: An Anthology with Critical Introductions*. Washington Square Press, 1966. 3 vols.

Davis, Thomas M., and Willoughby Johnson, editors. *An Anthology of American Literature*. Bobbs-Merrill, 1966.

Meserole, Harrison T., editor. *American Literature: Tradition & Innovation*. D. C. Heath, 1969.

Howe, Irving, editor. *The Literature of America: Nineteenth Century.* McGraw-Hill, 1970.

Brooks, Cleanth, R. W. B. Lewis, and Robert Penn Warren, editors. *American Literature: The Makers and the Making.* St. Martin's, 1973. 2 vols.

McMichael, George, general editor. *Concise Anthology of American Literature.* Macmillan, 1974.

Perkins, George, editor. *The American Tradition in Literature,* shorter 6th edition, Random House, 1985.

McQuade, Donald, general editor. *The Harper American Literature.* Harper & Row, 1987. 2 vols.

Baym, Nina, et al., editors. *The Norton Anthology of American Literature,* 3rd edition. Norton, 1989.

Elliott, Emory, general editor. *American Literature: A Prentice Hall Anthology.* Prentice Hall, 1990. 2 vols.

Millman, James E., Jr., editor. *Heritage of American Literature.* Harcourt Brace Jovanovich, 1991.

Lauter, Paul, general editor. *The Heath Anthology of American Literature,* 3rd edition. Houghton Mifflin, 1998. 2 vols.

———. *The Heath Anthology of American Literature,* concise edition. Houghton Mifflin, 2004.

Perkins, George, and Barbara Perkins, editors. *The American Tradition in Literature,* concise 12th edition. McGraw-Hill, 2009.

McMichael, George, general editor. *Anthology of American Literature,* 10th edition. Longman, 2011. 2 vols.

Belasco, Susan, and Linck Johnson, editors. *The Bedford Anthology of American Literature,* shorter 2nd edition. Bedford/St. Martin, 2014.

Levine, Robert, general editor. *The Norton Anthology of American Literature,* 9th edition. Norton, 2017. 5 vols.

PART III

SETTING TONES AND MOODS: GENRE ANTHOLOGIES AND AUDIOBOOKS

CHAPTER NINE

~

"Usher II"

Poe, Anthologies, and the Rise of Science Fiction

Stephen Rachman

Anthology-Functions

Notwithstanding their commercial exigencies, literary anthologies frequently take the form of story collections with an argument. The rationales
for the process of selection provided by preface or introduction, or implied
by the choices on display, typically offer a representative logic and a logic
of literary representation. Anthologies of this type—what Barbara Mujica
has termed "focus anthologies" (212–13)—indicate or advocate that there
is a trend, a movement within the culture, as it were, and, as the word "anthology" derives from a gathering of flowers, anthologies often flourish at a
moment when the lineaments of a genre can be made visible. Labels become
crucial at such moments of definition, consolidation, and differentiation.
What we might call the anthology-function operates by uniting the diverse
works of different authors into a generic whole—pointing toward the common features of the genre, movement, or topic covered in the particular
anthology, not the individual author.[1] In the anthology-function, authors
become relevant to the extent that they represent crucial generic elements
or innovations.

Twentieth-century science fiction anthologies exhibited this property
in that they showcased a variety of authors and were dedicated to the
enunciation of the genre itself, what defined it, who its venerable literary
pioneers and visionaries were, who its leading and emerging contemporary
practitioners might be, and how it might flourish. These anthologies came
in a number of forms: edited volumes, scholarly studies, annuals, and pulp

magazines.[2] Because science fiction entered its golden age around 1937, the pulp magazines that preceded this period self-consciously built on the foundational work of Mary Shelley, H. G. Wells, Jules Verne, Ambrose Bierce, Nathaniel Hawthorne and, most crucially for this essay, Edgar Allan Poe, and the anthology was often the vehicle of choice through which the emergent genre articulated its lineaments, made claims for its legitimacy, and proffered its polemics.

Prior to 1950, the pulp magazines were the main venue for new science fiction. These cheaply produced, inexpensive monthlies allowed for the development of readership and fan communities in a public way that was in actuality and perception outside of the literary mainstream. The genre was not taken seriously by the general public as a form of literature because of the magazines' cheapness, their often lurid covers, and their relatively small market share. More importantly, pulp magazines were overshadowed by the popular radio and film serials that dealt with science fiction as a vehicle for melodrama and gimmicky representations of advanced technology (especially rayguns and rockets). This remained a concern through the 1950s, when the genre was gaining a critical and popular foothold. As Ray Bradbury remarked in a radio documentary on science fiction from 1956, "In the past [science fiction] suffered from a bad reputation, a carryover from the comics and the bad science fiction and movies and what have you" ("Ticket"). Many issues of these pulp magazines functioned in practice as a form of anthology, showcasing representative works from the past and present, but they were insular, and scholars have come to view that germinative period from the mid-1920s to the mid-1940s as "its pulp ghetto"—a cultural space in which its "brash and crude" energies were on full display but "ignored by everyone except its fans" (Gunn 234).

Anthologies played an important role in enhancing the reputation of science fiction by demonstrating its power and relevance, especially as the world entered the atomic and space ages. The culling of excellent works by knowledgeable editors in durable book formats allowed for greater visibility and longevity. The paperback revolution allowed for these books to reach wide readerships—especially younger readers—and it was common for many to have had their first encounters with the genre by way of an anthology.[3] Several of these anthologies were exclusively gatherings of contemporary fiction, but many others attempted to create distinct lineages, to trace themes or the development of motifs and issues central to science fiction. In general, this last type of science fiction anthology is the most relevant to the study of Poe's impact on the genre, as demonstrated throughout the first section of this chapter.[4]

Poe's role in the emergence and definition of science fiction was complicated by the generic diversity found in his narrative and speculative works themselves. Some of his tales fit squarely into what might be called the main currents of science fiction as they would emerge in the twentieth century—extraordinary voyages with what was at the time considered advanced technology ("Hans Pfaall" and "The Balloon Hoax"), mesmeric out-of-body experiences ("The Facts in the Case of M. Valdemar" and "Mesmeric Revelation"), and time travel ("A Tale of the Ragged Mountains"). However, a significant number of his writings were generic blends. Poe's gothic fictions of the bizarre ("The Premature Burial"), homicide ("The Imp of the Perverse"), and detection ("The Murders in the Rue Morgue") begin with quasi-philosophical treatises that have the air of scientific method about them, but then move into narrative realms that render problematic the investment in science and defy any straightforward attempts to define or categorize them generically. Of all the popular genres, science fiction is the most variegated in terms of generic definitions and subgenres, and Poe's generic diversity in his science fiction-related output reflects this to a certain extent, but it would be a mistake to assume that his work was aligned with all the currents and countercurrents in the genre's development. The self-consciousness with which the scholarship and the many reading communities have attempted to define and distinguish themselves is intense and has led to a great deal of subcategorization within the genre.[5]

The problems of Poe in relation to science and science fiction, then, begin in his own work; he was an author who, early in his career, called science a "vulture" that preys "upon the poet's heart" ("Sonnet—To Science"), but he finished his career with *Eureka*, a self-described "prose poem" treatise on the origins of the universe. The early poem "Al Aaraaf" has a quasi-science-fictional premise involving the artist Michelangelo inhabiting a star—the supernova discovered by Tycho Brahe in the constellation Cassiopeia.[6] The mixture of interest and commitment to science, and disavowal or undermining of scientific principles, runs through much of his work. It is not merely that he called *Eureka* a prose poem that suggests generic instability, but that it is a work dedicated to the proposition that the universe derives from an original unity of all things and all thoughts of things, which is nevertheless eroded by the prefatory remark that there is "no such thing as demonstration" (*Eureka* 7). Poe's anthology-function, as it were, was highly variable because his works were both inspirational and ambiguous in their varying expressions of science, scientific thought, or the experimental within his fictional and nonfictional writing. Poe would serve many purposes for twentieth-century authors and anthologists who sought to claim him as a founding figure in the emergent and highly contested field of science fiction.

After a look at a few key precursors who recognized the importance of Poe's works for scientific and speculative fiction, the next section of this chapter surveys Poe's emergence as a foundational figure in science fiction during the heart of the twentieth century, just as the genre was gaining popularity and seeking to establish its own oft-disputed generic boundaries and lineages. The starting point for this survey is the 1926 publication of Hugo Gernsback's first issue of *Amazing Stories*, and the endpoint is Harold Beaver's 1976 Penguin anthology, *The Science Fiction of Edgar Allan Poe*. In that fifty-year span, science fiction achieved a level of maturation as a genre, laying the groundwork for its even deeper penetration into the mainstream. Film adaptations by bona fide auteurs of important science fiction novels like Francois Truffaut's *Fahrenheit 451* (1966) and Stanley Kubrick's *2001: A Space Odyssey* (1969) were harbingers of a cultural shift that *Star Wars*, which was released in 1977, made evident. The novels of J. G. Ballard, film adaptations of Philip K. Dick's works like the 1982 *Blade Runner*, and Donna Haraway's "A Cyborg Manifesto" in 1985 all helped to cement the viability of science fiction as a vehicle for dystopian vision, cybernetics, and cyberpunk deconstructions in both the popular sphere and the academic world of socio-literary criticism. This journey, "from the pulps to the classroom" (233–34), as James Gunn has described it, delineates the trajectory of the status of science fiction in the twentieth century, and it naturally describes the arc through which Poe's influence is most crucial and can best be seen.

The final section of this chapter takes up Ray Bradbury's short story, "Usher II," as a prime example and expression of Poe's legacy in twentieth-century science fiction. I would argue that Bradbury is *the* major science fiction author most deeply influenced by Poe and that "Usher II" expresses his most sustained engagement with Poe and the darkest potentialities of Poe's work on and within science fiction. Written in the late 1940s and published in the pulp magazine *Amazing Wonder Stories*, and then fitted into the American edition of *The Martian Chronicles*, "Usher II" takes up Poe's work in an anthological way. It also takes up the theme expressed in Bradbury's comments in the aforementioned mid-twentieth-century radio documentary: "Because the problem of modern man is the modern man and machine, and the machine is coming more and more into use every day. . . . I should think we would have more writers interested in the problem of the machine and mankind" ("Ticket"). Though the technologies of the twentieth century differed from those of Jacksonian America, the question of man and machines was nearly as central to Poe's science fiction work as it was to that of Bradbury, and to science fiction as a whole. In Bradbury's recasting of Poe's "The Fall of the House of Usher" on Mars, much more than homage or tribute takes place. As the story gathers together the collective power of many elements of Poe's tales, it places them at the embattled service of science fiction as a genre through which the fate of speculative and imaginative literature might be weighed as a disruptive and, ultimately, transformative cultural force.

Poe's Fictions of Science

The acknowledgment of Poe's engagement with science fiction occurred in small ways during his career. There were credulous reactions by readers who, to varying degrees, mistook fiction for fact in *The Narrative of Arthur Gordon Pym*, the article that came to be known as "The Balloon Hoax," and "The Facts in the Case of M. Valdemar" (Rachman, "Poe" 31–34). A reviewer of *Eureka* in the *Home Journal* remarked that Poe's late work of cosmological speculation was an instance of a new feature of "modern culture," namely "the application of rhetoric and imagination to science" (3). Not long after Poe's death and the appearance of Charles Baudelaire's French translations of his work in the 1850s, writers and critics—especially in Europe—perceived this distinctive scientific strain within Poe's literary output and hailed him as a pioneer in the new literary genre. As early as 1856, the Goncourt Brothers, after reading Poe in Baudelaire's translations, remarked that there was something in Poe that "critics have not noticed." He opened up "a new literary world, pointing to the literature of the twentieth century. Scientific miracles, fables on the pattern of A+B" (qtd. in Schmidt 250). In 1858, in the preface to the first Spanish edition of Poe's tales, Nicasio Landa claimed that Poe "was the first to exploit the marvelous in the field of science" (Smith 12). Of the five Poe stories translated in this early collection, two would be closely associated with Poe's signal contributions to science fiction: "The Facts in the Case of M. Valdemar" and "Hans Pfaall."[7]

Jules Verne's explicit acknowledgment of Poe's influence on his work—including his 1897 sequel/extension of Poe's 1838 *The Narrative of Arthur Gordon Pym*, entitled *Le Sphinx des Glaces* [*The Sphinx of the Ice Fields*]—reinforced Poe's centrality in the formation of the genre, but with a different inflection. Broadly speaking, in terms of plot Verne took up the mantle of Poe through narratives of adventure into realms unknown, but on the level of language, he emulated the line between fact and fiction that Poe routinely exploited. Verne's *From Earth to the Moon* (1865) and *Round the Moon* (1870) both directly follow from "Hans Pfaall." However, which elements of Poe's scientifically speculative works an author chose to emulate or develop mattered for the emerging field of science fiction. J. O. Bailey, who published the first systematic study of the genre in 1946, *Pilgrims Through Space and Time*, felt that Verne had fallen short in his moon "romances" precisely because he "'idolized' his master Poe," but misunderstood the intent behind the original, embracing "the spirit of its facetious enveloping plot rather than . . . its central story" (47). In this assessment, Bailey exhibited a commonly held perception of how science fiction was to best proceed. He wished that Verne had veered more toward scientific accuracy rather than the "rollicking" (47) absurdities he found in Poe that test the credulity of the reader. In this way, the mixture of modes one continually encounters in Poe (the scientific *and* the absurd) appeared to be a liability rather than an asset as science fiction emerged in the mid-twentieth century.

H. G. Wells's usage of Poe was more in line with the critical concerns that Bailey viewed as Poe's chief value to science fiction, but rather than focusing on scientific information, Wells stressed method and approach. In an 1896 essay entitled "Popularising Science" [sic], he wrote, "the fundamental principles of construction that underlie such stories as Poe's 'Murders in the Rue Morgue,' or Conan Doyle's 'Sherlock Holmes' series, are precisely those that should guide the scientific writer" (301). In this case, rather than the stories that deal with cosmological or technological speculation, it is Poe's tales of ratiocination and detection with their air of scientific method that provided the generic template. Like the Goncourt Brothers, Wells perceived in Poe a new literary mentality, modes of thought and expression, rather than a particular topic or branch of knowledge. The elements of this practice can be traced through Wells's "The Red Room" (1895), *The Time Machine* (1895), *The Island of Dr. Moreau* (1896), *The First Men in the Moon* (1901), and *Tono-Bungay* (1908).

The modern term for the genre itself—science fiction—was defined by Hugo Gernsback (he originally used the portmanteau "Scientifiction") in the inaugural issue of *Amazing Stories* for April 1926. The cover highlighted that the monthly pulp contained tales by Verne, Wells, and Poe. "The Facts in the Case of M. Valdemar" was featured in that first issue, and "Mesmeric Revelation" appeared in the second one. While Verne and Wells are more prominently associated with the genre, Poe is there, from the very coining of the genre's name, front and center as its foundational American avatar.

Gernsback's vision for the genre aligned with Wells's call for fictional vehicles through which actual science might be popularized. In the inaugural editorial, Gernsback opined that the genre in its best examples should consist of "a charming romance intermingled with scientific fact and prophetic vision" (3). By "prophetic vision" Gernsback meant futurology, especially the kind that is predictive of new technologies. He provided the example of Verne's Nautilus submarine from *Twenty Thousand Leagues Under the Sea* as an instance of a technology that once only seemed possible in the imagination or on the page but that, by the 1920s, had become a reality. In keeping with this approach, the note accompanying "Valdemar" suggested that in this tale Poe used mesmerism "as a vehicle for telling us his views about the higher philosophy and the future world" (92). However, readers of Poe's tale about a "test subject" crossing the line between life and death in a mesmeric trance may have wondered just exactly to what extent the story engages with the future in the way Gernsback indicated in his preface. Perhaps "Valdemar," with its aura of scientific method—suggested by the titular "The Facts in the Case"—participated in the kind of analytic fantasy that the Goncourt brothers first noted, and this was what Gernsback meant by "higher philosophy." It is more certain that, despite his claims to its relevancy for the future, the main attraction of Poe's tale for Gernsback lay in its "amazing" qualities—its shock value, or, as he described the denouement (the instantaneous putrefaction of the test subject's flesh), "the most horrifying and terrible in all modern storytelling" (92). Even as Gernsback attempted to define the genre with Poe at its core and to map out its future, the generic tensions inherent in Poe's fiction manifested themselves.

With these tensions in mind, Gernsback's full-throated embrace of Poe as an avatar and model was not unanimous in the formative years, given Gernsback's general position that science fiction should retain at its core a popularization of scientific fact.[8] In the twenty years following Gernsback's founding of *Amazing Stories*, pulps flourished in a hothouse culture in which editors like Gernsback and John W. Campbell, Jr. (editor of *Astounding*) wielded their editorial power in ways that could be quite doctrinaire, precipitating factions and a proliferation of generic mergers and subdivisions, arguments and counterarguments, as to what constituted science fiction's proper domains.

The anthologies of the 1940s and 1950s reflected these tensions in interesting ways, and Poe's deployment in this period allowed for an articulation of these cross-currents. It was not merely that Poe or his key tales were being held up as exemplary forerunners worthy of imitation, but Poe's oeuvre also became a question of negative influence. Phil Stong's 1942 anthology, *The Other Worlds: 25 Modern Stories of Mystery and Imagination*, serves as a case in point. Stong's anthology culled stories from the pulp magazines (drawing on *Weird Tales*, *Astounding Stories*, *Amazing Stories*, *Westminster Magazine*, *Esquire*, and *Thrilling Wonder Stories*), and it featured early work by notable science fiction authors, such as Theodore Sturgeon and Murray Leinster. Divided into three sections—"Strange Ideas," "Fresh Variants," and "Horrors"—the anthology indicated how the impetus toward science fiction had proliferated categorization, the parceling out of "romance" or the romantic elements of scientific fiction into distinct markets and venues. With respect to Poe, Stong's key selection was H. P. Lovecraft's "In the Vault," a premature entombment story, first printed in *Weird Tales*, the pulp outlet *par excellence* for stories in which the occult, gothic, and horror elements might meld with science fiction. Stong traces Lovecraft's fantastic cosmology (most widely recognized in Cthulhu) to "what might be called the Later-Georgian-English-Weird-School" but sees his style as "reminiscent of Poe at his most precious," and the liability of that preciousness was a kind of brilliancy that called its own veracity into question (327–30). Stong maintained that Poe's diction was "measured and ornamented" in such a manner that alerted the reader that "though the narrative was diverting it was not *true*" (327). Poe and Lovecraft were promising, but they were "too much bedizened both in language and setting" (328). Stong called for an editorial balance of matter-of-fact prose as a means to impose a realism of language and tone to achieve the proper horrifying effects of the weird or what we might call weird science. "Mr. Lovecraft erred," Stong concluded, "because of Poe" (330). As science fiction came of age at a moment when realistic prose was in vogue and the discourse of science—even in its most futuristic or apocalyptic modes—was committed to an editorial reality principle, Poe's style and generic latitude—even at a moment of powerful influence, as in the case of Lovecraft—could be construed as an aesthetic or even conceptual liability.

After World War II, when science fiction anthologies actively sought out and gained wider mainstream audiences, Poe's place in these works was less predictable. One important instance of this was Donald A. Wollheim's 1943 anthology, *The Pocket Book of Science Fiction*, the first titular usage of the term "science fiction" (Truesdale). Wollheim selected Ambrose Bierce's 1899 "Moxon's Monster" as his American precursor rather than use anything from Poe, but this choice clearly connects back to Poe. "Moxon's Monster," a tale about a chess-playing automaton that kills its human inventor in a fit of pique after being checkmated, works in the same terrain as Poe's analysis in his 1835 "Maelzel's Chess-Player." Bierce's tale is an early example of the recurrence of the man-and-machine issue that Poe's essay foretells and that Paul Grimstad sees played out in the works of several science fiction icons of the twentieth century. Grimstad states, "Poe's analysis of proto-artificial intelligence in his essay 'Maelzel's Chess-Player' puts in place the basic philosophical intrigue found in everything from Isaac Asimov's robot stories to Philip K. Dick's *Do Androids Dream of Electric Sheep?* Poe's example may be found resurfacing throughout the genre's evolution" (736). Grimstad's recognition of the connection from Poe to Asimov and Dick also runs in a latent way through Bierce, Wollheim, and Bradbury.

While Poe only had a latent presence in *The Pocket Book of Science Fiction*, he appears as the origin of science fiction in Edward Groff Conklin's *Best of Science Fiction*. Conklin's 1946 anthology included a preface by John W. Campbell, Jr., editor of *Astounding Science Fiction*, and it reprinted Poe's 1844 "A Tale of the Ragged Mountains" as its earliest example of the genre.[9] The sophistication of Conklin's classifications of the genre was a new feature as well. He divided the stories he included into six categories: The Atom, The Wonders of the Earth, The Superscience of Man, Dangerous Inventions, Inventions in Dimension, and From Outer Space. He placed Poe's tale under "The Superscience of Man" in which he featured the exploration of the hidden powers of the mind (312).

By the 1960s, science fiction had not only reached a serious mainstream audience in which figures like Isaac Asimov, Ray Bradbury, Arthur C. Clarke, Robert A. Heinlein, and Ursula K. LeGuin all enjoyed breakthrough popular and critical acclaim, but it had also been taken up in earnest by the academy. Sam Moskowitz, a veteran science fiction editor, assembled a collection in 1969, *The Man Who Called Himself Poe*, that attempted to gather the many generic facets of Poe that had been explored in the seemingly evanescent pulp era, with special emphasis on the biographical and a thorough embrace of Lovecraft's preoccupations with Poe. More than any editor, Moskowitz connected Poe's science fiction to his generic versatility. "Like all good science fiction," he explained of his collection, "each story begins from a factual premise . . . and proceeds from there. Yet only a few of these stories are science fiction, for quite logically they tend to cover the gamut of Poe's own genius: the detective story, murder mystery, horror tale, supernatural, humor, bittersweet remembrance, and even verse" (xiii). However, Moskowitz does not ascribe interest in Poe to the popularity of the genres he is associated with establishing, but to the fascination that authors and readers continually feel for Poe himself, which he likens to the perennial interest in the character of Sherlock Holmes (xi–xii).

H. Bruce Franklin's pathbreaking study—*Future Perfect: American Science Fiction of the Nineteenth Century: An Anthology* (1966, 1978, 1997)—virtually reversed the terms on which science fiction was understood by promoting the thesis that every major nineteenth-century American author was influenced by science fiction or the utopian tale. Science fiction was not a sidelight but a main thread in the production of national literature. Franklin makes the case for Poe's centrality as a foundational figure in science fiction while try-ing to decentralize, or at least diminish, his contributions. From Poe's works, Franklin selected "A Tale of the Ragged Mountains," "The Facts in the Case of M. Valdemar," and "Mellonta Tauta" as prime examples of what Franklin argues is the salient feature of Poe's contribution to the genre. "Science fic-tion as a form of physical (as distinguished from utopian, moral, psychologi-cal or religious) speculation," he argues, "is what Poe may have provided with significant new dimensions" (92).

Franklin's approach to science fiction privileges the varieties that empha-size the impact of science on society, and his reading of Poe is constrained by his relative inattention to what Jonathan Elmer has termed "the social limit" in Poe's fictions (20–21). For example, Franklin finds the horrors of "Valde-mar" as a form of escapism that seems, in his opinion, beyond any social ends—a kind of horror for horror's sake. He interprets "Valdemar" as a turn-ing away from harsher social realities, and he cites the horrors of slavery as described in Frederick Douglass's *Narrative of the Life of Frederick Douglass, an American Slave* (1845) as a counterexample of the kind of antebellum social reality Poe might have confronted but did not. Rather than "romancing the shadow," as Toni Morrison and others might phrase it, Franklin reads Poe as failing to encode any of the horrors of slavery or other ugly/dehumanizing social realities in his works.[10]

Harold Beaver's *The Science Fiction of Edgar Allan Poe* (1976), the first comprehensive assemblage of all of Poe's writings that might be construed as science fiction—from the early "MS. Found in a Bottle" in 1831 to the late *Eureka* (1848) and "Von Kempelen and His Discovery" (1849)—stands as a consolidation of how science fiction's place had shifted during the twentieth century and as a forceful rebuttal to Franklin's arguments. "Poe has never been without his detractors," (xv) Beaver wrote. "When his originality has not been ignored, it has been undermined. H. Bruce Franklin is the most recent to launch a two-pronged attack" (xv). If Franklin found Poe to be an empty popularizer without social relevance, Beaver countered that Poe's blend of the mathematical and the ideal did indeed have significant social relevance and subtexts. Beaver offered the examples of the "angelic collo-quies" of "Monos and Una" and "Eiros and Charmion," in which the tensions of science and society are manifest (xvii). "The Colloquy of Monos and Una" explains the destruction of the world by way of a corruption of taste that led to a world built of "rectangular obscenities" (612). As I have written else-where, "the object of Monos's criticism is not art or even fine arts, narrowly defined, but a broad almost ecological sense of the beautiful that pertains to the ways that our environments and economies are structured" ("Rectangular" 90). Reading "Monos and Una" as a direct expression of its author's beliefs, Beaver argued that "it was not science" that Poe "abhorred so much as the triumph of mechanical reason" (xvii).[11] In terms of science fiction in the twentieth century, however, Poe's angelic colloquy expresses a profound skepticism about man's technological control of nature—the Anthropocene itself as a fundamental wrong turn: "principles which should have taught our race to submit to the guidance of the natural laws, rather than attempt their control" (610). Even as one makes a convincing case for Poe's interest in the social impact of science on the fate of man and the world, one discovers a cautionary critique of the machine age that is at odds with the technological embrace that dominated twentieth-century science fiction. We find in Poe's science fiction writing a deep engagement with machines and technology that mixes with a profound skepticism about human agency with regard to such interventions.

"Usher II"

Where the first two sections of this essay have sought to provide an overview of the process of anthologization through which Poe came to be seen as a foundational figure in the science fiction genre and in which science fiction joined the main currents of literary culture, this concluding portion seeks to describe a singular engagement with Poe as a means to explore what it meant for science fiction and literary culture to embrace Poe in the white-hot moment of that process, in the late 1940s and early 1950s. The American edition of Ray Bradbury's 1950 science fiction classic, *The Martian Chronicles*, contains "Usher II," an account of the "rebuilding" of Edgar Allan Poe's House of Usher on Mars in the year 2005, as an act of terrorist subversion and a stratagem to thwart the cataclysmic censorship that began in the late 1940s and 1950s and had culminated in a holocaust of book-burning in the mid-1970s. While it is generally known that Poe was one of Bradbury's literary heroes, one whom he frankly imitated in much of his early work, and that "Usher II" is perhaps the deepest instance of tribute to Poe, I wish to take up the story in a way that goes beyond influence. Rather, I would like to consider "Usher II" as a deployment of Poe in the discourse of science fiction. This story is more than a literary tribute to Poe; it is a weaponization of Poe and of the literary territorialization of Mars that was central to the project of science fiction as it was imagined in the 1950s by Bradbury and other writers such as Isaac Asimov, Robert A. Heinlein, and Arthur C. Clarke. It is a tale that takes up many of Bradbury's abiding themes—censorship, the literary imagination, technological power, futurity, realism, and fate—but rather than focus on how this story is central to Bradbury's oeuvre, I will turn to the moment in which the story was written and the response it generated as a means to assess what Poe and his fictions came to stand for in the mid-twentieth century explosion of science fiction and fantasy writing. "Usher II" is, in fact, a story that moves from the pulps to mainstream fiction and reflects the tension between the ghettoization of science fiction and its concerns about "mainstream" American culture. It is also, in its way, a meditation on the relationship between man and machine that Bradbury discussed in the mid-1950s. "The machine is coming more and more into use every day," he opined, "and I should think we would have more writers interested in the problem of the machine and mankind. And yet, when you stop and think of it, how rarely has a good novel, for instance, been written on the impact of the automobile on life in America" ("Ticket"). But rather than merely reflecting upon the impact of the automobile on society, in "Usher II" Bradbury considers many kinds of machines and mechanisms and, at his most daring, he uses Poe to craft a narrative about the mechanization of storytelling itself.

Composed in 1949, the same year that George Orwell released *1984*, and first published the following year under the title "Carnival of Madness," "Usher II" (as printed in *The Martian Chronicles*) has an Orwellian timetable for the acceleration of literary destruction.[12] The libraries of the world had been purged of Poe

> and Lovecraft and Hawthorne and Ambrose Bierce and all the tales of terror and fantasy and horror and, for that matter, tales of the future. Heartlessly. They passed a law. Oh, it started very small. In 1950 and '60 it was a grain of sand. They began by controlling books of cartoons and then detective books and, of course, films, one way or another, one group or another, political bias, religions prejudice, union pressures; there was always a minority afraid of something, and a great majority afraid of the dark, afraid of the future, afraid of the past, afraid of the present, afraid of themselves and shadows of themselves. (163)

Evidently, Orwell, Arthur Koestler's *Darkness at Noon*, and figures like Frederic Wertham (who in the late 1940s began a crusade to suppress comic books and graphic detective fiction on the grounds that they contributed to juvenile delinquency, criminal violence, and deviant sexuality), along with Senator Joseph McCarthy and the House Un-American Activities Committee, had fueled Bradbury's imagination enough to convince him that the Stalinist and Nazi eras were far from aberrations in human history.[13]

As he would more fully imagine in *Fahrenheit 451*, Bradbury provides a rough-draft account of the historical sequence that created these repressive conditions. In the earliest phase, the word "politics," which had become a conservative byword for "communism," was equated with retribution and even death. The inhibition of political discourse would lead to the closure of the cinemas and theaters, and a constricting "purification" of print media, but it would do so through a curious mechanism of cultural violence: "with a screw tightened here, a bolt fastened there, a push, a pull, a yank, art and literature were soon like a great twine of taffy strung about, being twisted in braids and tied in knots and thrown in all directions, until there was no more resiliency and no more savor to it" (163). If Orwell imagined the denaturing of language in terms of the radical distortions and euphemisms of Newspeak, Bradbury imagines the state as a denaturing apparatus—a taffy-pulling machine gone haywire, in which mechanization has taken command and art and literature, tethered by bolt and screw, lose all elasticity and flavor like an overchewed piece of gum. This attenuation of the literary is a prologue—a preparing of the cultural space, so to speak—for a censorship proper in which all forms of escapist literature were deemed radical and placed in the crosshairs of the censors. The censorship did not stop at the level of authors; fictional characters also became the targets of this state action. As if in anticipation of a ghastly version of *Shrek*, Bradbury imagines the summary execution of Snow White, Mother Goose, and a host of fantasy and fairy tale characters. A tyranny of the matter-of-fact is strictly imposed on society. As his vengeful protagonist would explain, "Every man, they said, must face reality. Must face the Here and Now! Everything that was not so must go. All the beautiful literary lies and flights of fancy must be shot in mid-air. So they lined them up against a library wall one Sunday morning thirty years ago, in 1975; they lined them up . . . and shot them down, and burned the paper castles" (164).

Bradbury's character, Stendahl, the visionary rebel who continues defiantly to read imaginative works, had fled to Mars to escape the earthly censors (The Moral Climate people and their chief investigator, Garrett) only to find that these conservative forces of thought-policing, not satisfied with having burned his library on Earth, were now encroaching upon the red planet he had made his own preserve. This prompts Stendahl to lament: "Oh, realism! Oh, here, oh, now, oh hell!" (163). Aaron Barlow explains that when Bradbury refers to "realism" in "Usher II," he is not referring to the literary trend associated with William Dean Howells but "to the opposite of the imaginative" (105). While Barlow is certainly correct not to equate Bradbury's concept of realism with a specific period, we can offer a little more precision than the imagination's opposite—as if the target were some kind of unreconstructed Gradgrindian factitiousness. The particular kind of imaginative opposition is rather rooted in the classic spatio-temporal premises of fantasy and science fiction—not the here and now, but the there and then—other realms and other times. As the title of Bailey's seminal 1947 study of the genre puts it, *Pilgrims through Space and Time*.

It is not entirely accurate to say that Bradbury has no particular realistic literary targets in mind. "Oh, Poe's been forgotten for many years now, and Oz and the other creatures," Stendahl laments. "Just as you put a stake through the heart of Halloween and told your film producers that if they made anything at all they would have to make and remake Ernest Hemingway. My God, how many times have I seen *For Whom the Bell Tolls* done! Thirty different versions. All realistic" (168). It is not merely the erasure of Poe and Baum's Oz (note here the conflation of the erasure of authors from collective memory with the erasure of fictional spaces), but the expunging through the proliferation of film versions of Hemingway that literally drives Stendahl to Mars in the first place. The problem for Bradbury is, as it was for Walter Benjamin, the work of art (literary art in this instance) in the age of mechanical reproduction. But whereas Benjamin concerned himself with the impact of mechanical reproduction on the original, positing the diminution or even degradation of the aura of the original, Bradbury concerned himself with competitive forms of mechanical reproduction—the ways in which literature could be denatured by torsion (as in the taffy-pulling machine analogy) or erased when the mechanical reproductive power has been harnessed selectively by ideologically motivated power elites. For this reason, any reading of Bradbury's ultimate position as dividing neatly along lines of mechanized realities and the airy world of literary imagination is incomplete because Stendahl's literary platform—his Martian simulacrum of Poe's "House of Usher"—is just as wedded to the mechanical as that of his antagonists investigating Moral Climates.

But rather than a machine committed to the enforcement and proliferation of the "here and now," Stendahl is eager to build a machine through which one could proliferate literature committed to and welded to the "there and then"—the "other-worldly" that might oppose the "this worldly." It is to this end and in this fashion that Bradbury mobilizes Poe on Mars. In the face of the imminent threat of a Martian incursion by Moral Climate elite, Stendahl hires a young, unwitting architect named Bigelow, who was raised in the dogmatically realistic atmosphere of the Moral Climate to build the House of Usher in all its bleak, black, and lurid splendor. Pleased with his own handiwork and ingenuity, the young architect explains to his client,

"You notice, it's always twilight here, this land, always October, barren, sterile, dead. It took a bit of doing. We killed everything. Ten thousand tons of DDT. Not a snake, frog, or Martian fly left! Twilight always, Mr. Stendahl; I'm proud of that. There are machines, hidden, which blot out the sun. It's always properly 'dreary'" (161–62). What the architect does not know is that his ingenuity has been enlisted by Stendahl to lure all of the leaders of the Moral Climate elite to the Usher house in order to execute them en masse and to do so using an array of horrors from Poe's tales ("The Murders in the Rue Morgue," "The Masque of the Red Death," "The Cask of Amontillado," and "The Pit and the Pendulum" being the most prominent ones). The architect is essentially employed in a machine-like fashion, carrying out instructions the intent of which he does not fully comprehend and, had he comprehended them, would likely have opposed. The architect is equally ignorant of the fact that the house and its Usheresque atmospherics are just a component of Stendahl's plan, that he has a second, more witting partner named Pikes who has populated the house of Usher with an array of killing machines and lifelike robots drawn from Poe's tales.

In a tour de force passage, Bradbury renders an image of Poe-robots in readiness—as if on the eve of the Macy's Thanksgiving Day Parade—that is the apotheosis of his vision of the cultural work of mechanization on fantastic storytelling.

> Full grown without memory, the robots waited. In green silks the color of forest pools, in silks the color of frog and fern, they waited. In yellow hair the color of the sun and sand, the robots waited. Oiled, with tube bones cut from bronze and sunk in gelatin, the robots lay. In coffins for the not dead and not alive, in planked boxes, the metronomes waited to be set in motion. There was a smell of lubrication and lathed brass. There was a silence of the tomb yard. Sexed but sexless, the robots. Named but unnamed, and borrowing from humans everything but humanity, the robots stared at the nailed lids of their labeled F.O.B. boxes, in a death that was not even a death, for there had never been a life. And now there was a vast screaming of yanked nails. Now there was a lifting of lids. Now there were shadows on the boxes and the pressure of a hand squirting oil from a can. Now one clock was set in motion, a faint ticking. Now another and another, until this was an immense clock shop, purring. The marble eyes rolled wide their rubber lids. The nostrils winked. The robots, clothed in hair of ape and white of rabbit, arose. (71)

In a kind of mutually assured destruction befitting the Cold War, Bradbury's Stendahl has plotted a robotic killing before the Dismantlers and Burning Crew can do their work. The use of the literary plot as cultural conspiracy plot can, in a sense, only take place when welded to the mechanical and embodied in and acted out through mechanical forms. The plot of Poe's "Usher" determines that the house must fall, but in Bradbury's re-vision, that inevitability sets into motion the mechanized destruction of human censors. Fantastic literature lies in wait as a mechanical simulacrum in F.O.B. (Freight on Board) boxes, ready to kill those who cannot or fail to read its plots.

What are we to make of Bradbury's plot of vengeance through Poesque literary robots? It is a science fiction fantasy call-to-arms, but it also represents a delineation of what mainstream culture refused to read, or read in a particular way with a particular kind of enthusiasm. "Usher II" represents Poe's house of Usher as a site of mechanical destruction in which robots masquerade as "stories" or figures from stories in order to kill. The tale's original title, "Carnival of Madness," still resonates in this respect, for a carnivalesque masquerade pervades its course of inevitable destruction. The house masquerades as a library of censored books in order to lure the censors to their deaths at the hands of story-figures converted into machines. The literary vocabulary supplied to the twentieth century through the plots and characters of Poe offers a dark answer to the question of man and machines that Bradbury considered central to serious writing in the 1950s. Stories and censors alike have the potential to be mechanized as weapons in a battle for cultural control.

In "Usher II," the censors are undone because they have risked ignorance by failing to cultivate the imagination through fantastic, fanciful, or speculative literature and, as such, this plot element reflects what the pulpy science fiction world felt like to Bradbury and his like-minded cohort. And yet, the risks of science fiction going mainstream and gaining literary respectability also presented their own concerns. Perhaps this can best be seen by a response to the story that appeared in the pulp magazine in which the story was first printed. One reader, a budding science fiction writer from New York, Betsy Curtis, wrote a reply—"The Verse One"— that included a clever doggerel in which she imagines a future student looking back for the work of Bradbury from this era. In the spirit of Bradbury and Poe, the poem begins with an echo of "The Raven" and then addresses questions of censorship and the wages of becoming part of "mainstream" literary culture. Curtis claims that no fire was needed to purify the earth, "For we have schools and noted lecturers / To disinfect our swift-maturing minds" (155).

She goes on to describe a world in which literature is deadened and dulled through canonization, where works and authors are noted, cited, but unread. Her dream actually commends the student of the future who would truly know Bradbury to read his works in the old pulp magazines with the outlandish covers (155). Curtis offers an epistemological critique of Bradbury's scheme of literary censorship, erasure, and revenge: We might call it a proto-Wiki-ization of the literary, the reduction of literary knowledge to superficial citation and "quotation typical." Curtis locates the denaturing of fantastic literature in which science fiction came to maturity, not in its incineration but in predatory and superficial modes of reading. Curtis suggests, despite all the canonical invocations in "Usher II," that Mars becomes a spatial figure for an equally remote and marginal location: the pulp magazine at the very moment its cargo was becoming mainstream.

But whether literary vitality is denatured through censorship or rote learning, Bradbury's vision of Poe retains a volatile element that abides in the cultural discourses of science, of which fiction is one crucial plank. Literature, like science itself, has the power to be weaponized, and Mars and all that it represents is an apt space for such literary colonization—a space in which authors and the plots they have made famous become mechanical proxies in ongoing culture wars. The mechanization of the literary imagination can take place, it turns out, in the robotic minds of students and teachers. It is inevitable that a story like Bradbury's "Usher II," which attempts to include all the threads of Poe's imaginative gambits, would present a complex and ambiguous picture of that legacy. "Usher II," as a literary compendium set on Mars, wrestles then with the double-edged legacy of Poe's multidimensional, polygeneric science fiction, its currents and countercurrents, its capacity for creative inspiration, and its cautions about the dangers of the imagination.

Anthology Fictions

What, then, might this mean for the history of science fiction anthologies and their usage of Poe? By rebuilding and then destroying once more Poe's "House of Usher," Bradbury's "Usher II" transforms that gothic space from one that contained the secrets of Roderick and Madeline Usher into one that housed an array of characters from Poe's tales (as well as those from the works of Lewis Carroll and L. Frank Baum), programmed to reenact the most murderous and terrifying aspects of the plots in which they were originally designed. In so doing, Bradbury has conscripted Poe into the Cold War imaginary of the atomic age, in which the outcome is a mutually assured destruction between the agents of censorship and the allied agents of imaginative license. The final image of the story depicts Stendahl helicoptering away, watching the house crack and collapse as his co-conspirator, Pikes, intones the final sentence of Poe's tale; both stories, the gothic original and its Martian double, entwined in a shared oblivion. "Usher II" is not only an anthology of Poe's fictions; it is an anthology fiction, that is to say, a fiction that presents the reader with the literary anthology as a powerful weapon in a war of words and as a self-consuming artifact. "Usher II" no longer merely contemplates the extent to which Poe's works presage or fit into the paradigms of twentieth-century science fiction; rather, it deploys science fiction's topoi (Mars) and technology (rockets and robots) to mobilize Poe's work in a literary battle in which the partisans of censorship *and* the libraries of gorgeous imagination are destroyed. Perhaps this is what Bradbury meant to contemplate in using literature to think through the problem of man and machines. Bradbury's tale offers such an ambiguous message—Poe's limit cases of terror come most alive when realized as a part of a spectacle of destruction—but it is hardly transcendent, even on Mars. Furthermore, the fact that literary characters have been transformed into robots suggests that Poe and the agents of imagination have become part of an apparatus, the intellectual machinery of a culture war, and that anthologies of imaginative literature, on some level, cannot escape that potential use.

Anthologies are tools of potential canonization, and if they succeed, then they carry with them the challenges of cultural authority. Like the house of Usher's collapse, one senses the end of an era being signaled in "Usher II"—this is what Betsy Curtis picked up on. The threat of rote learning and the reduction of great authors to their CliffNotes versions remains part and parcel of the cultural imprimatur that comes with canonical status. Mainstream acceptance, for all its benefits, seldom matches the subcultural ferment from which literary movements spring forth. "Usher II" and the 1950s marked the end of the pulp ghetto where happy bohemian consumers and practitioners of science fiction in *Amazing Wonder Stories* could read intently and write with verve and energy. Science fiction was going to have to find a new oppositional politics, new literary marketplaces, and new bohemias from which to launch itself. That future needed to be imagined, as well, and it is part of Poe's lasting vitality as an author and a literary figure that he could continue to serve in some measure as both a canonical and a bohemian/outsider figure in this ongoing enterprise. The appearance of academic anthologies of science fiction in the 1960s and 1970s signaled that the mainstream acceptance had already happened and that Poe's place in it was safely a matter of scholarly debate. But in a moment of white heat in the late 1940s and early 1950s, that strange anthology fiction that is Bradbury's re-vision of "Usher" was a turning point, and Poe's corpus was the agent of destruction and creation from which a new science fictional world might emerge.

Notes

1. We can contrast the anthology-function with Michel Foucault's author-function, which argues that authors are posited as unifying fields for all the various thoughts and works that an author might have produced, imposing a unifying coherence on a multiform oeuvre.

2. Most genres are propelled by seminal works, but science fiction has been shaped by seminal works and multi-authored collections. The multi-authored works under consideration in this chapter are Phil Stong's edited volume, *The Other Worlds: 25 Modern Stories of Mystery or Imagination*; J. O. Bailey's scholarly study, *Pilgrims Through Space and Time*; and Hugo Gernsback's pulp magazine, *Amazing Stories*. Science fiction annuals played a role in this process as well, but they do not come under consideration here because they made little use of Poe and because they flourished after the establishment of the genre with Hugo and Nebula Awards in the 1950s and 60s. It is worth noting that the first single-issue magazine dedicated exclusively to speculation about the future was Millicent W. Shinn's *The Overland Monthly* for June 1890, which took inspiration from Edward Bellamy's socialist speculative fiction, *Looking Backward* (1888), and published a translated excerpt of the German speculative fiction of Kurd Laßwitz.

3. On the paperback revolution, see Warren French's "The First Year of the Paperback Revolution." While paperback printing had existed since the 1830s, the "revolutionary" development of mass-market paperback novels in the United States generally dates to June 1939 with the introduction of "Pocket Books" by publisher Robert Fair de Graff. Pocket Books first published mainstream best-sellers, previously only available in hardback, in inexpensive, easily portable paper editions. They soon branched out into other genres, such as mysteries. Their popularity was unprecedented and transformed the market. *The Pocket Book of Science Fiction* first appeared in 1943.

4. There are some exceptions, in particular those anthologies of new works that happen to engage directly with Poe's tales. See, for example, Phil Stong's *The Other Worlds*.

5. The intensity in science fiction's ongoing attempts to define its generic differences arose in part from strong fan communities that developed through magazine readership from the 1920s onward and the need for these groups to differentiate themselves from one another and to define this multifaceted genre in ways that suited their interests. The *Science Fiction Encyclopedia* contains a detailed entry on "Terminology" with several clusters of terms to distinguish one form of science fiction from another (e.g., Cyberpunk, Dystopias, Game-Worlds, Genre SF, Hard SF, Science Fantasy, Scientific Romance, Scientifiction, Soft SF, Steampunk). This includes a distinction between "SF" and "sci-fi" as designations for science fiction, "SF" being the preferred term of "insiders" and "sci-fi" being a term used by journalists.

6. See my article, "From 'Al Aaraaf' to the Universe of Stars."

7. For a discussion of the contents of this early Spanish edition, see Margarita Rigal-Aragón's "A Historical Approach to the Translation of Poe's Narrative Works in Spain" in *Translated Poe* (14).

8. Despite the myriad trends that have become parts of science fiction, this strain is still quite durable. Witness the lengths that Andy Weir, author of *The Martian*, went to crowd-source his novel so that it might be based on the best current scientific and engineering principles.

9. Campbell's *Astounding Science Fiction* was a seminal anthology in its own right, and it ran through several editions.

10. "Romancing the Shadow" is the title of the second chapter of Toni Morrison's *Playing in the Dark*, a chapter she begins with a trenchant analysis of Poe's *Pym*. Following Morrison's lead, J. Gerald Kennedy and Liliane Weissberg use this same title for their edited volume on Poe and race.

11. For another perspective on Beaver's *The Science Fiction of Edgar Allan Poe* as the most academic of Poe's popular anthologies in Britain, see Christopher Rollason's chapter 14 in this volume.

12. "Usher II" was first published in the April 1950 issue of *Thrilling Wonder Stories*.

13. Wertham's influential attack on comics appeared in the *Saturday Review of Literature* in May 1948. The House Un-American Activities Committee (HUAC) was a standing congressional committee from 1945 to 1975, achieving its greatest influence between 1947 and 1950 with investigations of Soviet spies Alger Hiss and Whittaker Chambers and the summoning of several Hollywood actors, writers, and directors.

Works Cited

Bailey, J. O. *Pilgrims Through Space and Time: Trends and Patterns in Scientific and Utopian Fiction.* Argus Books, 1946.

Barlow, Aaron. "Loss in the Language of Tomorrow: Journey Through Tucson on the Way to 'Usher II.'" *Orbiting Ray Bradbury's Mars: Biographical, Anthropological, Literary Perspectives,* edited by Gloria McMillian, McFarland, 2011, pp. 105–16.

Bradbury, Ray. "Usher II." *The Martian Chronicles,* Doubleday, 1950, pp. 137–56.

Conklin, Edward Groff, editor. *The Best of Science Fiction.* Crown Publishers, 1946.

Curtis, Betsy. "The Verse One." *Thrilling Wonder Stories,* Vol. 36, no. 2, June 1950, p. 155.

Elmer, Jonathan. *Reading at the Social Limit: Affect, Mass Culture, and Edgar Allan Poe.* Stanford UP, 1995.

Foucault, Michel. "What is an Author?" *Language, Counter-Memory, Practice,* edited by Donald F. Bouchard, Cornell UP, 1979, pp. 113–38.

Franklin, H. Bruce, editor. *Future Perfect: American Science Fiction of the Nineteenth Century: An Anthology.* Rutgers UP, 1995.

French, Warren. "The First Year of the Paperback Revolution." *College English*, vol. 25, no. 4, 1964, pp. 255–60.

Gernsback, Hugo. "A New Sort of Magazine." *Amazing Stories*, vol. 1, no. 1, April 1926, p. 3.

Grimstad, Paul. "Poe and Science Fiction." *The Oxford Handbook of Edgar Allan Poe*, edited by J. Gerald Kennedy and Scott Peeples, Oxford UP, 2019, pp. 735–51.

Gunn, James. "From the Pulps to the Classroom: The Strange Journey of Science Fiction." *The Science Fiction Reference Book*, edited by Marshall B. Tymn, Starmont House, 1981, pp. 233–45.

Morrison, Toni. *Playing in the Dark: Whiteness and the Literary Imagination*. Harvard UP, 1992.

Moskowitz, Sam, editor. *The Man Who Called Himself Poe*. Doubleday, 1969.

"Mr. Poe's Eureka." *Home Journal*, 12 August 1848, p. 3. Edgar Allan Poe Society of Baltimore, www.eapoe.org/papers/misc1827/hj480812.htm.

Mujica, Barbara. "Teaching Literature: Canon, Controversy, and the Literary Anthology." *Hispania*, vol. 80, no. 2, May 1997, pp. 203–15.

Poe, Edgar Allan. "The Colloquy of Monos and Una." *Collected Works of Edgar Allan Poe, Volume II: Tales and Sketches, 1831–1842*, edited by Thomas Ollive Mabbott, Harvard UP, 1978, pp. 607–19.

———. *Eureka: A Prose Poem*. George P. Putnam, 1848.

———. *The Science Fiction of Edgar Allan Poe*, edited by Harold Lowther Beaver, Penguin, 1976.

———. "Sonnet—To Science." *Collected Works of Edgar Allan Poe, Volume I: Poems*, edited by Thomas Ollive Mabbott, Harvard UP, 1969, pp. 90–92.

Rachman, Stephen. "From 'Al Aaraaf' to the Universe of Stars." *Edgar Allan Poe Review*, vol. 15, no. 1, 2014, pp. 1–19. doi:10.5325/edgallpoerev.15.1.0001.

———. "Poe, Annotation, and the Other." *Symbolism*, vol. 15, 2015, pp. 21–35. doi.org/10.1515/9783110449075.

———. "Rectangular Obscenities: Poe, Taste, and Entertainment." *Approaches to Teaching Poe's Prose and Poetry*, edited by Jeffrey Andrew Weinstock and Tony Magistrale, MLA, 2008, pp. 88–96.

Rigal-Aragón, Margarita. "A Historical Approach to the Translation of Poe's Narrative Works in Spain." *Translated Poe*, edited by Emron Esplin and Margarida Vale de Gato, Lehigh UP, 2014, pp. 13–23, 339–44.

Schmidt, Michael. *The Novel: A Biography*. Harvard UP, 2014.

Smith, Charles Alphonso. *Edgar Allan Poe: How to Know Him*. Bobbs-Merrill, 1921.

Stong, Phil, editor. *The Other Worlds: 25 Modern Stories of Mystery or Imagination*. Garden City Publishing Co., 1942.

"Terminology." *SFE: The Science Fiction Encyclopedia*. www.sf-encyclopedia.com/entry/terminology.

"Ticket to the Moon: A Biography in Sound." *Ticket to the Moon: A Biography in Sound*, NBC, 4 December 1956. https://www.youtube.com/watch?v=gFvAbX5tHeY.

Truesdale, Dave. "Interview with Donald A. Wollheim." Tangent Online, May 1975. https://tangentonline.com/interviews-columnsmenu-166/interviews-columns-menu-166-interviews-columnsmenu-166/classic-donald-a-wollheim-interview/.

Weir, Andy. *The Martian*. Crown Publishing, 2014.

Wells, H. G. "Popularising Science." *Nature*, vol. 50, no. 1291, 26 July 1894, pp. 300–1. https://doi.org/10.1038/050300a0.

Wertham, Frederic. "The Comics . . . Very Funny!." *Saturday Review of Literature*, 29 May 1948, pp. 6–14.

Wollheim, David A., editor. *The Pocket Book of Science Fiction*. Pocket Books Inc., 1943.

∼

CHAPTER TEN

Edgar Allan Poe and the Codifying and Anthologizing of Detective Fiction

John Gruesser

I tell you, my friend, that if a detailed account of that silent contest could be written, it would take its place as the most brilliant bit of thrust-and-parry work in the history of detection.

—Arthur Conan Doyle ("The Final Problem")

Edgar Allan Poe wrote five tales that scholars have categorized as detective stories, as well as a sixth one that is sometimes designated as such.[1] Three of these constitute a trilogy featuring the Parisian sleuth C. Auguste Dupin—"The Murders in the Rue Morgue," published in the April 1841 issue of *Graham's Magazine*; "The Mystery of Marie Rogêt," published in the November 1842, December 1842, and February 1843 issues of *The Ladies' Companion*; and "The Purloined Letter," published in *The Gift* for 1845, an annual gift book available in late 1844. Two others have likewise been classified as tales of detection—"The Gold-Bug," a story featuring a map in code leading to buried pirate treasure, published in the June 21 and June 28, 1843, issues of the Philadelphia *Dollar Newspaper*, and the humorous tale "Thou Art the Man," a piece in which a corpse appears to identify the murderer, published in the November 1844 issue of *Godey's Lady's Book*. An additional fiction that predates the others, "The Man of the Crowd," published in the December 1840 issues of both *Burton's Gentleman's Magazine* and *The Casket*, has been seen as a proto-detective story because, although the narrator shadows an old man he associates with "deep crime," the conclusion provides no resolution.[2]

Similar to Benjamin Franklin, who never used the word autobiography and yet has been credited with producing its first true, first modern, and first secular iteration, Poe has long been regarded as the originator of modern detection despite the fact that the word "detective" cannot be found in any of his writings. Rather, in a letter to Philip P. Cooke on August 9, 1846, he referred to his Dupin stories as "tales of ratiocination":

> These tales of ratiocination owe most of their popularity to being something in a new key. I do not mean to say that they are not ingenious—but people think them more ingenious than they are on account of their method and *air* of method. In the "Murders in the Rue Morgue," for instance, where is the ingenuity of unravelling a web which you yourself (the author) have woven for the express purpose of unravelling? (*Collected Letters* 1: 595)

Significantly, Poe refers here to multiple stories with shared characteristics. Roughly fifty years later, writers, critics, and anthologists would make the case for detective fiction as a distinct genre with established conventions, and they would credit Poe with initiating it.

Detective fiction anthologies only began to appear after detection had become recognized as a distinct and legitimate literary genre and after Poe had been acknowledged as a major world writer who had made indispensable contributions to several forms of writing. The first section of this chapter addresses the initial references to detection in print, as well as early collections featuring Poe's detective fiction. The second section concerns early critical discussions of detection, the first anthologies devoted exclusively to detective fiction, collections for children, and Poe's place in such works.

First Mentions of the New Genre and Early Collections of Poe's Detection

Prior to the 1840s, the only comparable word for detective was "thief-taker," a term appearing as early as 1535 and defined by Dr. Johnson as "one whose business is to detect thieves and bring them to justice" (Bendel-Simso and Panek 40; "thief-, taker, n.,"; Johnson 932). In 1829, Britain's Home Secretary, Robert Peel, established the first official "police" force in London, although the word itself, in the sense of a government department "concerned with maintaining order . . . and enforcing the law," dates from the 1740s (Queen, "The Detective" 477; "police, n."). In the mid-1830s, periodicals used "Vidocq," the name of the founder of the French department of criminal investigation, the Sûreté, to describe a pursuer of criminals (Bendel-Simso and Panek 171). According to the *Oxford English Dictionary*, the word "detective" first appeared as an adjective in 1843 ("detective, adj. and n.") and, as early as 1844, Irish newspapers used the term as a noun to refer to members of the plainclothes police force in the British colony, with several articles denouncing their unscrupulous practices.[3] In 1850, Charles Dickens published three true-crime "'Detective' Anecdotes" (the second of which was entitled "The Artful Touch—A Detective Story"), and during the 1850s and 1860s, British and American periodicals published "pseudo-biographical notebook stories" (Panek 178)—fictions masquerading as autobiographical accounts by policemen, detectives, and lawyers. An item about crime in India in the June 6, 1857, issue of the *Hereford Times* referred to "Edgar Poe's detective stories" ("Gleanings"), and two years later a review of Wilkie Collins's collection *The Queen of Hearts* in the October 20, 1859, issue of the London *Morning Post* identified four of the tales as belonging to a "detective school" that the reviewer connected with Poe. Shortly thereafter, the phrases "Detective's Story" and "Detective Story" (with or without a hyphen between the two words) began to be used as subtitles for American periodical fiction: Harry Harewood Leech's "The Robbery of Plate: A Detective's Story" appeared in the December 17, 1859, issue of *The Flag of Our Union*, a weekly newspaper that printed several of Poe's writings in 1849, and John B. Williams's "The Tell-Tale Signature: A Detective Story," whose main title evokes Poe's "The Tell-Tale Heart," was published in the April 22, 1860, issue of the *Memphis Daily Appeal* after appearing in *The Family Journal*.

Poe's detective tales were reprinted in book or pamphlet form on two occasions during his lifetime in the United States and with increasing frequency following his death. *The Prose Romances of Edgar A. Poe*, which appeared in 1843, included "The Murders in the Rue Morgue"; meanwhile, Poe's *Tales*, brought out by Wiley and Putnam in 1845 and comprising a dozen stories, began with "The Gold-Bug" and concluded with the three Dupin stories and "The Man of the Crowd." Because it was the first collection to contain the complete trilogy, Ellery Queen declared *Tales* "the first important book of detective stories, the first and the greatest, the cornerstone of cornerstones in any readers' or collectors' guide, the highest of all highspots" (*Queen's Quorum* 11). Shortly after his death, Poe's detection was reissued (interspersed among his other fiction rather than as a unit, although the Dupin stories were grouped together) in the first two volumes of *The Works of the Late Edgar Allan Poe* (1850), edited by Rufus Griswold. Two years later, "Rue Morgue," "Marie Rogêt," "The Purloined Letter," and "The Gold-Bug" appeared in *Tales of Mystery, Imagination and Humour; and Poems*, published in London by Henry Vizetelly, along with four other stories and twenty-six unattributed illustrations—eight inspired by "The Gold-Bug," four by "Marie Rogêt," two by "Rue Morgue," and one by "The Purloined Letter."

According to Burton R. Pollin's *Images of Poe's Works: A Comprehensive Descriptive Catalogue of Illustrations*, "The Gold-Bug" has inspired more illustrations than any other Poe text by a wide margin, with "The Murders in the Rue Morgue" accruing the second highest total, followed by "The Fall of the House of Usher" and "The Raven."[4] In addition to its comparatively high word count and its immediate, widespread, and sustained popularity, "The Gold-Bug" has attracted illustrators because of its appeal to juvenile and adult audiences and its unique combination of elements, including detection, adventure, cryptography, local color, and (minstrel show–type) humor. Over six decades before American pulp magazines such as *Detective Story* and *Black Mask* featured sensational cover images of crime scenes, the illustrated paper over boards of Vizetelly's 1852 selection of Poe's writings depicted the ape killing the two women in "The Murders in the Rue Morgue." Later the same year, the publisher brought out a second volume under the same name, *Tales of Mystery, Imagination and Humour* (dropping "Poems" from the end of the title this time) that included "Thou Art the Man" (and one illustration inspired by that story).

In 1857, "The Purloined Letter" appeared in *Stories for the Home Circle*, the final volume of Putnam's Story Library series, the other four being *The Modern Story-Teller; The Baked Head, and Other Tales; Stories of Christmas and Winter Evenings;* and *Sea Stories.* In a short preface, George Palmer Putnam expresses some reservations about the *Home Circle* tales, which include one other detective story, humorous pieces, and historical fiction, most of which were originally published in British periodicals: "This selection of Stories is not entirely in accordance with the publisher's view of fitness. A thoroughly 'good story'—good in all respects—is more rare than many would suppose. This volume comprises, however, several of more than ordinary merit, as 'Fugitive Tales,'—sufficient, it is hoped, to overshadow the faults and deficiencies of the rest."[5] With one key exception, the Story Library series does not identify the writer of any of the tales, including Poe's "MS. Found in a Bottle," which is included in *Sea Stories.* This makes all the more conspicuous the fact that the second and final paragraph of the Putnam preface to the *Home Circle* volume states, "the Story of 'THE PURLOINED LETTER' is taken by permission from Poe's works." In 1864, Jules Verne published "Edgard Poe et ses oeuvres," which, while summarizing several of the tales, offered some critical commentary. Notably, he declared, in connection with "The Gold-Bug": "In my opinion, it is the most remarkable of all of these extraordinary stories, the one in which is revealed to the highest degree what is now called the *Poe* genre" (202).[6] In 1875, Houghton reprinted "The Gold-Bug" in the collection *Stories of Fortune*, along with fictions by Edward Everett Hale, Nathaniel Hawthorne, and three other authors, none of which are detective stories. In 1879, the London firm Chatto and Windus issued *The Mystery of Marie Rogêt and Other Tales*, and, during the 1880s and the 1890s, publishers in the United States and Great Britain issued collections of Poe's writings under such titles as *The Murders in the Rue Morgue and Other Tales*, *The Murders in the Rue Morgue and Other Tales of Mystery*, *The Murders in the Rue Morgue and Other Stories*, *The Gold-Bug and Other Tales*, and *The Gold-Bug, The Purloined Letter, and Other Tales*—none of which were exclusively devoted to detective fiction. With the exception of the latter, which comprises only four tales, they group the Dupin stories together, typically including "The Gold-Bug" and sometimes "The Man of the Crowd" and/or "Thou Art the Man."

Indeed, following Poe's death several decades would elapse before detection came to be codified as a literary genre and Poe received widespread acknowledgment for his indispensable contributions to it.[7] Anthologies could not and did not appear until detection became recognized as a separate and legitimate genre. This only happened during the 1890s in the wake of the tremendous popularity of the Sherlock Holmes stories. An admirer of Poe's fiction and poems from his youth, Arthur Conan Doyle, who published a story in 1883 in which a ghost declares himself the "embodiment" of Poe (Sims 29, 74–75), frequently acknowledged his profound debt to the author of "Rue Morgue." In fact, in staging the first meeting of John Watson and Sherlock Holmes in *A Study in Scarlet*, he explicitly evokes his American forerunner:

> "You remind me of Edgar Allan Poe's Dupin. I had no idea that such individuals did exist outside of stories."
>
> Sherlock Holmes rose and lit his pipe. "No doubt you think that you are complimenting me in comparing me to Dupin," he observed. "Now, in my opinion, Dupin was a very inferior fellow. That trick of his of breaking in on his friend's thoughts with an apropos remark after a quarter of an hour's silence is really very showy and superficial. He had some analytical genius, no doubt; but he was by no means such a phenomenon as Poe appeared to imagine." (31)

Furthermore, in the novella's concluding passage (which explains its title), Doyle, in another nod to Poe (who uses not only the word "unravel" but also "disentangle" in connection with detection),[8] portrays Holmes employing weaving imagery to characterize the solving of crimes: "Why shouldn't we use a little art jargon? There's a scarlet thread of murder running through the colorless skein of life, and our duty is to unravel it and isolate it and expose every inch of it" (67). This early Holmes story, in which the protagonist and Watson discuss Dupin at their very first meeting, thus popularized both Poe and crime fiction. A review in the *Scotsman* described it as being "as entrancing a tale of ingenuity in tracing out crime as has been written since the time of Edgar Allan Poe" (qtd. in Sims 156–57), indicating that by the late 1880s critics had begun to conceive of detection as a genre with an identifiable lineage.

The delayed but, by the end of the nineteenth century, unstoppable recognition of Poe as a major writer with a profound and sustained influence abroad and at home coincided with and contributed to the coalescing of detection into a discrete literary genre meriting its own anthologies. In volume 3 of *The Works of Edgar Allan Poe* (1894–95), Edmund Clarence Stedman and George Edward Woodberry published "The Gold-Bug," the Dupin tales, and "Thou Art the Man" under the heading Tales of Ratiocination. Stedman's "Memoir" in volume 1 ascribes the founding of detection to Poe: "His first success [at *Graham's Magazine*] was the tale of 'The Murders in the Rue Morgue,' which appeared in the number for April, 1841, the first of his editing. He had been led to this new ratiocinative vein, perhaps, by his studies in cryptography, which he had kept up; and he continued to work it, becoming thereby the father of the modern detective novel" (38). Moreover, in the same volume's "Introduction to the Tales," Stedman not only refers to Poe's "detective-stories" (101) and notes their influence in "France, England, and America" but also asserts that "no amateur, with a genius approximating that of 'Monsieur C. Auguste Dupin,' has appeared, and had his exploits recounted, in our own or foreign literature" (119).

In 1900, Street & Smith published *Detective Tales*, the first collection exclusively devoted to Poe's detection, and a year later reprinted it under the title *The Detective Tales of Edgar Allan Poe* as part of its Magnet Detective Library. In the one-page preface, George A. Seaman, "The Compiler" of the volume, states that he "has endeavored to present not only the wonderful detective tales of Edgar Allan Poe, which so amazed the public at the time they were written, but has also aimed to lead the reader through the intricate methods of calculation employed to reach the conclusions" (n.p.) To accomplish the latter, he augments the Dupin trilogy with not only "The Gold-Bug," which, by dissolving "the hypothetical into the material calculation," provides "the connecting link between the assumed and the actual analysis," but also "Cryptography" (aka "Secret Writing"), Poe's December 1841 *Graham's Magazine* article embracing "the very essence of the detective instinct" (n.p.) Seaman's decision to omit the comic "Thou Art the Man" and include "Cryptography" might be seen as an effort to present detection as a serious genre.

In 1904, McClure, Phillips & Co. brought out *Monsieur Dupin: The Detective Tales of Edgar Allan Poe* with the same selections as those appearing in Stedman and Woodberry's edition of *Works*, accompanied by eight illustrations by Charles Raymond Macauley and a twelve-page introduction by McClure's literary advisor, William Aspinwall Bradley (who, the next year, published a book on William Cullen Bryant in which Poe figures significantly). This introduction to *Monsieur Dupin* deserves to be better known because of when it appeared and what it says about Poe and detection. Bradley acknowledges that his anthology comprises the five tales that Stedman and Woodberry were the first to group together under the heading "tales of ratiocination," but he explains that he has changed the sequence in order to "throw emphasis upon the stories as detective stories and upon the character of M. C. Auguste Dupin" by presenting the Parisian trilogy first, followed by "Thou Art the Man" and "The Gold-Bug" (iii). Of the author he states, echoing Stedman, "Poe is universally recognized as the father of the detective story. He was the first to perceive the literary possibilities of that form of mental activity involved in the ferreting out by the sleuths of the law, from dark clues and apparently insufficient data, the secrets of baffling and mysterious crimes" (iv). Bradley distinguishes Poe's tales from the crime stories that preceded them and describes the means by which he wrote them. Unlike the tales that appeared in *Blackwood's Magazine*, in which the "revelation of the guilty person" typically relies on "some strange accident or coincidence, some quasi-supernatural agency of nature or of conscience, wherein one seemed to detect the hand of God" (v), Poe's tales highlight ratiocination. As Bradley explains,

> his interest in the subject matter of criminology was of an entirely different order. For the murder itself he cared little, and for the moral issues and dramatic value even less; but when it was attended by circumstances that obscured the motive and the identity of the perpetrator, he was attracted as by a problem in chess or mathematics, and proceeded to frame a theory based upon the clues in the case and the general laws of chance. (vi)

Elaborating on Poe's methodology in composing his detection, Bradley adds, "And in the same way, but in reverse order, he would, failing an actual case, premise a set of clues and then proceed to induce from them, working backwards, a complete and elaborate fiction of his own invention. He had then only to eliminate the intermediate stages in the process, in order to have in all its essentials the basis of the modern detective story" (vi). Although the observation that Poe wrote his detective stories "backwards"—a notion that the author himself hints at in his letter to Cooke quoted earlier—would become a commonplace in criticism of the genre, it is worth noting that Bradley was apparently the first person to state it explicitly in print and to connect it with the method of ratiocination required of the detective tale.

All but ignoring "Thou Art the Man" and "The Gold-Bug" other than to note the "grotesque and extravagant" nature of the former and the "brilliant reasoning powers" showcased in the latter (iv), Bradley concentrates on the trilogy. Poe's primary purpose, he says, "was to create in Dupin a character who should embody in its highest degree the power of the human intellect to proceed from the slightest clues and the 'faintest prominences above the plane of the ordinary,' to use his own phrase, to the penetration of the most remote and baffling mystery" (ix). According to Bradley, Poe regarded "The Murders in the Rue Morgue" (which introduces "the talented amateur" Dupin) "merely as a character study" and "The Mystery of Marie Rogêt" as "an indication of the manner in which his own methods might be applied, not only to a fictitious set of circumstances carefully arranged to yield to the pressure of the key for which the lock had been constructed, but to an actual case that had occurred in New York and in which the mystery had remained unsolved" (ix–x). Conceding, as so many (but by no means all) critics have done, that Dupin's second outing "is somewhat of a disappoint-ment" on account of its less than satisfactory denouement, Bradley reserves his highest praise for "The Purloined Letter." The "masterpiece of the series," which "has, indeed, and with reason, been called the best detective story ever written," the finale "is less an essay in inductive analysis and more of a story than either of the others," and it succeeds because "the solution is reached by means that are really startling in their ease, simplicity and naturalness" (x–xi).

Bradley concludes with a discussion of Poe's considerable influence on modern literature generally and detection in particular and, in doing so, he places detective fiction among the established contemporary literary genres. He claims, with incredible prescience, that "all owe to him [Poe] more than will ever be realized, until the history of our age has been completely written a hundred years hence" (xiii). In view of "this larger indebtedness of the whole of the art of our time to Poe's genius," Bradley observes, "the fact of his having originated the form of the detective story seems a matter of relatively slight significance" (xiii); however, he does not fail to note that the genre has entered the modern canon: "the persistence of the form throughout a century, and the vitality which it still exhibits in our own day, prove its right to be regarded as one of the types of modern literature, like the sea story or the novel of manners" (xiii). In particular, Bradley lauds detection for its ability to convert "one phase of our complex social life, a phase in itself sufficiently sordid, into the material for romance" (xiii), echoing a key contention made in G. K. Chesterton's vigorous "In Defence of Detective Stories" (to be discussed below) three years earlier. Bradley's high praise of Poe reflects a change in attitudes that was in full swing during the early 1900s. After decades of mixed feelings about the writer and his legacy, scholars and the general public in the United States embraced Poe at the start of the twentieth century, initiating a love affair that reached a peak in celebrations of the hundredth anniversary of his birth in 1909. The appreciation of Poe has grown exponentially ever since, and that is amply reflected in the prominence granted to the writer in twentieth- and twenty-first century anthologies.[9]

Early Anthologies and the Codification of Detective Fiction

In the wake of the enormous success of Doyle's short stories featuring Sherlock Holmes that appeared in *The Strand* in the early 1890s, steps were taken on both sides of the Atlantic to delineate, defend, organize, and popularize detective fiction through the publication of articles, introductions, collections, and anthologies, resulting in the construction of a genealogy for the genre. Scholars, editors, and collectors were joined by writers in an effort to specify what detection was, when it arose, how it developed, who made significant contributions to it, and why it deserved to be read and studied. Multi-author anthologies began to appear at the turn of the twentieth century, and Edgar Allan Poe received credit for founding the form and influencing French and English authors, and, through them, American detective and mystery writers.

The recognition of Poe's founding role in creating the detective genre served to promote his image as a great American writer. 1895 saw the publication, in London, of *The Long Arm and Other Detective Stories*, detection's "earliest legitimate anthology" (Queen, "The Detective" 489), that is, the first collection of detective stories by more than one contemporary writer. In 1906, the New York publisher Collier issued the first retrospective anthology, *Great Short Stories: A New Collection of Famous Examples from France, England and America, Vol. I: Detective Stories*, which begins with Poe. The other volumes in the series, likewise edited by William Patten and devoted to "Ghost Stories and Romance & Adventure," contain no additional stories by Poe. Besides the Dupin trilogy, volume 1 includes a novella and a tale by Doyle (*The Sign of the Four* and "A Scandal in Bohemia"), the four-story cycle *The Rajah's Diamonds* by Robert Louis Stevenson, and one selection each by Anna Katharine Green, Broughton Brandenburg, and B. Fletcher Robinson. None of the *Great Short Stories* volumes has a preface or introduction, but Patten provides a headnote for each literary text. In the one for "The Murders in the Rue Morgue," he states that "[j]udged by the extent of his influence on writers of short stories, both here and abroad, Poe is the most important figure in American literature" (4), and, in the headnote for "The Purloined Letter," he quotes the high praise bestowed on the final installment of the series by the critics Edmund Clarence Stedman and Brander Matthews. The following year, another New York firm, Review of Reviews, published a second retrospective anthology, *Library of the World's Best Mystery and Detective Stories, Vol. I: America*, with a preface by the editor, Julian Hawthorne, entitled "Riddle Stories," in which "The Gold-Bug" was reprinted. Magazine pieces with advice on writing detection began appearing in the first decade of the twentieth century,[10] and after a lull during the 1910s, anthologies of detective fiction appeared with increasing frequency in the 1920s and have continued to do so ever since.

Because of its well-established appeal to juvenile readers, publishers frequently reprinted "The Gold-Bug" in the early 1900s, both as stand-alone volumes (often with explanatory notes, maps, illustrations, and glosses in footnotes or separate glossaries) and in anthologies for children. The subject of illustrations for "The Gold-Bug" deserves a much more detailed examination than can be offered here. It is not only fascinating because of the long history and large number of images inspired by the story, but also disturbing because of the frequent use of minstrel-show clichés (bug-eyes, exaggerated gestures, over-the-top emotionalism, etc.) to depict the ex-slave Jupiter and the tendency to relegate this Africanist character to the margins or the shadows so that his face is hidden, featureless, or indecipherable because of the lighting (or lack thereof).[11] Thus, one effect of an anthology (especially one for children) can be the inculcation and reinforcement of racist ideology.

The opening decades of the twentieth century were also notable for criticism on and apologies for the detective genre.[12] In his influential "In Defence of Detective Stories" (1901), G. K. Chesterton pronounces the genre "the earliest and only form of popular literature in which is expressed some sense of the poetry of modern life" (119) because its typically urban setting is "more poetic even than a countryside" (120) and its crime solving hero engages in "successful knight-errantry" (123).[13] Brander Matthews published a major statement, "Poe and the Detective Story," in the September 1907 number of *Scribner's Magazine*, which heaps praise on Poe for 1) focusing attention on "the unravelling of the tangled skein rather than on the knot itself" (289), 2) adding the Greek chorus-like narrator to the equation (291), 3) doing something "wholly different" in each of the three stories, "The Murders in the Rue Morgue," "The Gold-Bug," and "The Purloined Letter" (292), 4) bringing his poetic imagination to the form (293), and 5) "accomplish[ing] the first time of trying that which others have failed to achieve even after he had showed them how" (293).[14] Five years later, in an essay entitled "History of the Detective Story," University of South Carolina professor Reed Smith confidently declares, "Owing partly to its popularity and partly to the literary value of the work of Poe and Conan Doyle, the detective in fiction has become a personage of importance and has been investigated and written about from various viewpoints. Thanks to the work of previous investigators his literary genealogy is reasonably well known" (7). Smith's statement attests that the genre and its history were well established prior to the start of the First World War.

Led by Chesterton, who would go on to launch a series of stories about the sleuthing priest Father Brown beginning with "The Blue Cross" in 1910, writers of detection began playing a key role in codifying the form in the first two decades of the twentieth century and in editing anthologies of detective fiction in the 1920s and 1930s. Arthur Reeve, whose detective Craig Kennedy appeared in one hundred stories and novels beginning in 1910, wrote "In Defense of the Detective Story" for *The Independent* in 1913. The author of over seventy-five mystery novels, beginning with *The Clue* in 1909, Carolyn Wells published the first book-length study of the genre, *The Technique of the Detective Story* in 1913, which frequently mentions Poe. She went on to edit Oxford University Press's *American Detective Stories* in 1927.[15] Willard Huntington Wright, who amassed a collection of over two thousand works of crime writing in the early 1920s (Haycraft 33), published the first of twelve Philo Vance novels under the pen name S. S. Van Dine in 1926 and edited *The Great Detective Stories: A Chronological Anthology*, published by Scribner's in 1927. The following year, Dorothy Sayers, whose first novel featuring Lord Peter Wimsey appeared in 1923, edited *Great Short Stories of Detection, Mystery, and Horror* and brought out the first iteration of *The Omnibus of Crime* in 1929.

Like the anthologizers and critics who preceded them, the editors of 1920s collections, both established authors of detective stories and laypeople, credit Poe with founding the modern detective story. In doing so, they also build on the history of detection to be found in Reeve's "Defense of the Detective Story," which pays "tribute to the real founder of the modern mystery story" (91) and echoes an observation first made in the *New York Times* that "an American [Poe] took [the detective] into France and the French writers [Gaboriau and especially Fortune du Boisgobey through *The Crime of the Opera House*] sent him back to the land of his birth" (qtd. in Reeve 91).[16] In the 1926 anthology *Crime and Detection*, published by Oxford University Press, which begins with "The Murders in the Rue Morgue," the English critic E. M. Wrong declares that the genre "has proved capable of high development and has become a definite art" (31); he also distinguishes the Poe-Doyle amateur sleuth variety from the Wilkie Collins-Gaboriau police strain of detection (22). The next year, in his lengthy introduction to *The Great Detective Stories*, which also starts with Poe's "Rue Morgue," Wright distinguishes detection from the other types of "popular" or "light" forms—the romantic, adventure, and mystery novel—and traces its lineage from Poe to Charles Dickens and Collins, from these English writers to Gaboriau and du Boisgobey, from those French authors to the American Green and the Englishman Doyle, and from them to the modern practitioners.[17] Meanwhile, in the first *Omnibus of Crime*, Sayers distinguishes three types of detection that have been utilized by writers since the 1840s: "the Intellectual," "the Sensational," and "the Mixed," which she connects to Poe's "Marie Rogêt" (included in this anthology), "Rue Morgue," and "Purloined Letter," respectively.

In 1930, Sayers, Chesterton, Agatha Christie, Ronald Knox, and Baroness Orczy were among the founding members of the Detection Club, which propagated rules of "fair play" for writers. At roughly the same time that this influential group of authors was seeking to narrowly define and circumscribe the genre, American tough-guy writing was gaining prominence in pulp magazines. *Black Mask* was enormously influential, especially under the editorship of Joseph "Cap" Shaw, who nurtured the fiction of fledgling authors including Raymond Chandler as well as that of established writers such as Carroll John Daly and Dashiell Hammett from 1926 to 1936. Typically using first-person narration to focus on an independent, cynical, lower-middle-class private eye with a brash, idiosyncratic way of expressing himself, this new form of writing reached a high mark with Hammett's *The Maltese Falcon*, serialized in *Black Mask* from September 1929 through January 1930 and published in book form shortly thereafter. Assessing the genre of detective fiction at the middle of the twentieth century in his "Casual Notes on the Mystery Story," Chandler celebrated its "fluid" and "various" nature, the form's inherent ability, as he saw it, to defy "easy classification" (70). No fan of what he called the "deductive" variety of detection (69), Chandler, in his statement, takes aim, at least in part, at the previous generation of detective and mystery writers who, while actively participating in the effort to establish detective fiction as a bona fide literary genre with a history dating back to Poe through edited collections and critical assessments, sought to limit it by means of a rigid set of rules.

As a relatively recent literary form whose origin can be traced to a single author (Poe) and a precise moment in time (the early 1840s), detective fiction provides a unique opportunity to see how critics and writers, by means of anthologies, introductions, and essays, codified and created a genealogy for one of the most popular and influential types of literature. Just as Poe's reputation benefited from the recognition he received as "the father of the detective story" from scholars and writers at the turn of the twentieth century, so, too, did his newfound status as a major writer, with profound influence at home and abroad, aid and confer legitimacy on the efforts to establish detection as a distinct and significant literary genre, an enterprise in which anthologies played an indispensable role.

Notes

1. Thanks to Jeffrey Savoye, LeRoy Panek, David Schmid, and the editors of this volume for their helpful suggestions on this chapter.

2. In "The Limits of Reason," J. Gerald Kennedy refers to the narrator of "The Man of the Crowd" as a "deluded detective."

3. See, for example, "The Detectives."

4. An editor for several publications who had a long-held but never realized desire to launch his own monthly journal, Poe had definite ideas about illustrations, demanding that they be of "the highest order of art" and stipulating that those "only in obvious illustration of the text" be used ("Prospectus of the *Stylus*"). Felix Darley's images for the initial publication of "The Gold-Bug" in the Philadelphia *Dollar Newspaper* in June 1843 were among the handful of illustrations for texts by Poe published during his lifetime, and they have the distinction of being the only ones commissioned by Poe himself.

5. *The Oxford English Dictionary* defines "fugitive," when used in connection with "a literary composition," as follows: "Concerned or dealing with subjects of passing interest; ephemeral, occasional."

6. My translation.

7. The first story featuring Harlan Halsey's long-running dime novel detective Old Sleuth appeared in the *Fireside Companion* in 1872.

8. See the aforementioned letter to Cooke and "Rue Morgue."

9. Hoping to capitalize on the burgeoning interest in the author at the start of the twentieth century, D. W. Griffith made the highly fictionalized *Edgar Allen Poe* (1909), the title of which misspells Poe's middle name, apparently in the rush to distribute the movie so as to coincide with the centennial of the writer's birth. Reputed to be the first biographical film ever made, it conflates the composition of

"The Raven," published in 1845, and the death of Virginia Poe, which occurred in 1847, portraying the author as a tragic, impoverished, unappreciated genius, able to compose over a hundred lines of unforgettable poetry in a matter of seconds.

10. See, for example, M. Thornton Armstrong's "The Detective Story."

11. See Toni Morrison's discussion of the shadowy Africanist presence in white American literature in *Playing in the Dark: Whiteness and the Literary Imagination*.

12. In the October 1885 issue of the *Harvard Monthly*, C. O. Hurd published "The Logic of Poe's 'Murders in the Rue Morgue,'" apparently the first work of criticism devoted to Poe's detection which, perhaps because of its early date of appearance and its focus on a single story, had little or no impact. Hurd states, "the author's [Poe's] task now appears not one of clear and logical exposition, but rather that of clever mystification, and careful withholding of essential facts," and he emphasizes three logical failings in Poe's story (7).

13. In December 1905, "The Passing of the Detective," an anonymous essay appearing in *The Academy*, credits Poe with furnishing "[t]he germ of this fascinating personage" (1356) prior to announcing, rather prematurely, the figure's demise: "the regular [police] force has taken its revenge, and the lordly person who used to throw them his secrets, at whose feet they sat in awe, is beaten by the very weapons he taught them to use" (1357). "Art and the Detective," a November 1906 article in *The Living Age* by G. K. Chesterton's younger brother, Cecil, claims that although Poe lacks the French writer Emile Gaboriau's ingenuity and the Englishman Wilkie Collins's knack for characterization, "'The Purloined Letter' is imaginatively beyond the reach of any writer of this kind. And Dupin is more than a great detective, he is a great rationalistic philosopher, the incarnation of the logical and scientific conception of life" (507).

14. Although known primarily as a scholar who taught at Columbia University, Matthews contributed one of the pieces in *The Long Arm and Other Detective Stories* in 1895.

15. R. Austin Freeman, whose first Dr. Thorndyke mystery novel, *The Red Thumb Mark*, appeared in 1907, published an essay entitled "The Art of the Detective Story" (1924), discussing the form's popularity and structure, as well as the intellectual satisfaction it provides to readers.

16. In the foreword to *Masterpieces of Mystery: Detective Stories*, published by Doubleday in 1920, Joseph Lewis French echoes Reeve in stating, "The honor of founding the modern detective story belongs to an American writer [Poe]," asserts that the first and third Dupin tales "still stand unrivalled," and claims that Poe inspired both "the whole school of French detective story writers" and Arthur Conan Doyle, who, in turn, influenced "our American writers of to-day" (vii).

17. In the Modern Library anthology *Fourteen Great Detective Stories*, likewise published in 1927, Vincent Starrett addresses the genre's ability to "reach out and convert its millions," attributing detection's popularity to the "latent criminal" within readers that "is more than balanced by the instinct to support the rule of order" (ix, x). The following year, in the essay "The Detective Story," Valentine

Williams avers that only four writers—Vidocq, Poe, Gaboriau, and Doyle—deserve credit for contributing to the technique of detective writing.

Works Cited

Armstrong, M. Thornton. "The Detective Story." *The Editor*, vol. 23, 1906, pp. 218–19.

Bendel-Simso, Mary, and LeRoy Lad Panek. *The Essential Elements of the Detective Story*. McFarland, 2017.

Bradley, William Aspinwell. Introduction. *Monsieur Dupin: The Detective Tales of Edgar Allan Poe*, McClure, 1904, pp. iii–xiv.

Chandler, Raymond. "Casual Notes on the Mystery Story." 1949. *Raymond Chandler Speaking*, edited by Dorothy Gardiner and Katherine Sorley Walker, U of California P, 1997, pp. 63–70.

Chesterton, Cecil. "Art and the Detective." *Living Age*, Nov. 1906, pp. 505–10.

Chesterton, G. K. "In Defence of Detective Stories." 1901. *The Defendant*, 2nd ed., Johnson, 1902, pp. 118–23.

"Detective." *OED Online*. www.oed.com/view/Entry/51195. Accessed 29 November 2017.

"The Detectives." *Dublin Weekly Nation*, 22 June 1844, p. 7.

Dickens, Charles. "Three 'Detective' Anecdotes." *Household Words*, 14 September 1850, pp. 1577–80.

Doyle, Arthur Conan. "The Final Problem." 1893. *Sherlock Holmes: The Complete Novels and Stories, Volume I*, Bantam, 2003, pp. 736–55.

———. *A Study in Scarlet*. Ward, 1892.

Freeman, R. Austin. "Art of the Detective Story." 1924. *The Art of the Mystery Story*, edited by Howard Haycraft, Carroll, 1947, pp. 7–17.

French, Joseph Lewis. Foreword. *Masterpieces of Mystery*, Doubleday, 1920, pp. vii–viii.

"Fugitive." *OED Online*. www.oed.com/view/Entry/75264. Accessed 12 December 2017.

"Gleanings." *Hereford Times*, 6 June 1857, p. 15.

Griffith, D. W., director. *Edgar Allen Poe*. American Mutoscope & Biograph, 1909. https://www.youtube.com/watch?v=PeDOrpUgtO8.

Hawthorne, Julian, editor. *Library of the World's Best Mystery and Detective Stories, Vol. I: America*, Review, 1907.

Haycraft, Howard, editor. *The Art of the Mystery Story*. Carroll, 1947.

Hurd, C. O. "The Logic of Poe's 'The Murders in the Rue Morgue.'" *Harvard Monthly*, October 1885, pp. 7–10.

Johnson, Samuel. *Johnson's Dictionary of the English Language*. Williamson, 1839.

Kennedy, J. Gerald. "The Limits of Reason: Poe's Deluded Detectives." *American Literature*, vol. 47, no. 2, May 1975, pp. 184–96.

Leech, Harry Harewood. "The Robbery of Plate: A Detective's Story." 1859. *Westminster Detective Library*. https://wdl.mcdaniel.edu/node/88.

Matthews, Brander. "Poe and the Detective Story." *Scribner's Magazine*, September 1907, pp. 287–93.

Morrison, Toni. *Playing in the Dark: Whiteness and the Literary Imagination*. Vintage, 1993.

Panek, LeRoy Lad. *Before Sherlock Holmes: How Magazines and Newspapers Invented the Detective Story*. McFarland, 2011.

"The Passing of the Detective." *The Academy*, December 1905, pp. 1356–57.

Patten, William, editor. *Great Short Stories: A New Collection of Famous Examples from France, England and America, Vol. I: Detective Stories*. Collier, 1906.

Poe, Edgar Allan. *The Collected Letters of Edgar Allan Poe*. Edited by John Ward Ostrom, Burton R. Pollin, and Jeffrey A. Savoye, Gordian Press, 2008. 2 vols.

———. *The Detective Tales of Edgar Allan Poe*. Street, 1901.

———. *Prose Romances of Edgar A. Poe*. Vol. 1, Graham, 1843.

———. "Prospectus of The Stylus." 1848. Edgar Allan Poe Society of Baltimore. https://www.eapoe.org/works/misc/prosp012.htm.

———. *Tales*. Wiley, 1845.

———. *Tales of Mystery, Imagination and Humour*. Vizetelly, 1852.

———. *Tales of Mystery, Imagination and Humour; and Poems*. Vizetelly, 1852.

"Police." *OED Online*. www.oed.com/view/Entry/146823. Accessed 29 November 2017.

Pollin, Burton R. *Images of Poe's Works: A Comprehensive Descriptive Catalogue of Illustrations*. Greenwood, 1989.

Queen, Ellery. "The Detective Short Story: The First Hundred Years." 1946. *The Art of the Mystery Story*, edited by Howard Haycraft, Carroll, 1947, pp. 476–91.

———. *Queen's Quorum: A History of the Detective-Crime Short Story as Revealed by the 125 Most Important Books Published in the Field Since 1845*. 1948. Updated ed., Biblo, 1969.

Reeve, Arthur B. "In Defense of the Detective Story." *Independent*, 10 July 1913, pp. 91–4.

Review of *The Queen of Hearts*, by Wilkie Collins. *Morning Post* [London], 20 October 1859, pp. 3–4.

Sayers, Dorothy, editor. *Great Stories of Detection, Mystery and Horror*. Gollancz, 1928.

———. *The Omnibus of Crime*. Harcourt Brace, 1929.

Seaman, George, editor. Preface. *Detective Tales*, by Edgar Allan Poe, Street, 1900, n.p.

Sims, Michael. *Arthur and Sherlock: Conan Doyle and the Creation of Holmes*. Bloomsbury, 2017.

Smith, Reed. "History of the Detective Story: Its Development and Its Present Status—Voltaire, Poe, and Its Other Makers." *Farmer and Mechanic* [Raleigh, NC], 8 October 1912, p. 7.

Starrett, Vincent. "Of Detective Literature." *Fourteen Great Detective Stories*, edited by Starrett, Modern, 1928, pp. ix–xv.

Stedman, Edmund Clarence. "Introduction to the Tales." *The Works of Edgar Allan Poe*, vol. 1, edited by Edmund Clarence Stedman and George Edward Woodberry, Stone, 1894.

———. "Memoir." *The Works of Edgar Allan Poe*, vol. 1, edited by Edmund Clarence Stedman and George Edward Woodberry, Stone, 1894.

Stories of Fortune. Houghton, 1875.

Stories of the Home Circle. Putnam, 1857.

"Thief-taker." *OED Online*. www.oed.com/view/Entry/200744. Accessed 29 November 2017.

Verne, Jules. "Edgard Poe et ses oeuvres." *Musée des Familles*, vol. 31 (1863–1864), pp. 193–208.

Wells, Carolyn. *American Detective Stories*. Oxford UP, 1927.

———. *The Technique of the Detective Story*. Home Correspondence, 1913.

Wilkins, Mary E., et al. *The Long Arm and Other Detective Stories*. Chapman, 1895.

Williams, John B. "The Tell-Tale Signature: A Detective Story." 1860. *Westminster Detective Library*. https://wdl.mcdaniel.edu/node/96.

Williams, Valentine. "The Detective Story." *Bookman*, July 1928, pp. 521–24.

Wright, Willard H. Introduction. *Great Detective Stories: A Chronological Anthology*, Blue Ribbon, 1927.

Wrong, E. M., editor. *Crime and Detection*. Oxford UP, 1926.

~

CHAPTER ELEVEN

"I have spoken both of 'sound' and of 'voice'"

An *Analysis of* Doug Bradley's Spinechillers *Audio Anthology and the Works of Edgar Allan Poe*

Michelle Kay Hansen

Audiobooks have become a widespread phenomenon, acting as a method to reach readers/listeners who may not have the time or the circumstances to read hard-copy (or even electronic) versions of books themselves. While critics of audiobooks argue that the format contributes to the "dumbing down of America" and call the medium "a terrible development—as it inevitably means a loss of substance and may contribute to the appalling literacy problem in this country" (qtd. in Aron 212), the scholarship around audiobooks clearly argues that the benefits of this format far outweigh the disadvantages. Multiple studies have demonstrated how listening to books can increase literacy and reading comprehension levels, for example. As early as 1985, the U.S. Department of Education found that "the single most important activity for building the knowledge required for eventual success in reading is reading aloud" (Anderson et al. 23), and as Kylene Beers comments over ten years later, these findings "certainly indicate that hearing text read aloud improves reading ability" (33). Beers continues discussing the link between reading aloud and the "power" of audiobooks, claiming that audiobooks act as a "scaffold," allowing readers to build their vocabulary and comprehension, resulting in an eventual ability to climb above their initial reading level (33). In another study, Goldsmith finds that audiobooks improve oral reading skills, critical thinking, vocabulary, syntax, and speaking ability (50–53).

Another clear advantage of audiobooks is the ability they provide their audience to multitask while reading/listening. Stephen King, in *On Writing: A Memoir of the Craft*, writes, "You can even read while driving, thanks to the audiobook revolution. Of the books I read each year, anywhere from six to a dozen are on tape." In a survey done by Helen Aron in 1992, she found "The ability to listen to books while engaged in other activities was cited by most respondents as the main advantage listening has over reading. Only 4% were not engaged in any other activity when they listened" (211).

When it comes to the act of anthologizing through audio, there are even more benefits for readers (or listeners, as the case may be). A general reader, one who is not choosing an anthology for teaching purposes, for example, will likely choose an anthology because it is a quick way to discover writers within a certain genre that the reader is already inclined to enjoy—in this case, gothic and horror literature. In a survey done about the importance of anthologies, one reader commented on the usefulness of reading "a huge range of styles, forms, and perspectives—diversity in every sense of the word. It can be exciting compared to reading a novel by a familiar writer; there's something new every time you reach the end of a story" (qtd. in Johnson). Another response to the same survey states, "Most of the writers I have come to admire the most and who have had a lasting influence on me, I have discovered through anthologies" (qtd. in Johnson). For these reasons and more, when the editors of this volume approached me to write about the ways in which Edgar Allan Poe has been anthologized in the gothic and horror genre, I did not start reading—I started listening.

This chapter critically examines a specific anthology of gothic and horror literature titled *Doug Bradley's Spinechillers: Classic Horror Audio Books*, which is produced by Renegade Arts Entertainment. Each of the thirteen volumes of this anthology features Edgar Allan Poe at least once. Most of the time, however, Poe appears twice in each volume, with one short story and one poem (which always concludes the volume). This chapter analyzes the production company of *Doug Bradley's Spinechillers*, commenting on its use of nostalgia to influence a consumer-driven audience and on its reliance on popular culture "horror icons" in order to legitimize the works/authors included in the anthology as well as the company itself. The chapter then focuses specifically on Poe, offering a discussion of the short stories chosen for the anthology and the possible reasons behind these selections. Finally, just as the majority of the *Spinechillers* volumes end with poems, this chapter will end with an examination of the decision to conclude with a poem by Poe, what this implies about Poe as a poet, and what it suggests about the audio format in general. By anthologizing Poe in an audio format, Renegade Arts Entertainment has successfully proven that Poe's works can reach any and all readers/listeners, particularly the contemporary audience taking part in the audiobook revolution. Additionally, *Spinechillers* is continuing the long tradition of oral storytelling, which is at the heart of all narrative.

The volumes in *Doug Bradley's Spinechillers* were produced between 2010 and 2016, a period of intense consumerism, especially in relation to the audiobook revolution led by Audible.com, which joined the Amazon family in 2008. In 2012, Audible introduced Whispersync for Voice, "enabling book lovers to switch seamlessly between reading and listening without losing their place" ("About Audible"). Audible is known as "the biggest producer and seller of audiobooks" (Kaufman), and it is a thriving company in a time when book sales—both in print and digital formats—are in decline. From 2013 to 2016, the highest growing segment of publishing was audiobooks, with at least 36,000 titles published each year during this span (Kozlowski). In 2016, the global audiobook industry was "evaluated at $3.5 billion" (Kozlowski). In March 2016, CNBC reported that audiobook downloads "increased by 38.1 percent in 2015 and services such as Audible, where users pay a monthly subscription to access a library of audio books, are growing" (Graham). Though Renegade Arts Entertainment released its audio anthology first on CD, the company quickly moved to mp3 downloads and made their narrations available on Audible shortly thereafter. Doing so was both a smart and effective move, especially with the contemporary "click-and-purchase" capability and mentality of audiobook listeners. Instead of having to wait for shipped box sets of CDs, for example, anyone anywhere in the world could simply download the anthology (or even parts of the anthology) and begin listening within moments.

Within a consumer-driven culture, especially in the digital age, audiobooks are a way to market culture as a commodity in a late capitalist society. The consumerist drive is often related to a sense of nostalgia, and this is one of the main reasons *Doug Bradley's Spinechillers* finds success. With a contemporary audience, there is a lack of cultural memory, as well as a longing for a simpler past (or even a time and place that never was). Social media platforms like Facebook and Instagram, among others, allow people to not only share immediate moments with their contacts, but they also promote a sense of cultural nostalgia for memories from the past, no matter how recent that past may be. ("Throwback Thursday," also known as #TBT on certain mediums, would be an example of this attempt to cultivate nostalgia.) When it comes to the gothic and horror genre, one reason behind the cultural sense of nostalgia could be due to the world in which the audience currently lives. In an era of easy access to violence that can appear quite realistic through continuing advances in computer graphics technology, an audience might long for the now almost comic violence in the horror movies of the 1980s and even the 1990s. In a culture of binge watching, and particularly of an audience interested in episodic entertainment, the audience could long for the past when they had to check the TV Guide (in paperback, of course) to find which horror movies might be on during Halloween, or even to make sure they were home in time for *Tales from the Crypt*.

One way *Spinechillers* profits from these nostalgia-driven consumers is through the music included within the anthology. Under Douglas Bradley's direction, "original music and sound design is added to each story by composers with a background in movie soundtrack production" ("About Spinechillers"). Though others contribute to the music/sound production of *Spinechillers*, the person who most often composes the music for the anthology is Alistair Lock. Lock is a well-respected audio professional who has provided scores for the BBC series *Doctor Who*, among others, and whose work has been described by more than one reviewer as "cinematic" ("Alistair Lock"). The scores for the Poe stories and poems included in *Spinechillers* vary slightly from story to story, but they generally include similar refrains and techniques to create an atmosphere of reading that is akin to watching a horror movie. Each score is primarily in a minor key, and the lower notes of a piano are often emphasized on downbeats for dramatic effect every few measures. French horns, oboes, string instruments, and flutes tend to be the preferred instruments, played with eerie dynamics and evocative melodies to create a sense of dread and suspense. Additional sound effects are used sparingly, and the music is not present from beginning to end of the stories. Primarily, the music introduces the story, rises again at climactic moments, and returns once again as a way to end the piece and transition to the next selection. This music creates the majority of the nostalgia for the audience, as reading/listening becomes an immersive experience similar to either listening to radio programs or watching old horror films.

In addition to the music, the narrators—all popular culture horror icons—play a key role in determining whether or not the audio anthology is successful, while also lending a sense of nostalgia to the listener/reader. For most audiobooks, including *Spinechillers*, the narrators are usually trained, professional actors. These narrators "bring finely honed dramatic skills to an interpretation of the text" and are therefore able to "generate excitement and captivate a wide spectrum of listeners from the inept and unwilling to the expert and passionate" (Baskin and Harris 373). These types of recordings "often blur the line between book and performance" (Rubery 67). As Baskin and Harris point out in "Heard Any Good Books Lately?" the competent actor can select a style of delivery "calculated to elicit the desired literary effect" (374).[1] Elaborating on this, they write:

Trained actors who read texts for audiobook recordings, even when their native speech patterns do not reflect those of the books' characters, can simulate
local accents, phrasing, emphasis, and other phonological attributes that
clearly distinguish various types of speakers. Dialects, often problematic for
less than proficient readers to decode, are rendered intelligible in this format.
Archaic constructions, not readily fathomed in written form, may become
comprehensible when heard. (373)

One of the main appeals of *Doug Bradley's Spinechillers* audio anthology
is the reputation of the narrators. As Rubery points out, when the readers are celebrities, "name recognition promises to boost sales" (66). Of
course, Doug Bradley narrates the majority of the works included. Bradley
is touted as the "genesis" behind *Spinechillers*, and he is "best known as the
actor behind the horror icon Pinhead, the star of Clive Barker's *Hellraiser*
horror movies" ("Doug Bradley"). The anthology also includes narrations
by Robert Englund, best known for his role in *The Nightmare on Elm Street*
series as serial killer Freddy Krueger, and Jeff Combs from the cult classic Re-
Animator films based on H. P. Lovecraft's works. (Combs, of course, narrates
Lovecraft's Re-Animator stories included in the anthology). The exclusive
choice of "horror icon" narrators who give voices to the stories appeals to a
consumer-driven market and further makes this anthology successful due to
the concept of legitimation.

"Legitimation" occurs when a certain piece of art (or in this case, a text)
can be deemed "legitimate" based primarily on its proximity to other pieces
that have already been regarded as valid or worthy. Legitimation comes
about through consumerism and happens via institutions and social constructs rather than the actual products themselves. An item—whether it be a
text, a work of art, or another type of consumer product—can be legitimized
because of its affiliation with something that has already been accepted as
"art" or "text." For example, an unknown horror author who is anthologized
in a work with someone like Edgar Allan Poe or Stephen King now becomes
"legitimate" through proximity to these famous writers. In the case of *Doug
Bradley's Spinechillers*, legitimation is also at work due to the use of celebrity,
and this process is another reason why Poe's stories work so well in this anthology. Legitimation can most easily be seen on the covers of the volumes
and in the wording chosen to legitimize the project. The complete title of the
project is *Doug Bradley's Spinechillers: Classic Horror Audio Books*. The choice
to clarify that this is a project primarily done by Doug Bradley is something
that would appeal to an audience familiar with the horror genre, and Bradley himself appears on each of the covers as part of the art. However, just in

212 ~ Michelle Kay Hansen

case his name itself is not enough to tempt a reader/listener into a purchase, the covers of volumes 1 through 9 make Bradley's celebrity status even more evident. Each of these volumes has the following line on the cover (in all capital letters, as written here): "READ BY THE STAR OF *HELLRAISER* DOUG 'PINHEAD' BRADLEY." The words "HELLRAISER" and "PIN-HEAD" are often emphasized further with the use of a red colored font, while the other words are in white.[2] In volumes 6, 8, and 9, three of the times when the narrators include guest stars, they are listed specifically as "Robert 'Freddy Krueger' Englund" and "Jeff 'Reanimator' Combs." It is not until volume 10 that the epithets for the narrators are no longer included, listing simply "Doug Bradley" and "Guest Starring Robert Englund [and/or] Jeff Combs." If a reader/listener has already made the choice to purchase the initial volumes of the anthology, the labels of "celebrity" are no longer necessary toward the later parts of the series because the legitimation of the series itself is complete.

Spinechillers appears on Amazon/Audible through keyword searches of "Gothic/Horror Literature," mainly because the selections involve ghosts and/or deliberate or unintentional murder, among other facets of the genre. More importantly, however, the volumes also appear when a person simply searches for something written by "Edgar Allan Poe." Poe's name legitimates the anthology in this way because, in the thirteen volumes of *Spinechillers*, Poe appears more often than any other author, with twenty-two pieces of both fiction and poetry, including at least one story in each volume of the series.[3] Bradley offers some reasons as to why he chose Poe when developing *Spinechillers* in a biography he wrote for the Renegade Arts Entertainment website:

> When I was a boy, there was a small bookcase in one of the downstairs rooms that contained my father's books. Here, I first encountered Dickens and excitedly reached for a play called "Ghosts" only to be disappointed that Ibsen's play was a domestic drama and not about shades of the ghoulish kind. Here also nestled a slim volume with one of those titles that you can't pass by: *Tales of Mystery and Imagination*. Edgar Allan Poe sidled into my life.

The choice to include Poe in each of the volumes of *Spinechillers* extends to more than a simple admiration for the author. First of all, Poe's stories simply tend to work effectively when adapted into audio format due to his own style and philosophy of writing. In "The Philosophy of Composition," Poe states that effective storytelling should be built around three principles: length, method, and unity of effect. For length, Poe states there should be "a distinct limit . . . to all works of literary art—the limit of a single sitting." For method, Poe dismisses "intuition" and "spontaneity" as part of writing a story, and instead emphasizes that writing and storytelling are methodical and analytical. Finally, Poe writes about the "unity of effect," and it is his conviction that a work of fiction should be written only after the author has decided how it is to end and which emotional response, or "effect," the writer wishes to create. Once the effect has been determined, then the writer should decide all other matters pertaining to the composition of the work, including tone, theme, setting, characters, conflict, and plot (*Essays and Reviews* 13–25). The audio format of *Spinechillers* highlights each of these elements. Because a listener with an audiobook application—like Audible, for instance—has access to the "chapters" (individual stories) in each volume of the anthology, the listener then has the option of choosing one story at a time. In fact, if the audience is interested *only* in the Poe stories (or the stories by any specific author included in the anthology, for that matter), Renegade Arts Entertainment offers the ability to download individual stories rather than the entire collection. This serves Poe's own "length" principle, as the selections are all easily listened to in a single sitting. The "method" and "unity of effect" principles are primarily accomplished through the narrators themselves, as they have clearly taken the time to familiarize themselves with the pieces they are dramatizing and have included music and sound effects to further the emotional response of the audience, as discussed previously. The narrators use their voices—tone, pitch, and volume—to create feelings of suspense, dread, and horror for the audience.

Part of the ease of audio adaptation of Poe's narrative style is due to his reliance on first-person narration. In fact, almost all of Poe's collected short stories—not just those anthologized in *Spinechillers*—are written in the first person. Poe's most famous stories tend to rely on the concept of the "confessional." As stated by Bleakley, the confessional narrative "is offered as a revelation of an individual's interiority, usually centered on emotional life" (16). Of course, confessionals—even in the religious sense—are mainly accomplished aloud, so Poe's narrative choices seamlessly fit the audio anthology. Volume 1 of *Spinechillers* includes Poe's "The Tell-Tale Heart." This story contains no dialogue, and no other character speaks besides the first-person narrator himself, who is confessing his act of murder (and betraying his own insanity). The same applies to the Poe story in volume 4, "The Black Cat," in which the only lines of dialogue are from the narrator either speaking to himself, to the reader, or to the gentlemen at the end of the tale who apparently discover the cat within the enclosed wall. In volume 6, the editors have included "The Pit and the Pendulum," the testimonial of a man who has been tortured by unseen antagonists rather than a confession on the part of the narrator. In this story, there is only one spoken line: "'Death,' I said, 'any death but that of the pit!'" (*Poetry and Tales* 505). It is unclear due to the story's context whether this line is spoken out loud or within the mind of the narrator. One final example of a purely confessional story in *Spinechillers* is the selection of "William Wilson" included in volume 7.

All of the above selections, with the exception of "William Wilson," have something important and similar in common when discussing audio adaptation—the original stories contain very little (if any) dialogue. This puts less stress on the actor/narrator in terms of voice modification. As Rubery points out:

> Perhaps the most consequential decision to be made when recording an audiobook is how far to take 'voice characterization,' the narrator's performance of varied vocal registers to represent different characters in the narrative. This can be challenging for narrators reading stories outside the range of their own biography and may even call for a counterintuitive solution; for instance, male narrators often have more success speaking female parts in a whisper rather than a falsetto. (67)

The choice to include stories with very little dialogue allows the reader/listener—and even the voice actor himself—to become more immersed within the story, as there is no pressure to try to imagine the various characters aside from the main narrator. Even when a spoken line is included in one of the selections, it is primarily an exclamation. For example, volume 2 of *Spinechillers* includes Poe's "The Oval Portrait," in which the only spoken line occurs when the painter cries with a loud voice, saying "This is indeed Life itself!" before turning and finding his beloved has died (*Poetry and Tales* 484). Volume 8 includes "MS. Found in a Bottle," in which the only spoken line is the companion's scream, "See! see! . . . Almighty God! see! see!" (193). Poe's "Ligeia," chosen for volume 11, contains lines from various authors quoted by the narrator, but the only lines of spoken text occur at Ligeia's death and in the story's finale. In the former example, Ligeia cries out, "O God! . . . O God! O Divine Father!—shall these things be undeviatingly so?—shall this Conqueror be not once conquered? Are we not part and parcel in Thee? Who—who knoweth the mysteries of the will with its vigor? Man doth not yield him to the angels, *nor unto death utterly*, save only through the weakness of his feeble will" (269) before whispering the final sentence—supposedly from Joseph Glanvill—one last time. In the latter case, the narrator himself exclaims, "'Here then, at least, . . . can I never—can I never be mistaken—

these are the full, and the black, and the wild eyes—of my lost love—of the lady—of the LADY LIGEIA!'" (277). Finally, the concluding volume of the anthology offers "The Masque of the Red Death," a tale in which Poe includes only one line of spoken text from Prince Prospero: "'Who dares?' he demanded hoarsely of the courtiers who stood near him—'who dares insult us with this blasphemous mockery? Seize him and unmask him—that we may know whom we have to hang at sunrise, from the battlements!'" (489). The exclamations, of course, are part of Poe's "unity of effect" principle as discussed above. Exclamatory sentences function in providing an overall tone for fiction in general, whether they are positive or negative, declarative or interrogative (Rosengren 153). As Rosengren asserts, the exclamations function "through an inference process, triggered by the sentence type, the propositional content and emphatic stress, resulting in a generalized impli-cature" (153). In other words, the audiobook's narrator can easily interpret the use of exclamations in Poe's stories because these statements can be dramatized based on the implications of the type of exclamation being used. So the tone and emphasis that the narrator, in these cases Doug Bradley, uses while recording the story become inherently effective for the audience because Bradley has been implying his own "unity of effect" throughout his narration from beginning to end.

The rest of Poe's short story selections anthologized in *Spinechillers* have multiple lines of dialogue. However, the spoken lines still work easily within the audio adaptation format for various reasons. First, volume 3 includes Poe's "Hop-Frog," told through a first-person narration, but narrating events that possibly did not even include the speaker. Aside from the title character, the lines of dialogue are spoken by the king, the prime minister, and other courtiers, who function as a "chorus" of the king's ministry. Although there are multiple spoken lines by a variety of characters, when it comes to those in positions of power within the story, there is still little need for much voice modification to make the effect of the story work. All of these speakers (aside from Hop-Frog, of course) are fundamentally the same character, as proven by the narrative itself—Hop-Frog convinces them all to dress as orangutans, essentially putting them on the same level, because they all symbolize tyr-anny and oppression. Other Poe works anthologized in *Spinechillers* include "The Fall of the House of Usher" (volume 5), "The Facts in the Case of M. Valdemar" (volume 9), "The Cask of Amontillado" (volume 10), and "The Premature Burial" (volume 12).[4] From an audio adaptation standpoint, it is important to remember that all of these stories are still told through a first-person narrator. Therefore, even when two or more characters are speaking, the voice/pronunciation of the person reading does not need to drastically change because the audience is hearing only the narrator's version of the other characters' voices in the first place. Since the entire narration is told from the same voice or point of view, the reader's dramatized version of the story does not have to vary drastically in inflection or tone. This is yet another reason why Poe's narrative style—particularly his choice of first-person narration—is effective and suitable when adapted to the audio format.

Nine of the thirteen volumes of *Spinechillers* conclude with Doug Bradley reading a poem written by Poe. Poe claimed that, for him, poetry was "not a purpose, but a passion; and the passions should be held in reverence; they must not—they cannot at will be excited with an eye to the paltry compensations, or the more paltry commendations, of mankind" (*Poetry and Tales* 18). Since Poe believed that poetry was one of the highest forms of literary art, including his poetry in this anthology is a testament to his own rather tragic legacy when it comes to his lack of success in publishing his poetry during his lifetime. When read by an expert, and particularly a trained actor, the poems also benefit the listener in terms of comprehension and enjoyment. As Baskin and Harris point out: "Poetry, traditionally a problem for [readers], is presented on tape with expert phrasing, rhythm, accent, and pronunciation as well as sensitivity to mood and tone" (374). The choice made to "round off the volumes" with poetry is explained by Renegade Arts Entertainment as being a way to "nicely calm us down" at the end of each volume ("About Spinechillers"). However, there is much more to be said about the effective inclusion of poetry within an audio format than its ability to calm the listener. In fact, Poe himself argues, "a poem deserves its title only inasmuch as it excites, by elevating the soul. The value of the poem is in the ratio of this elevating excitement" (*Essays and Reviews* 71). He continues:

> That pleasure which is at once the most pure, the most elevating, and the most intense, is derived, I maintain, from the contemplation of the Beautiful. In the contemplation of Beauty we alone find it possible to attain that pleasurable elevation, or excitement, of the soul, which we recognize as the Poetic Sentiment, and which is so easily distinguished from Truth, which is the satisfaction of the Reason, or from Passion, which is the excitement of the heart. (78)

So instead of simply "calming" the reader, the poems from Poe's perspective are meant to "excite" the reader, and they do this through the genre of both the poems themselves and the audio format of the anthology as a whole. The poems bring a mood of incantation that often involves some sort of rhythm or piercing line. This incantation propels the audience into the next collection of the anthology by way of Poe's idea of "excitation" of the reader/listener.

The nine selected poems in *Spinechillers* include "The Raven," "A Dream within a Dream," "For Annie," "The Haunted Palace," "Annabel Lee," "Alone," "The Sleeper," "Dream-Land," and "The Conqueror Worm." In volume 13 of *Spinechillers*—the final volume of the anthology—Bradley incorporates an introduction with a clear rationale for his selection of "The Conqueror Worm," stating: "Quite appropriate for me that the final words in the *Spinechillers* series should belong to Edgar Allan Poe, and that the last words should be 'The Conqueror Worm,' in whose digestive tract we will—one way or another—all wind up" ("Introduction" 00:15:13–26). Though none of the other volumes offer insight into why or how Bradley chose which poems to include, the styles, genres, and moods of the chosen poems easily adapt into audio format. As a poet, Poe crossed and broke boundaries of genre and mode, and the two main genres anthologized in *Spinechillers* are narrative and lyric verse. Since narrative poems—such as "The Raven," "Annabel Lee," "For Annie," and "The Sleeper"—tell a story, they effectively function in audio format for reasons similar to the success of Poe's stories in this format, including the usage of the first-person approach and a "confessional" tone.

The remaining five poetry selections arguably belong to the lyric mode, which is meant to be sung or spoken aloud. A lyric is usually fairly short, not often longer than fifty or sixty lines, and often only between a dozen and thirty lines; and it usually expresses the feelings and thoughts of a single speaker (not necessarily the poet him/herself) in a personal and subjective fashion (Cuddon 481). Poe's style is obviously suited to the lyric genre based on his own philosophy of "length" as discussed above, as well as his preference for first-person speakers in his writing. Bradley beautifully reads the poems with what has been described as "care and panache" ("About Spinechillers"). By listening to the poems read aloud, readers/listeners are able to have a more pleasurable experience with these works, hearing the way the phrasing and the emphasis within the stanzas can make a difference in the overall meaning of the poem. Hearing the poems aloud helps the listener understand the fundamentals of lyric poetry. Additionally, the poetry selections are the only pieces in the anthology that contain no background music or sound effects.[5] This production choice allows the poems to become music in and of themselves, staying true to the nature of lyric.

The benefits of anthologizing Poe's works through audio are numerous, both to readers/listeners who are able to approach the texts in a contemporary manner, and to Poe's legacy itself and his own ideas and philosophies about writing and poetry. *Doug Bradley's Spinechillers* effectively uses the audio format to bring Poe's works to life for contemporary consumers of literature and popular culture. Furthermore, perhaps unknowingly, this anthology is a new step in the oral tradition of literature, which is at the heart of both storytelling and poetry. A book—or in this case, an anthology—does not simply consist of words printed on paper and bound together for one to read. This definition is just not adequate in an age where technology has transformed our abilities to consume literature in unique and personalized ways. As Baskin and Harris point out, "[t]he lineage of recorded books harkens back to ancient times when stories, commentaries, poems, and histories were transmitted by storytellers; the first literature was heard, not read" (372). By anthologizing Poe as part of the oral tradition, and by providing an innovative medium for reading, *Spinechillers* adds even more to the legacy of Poe himself and to his works in the gothic and horror genre. For a man who was often degraded by his contemporaries, with his name connected to many negative labels including "charlatan, plagiarist, pathological liar, egomaniac, whimpering child, braggart, and irresponsible drunk" (Van Doren Stern xxxviii), Poe's works have proven themselves above any of these stereotypes, as they are both lasting and adaptable to contemporary audiences. Further, through the emerging audiobook revolution, Poe—as both a fiction writer and a poet—has become legitimized within the long-standing and valued oral tradition of literature.

Notes

1. Baskin and Harris's comment on a voice actor's ability to create a "desired literary effect" clearly converses with Poe's ideas in "The Philosophy of Composition." I will return to this point later in this chapter.

2. The use of red font occurs in volumes 1 through 5, and the remainder have only white font (still in capital letters).

3. Other authors in the anthology include H. P. Lovecraft (14 selections), Ambrose Bierce (9 selections), Arthur Conan Doyle (8 selections), M. R. James (5 selections), Charles Dickens (3 selections), William Harvey (3 selections), Saki (2 selections), Rudyard Kipling (2 selections), and Wilkie Collins, W. W. Jacobs, Robert Louis Stevenson, John Milton Hayes, Arthur Machen, and Walter De La Mare (each with 1 selection).

4. Roderick Usher's character has three short spoken sections as well as one long monologue at the end of this story. The narrator has only one spoken line aside from reading passages aloud to Roderick. In "The Facts in the Case of M. Valdemar," the narrator has three spoken lines, which are questions to Valdemar. Then, Valdemar has three direct responses to these questions. Valdemar also speaks as he is dying, when asking the narrator to wake him up and, finally, when he claims that he is "dead! dead!" (*Poetry and Tales* 842). The majority of "The Cask of Amontillado" is

a dialogue between the narrator, Montresor, and Fortunato. Finally, "The Premature Burial" contains only limited spoken text as well.

5. The exception to this rule is found in volume 12, with the inclusion of Poe's "Dream-Land." This poem has background music all the way from beginning to end, and the poem becomes less effective because of this production choice. My supposition is that the producers realized the music was a distraction, as the music was then eliminated from the final poem in volume 13 ("The Conqueror Worm") by the time it was released.

Works Cited

"About Audible." Audible.com. http://about.audible.com. Accessed 21 October 2017.

"About Spinechillers." Renegade Arts Entertainment. http://www.renegadeartsentertainment.com/spinechillers-about. Accessed 25 October 2017.

"Alistair Lock." B7 Media. http://www.b7media.com/about/team/alistair-lock/. Accessed 2 November 2017.

Anderson, Richard C., et al. "Becoming a Nation of Readers: The Report of the Commission on Reading." *National Academy of Education*, U.S. Department of Education, Washington DC, 1985.

Aron, Helen. "Bookworms Become Tapeworms: A Profile of Listeners to Books on Audiocassette." *Journal of Reading*, vol. 36, no. 3, 1992, pp. 208–12.

Baskin, Barbara H., and Karin Harris. "Heard Any Good Books Lately? The Case for Audiobooks in the Secondary Classroom." *Journal of Reading*, vol. 38, no. 5, 1995, pp. 372–76.

Beers, Kylene. "Listen While You Read: Struggling Readers and Audiobooks." *School Library Journal*, April 1998, pp. 30–35.

Bleakley, Alan. "Writing with Invisible Ink: Narrative, Confessionalism and Reflective Practice." *Reflective Practice*, vol. 1, no. 1, 2000, pp. 11–24.

Bradley, Doug. "Edgar Allan Poe." Renegade Arts Entertainment. http://www.renegadeartsentertainment.com/edgar-allan-poe. Accessed 19 October 2017.

———. Introduction. *Doug Bradley's Spinechillers Volume 13: Classic Horror Short Stories*, narrated by Doug Bradley, Renegade Arts Entertainment, 2014. Audiobook.

Cuddon, J. A. *The Penguin Dictionary of Literary Terms and Literary Theory*. Penguin Books, 1998.

"Doug Bradley." Renegade Arts Entertainment. http://www.renegadeartsentertainment.com/about-us/doug-bradley. Accessed 21 October 2017.

Goldsmith, Francisca. "Earphone English." *School Library Journal*, May 2002, pp. 50–53.

Graham, Luke. "Book Sales Are in Decline but Audio Books Are Thriving." CNBC.com, 7 Mar. 2017. https://www.cnbc.com/2016/03/03/book-sales-are-in-decline-but-audio-books-are-thriving.html. Accessed 21 October 2017.

Johnson, Andrea. "MIND MELD: Why Are Anthologies Important?" *SF Signal*, Signal Web Media, 13 November 2013. https://www.sfsignal.com/archives/2013/11/mind-meld-why-are-anthologies-important/.

Kaufman, Leslie. "Actors Today Don't Just Read for the Part. Reading IS the Part." *New York Times*, 29 June 2013. http://www.nytimes.com/2013/06/30/business/media/actors-today-dont-just-read-for-the-part-reading-is-the-part.html.

King, Stephen. *On Writing: A Memoir of the Craft*. Kindle edition, Scribner, 2000.

Kozlowski, Michael. "Global Audiobook Trends and Statistics for 2017." *Good e-Reader*, 18 December 2016. https://goodereader.com/blog/digital-publishing/audiobook-trends-and-statistics-for-2017.

Poe, Edgar Allan. *Essays and Reviews*. Edited by G. R. Thompson, Library of America, 1984.

———. *Poetry and Tales*. Edited by Patrick Quinn, Library of America, 1984.

Rosengren, Inger. "Expressive Sentence Types—A Contradiction in Terms: The Case of Exclamation." *Modality in Germanic Languages: Historical and Comparative Perspectives*, edited by Toril Swan and Olaf Jansen Westvik, Mouton de Gruyter, 1997, pp. 151–82.

Rubery, Matthew. "Play It Again, Sam Weller: New Digital Audiobooks and Old Ways of Reading." *College Publications*, vol. 13, no. 1, 2008, pp. 58–79.

Van Doren Stern, Philip, editor. *The Portable Poe*. 1945. Penguin, 1973.

CHAPTER TWELVE

~

Poe's Poetry Anthologized

Philip Edward Phillips

Most modern readers in the United States first encounter the poetry of Edgar Allan Poe either in popular culture references or in anthologies of American literature.[1] In his own time, Poe became known to many readers through his acerbic reviews of the poetry and prose publications of his contemporaries. If antebellum American readers were initially unfamiliar with the "Tomahawk Man," they likely encountered Poe later, in 1845, when he published his most popular work, "The Raven." Although he ultimately made his living as a "magazinist," who appealed to and successfully exploited popular tastes and trends in his writings,[2] Poe's greatest aspiration from a young age was to be a poet and, ultimately, to own and edit his own five-dollar-per-annum literary magazine featuring poetry of the highest quality. Over the course of his career, Poe produced a remarkable range of literary works and critical writings in which he sought to establish new aesthetic standards for American literature. In fact, he published four collections of poetry during his lifetime: *Tamerlane and Other Poems* (1827), *Al Aaraaf, Tamerlane and Minor Poems* (1829), *Poems, by Edgar A. Poe* (1831), and *The Raven and Other Poems* (1845).[3] He also published and reprinted his poetry in various literary magazines, newspapers, and gift books, which were popular in antebellum America.[4]

In *Tradition and the Individual Poem: An Inquiry into Anthologies*, Anne Ferry argues that, "[f]or all their variousness, anthologies have features in common that invariably set them apart from other kinds of poetry collections made by authors of their own work or by editors" (13). Unlike an author's collection of his or her own poems—which reflect in the title, preface, arrangement, and revisions the poet's programmatic aims and self-fashioned literary persona— poetry anthologies reflect the literary tastes of their editors, often complicated or affected by the demands and expectations of the marketplace. Indeed, as Ferry writes, the anthology is "the work of a unique kind of maker, whose presence is felt, inescapably, only in this kind of book" (13). The poet's authorial presence, as it were, becomes subjected to and shaped by the aims of the anthologist. Whereas some poets attempt in collections of their own works to project a sense of development or thematic unity, anthologies, "lacking fixed requirements," usually do not demonstrate the "progress . . . evolution . . . or development" of a poet's literary productions,[5] and also remove those productions from the order imposed by a collection's title, for example, that attempts to make a claim regarding its contents (14–15).

Other chapters in this volume address Poe's poetry collections, literary magazines, and gift books as "anthologies" in their own right. This one concerns poetry written by Poe that was published in multi-author anthologies— from Rufus W. Griswold's *The Poets and Poetry of America* (1842) to David Lehman's *The Oxford Book of American Poetry* (2006). This chapter argues that reading Poe's poetry "anthologized" can reveal not only the changing literary tastes of different generations of editors and readers, but also the ways in which the inclusion or exclusion of his poetry affected his status as a poet alongside the emerging, and changing, pantheon of the "great" American writers.

To that end, this chapter surveys and critically examines some of the most significant anthologies in which Poe's poetry was included (or excluded), considering especially the editors' selection criteria. From Elihu Smith's *American Poems* (1793) to the volumes in the present-day Oxford series, this chapter explores Poe's place in the emerging "canon" of American poetry as largely established by the anthologies of American poetry. It also considers the extent to which Poe's reputation as a poet has been, and continues to be, affected by perceptions of the author himself and the inclusion, exclusion, and selection of his works in these volumes from the antebellum period to the twenty-first century.

The Earliest Anthologies of American Poetry

Elihu H. Smith edited the first known anthology of American poetry— *American Poems, Selected and Original, Vol. I*—in 1793. It is comprised mostly of obscure poets, of whom only Joel Barlow and Philip Freneau have enjoyed much staying power.[6] Smith sought to preserve in book form poems originally published in various magazines, as well as some previously unpublished original poems. In the spirit of the Greek roots for "anthology"—*anthos* (flower) and *legein* (to gather), Smith was motivated to gather together the poetry that had flowered in America, not necessarily to select the "best" specimens of American poetry. Although published before Poe's lifetime, *American Poems, Selected and Original* was a volume with which he and his contemporaries were familiar. It is also important historically because of its influence on future American poetry anthology editors. Many of the subscribers listed in the back of the volume hailed from Connecticut, and were friends of the editor.[7] According to Alan C. Golding, Smith's stated goals as an anthologist—to preserve the widest range of poems that otherwise would have fallen into oblivion—were at odds with his "unstated biases on which the selections [were] founded" (4). Indeed, Golding observes that "[p]ersonal, regional, and political loyalties all underlie his work. To represent American poetry, he compiled a book dominated by his friends, by Connecticut poets, by Federalists" (4). By affirming Federalist poets, Smith effectively used his anthology to "build America's sense of identity by gathering an independent national literature to match and strengthen the country's newly achieved independence" (5). Although a second volume was planned, the project was not realized because of the editor's death.

Another early, and more widely known, anthology is Samuel Kettell's *Specimens of American Poetry, with Critical and Biographical Notices*, published in three volumes by S. G. Goodrich and Company in Boston in 1829. Kettell's *Specimens* took the American poetry anthology to a new level with its more judicious selection of poetry—which included the major poets of the era—and its inclusion of critical and biographical notices for each author. This anthology, featuring "189 poets from Cotton Mather to John Greenleaf Whittier," became the "first scholarly anthology" of American poetry (Golding 11–12) and the standard upon which Rufus W. Griswold later modelled his own successful anthologies of American poets and poetry in the 1840s–1850s by incorporating its best features into his volumes. It is also an anthology that Poe knew well as an aspiring young poet eager to join the ranks of the literary elite.[8]

Griswold, the Gatekeeper of American Poetry, and His Contemporaries

Griswold was a native of Vermont, a preacher, and a magazine editor who became the gatekeeper of American poetry in the antebellum period. Jay B.

Hubbell claims that "the successive editions of [Griswold's] anthologies are a good index to the changing literary fashions of the mid-nineteenth century" (32). According to Hubbell, Griswold "was slow like his readers to recognize the greatness of the newer writers" and "slow also to realize the lack of intrinsic merit in many of the literary pioneers" (32). Nevertheless, Golding accurately identifies Griswold as "America's first professional anthologist" (13) with the first publication of *The Poets and Poetry of America* in 1842. Although Poe found fault in Griswold's methods for selecting poets for inclusion in (and exclusion from) his volumes, he also recognized and appreciated the importance of having one's works published in *The Poets and Poetry of America*.

The frontispiece to that seminal volume (figure 12.1) features what became known affectionately as the "Boilerplate Five," comprised of such literary luminaries as Dana (represented by a classical marble bust), Bryant, Halleck, Sprague, and the young Longfellow (all New Englanders). Griswold intended for his volume to be the definitive anthology of American poetry. Modeled on Kettell's *Specimens*, it surpassed its predecessor in scope and depth, including far more poets and adding biographical headnotes for each of those poets in the lavishly produced book. Griswold's anthology was the first such volume to include poems by Poe. In fact, over the course of his career, Griswold gradually increased the number of Poe's poems appearing in the anthology, although not to the degree that he promoted the poetical productions of his New England contemporaries.

In "To the Reader," Griswold explains: "This [anthology] is designed to exhibit the progress and condition of Poetry in the United States. . . . Although America has produced many eminent scholars and writers, we have yet but the beginning of a national literature" (v). Concerning his rationale for selecting material for inclusion, Griswold states:

> This volume embraces specimens from numerous authors; and though it may not contain the names of all who deserve admission, the judicious critic will be more likely to censure me for the wide range of my selections than for any omissions he may discover. In regard to the number of poems I have given from particular writers, it is proper to remark that considerations unconnected with any estimates of their genius have in some cases guided me. (vi)

Although his anthologies, like those of Smith and Kettell, sought to preserve the range of American poetry, regardless of quality, Griswold was aware of the potential pitfalls of suggesting a hierarchy of American poets based on the number of poems included, or not included, in them. On the one hand,

Figure 12.1.   Frontispiece, *The Poets and Poetry of America*, edited by
Rufus W. Griswold, 1st ed. (1842).
Photograph by Philip Edward Phillips, with permission. Boston Athenæum.

he was attempting to perform a balancing act by paying due reverence to the great New England poets, both past and present. On the other hand, he included the works of more innovative writers, such as Poe, but perhaps in a more limited way. Like Poe, Griswold was aware of the literary marketplace, and he likely adjusted his content accordingly.

In the first edition of his landmark volume, Griswold includes three poems written by Poe: "Coliseum," "The Haunted Palace," and "The Sleeper" (387–88). The headnote to the selections erroneously gives Poe's birthdate as 1811 (instead of 1809), and it presents other false information (including references to certain exploits in Greece and St. Petersburg). The omission of Poe's service as an enlisted soldier in the U.S. Army and the inclusion of fictitious dates and travels, for the most part, were the result of Poe's own efforts to romanticize his life along the lines of George Gordon, Lord Byron, whom he idolized and who was very much in vogue on both sides of the Atlantic.[9] The headnote devotes almost half the space to Poe's lineage and education, and it ends with his editorial associations with the *Southern Literary Messenger*, the *New York Review*, and his contributions both to "several foreign periodicals" and to a "popular monthly magazine [probably *Graham's*] in Philadelphia" (387)

In his 1842 critical review of Griswold's volume, however, Poe writes:

> We disagree, then with Mr. Griswold in *many* of his critical estimates; although in general, we are proud to find his decisions our own. He has omitted from the body of his book, some one or two whom we should have been tempted to introduce. On the other hand, he has scarcely made us amends by introducing some one or two dozen whom we should have treated with contempt. We might complain, too, of a prepossession, evidently unperceived by himself, for the writers of New England. (221)

Because of his apparent disdain for Southern poets and his favorable treatment of New England poets, Griswold's anthology contributed to the growing "sectionalism" in American literature. Moreover, because Griswold believed that "American poetry should be represented by specimens of the utmost purity, [and] that poetry's function is inspirational" (Golding 14), his anthologies, and thus the emerging canon, tended to be "homogeneous," meaning that there was little room for "eccentric philosophies, that it was primarily written by men, and that it was created solely in New York and New England" (15). Poe's unfavorable assessment of Griswold's volume, as well as his later remarks during his many public lectures on the topic, very likely contributed to the anthologist's negative treatment of Poe's life and work when he edited Poe's writings for Redfield after the author's death.

Although Griswold included Poe in his *Poets and Poetry of America*, he did not include any of his poetry in a subsequent anthology, *Readings in American Poetry*, published in 1843. In the preface to that volume, Griswold addresses the didactic nature and national tendencies of the poems chosen for inclusion:

> This collection of specimens of American Poetry is designed principally for the use of schools. The books hitherto published for this purpose have been mainly or entirely compiled from the writings of foreigners. . . . The poems which it contains are essentially American, in spirit as well as by origin. The themes of many of them are from our country; they relate to the grand and beautiful in our scenery; or assert the dignity and rights of man, as recognized in our theory of government. (3)

He then asserts, "A distinguishing character of our poetry is its freedom from all licentiousness" (3). Assuming appropriate editorial modesty, Griswold concludes: "However imperfectly the editor may have performed his task, he anticipates for the volume a favourable reception, not more confidently for this reason, than because of the intrinsic excellence of its contents, and the generally deepening interest in American letters" (4).

That Poe does not appear in this volume should come as no surprise. After all, Poe was a relative newcomer on the poetic scene in 1843, and his poetry was not very "American" in the nationalistic sense of the times. Appropriately, the volume opens with "Thanatopsis" by William Cullen Bryant, and the poets most represented include Brainard, Bryant, Clark, Dana, Halleck, Holmes, Longfellow, Percival, Pierpont, Sigourney, Sprague, Whittier, and Willis. Interestingly, what was not suitable for schoolchildren in the 1840s has clearly changed in our times: Poe's works have become *de rigueur* for young American readers as early as middle school, and his name has become synonymous with Halloween because of the popular, although erroneous, perception that he was primarily a horror writer.

By 1846, Griswold's *Poets and Poetry of America* was in its seventh edition, and its frontispiece features the same "Boilerplate Five" as featured in the 1842 volume. It also includes a historical introduction, gilded edges, an ornamental cover, and fine engravings throughout the volume. In the note to the second edition that is reprinted in the front matter of the seventh, Griswold updates his earlier observations on American poetry and his rationale for selecting poets and poems for inclusion: "A new edition of this work having been called for much earlier than was anticipated by the publishers, but little time has been afforded for improvements. A few poems have, however, been added, and such errors as were discovered have been corrected" (vi). Griswold includes in this volume the same three poems by Poe that had appeared in the first edition of the volume in 1842.

Four years later, George B. Cheever published *The Poets of America*. Befitting a volume with such an inclusive title, the anthology includes a fine lithograph frontispiece produced by Kellogs and Comstock, which also carries the author W. C. Bryant's signature. Other fine lithographs in the volume include images of N. P. Willis, Fitz-Green Halleck, J. Pierpont, Washington Allston, and L. H. Sigourney. Henry W. Longfellow's image is also included in the text, but it is a remarkably bad likeness of the young author. Although the New England writers were well represented, as expected, Cheever's volume does not include any poems by Poe, not even "The Raven," which was arguably the most unique and memorable poem in American literature at the time. Poe's omission from Cheever's anthology is less surprising, though, when one considers its editor's enthusiasm for devotional poetry. While the stimulation of thought and the imagination (characteristic of Poe) was a priority for Cheever, it was more important to him that "[a]ll the pieces in this volume are of the purest moral character; and, considering its limits, and the comparative scantiness of American poetry, a good number of them contain, in an uncommon degree, the religious and poetical spirit united" (5). Cheever praises Bryant, Wilcox, Dana, Pierpont, Brainard (whom he compares favorably to Burns), Hillhouse, and Willis, and he concludes with the injunction, "May the volume, thus selected, please and do good" (6).[10]

Even with anthologies like Cheever's on the market, Griswold's *The Poets and Poetry of America* thrived and continued to be reprinted throughout the 1850s. The seventeenth edition, released in 1858, contained a new frontispiece—a fine engraved steel portrait of Rufus W. Griswold with the signature of the editor underneath. This is a significant departure from the singular "Boilerplate Five" that was a staple of Griswold's previous reprintings. The volume also features several steel engravings of notable poets, including one of Poe (468–69). While *Poets and Poetry* was already considered a high-quality publication, this edition provided Griswold another means by which to capitalize on his recently published edition of Poe's *Works*, and his inclusion of the engraving of Poe could even suggest his grudging acknowledgment of Poe's significance as a great American poet. Regardless, Griswold's substitution of his own portrait for that of the "Boilerplate Five" illustrates a narcissistic focus on himself as editor, as anthologizer, and as the gatekeeper of American poetry.

These anthologies enjoyed considerable literary and cultural significance during the early-mid-nineteenth century. As Alexandra Urakova reiterates in "The 'Flower-gemmed' Story: Gift Book Tradition and Poe's 'Eleonora'" in this book, early anthologies such as Griswold's patterned themselves after gift books, with their ornamental binding, gilded edges, and high-quality steel engravings (62). Such is the case with the later, more ornate editions of *Poets and Poetry*. Rather than presenting a *florilegium*, or gathering of poetical flowers, Griswold and those anthologists who followed him—especially the anthologists of poetry—were engaged, implicitly or explicitly, in establishing a canon of American literature. In that sense, ultimately, *Poets and Poetry* served a higher purpose than the typical gift book otherwise might serve.

Griswold's ultimate aims in the shaping of an American canon of poetry were further explicated in his preface to the sixteenth edition (reprinted in the seventeenth edition). He provided readers with his reasons for his selection of authors and their work, defending first the exclusion of women writers from *The Poets and Poetry of America* and reaffirming his primary purpose for his collection: to display the notable work done by artists who were in the process of creating the American literary tradition. In the seventeenth edition the volume, he describes the process of selection as follows: "By the publication of 'The Female Poets of America,' in 1849, this survey of American Poetry was divided into two parts. From 'The Poets and Poetry of America' were omitted all reviewals [sic] of our female poets, and their places were supplied with notices of other authors. The entire volume was also revised, re-arranged, and in other respects improved" (3).

Perhaps in anticipation of further resistance given his taste in selections, Griswold validates his critics, including Poe, admitting that he had "been censured, perhaps justly, for the wide range of [his] selections [and] did not consider all the contents of the volume Poetry" (3). Griswold states, "I aimed merely to show what had been accomplished toward a Poetical Literature by our writers in verse before the close of the first half century of our national existence" (3). Through admittedly questionable methods, Griswold continued to build his career as both a "taste-maker" and a "genre-maker." Desiring to produce *the* anthology of American poetry, Griswold sought thereby to influence the perceptions and expectations of readers, and to create a pedestal atop which the anthologizer could sit and gaze down on the poets he has selected for inclusion.

Despite his postmortem attacks on Poe's character, Griswold nevertheless includes in the later editions of *Poets and Poetry* sixteen poems by Poe, who had named him literary executor of his works upon his death in 1849. This was a considerable contrast to the three poems by Poe that had been published in previous editions of *Poets and Poetry*. The broader selection of Poe's work included "The City in the Sea," "Annabel Lee," "Ulalume: a Ballad,"

"To Zante," "To ——," "Dream-Land," "Lenore," "Israfel," "The Bells," "To F.S.O.," "For Annie," "To One in Paradise," "The Raven," "The Conqueror Worm," "The Haunted Palace," and "The Sleeper," which gave readers a greater sense of the range of Poe's poetry and helped to perpetuate a view of Poe as a dark, brooding, macabre poet detached from the material world.

Griswold also includes a much-expanded headnote in the later editions of *Poets and Poetry* in which he states his attempt as an editor "to present, with as much kindly reserve in regard to his life as was consistent with justice, a view of his extraordinary intellectual and moral character" (470). While this statement, at face value, may suggest that the editor is being as evenhanded as possible in his handling of Poe's life, Griswold's seemingly complimentary words are undercut by the next few lines in which he intimates that Poe was "[u]nquestionably . . . a man of genius, and those who are familiar with his melancholy history will not doubt that his genius was in a singular degree wasted or misapplied" (470). Concerning Poe's poetry, Griswold pronounces:

> In poetry, as in prose, he was most successful in the metaphysical treatment of the passions. His poems are constructed with wonderful ingenuity, and finished with consummate art. They illustrate a morbid sensitiveness of feeling, a shadowy and gloomy imagination, and a taste almost faultless in the apprehension of that sort of beauty most agreeable to his temper. His rank as a poet is with the first class of his times. "The Raven," "Ulalume," "The Bells," and several of his other pieces will be remembered as among the finest monuments of the capacities of the English language. (470)

Indeed, the method by which Griswold managed to destroy Poe's character while simultaneously assuring his reputation as one of the most notable America writers is as sinister as it is tragic.

Griswold's anthologies were the most popular anthologies of American poetry of their time—going through seventeen editions in fourteen years—and thus were influential in shaping and defining the "canon" of American poetry for several generations. Golding correctly suggests that Griswold deserves credit for raising his estimate of Emerson and Poe. As Golding notes, Griswold increased his representation of Emerson's poetry from five poems in 1842 to fifteen in 1855, and he increased his representation of Poe's poetry from three poems in 1842 to sixteen poems in 1855, "this despite Poe's feud with Griswold and the editor's posthumous character assassination of him" (16). At the same time, Griswold enhanced his own reputation in the literary world and profited financially from his efforts, effectively elevating and enriching himself off of the creative work of others. He carved out a place for himself in the antebellum literary marketplace as the "anthologizer" (of

American poetry) and the "editor" of *The Works of the Late Edgar Allan Poe*. In these roles, Griswold exercised considerable control over the valuing and distribution of much of the poetry written in the United States during this period. His presentation of Poe's works and his (mis)representation of Poe's life would influence perceptions of Poe in the United States and Europe for over a century.

Competing Anthologists: Dana, Lowell, and Emerson

Other anthologies besides Griswold's were published in the mid- to late nineteenth century. In 1858, Charles A. Dana edited the *Household Book of Poetry*.[11] In most ways, *Household Book* was organized in a manner that audiences had come to expect from anthologies. The volume offered notable selections from a wide range of sources intended to increase the collection's scope. Dana writes in the preface, "The purpose of this book is to comprise within the bounds of a single volume whatever is truly beautiful and admirable among the minor poems of the English language. . . . [I]t has been the constant endeavor of the Editor to exercise a catholic as well as severe taste; and to judge every piece by its poetical merit solely, without regard to the name, nationality, or epoch of its author" (v). One notable aspect of *Household* is that the editor offers a "novel" arrangement, dividing the selections according to their "ideas and motives" (or themes) rather than their chronology, birthplace, or sex, which is "a method more usual in such collections" (v). Dana includes poems of "indisputable greatness," whether of "English, Scotch, Irish, or American origin" (vi). Among these selections, Dana inserts three poems by Poe in his hefty volume: "The Raven" (under "Poems of the Imagination"), "Annabel Lee" (under "Love's History"), and "The Bells" (under "Poems of Sentiment and Reflection"). Yet again, Poe's place and date of birth are presented erroneously, 1811 instead of 1809.[12] Even while operating within the scope of several national literary traditions, Poe earned his place in Dana's anthology, thus providing evidence for some sense of his postmortem acceptance and appreciation.

In 1866, Anna Cabot (Jackson) Lowell published *Gleanings from the Poets, for Home and School*. Lowell's anthology shares certain features with Cheever's *Poets of America* in that her hopes for the volume center on providing certain foundations for impressionable young readers. In her preface, Lowell points out that "[w]hile school education especially aims to develop the understanding and form good mental habits, it must not neglect to interest the imagination and refine the taste" (iii). The editor explains her choices for inclusion, which seem to emphasize aesthetics, stating: "It is with this design of presenting beauty, both moral and natural, in its manifold shapes, as it is shown to us in the universe, that the present collection has been made" (iii). Another notable feature of *Gleanings* is that it contains what the editor claims to be "the whole range of English and American standard authors" (iii), with more selections of the former than the latter. Like Cheever's earlier work, Lowell's anthology omits both Poe and Whitman, whom she very likely did not consider "standard" figures for her stated purpose of providing moral instruction for children.

Similarly, Ralph Waldo Emerson published a thematically arranged poetry anthology, *Parnassus*, in 1875, consisting of selections from both British and American poetry. Emerson reveals a decided preference for British authors, and he omits most major American poets, including Poe and Whitman. In titling this anthology *Parnassus*, Emerson attempts to establish a fellowship of poets at the pinnacle of their artistry, who dwell with the Muses on top of this sacred mountain in Greece. With this in mind, his exclusion of Poe and Whitman from this volume could be interpreted as being a literary slight. In Poe's case, the cause for Emerson's actions may be because of the outspoken disdain that Poe held for Emerson's poetry, a subject about which the Transcendentalist proved to be sensitive. Regardless, Emerson's anthology appeared at a time when American poets had not yet begun to earn the same level of respect afforded to their British counterparts.

Into the Twentieth Century

It would not be until the turn of the twentieth century that Poe's poetry would be reconsidered seriously in the United States (although it had begun to be admired throughout France, and Europe in general, much earlier because of Charles Baudelaire's translations of Poe's prose works, his influential biographical essays on Poe, and Stéphane Mallarmé's translations of Poe's poetry). The same would be true of Walt Whitman and Emily Dickinson, whose poetry, for different reasons, would not appear in major anthologies until the twentieth century. Two major anthologies—edited by Edmund Clarence Stedman in 1900 and Curtis Hidden Page in 1905—ushered Poe's poetry into the twentieth century and introduced a higher level of critical perspective to the enterprise of anthologizing American poets and poetry.

Stedman's voluminous *An American Anthology, 1787–1899* both continues and departs radically from the tradition that Griswold established during his lifetime.[13] "By Stedman's time," according to Golding, "the tendency to politicize and moralize poetry (explicitly, at least) had largely dropped out of American anthologies. The country's sense of political and literary accomplishment no longer needed the support of anthologies documenting the unique national characteristics and moral purity of American verse" (20). In his introduction, Stedman contrasts his own anthology with that of Griswold by pointing out that his literary forebear's attempts were perhaps more notable for their cultural significance than scholarly achievements, stating that "Dr. Griswold performed an historical if not a critical service; he had a measure of conscience withal, else Poe would not have chosen him for a literary executor. But if this anthology were modelled upon his 'Poets and Poetry of America' it would occupy a shelf of volumes" (xvii). This summation of Griswold's efforts and Stedman's emphasis on volume size speaks to developing attitudes regarding Poe's literary executor. According to Golding, Stedman prefers the revolutionary voices of Poe and Whitman to the moralizing ones of Longfellow and Lowell, and he gives Emily Dickinson the "space she would not receive again for years" (20).

In his anthology, Stedman updates Griswold's "Boilerplate Five" with his own frontispiece (figure 12.2) that features eight poets (Poe, Longfellow, Whitman, Bryant, Whittier, Holmes, Lowell, and Lanier). His reconfiguration of the canonical pantheon of American poetry elevates Poe to the highest position, casting him as the greatest among his peers. Stedman tells his readers that he has included "nearly all the effective lyrics of Poe" in his anthology (xvi). Stedman does not, however, define or clarify what he means by "effective." Nevertheless, he includes twelve poems by Poe: "To Helen," "The Raven," "The Sleeper," "Lenore," "To One in Paradise," "The City in the Sea," "Israfel," "The Haunted Palace," "The Conqueror Worm," "The Bells," "Annabel Lee," and "Ulalume." The increased representation of Poe's poetry, and especially the inclusion of one of his finest short lyrics—"To Helen"—previously omitted by Griswold, reinforces Stedman's estimation of Poe's merits as a poet and Poe's placement above his fellow poets.

Only five years later, Curtis Hidden Page published *The Chief American Poets: Selected Poems by Bryant, Poe, Emerson, Longfellow, Whittier, Holmes, Lowell, Whitman, and Lanier* with notes, reference lists, and biographical sketches. In what is perhaps an unintentional show of solidarity, Page's frontispiece more or less reaffirms Stedman's estimation of the American pantheon of poets. It includes Bryant, Poe, Whitman (top row); Lowell, Longfellow, Holmes (second row); and Emerson, Lanier, and Whittier (bottom row). By adopting the definite article "The" in his title, Page subtly asserts that his anthology is the definitive one rather than Stedman's, whose title is phrased more tentatively as "An Anthology." Nevertheless, Page accepts Stedman's cast of luminaries but adds Emerson to the mix in what

Figure 12.2. Frontispiece, *An American Anthology*, edited by Edmund Clarence Stedman, (1900).
Photograph by Philip Edward Phillips, with permission. Boston Athenæum.

would become the last major anthology to include a visual "pantheon" of American poets in this way.

Hubbell calls attention to the fact that six of the nine poets selected by Page to comprise his "chief poets" are New Englanders and suggests, at least indirectly, that market factors and readers' expectations likely played a role in their inclusion, especially in the case of Lowell. Hubbell states that the publisher, the Houghton Mifflin Company, "held the copyrights on many of the best books by the older writers of New England" (112), and for this reason neither Page, nor any anthologist for that matter, "could safely deny [Lowell] a place in the canon of the great American writers—especially in a text published by the firm which held the copyrights on Lowell's writings and those of other New England poets" (113). That Page selected Poe to sit atop those same New England writers in his frontispiece is therefore all the more remarkable.

Contrasting Griswold's anthologies, which enjoyed almost annual revised editions during his lifetime, Page claims in his preface that his anthology

> must remain for many years without a rival. "Yet still the man is greater than his song." Many true lovers of literature care more for a few poets than for many poems, and would prefer to have always by them the best work of our few chief poets, rather than the few best poems of our many minor singers. The present volume, like my *British Poets of the Nineteenth Century*, attempts to give, for each one of the authors included, all the material needed to show his development and his achievement, and to give first knowledge of him as man and poet. (xvi)

His anthology is intended for scholarly audiences and classroom use, with its ample footnotes, lists of standard editions, and biographical sketches. Although generally more inclusive, the volume nevertheless excludes female poets, which is a serious shortcoming. Page further reveals his high esteem for Poe by including thirty-three of his poems, the most by any of these anthologists of American poetry. These poems range from his youthful "Tamerlane" to one of his last poems, "Eldorado."

In his biographical sketch, Page calls Poe "unique among the chief American poets" because of his life of "extreme poverty and loneliness . . . his hatred of commonplace and of convention . . . his intense devotion to poetry . . . his love of mere music in verse, [and] . . . his strange visionary conceptions of death" (663). Page's acknowledgment that the circumstances of Poe's life were markedly different from those of all the other "chief poets" exemplifies his sense of conflict regarding the poet's life. Ultimately, he does not know

how to handle Poe's "weak character and ill-repute" (663). In Page's estimation, Poe is to American poetry what Hawthorne is to American prose
fiction; Poe is "the only American who has been *intensely a poet*, and the
only American poet (as Hawthorne is our only prose writer) who can justly
be said, in any strict and narrow use of the word, to have had genius" (663).

Also published near the beginning of the twentieth century, the *Yale Book
of American Verse*, edited by Thomas R. Lounsbury, responds directly to the
anthologies of American poetry published in the previous decade. In his
prefatory note, "A Word About Anthologies," Lounsbury writes:

> [I]n case of works of the imagination, the settled judgment of the great body of
> cultivated men is infinitely superior to the judgment of any one man, however
> eminent. . . . A genuinely great production will in the end find its own public
> which in time will become the public; and that public will not be deterred
> from admiring it by the most bitter attacks of the ablest writers in the most
> influential periodicals. (xv)

Recalling the anthologies of his predecessors, Lounsbury opines: "[D]ur-
ing the last fifty or sixty years there have been published a full half-dozen
[anthologies] which have aimed at completeness. As they set out to cover
the whole field of English literature, much of the largest proportion of what
they contain has been taken from British authors. Still they have given full
recognition to whatever has come from America which they have deemed
worthy of inclusion" (xxv).

According to Lounsbury, Stedman's 1900 anthology "was not designed as
a collection of poems of undisputed worth, but as a general representation of
the work of American authors who had written verse of various degrees of
excellence" (xxvi). The Yale anthology reaffirms Poe's place in the emerging canon of American poetry—albeit with fewer representative poems—
eight—than either Stedman or Page. These include some of his very best
and most memorable: "Annabel Lee," "The Bells," "The Conqueror Worm,"
"The Haunted Palace," "The Raven," "To Helen," "To One in Paradise,"
and "Ulalume."

Golding remarks that the anthologies of both Page and Lounsbury "show
teachers of literature becoming more responsible for overseeing the canon in
the decades after 1900" (21). Indeed, as he notes, the power to sway public
literary taste and to change what constitutes the canon of American poetry
began to "shift from individual editors to an institution—the university"
(21).[14] Whitman, Dickinson, and Poe would endure as major poets whose

literary reputations would be affirmed and solidified by later twentieth- and twenty-first-century anthologists of American poetry.

The Oxford and Other Anthologies

While other anthology series could be considered, including the various Norton anthologies and others designed for undergraduate classroom use, I shall focus instead on the respected Oxford anthologies of American literature, which provide unique insight into the critical and aesthetic reception of Poe. They also constitute a tradition of the "anthology" genre, one that participates in and contributes significantly to the changing "canon" of American poetry, including Carman (1927), Matthiessen (1950), Ellmann (1976), and Lehman (2006).

The first of what would become a series of anthologies, *The Oxford Book of American Verse*, edited by Bliss Carman, was published in 1927. Recognizing the influence of Stedman's anthology, Carman writes in his preface that his own volume "does not attempt to be in the least encyclopedic. It is a comparatively small anthology, and cannot pretend to compete with a work such as Mr. Stedman's invaluable book was in its day, and still is for the period it covers. . . . *The Oxford Book* . . . takes a much more skimming view of the whole field of American verse" (iii). The editor states that he has been all the more judicious in his selection of poems because he was given such freedom to choose them, and he also apologizes to readers who may be disappointed that their favorite poems are not included. He also contrasts "old poetry and new" writing; "[t]he old poetry by comparison was to so great an extent imbued with a doleful spirit, or with a desperate resignation at best. In spite of the orthodoxy of the conventional age which produced it, the poetry of those days shows for the most part little of the valiant and joyous spirit which we find in the verse of our own times" (iv–v). He considers our poetry still "only in its beginning," leading him to implore a "younger generation of poetry lovers," including his students in Canada and the United States, to establish and protect "the future of American poetry," which he confidently entrusts to them (v). He prints nine well-known poems by Poe: "The Raven," "The Bells," "Ulalume," "The Haunted Palace," "The City in the Sea," "The Sleeper," "Annabel Lee," "To Helen," and "To One in Paradise."

When F. O. Matthiessen published *The Oxford Book of American Verse* in 1950, he asserted a preference for quality over quantity. Indeed, the individual sections dedicated to the poets provide thorough representations of their works. In his introduction, he details his editorial practices, expressing his preference for "fewer poets, with more space for each" (ix). He qualifies this preference by explaining that "[t]he space allotted to various poets is not always proportional to their relative importance" (xiii). Matthiessen asserts that Poe and Whitman are the "two great pivotal figures" in nineteenth-century American poetry, and they "present opposite problems" (xiii). On the one hand, Poe "wrote somewhat less than fifty pieces of verse altogether," aside from his early verse, and selecting what is best for his anthology "involves little more than the elimination of several . . . occasional poems and of one or two notorious stunts like 'The Bells,' which no adult reader can now face without pain. The visible body of Poe's work, the work from which France would date the beginning of modern poetry, amounts to barely thirty pages" (xiii). On the other hand, Matthiessen argues that "Whitman's place in American poetry is one of amplitude both of form and feeling" (xiii–xiv). Matthiessen includes nineteen selections from Poe with no author head-notes: "Dreams," "A Dream within a Dream," "The Happiest Day, The Happiest Hour," "Sonnet—To Science," "Song from *Al Aaraaf*," "Romance," "To Helen," "Israfel," "The City in the Sea," "The Sleeper," "To One in Paradise," "The Haunted Palace," "Dream-Land," "The Raven," "Ulalume—A Ballad," "Eldorado," "For Annie," "To My Mother," and "Annabel Lee."

Matthiessen's Oxford anthology, along with his previously published landmark study, *American Renaissance: Art and Expression in the Age of Whitman and Emerson*, served simultaneously to define and limit scholars' and general readers' perceptions of the value of the poets whose work contributed to and was omitted from the *American Renaissance*.[15] Despite the Oxford volume's merits, including the recognition of Poe and Whitman as major poets, Matthiessen did not include Poe among the authors lauded in *American Renaissance*, a decision that, perhaps, affected Poe's standing among scholars of that era and, most certainly, affected Poe's representation (or lack of representation) in many undergraduate- and graduate-level courses on the "American Renaissance." Poe's association with so-called dark romanticism, or the general perception that his subject matter is dark, contributed to his marginalization.

Richard Ellmann edited the next iteration of the Oxford series, *The New Oxford Book of American Verse*, in 1976. In his anthology, Ellmann takes a much more comprehensive approach than his predecessor. He begins boldly, claiming that "American poetry, once an offshoot, now appears to be a parent stem" (xv). Although the editor is positive about the growing tradition of stateside verse, he concedes that early Americans were more gifted prose writers than poets: "Almost from the beginning there must have been a glimmer that new exploits might be hazarded in creative literature as in other kinds of endeavor. . . . If memorialists were scarce, it is salutary to recognize in an age of chairpersons, that the first American poet of consequence was a woman. Anne Bradstreet, born before Shakespeare died, belonged to a pious and workaday world as unlike his as possible" (xv). Ellmann devotes much attention to both Poe and Whitman and then turns his attention appropriately to Emily Dickinson. Ellman notes that Poe and Whitman resemble each other only in respect to their ambition. They were very much "opposites" in their differing worldviews: "Poe's apocalyptic imagination saw love, the haunted palace of the mind, and the whole fabric of reality about to fall—like the house of Usher—into negativity. To Whitman's calls to awakening Poe responded with 'Nevermore'" (xxiii). Perhaps Ellman's estimation of their poetic projects can best be seen in this statement: "the world that Whitman was busy celebrating was the world that Poe was busy destroying" (xxii). In his characterization, Poe remains the dark romantic, always critical, always on the margins, and never in the mainstream.

Concerning his selection practices (departing from Matthiessen, who was also his friend) and his range (from Bradstreet to LeRoi Jones), Ellmann writes: "A number of the choices, and of the exclusions, may be controversial. I have attempted to select poems on the basis of intrinsic merit rather than the tendencies they represent. Still, taken, as a whole, the book gives a broad indication of the principal directions of American poetry, and of its accomplishment" (xxx). Ellmann includes a generous seventeen selections from Poe: "A Dream within a Dream," "Song from *Al Aaraaf*," "Introduction [to *Poems*]," "To Helen," "Israfel," "The City in the Sea," "The Sleeper," "The Haunted Palace," "The Coliseum," "Sonnet—Silence," "The Conqueror Worm," "Dream-Land," "The Raven," "Ulalume—A Ballad," "Eldorado," "For Annie," and "Annabel Lee." In addition to including some of Poe's best-known and frequently anthologized poems, such as "The Haunted Palace," "The Coliseum," and "The Raven," Ellmann adds an excerpt from Poe's most opaque poem, "Al Aaraaf," which reveals the poet's youthful, epic aspirations, as well as an excerpt from his "Introduction [to *Poems*]," which provides insight into Poe's developing aesthetic theories. This range of works offers readers a more complete picture of Poe as a visionary and an artist than did previous anthologies.

Published in 2006, *The Oxford Book of American Poetry*, edited by David Lehman, is the most recent contribution to the Oxford series. It measures artistic merit at face value and creates connections between and among major literary figures. In the introduction, Lehman explains to his readers, "To learn from a Richard Wilbur essay that 'Fairy-Land' was Elizabeth Bishop's favorite poem by Edgar Allan Poe . . . is not inconsequential if the information prompts one to look up the poem and see just how good it is" (xi). Acknowledging the work of Ellmann and Matthiessen, Lehman writes, "The goal of this volume is to establish a canon wider and more inclusive than those that formerly prevailed, but to do so on grounds that are fundamentally literary and artistic in nature. Not one selection was dictated by a political imperative. Matthiessen in 1950 picked fifty-one poets. Ellmann's anthology contained seventy-eight. There are two hundred and ten in this volume" (xii). While Matthiessen selected poets for their "star power" and included fewer poets with more space for each, Lehman tried to include more poets with less space for most. Interestingly, Lehman's anthology also pushes past his previous cutoff date of 1950, including material like the lyrics for Bob Dylan's "Desolation Row" because of the shifts in what "value" we place on certain work.

The volume includes ten poems by Poe and a headnote: "Dreams," "Fairy-Land," "To Helen," "The City in the Sea," "To One in Paradise," "The Haunted Palace," "The Raven," "Ulalume—A Ballad," "A Dream within a Dream," and "Annabel Lee."[16] Lehman's biographical sketch of Poe is far less biased against him than those appearing in many other anthologies. Nevertheless, he allows himself the liberty to suggest that Poe "lived a luridly sensational life" (61). He begins by telling readers that Poe invented the detective story, was a celebrated poet, and a professional writer and editor. There are several sentences devoted to his international influence and to his habitual contradictions as an editor and writer. Lehman concludes by stating that Poe "challenges readers not to read but solve him" (61). In doing so, Lehman pays homage to Poe's role in the creation of detective fiction as well as his skill with solving ciphers and analyzing poetry and prose. By mentioning Bishop's admiration for Poe's "Fairy-Land," Lehman brings Poe—as seen through the eyes of a major modernist American poet—into the twentieth century. Lehman's account of Poe's life remains faithful to his apparent intent to look at the artist's contribution. It also reflects the prevailing current critical attitude toward Poe, one that considers more objectively the poet's artistic merit and literary-historical context rather than a popular, that is to say, sensationalistic and commercialized, reading of Poe.[17]

Tracing Poe's place and presentation in anthologies of American poetry can tell us much about changing American literary tastes, anthologists' attitudes toward his life and works, and the significant role that anthologies play in establishing a "national literature" or a "canon" of American poetry. Among Poe's anthologized poetry, six poems—"To Helen," "The City in the Sea," "The Haunted Palace" (from the original three poems in Griswold, 1842),

"The Raven," "Ulalume—A Ballad," and "Annabel Lee"—appear in all four of the Oxford anthologies and remain among Poe's most loved, and most frequently anthologized, poems. They share none of the nationalistic or didactic qualities promoted by anthologists—such as Griswold and his contemporaries, who insisted that "the great American writer had to be a model of morality" (Hubbell 52)—and expected by readers in nineteenth-century America. They do, however, reflect Poe's own assertion that poetry's aim should be Beauty, and that art exists for its own sake. The first two poems and the final three concern *"Mournful and Never-ending Remembrance"* (Poe, "Philosophy" 167), and/or the longing for something that is seemingly just beyond our grasp. "The Haunted Palace" represents the mind of the artist and concerns the theme of madness while serving as the centerpiece of one of Poe's finest tales, "The Fall of the House of Usher." The focus on art, on interiority, on darkness, and on the quest for the unattainable are themes that resonated with many modernist poets and artists, and they resonate with readers today. So, while anthologists' selection processes may reflect their own literary tastes and efforts to define the "canon" for their times and, perhaps, for later generations, there are ways in which the poems themselves demand to be included, and are included, as they speak to and thereby shape the tastes of readers through time.

In "Inventing the Literati: Poe's Remapping of Antebellum Print Culture," J. Gerald Kennedy argues that the tendency since Griswold's infamous "Ludwig" obituary "to separate Poe from the American scene, to see his poetry and fiction as inherently disconnected from antebellum culture, has institutionalized a fundamental misrepresentation of him" (3). Not an anthologist himself, Poe nevertheless rivaled Griswold as an arbiter of American literary taste.[18] He reinvented himself throughout his literary career, as a "magazinist" on the one hand and as a lyceum lecturer on the other. In his lectures on "The Poets and Poetry of America," especially, Kennedy suggests, Poe "implicitly competed" with Griswold "for preeminence as a judge of American versifiers" even as he attempted to promote his own magazine (24). While Poe, in the short term, may have lost ground to Griswold, Poe's poems and aesthetic theories, in the long term, have gained the respect and representation that they deserve in current anthologies of American poetry.

Notes

1. I am grateful to Provost Mark Byrnes and Dean John Vile, Middle Tennessee State University, for supporting my research in Boston; Amy A. Harris-Aber, my doctoral research assistant, Middle Tennessee State University, for her contributions

to this essay; Patricia Boulos, head of Digital Programs, Boston Athenæum, for granting me permission to use the images featured in this essay; Carolle Morini, Caroline D. Bain Archivist/Reference Librarian, Boston Athenæum, for helping me locate materials essential to the completion of this project; and Emron Esplin and Margarida Vale de Gato for their careful editing and helpful suggestions to me throughout the process.

2. See Scott Peeples's "Teaching Poe the Magazinist"; Jeffrey Andrew Weinstock's "Magazines;" and my own "Poe the Magazinist."

3. The first effort to publish a complete collection of Poe's poetry appeared in *The Works of the Late Edgar Allan Poe*, edited by Rufus W. Griswold, after Poe's death.

4. On the topic of Poe and reprinting, see Meredith L. McGill's *American Literature and the Culture of Reprinting, 1834–1853*. For more on Poe and gift books, see Alexandra Urakova's chapter 3 in this book as well as her article "'The Purloined Letter' in the Gift Book: Reading Poe in a Contemporary Context," and Kathryn K. Shinn's "Gift Books."

5. Nonetheless, there are patterns of requirements that can be discerned throughout anthologies and that, even if they do not particularly mind the progression of a poet's career, record changes in poetic fashions. Many anthologies assume the role of interpreter of literary evaluation. See Barbara Korte and her colleagues' *Anthologies of British Poetry: Critical Perspectives from Literary and Cultural Studies*.

6. Freneau's name appears with that of Walt Whitman in the title of the Library of America anthology edited by John Hollander in 1993. Freneau's inclusion attests to his enduring appeal, and Whitman's inclusion reinforces Freneau's dominant place as a major American poet after generations of neglect and omission by earlier anthologists.

7. Several of these writers were known at the time as the "Connecticut Wits."

8. A decade later, John Keese published *The Poets of America: Illustrated by One of Her Painters* with S. Coleman in 1840. Its frontispiece depicts a beautifully drawn illustration of the three graces, and its dedication reads: "To the / Poets of Our Country, / this volume, / THE CREATION OF THEIR GENIUS, / is respectfully dedicated." In his preface, Keese writes that American poetry has heretofore "been produced mostly by minds devoted to sterner studies, and in brief intervals of leisure, snatched from more engrossing toils" (9). Emphasizing the "practical" character of his compatriots and the "prosaic" nature of the times, he suggests that now is the time for America to share the "brilliancy of our gems," asserting that "the design of the present volume, is in some degree, to repair this deficiency" (10). His aim, as was Kettell's, was primarily to preserve "specimens" (11) of varying quality. His anthology features ninety poems, almost exclusively written by poets popular at the beginning of the nineteenth century, and therefore includes no poems by Poe.

9. The inclusion of such fictitious, romanticized information (supplied by Poe) affected multiple generations of Poe biographies that relied on Griswold's headnote to make what were later proven to be false claims about Poe's biography.

10. Perhaps a more accurate title of Cheever's volume would been the "Christian" Poets of America. The volume may have been intended to "please" a more conservative, nostalgic American readership, one that would likewise approve of the volume's purported didactic aim to "do good" (6). Nevertheless, it is surprising that an anthology of American poetry published as late as 1850 would not feature poets who had proven themselves to be more accomplished than almost all of those praised by Cheever.

11. The Boston Athenæum holds the ninth edition, published in 1864, which illustrates the popularity of this anthology with its core audience for nearly a decade.

12. This flawed information is unsurprising, as it was probably gathered from Griswold's "Memoir."

13. According to Golding, "Stedman's was the first large anthology by a prestigious American editor since 1875, and the first of solely American poetry since Griswold's 1872 edition. This, combined with Stedman's reputation as a critic, assured the book substantial influence" (19–20).

14. As important as this observation is, Golding argues that "these texts [those of Page and Lounsbury] suggest that Stedman's reevaluations took some time to catch on" (21). "These anthologists," Golding concludes, "while demeaning popular taste, generally accepted the canon of poets which that taste had established" and, in doing so, "simply found a new way to validate the old poetry" (21).

15. Matthiessen, glaringly, does not include a single African American poet in his anthology. This deficiency immediately called for a major correction, but one that would take another twenty years.

16. Lehman acknowledges that he included Poe's "To One in Paradise" because Matthiessen had included it in his anthology.

17. Two other twentieth-century anthologies of American poetry merit acknowledgment. First, *American Poetry: The Nineteenth Century, Vol. 1: Philip Freneau to Walt Whitman*, edited by John Hollander in 1993 and the first volume in a two-part set produced by the Library of America, seeks to replicate for American readers what the Pléiade series offers to French readers: high-quality, standard volumes containing the most important national poets, published in a handsome and an enduring format. Hollander's anthology includes a straightforward, two-page biography of Poe. He also includes a generous selection of poems by Poe, twenty-four, compared to previous anthologies: "Stanzas," "The Lake—To——," "To Science," "Al Aaraaf," "Romance," "Fairy-Land," "Alone," "To Helen," "Israfel," "The Valley of Unrest," "The City in the Sea," "To F——," "The Coliseum," "The Haunted Palace," "Silence," "The Conqueror Worm," "Lenore," "Dream-Land," "The Raven," "Ulalume—A Ballad," "The Bells," "For Annie," "Eldorado," and "Annabel Lee." Only Page, in 1905, provides more at thirty-three. Second, *The Columbia Anthology of American Poetry*, edited by Jay Parini in 1995, highlights the writings of Emerson and Whitman among nineteenth-century poets and discusses ways in which they transformed American poetry. Parini argues that Whitman dominates the poetic landscape. Compared to six poems by Bryant, nine poems by Emerson, and eight poems by Longfellow, there

are only seven poems by Poe in the *Columbia Anthology*: "To Helen," "The City in the Sea," "Sonnet—Silence," "The Raven," "Eldorado," "For Annie," and "Annabel Lee." Both volumes are edited by respected American poets, suggesting that these presses wanted to identify and canonize poetry of the highest quality in these influential anthologies.

18. Poe published no anthologies, but Jana Argersinger's and Harry Lee Poe's essays in this book (chapters 1 and 2) examine the anthologizing processes Poe used in his literary relationships and in his own writing.

Works Cited

Carman, Bliss, editor. *The Oxford Book of American Verse*. Oxford UP, 1927.

Cheever, George B., editor. *The Poets of America*. Silas Andrus and Son, 1850.

Dana, Charles A., editor. *Household Book of Poetry*. D. Appleton and Company, 1858.

Ellmann, Richard, editor. *The New Oxford Book of American Verse*. Oxford UP, 1976.

Emerson, Ralph Waldo, editor. *Parnassus*. James R. Osgood and Company, 1875.

Ferry, Anne. *Tradition and the Individual Poem: An Inquiry into Anthologies*. Stanford UP, 2001.

Golding, Alan C. *From Outlaw to Classic: Canons in American Poetry*. U of Wisconsin P, 1995.

Griswold, Rufus W., editor. *The Poets and Poetry of America*. Carey and Hart, 1842.

———. *The Poets and Poetry of America*, 7th ed. Carey and Hart, 1846.

———. *The Poets and Poetry of America*, 17th ed. Perry and McMillan, 1858.

———. *Readings in American Poetry*. John C. Riker, 1843.

Hollander, John, editor. *American Poetry: The Nineteenth Century, Vol. 1: Philip Freneau to Walt Whitman*. Library of America, 1993.

Hubbell, Jay B. *Who Are the Major American Writers? A Study of the Changing Literary Canon*. Duke UP, 1972.

Keese, John, editor. *The Poets of America: Illustrated by One of Her Painters*. S. Coleman, 1840.

Kennedy, J. Gerald. "Inventing the Literati: Poe's Remapping of Antebellum Print Culture." *Poe and the Remapping of Antebellum Print Culture*, edited by J. Gerald Kennedy and Jerome McGann, Louisiana State UP, 2012, pp. 13–36.

Kettell, Samuel, editor. *Specimens of American Poetry, with Critical and Biographical Notices*. S. G. Goodrich and Co., 1829. 3 vols.

Korte, Barbara, Ralf Schneider, and Stefanie Leffbridge, editors. *Anthologies of British Poetry: Critical Perspectives from Literary and Cultural Studies*. Rodopi, 2000.

Lehman, David, editor. *The Oxford Book of American Poetry*. Oxford UP, 2006.

Lounsbury, Thomas R., editor. *Yale Book of American Verse*. Yale UP, 1912.

Lowell, Anna Cabot (Jackson), editor. *Gleanings from the Poets, For Home and School*. Crosby and Ainsworth/Oliver S. Felt, 1866.

Matthiessen, F. O. *American Renaissance: Art and Expression in the Age of Whitman and Emerson.* Oxford UP, 1941.

———, editor. *The Oxford Book of American Verse.* Oxford UP, 1950.

McGill, Meredith L. *American Literature and the Culture of Reprinting, 1834–1853.* U of Pennsylvania P, 2003.

Page, Curtis Hidden, editor. *The Chief American Poets: Selected Poems by Bryant, Poe, Emerson, Longfellow, Whittier, Holmes, Lowell, Whitman, and Lanier.* Houghton, Mifflin, and Co., 1905.

Parini, Jay, editor. *The Columbia Anthology of American Poetry.* Columbia UP, 1995.

Peeples, Scott. "Teaching Poe the Magazinist." *Approaches to Teaching Poe's Prose and Poetry*, edited by Jeffrey Andrew Weinstock and Tony Magistrale, MLA, 2008, pp. 26–32.

Phillips, Philip Edward. "Poe the Magazinist." *The Oxford Handbook of Edgar Allan Poe*, edited by J. Gerald Kennedy and Scott Peeples, Oxford UP, 2019, pp. 479–98.

Poe, Edgar Allan. "Griswold's American Poetry." *Boston Miscellany of Literature and Fashion*, vol. 2, November 1842, pp. 218–21. Edgar Allan Poe Society of Baltimore. https://www.eapoe.org/works/criticsm/bm42gr01.htm.

———. "The Philosophy of Composition." *Graham's Magazine*, vol. 28, no. 4, April 1846, pp. 163–67. Edgar Allan Poe Society of Baltimore. https://www.eapoe.org/works/essays/philcomp.htm.

———. *The Works of the Late Edgar Allan Poe*, edited by Rufus W. Griswold, J. S. Redfield, 1850–1856. 4 vols.

Shinn, Kathryn K. "Gift Books." *Edgar Allan Poe in Context*, edited by Kevin J. Hayes, Cambridge UP, 2013, pp.179–87.

Smith, Elihu H., editor. *American Poems, Selected and Original*, vol. 1, Collier and Buel, 1793.

Stedman, Edmund Clarence, editor. *An American Anthology, 1787–1899.* Houghton, Mifflin and Company, 1900.

Urakova, Alexandra. "The 'Flower-gemmed' Story: Gift Book Tradition and Poe's 'Eleonora.'" *Anthologizing Poe: Editions, Translations, and (Trans)National Canons*, Lehigh UP, 2020, pp. 59–72.

———. "'The Purloined Letter' in the Gift Book: Reading Poe in a Contemporary Context." *Nineteenth-Century Literature*, vol. 64, no. 3, 2009, pp. 323–46.

Weinstock, Jeffrey Andrew. "Magazines." *Edgar Allan Poe in Context*, edited by Kevin J. Hayes, Cambridge UP, 2013, pp. 169–78.

PART IV

WOR(L)DING POE ABROAD: ANTHOLOGIZERS, EDITORS, ILLUSTRATORS, AND TRANSLATORS

CHAPTER THIRTEEN

~

Startling Restitutions, Significant Partialities

The French Come to the Rescue of Edgar Allan Poe

Margarida Vale de Gato

In his groundbreaking analysis of the reception of Edgar Allan Poe in France, *The French Face of Edgar Poe*, Patrick F. Quinn famously asks, "But what do they see in him?" (28). Quinn defers to earlier studies that point to Poe's mathematical mind and apparent discursive lucidity, even in the face of the macabre, as conditioning his acceptability in the French neoclassic system more favorably than most of his European romantic counterparts (40–41). The American critic argues, nonetheless, that if Poe had not also brought a deeply foreign element that was seen as adoptable in the new social order of mid-nineteenth-century France, the French literati might well have kept to their own models.

Through the study of how Poe was presented, ranked, selected, related with, and written about in translated French anthologies of poems and tales, I will attempt to contribute to the understanding of why and how Poe was appropriated by successive generations of important stakeholders in the French literary field.[1] I am also interested in the ways such appropriations configure broad gestures of *restitution*. This is a notion I find useful for reception studies, as a kind of ideal, a conflation of George Steiner's ultimate design for the hermeneutics of translation—to "make good" the advances of "rapacity and profit" by offering "in reparation . . . something *new that was already there*" (111–12)—and Mallarmé's cryptic first lines of "The Tomb of Edgar Poe": "As into Himself at last eternity changes him" (*Selected Poetry* 51). We cannot know for certain how eternal Poe's reputation will be, and his afterlife is in no way essentialist—that is, it does not change the author

249

into himself but corresponds to a projection of several selves, borrowed largely from the receiving agents, or rewriters (in the sense perceived by André Lefevere), which makes "partiality" a complement to "restitution."[2] Although Charles Baudelaire was not the first to translate nor even to anthologize Poe in France, his Histoires extraordinaires (1856) and Nouvelles histoires extraordinaires (1857) put forth the influential model of restoring the "real" Poe, ransomed through a kindred spirit—one whose learned French background was (self-)perceived as an advantage over the underestimation of Poe's literary talent in his home country.[3]

In this chapter, I particularly attend to Poe's multiple French selves, to some of his French offspring, and to genres and formats into which Poe, the storyteller and poet, was framed through anthologizing practices. After tracing the selection rationale of Baudelaire's Poe, I will look into a very productive mode in French modern literature, le fantastique, where Poe was cast as a forerunner not only by Baudelaire but by several "focus anthologies" (to use Barbara Mujica's taxonomy) that proliferated in France in the late 1950s and throughout the twentieth century.[4] In the third section, I examine poetry selections, going back in time to the symbolist outlook of Poe's French face that started to be delineated by Stéphane Mallarmé. In the chapter's final section, I discuss the anthologizing processes of a hybrid format—monographies illustrées or illustrated pocket readers—a format that combines extracts of authorial oeuvre with biography and commentary.

Charles Baudelaire: The Maker of Poe in French Prose

It remains controversial whether Baudelaire had access to a wide variety of Poe's pieces before the Griswold edition, despite his claims that he had sought to assemble the works of his transatlantic brother from newspaper collections belonging to "Americans living in France."[5] What is ascertainable, from a comparison of Griswold's four volumes of The Works of the Late Edgar Allan Poe (1850–1856) and the selections of Baudelaire's translated anthologies, is that all the latter texts were comprised in the former American edition; and furthermore, it is plausible that Baudelaire's pool of choice was dependent on the texts being made available by Griswold.[6]

On the other hand, Baudelaire set up a large-scale operation to avenge Griswold's profile of Edgar Allan Poe, having made up his mind about the reverend's character: "This pedagogue vampire defamed his friend at length, in an enormous, boring and venomous article placed at the head of the posthumous editions of Poe's works. Is there no by-law in America to prevent dogs from entering cemeteries?" (Baudelaire, Selected Writings 164). These lines reveal Baudelaire's self-appointed role as mediator for Poe. He would be the dignified guardian of Poe's grave, as was incumbent upon a representative of the nation that then possessed the symbolic capital to construct what Pascale Casanova has dubbed a "world republic of letters" (11), against what Baudelaire called a materialistic and "juvenile country, naturally jealous of the old continent" (*Selected Writings* 165).

Baudelaire's interests were in monomania as a sign of spirituality, madness as a token of the sublime, the hallucination of modern nervousness as poetic, and the phosphorescent halo of minds derailed by artificial stimulation as enlightenment. Indeed, Baudelaire underscored a great part of the agenda of his own work, namely *Les paradis artificiels* (1860), in the preface to the first volume of *Histoires extraordinaires*:

> The solitude of nature, the bustle of great cities, are all evoked tensely and fantastically. . . . So-called inanimate Nature participates in the nature of the living beings, and, like them, is seized with a supernatural and galvanic shuddering. Space is extended by opium . . . full of light and colour, where sparkling in the sun's golden rain, oriental cities and diverse buildings appear in the distant gaze. (*Selected Writings* 186)

There is evidence that in organizing his first two volumes of Poe translations, Baudelaire aimed to gradually prepare the audience for the allurement of the fantastic that could hoist supernatural intimations. He would first give the French what they recognized as familiar (riddles and rationalism), following the plan he disclosed in a letter dated March 26, 1856 to Sainte-Beuve, arguably the most important literary critic of his time: "The first volume was designed as a bait for the public: tricks, divination, leg-pulls, etc. *Ligeia* is the only important piece connected, from the moral point of view, to the second volume. The second volume is of a loftier kind of fantastic: hallucinations, mental illness, pure grotesque, supernaturalism, etc." (Baudelaire, *Selected Letters* 84). The original French phrase "un fantastique plus relevé" (*Correspondance* 1, 344)—which translates as "loftier," or "heightened," fantastic— is important because it agrees with a series of hyperboles of elevation used by Baudelaire in his prefaces to refer to "the man of heightened faculties" that "marked him out as one of the elect" (*Selected Writings* 187, 177). There is also, in these exaggerations, an implicit merging of the stories, the storyteller, and the empiric author: "Poe's characters, or rather his one character . . . is Poe himself" (187).

Histoires extraordinaires opens with Baudelaire's text "Edgar Poe: Sa vie et ses oeuvres" ["Edgar Poe: His Life and Works"] and gives us first the ratiocinative tales ("The Murders in the Rue Morgue," "The Purloined Letter," The Gold-Bug").[7] It continues with the scientific fantasies of "The Balloon Hoax" and "Hans Pfaall," then moves on to the maritime adventures, "MS. Found in a Bottle" and "A Descent into the Maelström." This first volume becomes more fantastic, if not "loftier," with "The Facts in the Case of M. Valdemar," and then pursues with the more metaphysical inquiry about a near-death situation and what it might tell of the afterlife in "Mesmeric Revelation." (Baudelaire's own interest in magnetism probably explains why this was his first-ever Poe translation in 1848.) The four final tales all allude to metempsychosis —"A Tale of the Ragged Mountains," "Morella," "Ligeia," and "Metzengerstein."[8]

In March 1857, Baudelaire would again procure Sainte-Beuve's critical favors for his cause: "This second volume is more lofty in character, more poetic, too, than two-thirds of the first volume" (*Selected Letters* 91). His appeal was unheeded, but *Nouvelles histoires extraordinaires*, boasting twenty-three tales, seems to represent what Baudelaire valued in Poe. It opens with a new preface, "Notes nouvelles sur Edgar Poe" ["New Notes on Edgar Poe"], and the tales by Poe start with a series in which personal resentment and revenge seem to follow a greater, mysterious plan, often also pairing hints of self-loathing and reluctant sacrifice with an unfathomable intelligence of psychic relations. This is the case with "The Black Cat," "The Tell-Tale Heart," "The Fall of the House of Usher" and "The Cask of Amontillado," as well as with the essayistic tale "The Imp of the Perverse." This corroborates the critical understanding that Baudelaire associated such impulses with his own concept of *l'héautontimoroumenos* [the self-torturer], thereby fusing it with an emphasis on translation and paraphrases around *le démon de la perversité*.[9] Furthermore, tales such as "William Wilson," "The Man of the Crowd," and "The Fall of the House of Usher" all develop the trope of doubling and delusion, or romantic irony anticipating modern schizophrenia. In its middle part, *Nouvelles histoires extraordinaires* presents "The Masque of the Red Death," followed by "King Pest," showing an understanding that the change of tone in the treatment of a similar theme (the plague of death and decadence in the midst of a closed society of aristocratic pretense) might favor the transition from somberness to satire, and the brief interlude of four humoristic tales, "The Devil in the Belfry," "Lionizing," "Four Beasts in One," and "Some Words with a Mummy." The volume then turns to the metaphysical, with the three postmortem dialogues ("The Power of Words," "The Colloquy of Monos and Una," and "The Conversation of Eiros and Charmion") to finish, according to Baudelaire's design of "more poetic," with the lyrical tales "The Island of the Fay," "Silence," and "Shadow," while the very last choice, "The Oval Portrait," is perhaps meant to hint at the *ars poetica* of aestheticism at the moral cost of the lives of loved ones.[10]

The reception of Baudelaire's "extraordinary stories" granted them not only successive reprints to this day, but also an undisputed place in the receiving literary system. Poe became the second author of the nascent Pléiade series in 1932, possibly through the contamination of the authorial status of Baudelaire, who was chosen as the first anthologized author for this prestigious series. The editor Y. G. Le Dantec, also responsible for Baudelaire's Pléiade collection, explained in the preface to Poe's book that he rejected two initial ideas—preparing a complete works, and organizing Poe's pieces chronologically—choosing instead to give us only *Histoires* and to repeat the choice of texts and the order in which Baudelaire published his translations. For, he argued, it would be a sacrilege to pair other translations with the "stories masterly transcribed" by the poet, and any other arrangement risked losing the "familiarity" of the location of the readers' favorite pieces (qtd. in Poe, *Histoires* ix).[11]

The anthological enterprise therefore had an important role in making, as it were, Poe's works part of the Baudelairean *oeuvre*, an entanglement that was due to important paratexts as well as to slight but indelible translation changes.[12] Several critics have underscored Baudelaire's partiality to the somber, clever, and malicious Poe, either because Poe's humoristic pieces did not attract him or because he simply did not get the jokes. Henri Justin observes, "Twenty-three [stories] he definitely left out, more than one third of Poe's production, and they were all of them comedies. So Baudelaire's choices implied an alteration of the nature of the corpus as a whole, an alteration in favor of the so-called *serious* tales" ("Paradoxes" 81). The affirmation is slightly exaggerated, since the dislike for the most blatant grotesqueries is already visible in Griswold's edition, which relegated the greater part of those stories to the "miscellaneous" fourth volume, and even in Evert Duyckinck's selection of the 1845 *Tales*, of which only "Lionizing" was satirical. Furthermore, one should not forget that humor is context-based and often relies on puns that depend on the sounds and cognates of the source language, and thus Baudelaire might have left out many of the comic tales because his English and his cultural competence were not adequate, just as he did not venture to translate Poe's poetry.

In a previous study that compares Poe's own plans for collections of his works with the French and Portuguese selections, I have relied on the idea of "ironical double-vision," advanced by G. R. Thompson (105–37), to suggest that there is not an edition of Poe that follows the speculative intention of alternating between the sinister and the ludicrous, with the exception of

254 ~ Margarida Vale de Gato

the two-volume set by Lea and Blanchard, closely supervised by the writer in 1840.[13] Harry L. Poe's chapter on Poe as an anthologizer of himself, in this book (chapter 2), concurs with this impression though it allows for a greater variety of design in Poe's mind, rather than just a double-intention model. Baudelaire's later volume, *Histoires grotesques et sérieuses*, was perhaps the one space where he tried to convey a vein of Poe that is not only duplicitous but all over the place—from detective story, to hoax, to fairy/gothic, to humorous parable.[14] However, Baudelaire published this volume eight years after the first two, and with no paratextual apparatus.

There have been a few alternative editions to Baudelaire's prose in France. The first one was *Contes inédits*, translated as early as 1862 by William L. Hughes, before Baudelaire released his last volume. This edition did not alter Poe's image very much; it included seven humorous tales (though a few of them, like "The System of Doctor Tarr and Professor Fether" and "The Man That Was Used Up" can have ghastly interpretations) and only two serious ones, but this might have been because Baudelaire had limited the available choices. The two more so(m)ber stories—"Eleonora" and "The Assignation"—were placed upfront, and the lighter pieces were sandwiched between "Politian" and the poetry that closed the volume. Poe's facetious side was underscored in 1882, when Emille Hennequin brought to the French audience eight tales not previously translated by Baudelaire—"The Premature Burial" (that might be considered ambivalent in terms of mode), "Loss of Breath," "Mystification," "Bon-Bon," "Von Kempelen and His Discovery", "X-ing a Paragrab," "The Oblong Box," "Never Bet the Devil Your Head"—in *Contes grotesques*. However, the fact that the table of contents is rounded up with the publication of "a fragment ['The Journal of Julius Rodman'] and a sequence of notes and maxims titled *Marginalia* . . . [of which] we have selected those that might be of interest to the French reader, thereby omitting more than half" (Hennequin 47) gives the impression of an unfinished polish, a miscellany of leftovers.

This kind of arrangement of compromise was assumedly undertaken also by the translator F. Rabbe in *Derniers contes* of 1887, with eight humorous tales—"The Duc de L'Omelette," "The Thousand-and-Second Tale of Scheherazade," "Mellonta Tauta," "How to Write a Blackwood Article," "Diddling Considered as One of the Exact Sciences," "The Business Man," "The Premature Burial," and "Bon-Bon"—followed by three very different nonfiction pieces ("Cryptography," "The Poetic Principle," "Some Secrets of the Magazine Prison-House"). Rabbe's admission that his selected stories "do not share in the same degree the points of interest and pathetic poignancy, nor the picturesque or dramatic qualities of certain more renowned narratives we have agreed to call the masterpieces of Poe" (9) relegates the satirical works to an afterthought that will very seldom come to the fore. As late as 1989, when Alain Jaubert collected a total of twenty-five stories in *Ne pariez jamais votre tête au diable et autres contes non traduits par Baudelaire*, he, too, ascertained the continuing hegemony of the translations by Baudelaire, calling them "*à jamais* intouchables" [forever untouchable] (65).[15]

The consensus over the inviolate status of Baudelaire's translations of Poe still prevails, contradicting the tenet that translated texts age fast and that periodical retranslation offers the chance to update old texts in light of new readings. The two more recent critical editions that further disseminated Poe to the French audience still bowed to Baudelaire's imprint regarding Poe's fiction. *Edgar Allan Poe: Contes-essais-poèmes*, in 1989, was the "life-long work of French Poe scholar Claude Richard" (Vines, "Poe Translations" 52), finalized by Robert Kopp. Poe's works were presented chronologically, but Baudelaire's translations (as well as Mallarmé's for poetry) were not replaced by new ones. In 2006, *Edgar Allan Poe: histoires, essais et poèmes*, edited by Jean-Pierre Naugrette and four collaborators (including James Lawler, an advocate of Poe's essays), opened with the three Baudelaire volumes (order of the tales unchanged) followed by "Autres histoires" (other stories) translated by François Gallix.

In the early twenty-first century, Henri Justin, considering that Baudelaire smoothed out linguistic quirks that were relevant to Poe's narrators' deranged senses, as well as overlooked certain "geographical gaps" among other disparities, accepted the challenge to break the consensus ("Retranslating Poe" 210). His *Contes policiers et autres* (2014) recovered the translation history for each of the twelve tales he chose and explained the problems of Justin's own work, besides clarifying cultural references. He included two stories that were not of Baudelaire's choice, and the book opens with one of them, "A Decided Loss," in keeping with a chronological organization of the texts. A paperback edition was issued in 2016, but the popularity of Baudelaire's translations is seemingly unshakeable, with Amazon France indicating seventy-eight formats and editions for just *Nouvelles histoires extraordinaires*.

Curiously, the Pléiade edition—reissued in 1951 as *Oeuvres en prose* and still in print—is the only one that takes up Baudelaire's hint, in a paratext left unpublished in his lifetime, of combining in a single volume the tales and the longer pieces (*Pym* and *Eureka* along with some criticism); furthermore, to this day no one has attempted to realize a potentially different organization, that is, the thematic one that Baudelaire envisioned in the same "translator's note": "very soon the editors of the popular edition of Edgar Poe's works will feel the glorious necessity of publishing them in a more solid material form . . . in an edition in which the component parts will be more definitively and more *analogically* classified" (*Oeuvres* 2, 348, my emphasis). Unlike what happens with Poe in English, explicit analogical (thematic) categorization does not play a part in Poe's selected or collected prose works in France, suggesting that the greatest difference between the two cultures' uses of Poe is not in canon but in arrangement. Defining subject topics, however, was a fairly common practice in the multi-author focus anthologies featuring Poe that I will discuss below.

Anthologies Promoting *le fantastique*

The selection proposed by an anthology at a given point in the history of translation and/or literature invites speculation as to what might have happened to the fate of an author, in this case Poe, had he become known for different texts than the consensual canon established around his prose, be it under the variations of the English "tales of mystery and imagination" or under the French rubric of "extraordinary stories."[16] A volume of "Edgard Poe," edited and translated by G. [Gaston] Lavergnolle in 1879, *Nouvelles américaines*, is prone to such speculation. First, its title is intriguing: it derives from the oscillation between *histoires*, *contes*, and *nouvelles* in the French literary system of the time, accustomed to larger prose pieces, while also pointing to the possibility of something original or new (*nouvelles*) coming out of "America" via Poe's craft. Secondly, almost all the selections in the volume seem to be comprised of "American news": the treasure hunt in the "The Gold-Bug," the struggle with the unexplored depths of science in "A Descent into the Maelström," and then two balloon stories, of which "Hans Pfaall" (translated as "Dix-neuf jours em ballon") is followed by a "Note sur les aérolithes" whose source is unknown to me but is not Poe. The fact that the closing story is the somber and more poetic "Silence" does not dispel the book's partiality to scientific wonders, and instead lends it a prophetical tone of fear for meddling with the mysteries of the unknown.

Nouvelles américaines illustrates a parallel afterlife of Poe that may have influenced the literary career of certain French followers, for instance Jules Verne. However, it might have been a stand-alone case, since in what concerns multi-author anthologies that have circulated in France including Poe stories, the majority are devoted to *le fantastique*. Baudelaire's design, therefore, had an impact over time. However, Baudelaire did not define the mode (or genre?) fantastic. It is not easy to measure how much the fantastic might partake of the marvelous and the supernatural against a certain degree of plausibility; there seem to be too many borderline cases in the distinction, famously established by Todorov in *The Fantastic*, between the supernatural explained and the one the reader accepts as given. Moreover, the fantastic might overlap with the realms of romance or fairy tale on one end of the spectrum and with the worlds of science fiction on the other. According to Roger Caillois, the fantastic holds the unique claim of "manifesting a scandal, a tear, an uncanny irruption that is almost unbearable in the real world," whereas in other related modes, fantasy and reality only exist in parallel worlds (*Anthologie* 8). This could be a way to separate the waters, but there is still another dangling, more Anglo-Saxon, notion, the "gothic," and indeed some contributors to this book, namely Christopher Rollason in his comparison of the British and French mainstream dissemination of Poe, use "gothic" rather than "fantastic" to describe the more influential trend.

Crossing the thresholds of time—past/present—with those of cognitive space—the realms of fantasy and reality—the fantastic may be considered inclusive of (if not co-extensive with) the gothic, although not a preferred term in French literary criticism. For the sake of comparing what the literary stakeholders state as landmarks for these categories, I point out that Chris Baldick's *Oxford Book of Gothic Tales* (1992) is ordered chronologically and features "The Fall of the House of Usher" among a selection of fourteen tales for the nineteenth century, among which twelve were originally written in English and five by American authors. Hoffmann does not appear, and no other German writers are included in the entire volume. On the other hand, Jacques Goimard, in *La grande anthologie du fantastique* co-edited with Roland Stragliati, ascribes to Hoffmann the paternity of the "fantastic, in the French sense . . . at the end of a process of consolidation that mostly took place in Germany" (9), but only features Hoffman twice in his collection (in the sixth and tenth volumes), whereas Poe appears twice in the first volume (the only repeated author) and four times in total. Roger Caillois orders his *Fantastique: Soixante récits de terreur* (1958) geographically rather than chronologically; it opens with England (seven tales), then Ireland (three), followed by the United States (six tales, two of them by Poe). Germany (three) and Flanders (one) come next, and then we get to France, whose central appearance with the more robust selection (eight) is reinforced by the scarcity or vagueness of the latter configurations (e.g., two titles from Italy and four from the too-general "Iberian-America").

The research hypotheses that an excavation of the positions (and perhaps omissions, too) of Poe in multi-author anthologies might yield are far-reaching. In the case of international anthologies, we might gain outsiders' overviews of the contributions of a certain literary tradition (in this case, the tradition of the United States), while following the development/configura-tion of a certain genre (the fantastic) and the framing of a specific author's production (Poe) within an editorial design. In French focus anthologies of the fantastic, the latter has implied more often than not an embedding of Poe in an "American" section, tailored to the presumption that he was the rescuer of outcasts, of *poètes maudits*.

The appeal of the doomed artist, at the heart of late nineteenth-century symbolism, resurged in France in the context of postwar surrealism. The aforementioned Roger Caillois was very influential in the trend that had the fantastic complementing the journey to the unconscious depths of individual or collective imageries—an essentially modern genre, reconciling civilization and imagination. As already suggested, Caillois separated the fantastic from other related forms where the extraordinary did not overlap with reality. Moreover, in *Puissances du rêve*, a 1962 anthology, he presented a subgenre of the fantastic, comprising what we call today "speculative fiction": "tales that are also fantastic [and] whose common trait is to speculate about differ-ent qualities of dreaming, be it to confound reality, to predict it, to level it, or to surpass it" (*Anthologie* 26). This anthology includes Poe's "Souvenirs de M. August Bedloe" ["A Tale of the Ragged Mountains"], a story that had recently been featured in a 1960 issue of the magazine *Fiction: Revue littéraire de l'étrange*, which had mostly served to promote the sci-fi genre since 1953 but shifted configuration under different editors, attesting to the fluidity between fantasy, the speculative, horror, and the fantastic.

Nonetheless, critical efforts of categorization play a part in the design of anthologies, maybe even in the desire to make them. In 1966, Caillois presented the two-volume *Anthologie du fantastique*—which was basically a revision of the 1958 *Fantastique*, but this time with a clearer division between dreamlike fantasies (in the previous *Puissances du rêve*) and the infusion of the supernatural within reality (in the current anthology). The preface in the first volume of *Anthologie du fantastique* devotes a couple of pages to the enumeration of the breaches of the impossibilities of life that constitute, ac-cording to Caillois, the themes of the fantastic: the pact with the devil, the vengeful revenant, the restless spectre, the materialization of death among the living, the presence of a "thing" with destructive powers, the dead that feed upon the living, the automaton that acquires independence, a sorcerer's curse, the phantom-woman, the dream that makes reality a nightmare, the apartment or building represented as a crossover space, the repetition or suspension of time (19–21). Poe's "The Fall of the House of Usher" is given as an example of the latter, and the "Masque of the Red Death" is cited as prototype of the personification of death.

Variants of the above categories served the organization of impressive anthologies in subsequent years. *Les chefs d'oeuvre de l'épouvante* (1965) and *Les
chefs d'oeuvre du fantastique* (1967), edited by the trio Sternberg, Grall, and
Bergier, contain, respectively, Poe's "The Masque of the Red Death"—under
the theme "Do not open the forbidden doors"—and "The Facts in the Case
of M. Valdemar" in the "after Death" category. In 1977, the popular Pocket
Editions launched the aforementioned *La grande anthologie du fantastique*
in ten volumes, edited by Jacques Goimard and Roland Stragliati. In "Les
morts-vivants" [Dead-alive], the first volume, Poe's "The Fall of the House
of Usher" and "Ligeia" are interspersed with Villiers de l'Isle-Adam's "Véra,"
a tale of avowed Poesque influences, suggesting the transatlantic cross-
fertilization of the genre was boosted by the impact of the French face of Poe.

The bias toward the Anglophone, in regard to the intersection of national and linguistic traditions, is pronounced in the choice of authors in the
"boom" of the fantastic that motivated voluminous anthologies in France
in the last four decades of the twentieth century.[17] While from the English
side Dickens is a likely choice, from the American side, Poe and Hawthorne
are the most featured nineteenth-century authors. Even so, Poe's and Hawthorne's brands of the fantastic do not seem to be quite compatible, for the
presence of the two authors is unbalanced in many anthologies, with Hawthorne being chosen more often for anthologies of "weird" or "satanic" tales
(e.g., "Young Goodman Brown" in Jean Palou's *Histoires étranges* of 1963 and
in the volume titled *Histoires démoniques* of Goimard and Stragliati's series).

Although anthologies of the fantastic are still popular in France, with
new volumes coming out along with reissues of some of the old titles, the
timeline from the late 1950s to the end of the twentieth century that frames
the above-mentioned "boom" corresponds to a greater attraction of the
unconscious/irrational as a consequence of the civil crisis caused by major
world conflicts. In his prefatory words to *La grande anthologie du fantastique*
in 1977, Jacques Goimard mentions the Vietnam War—and the interest in
zombies (28)—while Bergier, in the introduction to the *Chefs d'œuvre du
fantastique* in 1967, had alluded to the Holocaust and the terror of the Ge-
stapo. His preface closed by suggestively shifting the emphasis from authors
to *faits maudits* (18), and Goimard's evoked the greatest menace of the old
terror of the dismembered body, shattering our unconsciousness in moments
of crisis: "the eyes spy, the teeth bite, the hands strangle" (28). The favoring
of "Berenice" might thus reflect the anxiousness of an age of broken bodies.
It appears thrice in the multi-author anthologies examined here, the same
amount of times as "The Fall of the House of Usher."

The anthologies of the fantastic in France in the late twentieth century testify not only to the influence of a small core of Poe tales in the configuration of a genre/mode, but also to Baudelaire's lasting perception of the value of his transatlantic brother, since all the stories previously appeared in his selections and are presumably reprints of his translations (even if some do not state the source). The discussion of the French "fantastic," the submarine that travels the waters of literature and of the popular unconscious, sharing ammunition with the gothic and the ghastly, would not be the same—nor as modern and truly quite contemporary—without "Poedelaire."[18]

The Poetry

To turn to Poe's extremely fruitful poetic reception in France, and to unfold other perspectives of the Poe that mystified not only symbolists but surrealists and other emerging agents in the literary field, including female artists, we must go back in time again to Baudelaire's impact in the modern(ist) form of the lyric genre, and to Stéphane Mallarmé, his appointed successor. Mallarmé—who stated in a letter of September 1867 to Villiers de l'Isle-Adam that he had "accept[ed] the task" of translating Poe's poems "as Baudelaire's legacy" (Oeuvres 1, 727)—made of Poe's poetry a work of art for choice collectors, with the complement of Edouard Manet's illustrations. The thirty-three letters, kept with care by Louis Deman in his own specially bound album of Poèmes d'Edgar Poe (1888),[19] testify to Mallarmé's fastidiousness in erecting "a monument of the French taste to the genius who, just as our most dear or venerable masters, exercised an influence upon us" (Oeuvres 2, 765–66). All Mallarmé's comments about this book appear in "Scolies" (from scholium, whence comes, in English, scholar). The above-cited words are from the first note that, rather than addressing Poe's own verse, ponders Mallarmé's own sonnet, "Le tombeau d'Edgar Poe," which opens the volume. The poem, already quoted, famously recalls Mallarmé's own plight for "pure poetry," implicitly comparing Poe's effort with "the angel" who in the past gave "a purer sense to the words of the tribe" (Selected 51).

The Mallarméan ideal of poetry as language rescued from the dross of everyday speech transpires as the rationale for his own translation choices. The current Pléiade edition of Mallarmé's Oeuvres complètes (vol. 2) reveals Mallarmé's youth notebook "Glanes" (1860) with nine Poe poems translated in verse form, including "Le corbeau" ("The Raven"), which would appear in print for the first time in 1975 in a very large artbook, but in prose paragraphs. By 1888, all thirty-seven of Poe's works translated in Poèmes d'Edgar Poe are in prose. Baudelaire had already presented a prose version of

"Le Corbeau" as an appendix to "La genèse d'un poème" ("The Philosophy of Composition"), claiming he feared to turn poetry that "shimmered as a dream" into the mockery of "aping rhymes" (*Oeuvres* 2: 317). Mallarmé, for his part, made the willful decision to render "what for Poe was always, either fiery or translucent, pure as diamond, poetry" (*Oeuvres* 2: 770) in prose form. He refers to such prose as *calque*, which defers to fidelity as the scholar's best interest; however, Jany Berretti has noted that Mallarmé gives a new sense to the term when he adds that it "intends nothing else than rendering some of the extraordinary sonorous effects of the original music, and, here and there, perhaps, even the feeling itself" (773). By remarking that Mallarmé further insists on the alliterations the *calque* strives to capture, Berretti (146–48) convincingly sustains that Mallarmé used the process of translating Poe to enable him to fulfill his project for modern poetry: to mute self-expressive illocution and let words take the initiative themselves, as Mallarmé would put it in the essay "Crise de vers" in 1892. There is then a possible correlation between Mallarmé's defense of a desirable slippage of poetry into all kinds of language and the affirmation of the prose poem evinced both in the translation of *Poèmes* and in Mallarmé's concomitant experiments with the possibilities of the genre, later collected in *Divagations* (1897).[20]

In his edition of Poe's poems, Mallarmé exercises a ranking judgment of the thirty-seven selected poems by basically dividing the pieces into "Poèmes" (21), such as "Ulalume," "Annabel Lee," "The Bells," and "The Raven," and "Romans et vers d'album" (16), where he places the shorter and the less interesting poems for him (*Oeuvres* 2 785). The division corresponds also to a retrospective chronology, since he tags the latter section as juvenilia ("Poèmes de jeunesse"), which is erroneous in terms of the actual timeline (the last part includes "To M. L. S.," "To F——," "To My Mother," and "Eldorado," not written in Poe's youth).

The distribution of Poe's poetry would be more accurately organized by Gabriel Mourey, a poet who also conversed in the symbolist circles and whose amicable relations with Mallarmé did not, apparently, interfere with the undertaking of *Poèmes complets d'Edgar Allan Poe*, first released in 1889. Mourey organized his collection of translations under the influence of Ingram, from whom the second edition of the book (1910) includes a letter of support. The tradition of starting with Poe's "stronger" poems, generally "The Raven," and proceeding backwards arguably started during the author's lifetime with *The Raven and Other Poems* (1845), and Ingram as well divided between "later poems" and "poems of youth." Mourey inserted an intermediary division, "Poèmes d'âge mûr (1833–1844)" ["Poems of mature age"]. He started the book with a dedication to Baudelaire and a preface by Joséphin

Péladan that praised Poe's genius and criticized the American people as ugly, violent, hard, and largely inferior to the dispossessed natives (viii). Contrary to subsequent editions of Poe's complete poetical works (Victor Orban in 1909, Léon Lemonnier in 1949), Mourey presented a verse translation.

Complete editions fall outside the scope of this section, since its focus is rather on the canonical narrowing of the anthologization process. Nevertheless, the fact that both editors of collected and selected poems of Poe in French constantly supplied new translations indicates that Mallarmé, though prominent in disseminating Poe among symbolist fellow poets (as were Maurice Rollinat and Verlaine), did not attain, in the translation of Poe's poetry, as unshakeable a status as Baudelaire did with the prose works.[21] Unlike his predecessor, moreover, Mallarmé was time and again taken to task on choices and flaws of language (Berretti 143; Claude Richard, *Edgar Poe journaliste* 657).

Translating Poe's poetry in France was a belletristic occupation, combining a sense of affinity with a more or less thorough scholarly framework in support of the American author—as shown by four selections in print through the mid-twentieth century. Émile Lauvrière, who was a philologist and historian, included in his *Edgar Poe: Contes et poésies* (1917) fourteen poems whose tone, starting with "The Haunted Palace" and ending with "Annabel Lee," matched his doctoral thesis, titled *Un génie morbide* (1904). The other translators were artists and creative writers. Lucie Delarue-Mardrus, responsible for *Six poèmes d'Edgar Poe* (1921), was a poet, fiction writer, journalist, sculptor, and feminist who fought for sexual freedom. Jean Rousselot, who chose twenty poems for the concise Poe anthology, *Edgar Allan Poe*, in the series Poètes d'aujourd'hui (1953), left a tremendous body of poetry and was a legend of heroism in the French resistance.[22] Suzanne d'Olivèra Jackowska is the most mysterious character in our corpus, as the Bibliothèque Nationale France has no register for her birth or death, despite listing a dozen works authored by her, mostly related to her activities as a lyrical singer. *La réhabilitation d'Edgar Poe* (1933) contains twelve poems, and it is dedicated both to "Madame Maria Clemm" and to her mother, "La C.tesse [the Countess] Marie d'Olivéra Jackowska," of whom I could find no record. She is presented in the foreword as a French-Polish artist and speaks of herself as having obtained "authorization by the government to reside during three years in New York" (12). Her two volumes of Poe's poems (the second, in the same year, is *Le corbeau d'Edgar Poe*) contain versions that she performed in song, along with other unique aspects: the perception of Poe, still in 1933, as an author in need of "rehabilitation"; the fervor toward an author that underlies the association with an (apparently) tailored press, "Les Amis d'Edgar

Poe"; the aura of legitimacy that surrounds the work, with several layers of paratexts, including endorsements by American and French scholars; an allocution of the author to the university of Paris; a long biographic essay and headnotes for the translated poems; and, perhaps the most singular element of all, the gendered female perspective, a rare thing in the editorship of Poe.

It is interesting to compare the choices of both Delarue-Mardrus and Jackowska with each other, both straying from the matrix set by Mallarmé and generally followed by their male counterparts. In Delarue-Mardrus's case, one should note that despite the paucity of poems, five out of six have the common trait of constituting conversations with beautiful dead women: "Ulalume," "The Raven," "The Sleeper," "To Helen [Whitman]," and "Lenore." The odd case is "The City in the Sea." Delarue-Mardrus has the additional particularity of filling in the ranks, along with Princess Marie Bonaparte, of the early female French scholarship on Poe, with the essay "Oeuvre, vie, amours d'Edgar Poe," published in *La Revue de Paris* in November and December 1925.[23] Anne-Marie Van Bockstaele's study, "Traduction ou réécriture des genres," argues that in translating "The Raven" Delarue-Mardrus has infantilized "Lenore" (using "enfant" for "maiden") and feminized the narrator with a pronoun shift. Picking up on Poe's "soul," she chooses "une âme" (a feminine noun in French) as referent for the speaking voice, marked as "elle" (she), thus displacing the longing to that of a female bonding. To corroborate the womanly slant, Delarue-Madrus's essay on Poe presents a feminist take: "we are thoroughly convinced, on account of his romantic life and on account of his books, that a woman, for him, could only be eminently intellectual, superior, and passionately cultivated" ("Oeuvre" 583).

Without being overtly feminist, Jackowska's presentation of Poe resembles Delarue-Mardrus's in that she greatly tries to disavow the image of Poe as a psychopath and drunkard. On the other hand, she does so by largely avoiding the Poe of Baudelaire's *Histoires extraordinaires* (disconcertingly, Jackowska ignores the previous French reception), instead focusing on the poems, *Eureka*, and the landscape pieces. The apparatus of her *La réhabilitation d'Edgar Poe*—boasting as subtitle that his "most beautiful poems" will be presented in "French verse" side-by-side with the English text, as well as a preface (quite anodyne) by "M. Le Professeur C[harles] Cestre"—is telling of an outsider's effort to enter the French *belles lettres*. The attempt is somewhat slighted by an aura of candor that seems to flow from the translator to the poet (the headnote to "To Science" reproduces the myth that Poe wrote the poem *ipsis verbis* at fourteen) and too much bragging—for example, the claim of having found the poem "Alone" or the first stanza of "Catholic Hymn" in "documents d'époque" [epoch documents]. The latter poem's inclusion is a unique choice that is symptomatic of the sentiment of piety and decorum that pervades the work. The other selected pieces are "To Science," "A Dream" (from the 1827 *Tamerlane and Other Poems*), "Alone," "Fairy-Land," "Israfel," "The Haunted Palace," "Eulalie," "Annabel Lee," "Eldorado," "The Bells," and "To My Mother"—all supporting the image of the lone visionary whose love of poetry was equal to his admiration of women. Even the most problematic case in the ensemble, "The Bells," is amputated, represented only by its first two parts, without any mention to the remainder of the poem, where the shift from silver and golden bells to brazen and iron bells completely alters the tone. Some cover-up was needed for the rehabilitation that the singer sums up in the sentence: "to do the justice deserved by that great soul, thirsty of the ideal and of beauty, and make people understand that Poe is not the man of *Contes fantastiques* nor the man who assassinates, but the man who was assassinated by his century" (42). Albeit with sentimental partiality, and without the audacity of Delarue-Madrus, Jackowska testifies to an alternative rescue of Poe—not of the French decadent ideal of the poet who tortures in revenge of a torturing milieu, but of the secretive feminine flame of the art seeker. Being a minority in the construction of Poe's French canonicity, these two women strive to attain the symbolic credibility of their more authoritative male counterparts, framing Poe's poems with a scholarly apparatus and making use of legitimacy strategies such as the transcription of letters or philological enquiry.

The Poe(s) *à porter*

In the vein outlined above, I only glossed over the important work and anthologizing criteria of Jean Rousselot, who took upon himself the task of retranslating the majority of the poems included in his *Edgar Allan Poe* (1953, augmented in 1962), thirty-ninth in Seghers' Poètes d'aujourd'hui [Poets of Today] series. This little, square volume, profusely documented with drawings, portraits, bibliographic lists, and facsimile letters, fits better in this last section dedicated to a sort of hybrid format much in vogue in twentieth-century France, particularly after the Second World War. The format compares roughly to the American "portables," though these were more compact editions, acquainting the general public with celebrated writers through a blend of author-centered research (much in the style of the monograph, which is why French scholars have referred to them as *monographies illustrées*), and the compilation of bio-bibliographic material as well as selected works (or excerpts of works).[24] In 2015, a special issue of the online academic journal *Mémoires du Livre* was devoted to how these particular pocket editions revolutionized the French literary field, operating as a "collective factory of literary heritage."[25] The emphasis on iconographic contextualization and on a blending of authorial, editorial, professional, and artistic discourses likewise sets these pocket books apart from other apparently similar "readers." Martins and Labbé convincingly underscore the network of literary "sociabilities" created by these artifacts: "The three aspects of the collective dimension of such collections—network of sociabilities governing the making of books, work process involving several actors, and the representation of the literary sociabilities of writers—are interconnected conditions of their editorial enterprises."

In the introduction to the special issue, the two editors also track the emergence of the illustrated pocket edition to a critical turn at the end of the nineteenth century, entailing a claim for *la critique de sympathie*, arguably pioneered by Baudelaire himself, whereby a "commerce of [kindred] spirits" is foregrounded, at the expense of objectivity. In other words, "sympathetic criticism" required a subjective, if not passionate predisposal to affinity with the mindset underlying authorial intention. This predisposal potentially expands to authors and their disseminators inside the series, creating a community. Hence, in the Seghers collection, Edgar Allan Poe joined the company of Paul Éluard, Walt Whitman, Rainer Maria Rilke, or Lewis Carroll through the congenial pen of Jean Rousselot. The latter's poetical production is hardly an evidence of such affinity (Rousselot's poetry tends to deconstruct familiar tropes with humor, and he seems to take Poe too seriously), but it comes across in the insights on translations he calls "transcriptions." More restricted than Mallarmé's, Rousselot's selections of poems are almost all comprised within those of the earlier *Poèmes d'Edgar Poe*, with the exception of extracts from the lengthier poems "Tamerlane" and "Al Aaraaf." The effort to represent the longer and earlier poetical endeavors follows the concept of these illustrated pocket collections, striving for a holistic view of the writer as reflected also on the choices of other parts of Poe's *oeuvre*, except for the comic tales—neglected once again. By order of appearance, we have passages from "The Poetic Principle," the above-mentioned choice of twenty poems, short stories—"Morella" and "Manuscrit trouvé dans une bouteille"—along with excerpts from *Eureka* and "Marginalia."

Rousselot's critical orientation and selection of texts overall honor the collection's purpose of presenting portraits of poets. "La poésie comme passion" [poetry as passion] occupies a central chapter. There is another chapter devoted to the difficulties of translating Poe's poetry, showing well Rousselot's take on Poe: "the 'sensitive' effects, of iridescence, of dissonance, of trembling, of discordance, of grating, that the poet himself preferred" (72). Acknowledging the relation with Baudelaire, there is a chapter titled "Histoires extraordinaires," suggesting ingeniously that both the writer Poe and the translator Baudelaire were poets writing prose, with the corollary: "the *Histoires extraordinaires* are in reality the continuation of *Poèmes* and not their complement; *Eureka* is their metaphysical and cosmic infrastructure; the *Genèse d'un poème* is their justification" (81).

The biographical and contextual chapters that open Rousselot's volume corroborate an image of Poe as tormented genius, morbid at times but in quest of an impossible spiritual ideal. The first chapter is titled "Les voûtes du ciel m'écrasent" [Heaven's vaults crush me], which are given as Poe's last words from a highly fictionalized account, "Les derniers moments d'Edgar Poe," that circulated in France as an appendix of the "unpublished romantic drama," "Politian," in 1926. The preference of sentimental over accurate documents pervades the book (which includes, for instance, the mystification of Poe's "self-portrait"). Lastly, the second chapter, "Parmi les féroces calibans" [Among the ferocious Calibans], is indebted to Joséphin Paladin's preface to G. Mourey's aforementioned edition of Poe's poems, repeating a simile that compared Poe to a Prospero surrounded by the brutish and ungrateful masses of his nation and understood only by the sophisticated and sensitive French literati.

Jacques Cabau offers a competing illustrated pocket edition of Poe in a broader series, Seuil's Écrivains de toujours [Writers of All Times]. Cabau's *Edgar Poe par lui-même* (1960) provides a remarkably different perspective on two significant counts: the vocation of Poe, said to be the scientific and aesthetic contributions to fictional prose, and the squaring of the author with his American compatriots. Designed in a similar fashion to the compact edition described above, this series held for some time the somewhat misleading title *par lui-même*: Poe's book had the subtitle in the first edition, but not in the second (1977). Poe was the forty-ninth author, the ninth foreigner, and the third American (after Hemingway and Melville) in this series. Cabau, who was a Sorbonne professor teaching at the Institut du Monde Anglophone and not a creative writer, chose to start his work with what, as he explained, would have been a platitude were it not for Baudelaire and the superior reputation of Poe in France: "Edgar Poe is an American writer" (5). This is the opening sentence of the chapter "Les Trois coups" [The Three Strikes], presumably the death of three mother figures in Poe's life. The facing page is occupied by a map of the East Coast of the United States, with amplified lettering for the cities of "New-York" [sic], "Philadelphia," "Baltimore," and "Richmond" and the legend, "For a true nationality of American letters." Much of Cabau's prose seems intent on a reverse rehabilitation of Poe—this time as a man of his place; for that purpose, Cabau supplies accurate documentation, such as the records of the inventions that fascinated Poe, a facsimile of the *Stylus* cover, and portraits of the important women in Poe's life.

Besides the psychoanalytic slant of the first biographical chapter, two chapter titles show Cabau's preferred face of Poe: "L'apprentissage de l'illusionisme" [Learning how to be an illusionist] and "Les engrenages de la logique" [The workings of logic]. He briefly addresses and discards Poe's poetry, following his opinion that Poe's rhetoric in the defense of a more deliberate poetry practice made his place in modernism, but not the practice itself, which Cabau regards as "nothing more than a very ingenious musical box" (41). Along with his praise for Poe's logical mind, Cabau also lauds Poe's capacity to philosophize fear, even impersonate it, and speculate on the afterlife. The book sports an epigraph taken from Baudelaire's translation of "The Pit and the Pendulum," which in the original reads, "It was not that I feared to look upon things horrible, but that I grew aghast lest there should be nothing to see" (Poe, *Collected Works* 2: 684). Poe and the metaphysical void, with a somewhat existentialist streak, and a glance at Poe's grappling with business and domestic life govern the selection of letters that opens the short anthology. Next comes mostly fiction, also liable to an existentialist or even nihilist reading, beginning with "The Man of the Crowd" and closing with the "The Pit and the Pendulum." In the middle, there is space for "The Cask of Amontillado," "The Raven," and "For Annie," under the rubric "Esthétisme et volonté de puissance," thus betraying a Nietzschean take on the American author. The selection, surprisingly, does not include any essay nor excerpt from *Eureka*, but it finds a place for "Lionizing," presented under the headnote "Le burlesque equivoque" [The equivocal burlesque], thus fulfilling the editor's panoramic intention, with a nod to Poe's humoristic vein. Cabau's volume strives for balance and diversity and also, as pertains to the academic, for detachment from more passionate and partial views, as well as from the tradition of French nationalization.

A pervading aspect of the reception of Poe in French anthologies is the considerable critical apparatus framing them—supporting, as it were, the shrewdness of their editors' insights. Baudelaire, moved by a sense of affinity that was also self-serving, framed Poe's prose in the critical model he had put forth in the *Salon 1846*: "criticism must be partial, passionate, political, that is to say it must adopt an exclusive point of view, provided always the one adopted opens up the widest horizons" (*Selected Writings* 50). Passionate and political, Baudelaire fashioned the acceptance of the morbid and spiritual Poe, writer of tales that belonged to a "high" mode of the fantastic, against the businesslike entrepreneurship of a materialistic and ill-schooled democracy.

Multi-author anthologies featuring Poe in France have relied pervasively on Baudelaire's translations and arguably on his judgment of the best tales, which helps to explain why the American writer is mostly prominent in anthologies of the fantastic, with his contribution to the modern form of the genre being represented by tales such as "Berenice" or "The Fall of the House of Usher." Looking at different conceptions of anthologies helps to envisage the different ways in which they map the literary field. In the case of the fantastic, we have seen how it seems broader than the gothic, how it might be adjacent to "terror," and how Poe might serve to illustrate or bridge definition gaps between these genres.

In the case of poetry anthologies dedicated to Poe, we have primarily focused on two tendencies: the elevation of his status as a musician of words and the "rehabilitation" of Poe the poet, with his idealistic and spiritual drive, against the reputation of the psychopath writer. The overview of poetry anthologies also opened up issues of a gendered reception of Poe, with multifaceted female artists pursuing personal interpretations of affect in Poe's poems.

A consensus around Poe's important works in French seems more or less established, both in the fictional prose and in the poetry, as can be surmised from this survey, even though it is not exhaustive. It does not include, for instance, multi-author anthologies of American poetry (like Alan Bosquet's influential *Anthologie de la poésie américaine* in 1956, singling out Poe, Whitman, and Dickinson as the three great poetical figures of the century), and it hardly refers to the publications of Poe's essays, anthologized separately and more rarely. Praise of Poe's critical and speculative mind attained its height with Paul Valéry, but lack of space and the fact that his only anthologizing enterprise of Poe was a narrow selection of "fragments" from "Marginalia" justify the absence here of this figure, whom T. S. Eliot famously studied along with Baudelaire and Mallarmé, calling him to task for pushing his interpretation of Poe to an untenable "advance of self-consciousness" (342).[26]

References to Poe's criticism, however, abound in the paratexts to most of the anthologies under study, particularly in the illustrated pocket editions. The latter are composite works that made a place for themselves in the literary field in France, charting, as it were, reading maps through a blend of scholarship, journalistic prose, and the illusion of authorial intimacy. The pocket books are also an example of the variety of presentation that underlays the majority of Poe editions in France. Backed up by dedications with a pretense of familiarity, correspondence, autograph documents, portraits, and most often superior layout, the anthologies featuring Poe underwrote different and compelling narratives of an author in constant need to be truly revealed and sympathetically adopted.

Notes

1. Due to space limitations, I do not examine French anthologies of Poe's essays in this chapter.

2. Both Emron Esplin and I are indebted to the idea of the manipulation of literature put forth by Lefevere in his writings on literary translation, as stated in our introduction, and the theoretical background and structure of *Translated Poe* already relied on his idea of rewriting.

3. According to W. T. Bandy, the first translation of Poe in France was "Le scarabée d'or" ["The Gold-Bug"] in the *Revue Britannique* of November 1845, signed by A. B., which stood for Alphonse Borghers, in turn a pseudonym of Amédée Pichot, a novelist, historian, and the director of the *Revue Britannique* (see Bandy, "Poe's Secret Translator: Amédee Pichot"). Alphonse Borghers was also responsible for *Nouvelles choisies* of 1853, a minimalist anthology, with "L'Aéronaute" ["The Unparalleled Adventure of One Hans Pfaall"] and "Le scarabée d'or."

4. Barbara Mujica divides anthologies into three general categories: 1) national or ethnic; 2) thematic, women's writing, and focus; 3) anthologies of critical studies. In her words, "the 'focus anthology' combines work by disparate writers united by some common element" (213). Note that the same can be said of thematic anthologies, but with "focus" she specifically refers to orientations such as one generation or genre.

5. It is believed that Baudelaire's assertion, "The first time I opened one of his books, I saw, with horror and delight, not only topics that I had dreamt of, but sentences that I had thought of, and that he had written 20 years before" (*Selected Letters*, 204), refers to his first encounter with Poe via Isabelle de Meunier's translation of "The Black Cat." The other three stories "anthologized" by Meunier in the newspaper *La Démocratie Pacifique* of 1847 were "The Murders in the Rue Morgue," "The Gold-Bug," and "The Conversation of Eiros and Charmion," see L. Lemonnier's *Les traducteurs d'Edgar Poe en France* (39–42). Baudelaire's claim of having engaged friends in the United States to search Poe texts for him, stated in a letter to Armand Fraisse, dated February 18, 1860 (*Correspondance* 1, 676), was nuanced by W. T. Bandy in "New Light in Baudelaire and Poe."

6. For instance, "The System of Doctor Tarr and Professor Fether" and "The Angel of the Odd" come out in Griswold's fourth volume, 1856, and their late appearance is the likely reason for Baudelaire having included them only in his third volume, in 1865.

7. Titled, in French, "Edgar Poe: Sa vie et ses oeuvres," Baudelaire's preface revised the longer, less informed and arguably even more romanticized biographical essay, "Edgar Allan Poe: Sa vie et ses ouvrages," published in 1852 in the influential *Revue de Paris*—see W. T. Bandy's edition of this work referenced in the bibliography.

8. This is the sequential list of the table of contents with the French titles of Poe's tales in *Histoires extraordinaires* (1856): "Edgar Poe: Sa vie et ses oeuvres" (preface by Baudelaire), "Double assassinat dans la rue morgue," "La lettre volée," "Le scarabée d'or," "Le canard au ballon," "Aventure sans pareille d'un certain Hans Pfaall," "Manuscrit trouvé dans une bouteille," "Une descente dans le maelstrom," "La vérité sur le cas de M. Valdemar," "Révélation magnétique," "Les souvenirs de M. Auguste Bedloe," "Morella," "Ligeia," "Metzengerstein."

9. Patrick F. Quinn was the first to note Poe's appropriative gesture of "raising the word *imp* to the power of *demon* . . . weighted with an expressly theological sense of guilt and retribution" (131). Both Jonathan Culler and Laurent Semichon have subsequently added evidence for Baudelaire's exclusive understanding of "perverseness" as "perversity" (Semichon 119–20).

10. This is the sequential list of the table of contents with the French titles of Poe's tales in *Nouvelles histoires extraordinaires* (1857): "Notes nouvelles sur Edgar Poe" (preface by Baudelaire), "Le démon de la perversité," "Le chat noir," "William Wilson," "L'homme des foules," "Le coeur révélateur," "Bérénice," "La chute de la maison Usher," "Le puits et le pendule," "Hop-Frog," "La barrique d'Amontillado," "Le masque de la mort rouge," "Le roi Peste," "Le diable dans le beffroi," "Lionnerie," "Quatre bêtes en une," "Petite discussion ave une momie," "Puissance de la parole," "Colloque entre Monos et Una," "Conversation d'Eiros avec Charmion," "Ombre," "Silence," "L'île de la fée," "Le portrait ovale."

11. All translations from French to English that are not specifically cited as published translations are my own.

12. Maria Filippakopoulou, in *Transatlantic Poe*, has a chapter titled "Papery Poe" in which she discusses how Baudelaire used italics throughout the prefaces for his translations, both to signal phrases by others (i.e., Poe and his critics) and to emphasize his own thoughts, thus merging personal opinion with what could be taken for translation (see especially 97–105).

13. See my essay, "100 Years and Something of Poe in Portuguese Anthologies."

14. This is the sequential list of the table of contents with the French titles of Poe's tales in *Contes grotesques et sérieuses* (1865): "Le mystère de Marie Roget," "Le joueur d'échecs de Maezel," "Éléonora," "Un événement à Jérusalem," "L'ange du bizarre," "Le système du docteur Goudron et du professeur Plume," "Le domaine de Arnheim," "Le cottage Landor," "Philosophie de l'ameublement," "La genèse d'un poème" ("Corbeau" + "Méthode de composition").

15. Christopher Rollason examines Jaubert's preface to his Poe collection in greater detail in chapter 14 of this book.

16. See Rollason's chapter 14 in this book.

17. By order of publication, these are the titles whose contents I have checked: *Fantastique: soixante récits de terreur*, edited by R. Caillois in 1958; *Puissances du rêve*, edited by R. Caillois in 1962; *Histoires étranges*, edited by Jean Palou in 1963; *Les chefs d'oeuvre de l'épouvante*, edited by Sternberg, Grall, and Bergier in 1965; *Histoires étranges et récits insolites*, edited by Hubert Juin in 1965; *Anthologie du fantastique*, edited by R. Caillois in two volumes in 1966; *Les chefs d'oeuvre du fantastique*, edited by Sternberg, Grall, and Bergier in 1967; *La grande anthologie du fantastique*, edited by J. Goimard and R. Stragliati between 1977 and 1981 in ten volumes; *Histoires terribles de revenants*, edited by Jean-Baptiste Baronian in 1979; *Les grands maîtres de la littérature fantastique* in two volumes in 1980; *Contes inquiétants et sardoniques*, edited by Pierre Leyris in 1985; *Nouvelles fantastiques anglaises*, a bilingual edition translated by Jean-Paul Naugrette in 1990; and *La dimension fantastique. Treize nouvelles d'Hoffmann à Claude Seignolle*, edited by Barbara Sadoul in 1996.

18. The neologism "Poedelaire" is credited to Fritz Gutbrodt in "Poedelaire: Translation and the Volatility of the Letter."

19. This volume belongs today to the Rosenwald Collection of the Library of Congress, where I have consulted it.

20. I have explored this idea in my doctoral thesis, *Edgar Allan Poe em Translação* (257–60).

21. See Lemonnier, *Edgar Poe et les poètes français*.

22. The list of the poems presented by Rousselot is more precisely twenty-two, since he included two in text (of the author and a work overview).

23. Marie Bonaparte published her influential psychoanalytical study of Poe, prefaced by Sigmund Freud, in 1933. In her essay "Oeuvre, vie et amours d'Edgar Poe," Delarue-Mardrus also mentions a chapter on Poe in a 1908 book, *Poètes et névrosés* by Mme. Arvède Barine (1908).

24. *Monographie illustrée* is the term used in the special issue of the journal *Mémoires du Livre*, mentioned in the following discussion; even if *monographie* in French has a broader range than the cognate English term, and is not confined to the book format (it can be any loose or accurate effort to describe and discuss in writing a cultural artifact or event), it is still a misnomer, precisely because the inclusion of a select anthology dispels the concept of singular study and single object.

25. This is a partial translation of the issue's title, "Une Fabrique collective du patrimoine littéraire: XIXème-XXème siècles. Les collections de monographies illustrées," edited by Mathilde Labbé and David Martens.

26. Paul Valéry's brief selection of *Quelques fragments des Marginalia* (1927) would, nonetheless, afford a compelling case study of anthologization in its own right. In accordance with an agenda of the theory of notes and defense of the fragmentary, this French author inserted profuse comments in the margins of Poe's excerpts, producing a *mise-en-abîme* of "Marginalia," defying notions of representation and continuity, and instead enhancing parallel reading, rewriting, and dialogue. For a full-length study on the Poe-Valéry connection, see Vines, *Valéry and Poe*.

Works Cited

Baldick, Chris. Introduction. *The Oxford Book of Gothic Tales*, Oxford UP, 1992, pp. xi–xxiii.

Bandy, W. T. "New Light on Baudelaire and Poe." *Yale French Studies*, no. 10, 1952, pp. 65–69.

———. "Poe's Secret Translator: Amédée Pichot." *MLN*, vol. 79, no. 3, 1964, pp. 277–80.

———, editor. *Edgar Allan Poe: Sa vie et ses ouvrages*, by Charles Baudelaire. U of Toronto P, 1973.

Baronian, Jean-Baptiste, editor. *Histoires terribles de revenants*. Librairie des Champs-Élysées, 1979.

Baudelaire, Charles. *Correspondance*. Edited by Claude Pichois and Jean Ziegler, Pléiade (Gallimard), 1973. 2 vols.

———. *Oeuvres complètes*. Edited by Claude Pichois, Pléiade (Gallimard), 1975–1976. 2 vols.

———. *Selected Letters of Charles Baudelaire*. Edited and translated by Rosemary Lloyd, U of Chicago P, 1986.

———. *Selected Writings on Art and Artists*. Edited and translated by P. E. Charvet, Cambridge UP, 1981.

———, editor and translator. *Histoires extraordinaires*. By Edgar Allan Poe, Éditions Michel Levy, 1856.

———. *Histoires grotesques et sérieuses*. By Edgar Allan Poe, Éditions Michel Levy, 1865.

———. *Nouvelles histoires extraordinaires*. By Edgar Allan Poe, Éditions Michel Levy, 1857.

Bergier, J. "Preface." *Les chefs d'œuvre du fantastique*, edited by Jacques Sternberg, A. Grall and J. Bergier, Planète, 1967.

Berretti, Jany. "Mallarmé traducteur de Poe: Quelques 'Vers d'album.'" *Atala*, no. 2, 1999, pp. 143–54.

Bonaparte, Marie. *Edgar Allan Poe: Etude psychanalitique*. Preface by Sigmund Freud, Denoel et Steele, 1933. 2 vols.

Borghers, Alphonse [Amédee Pichot], editor and translator. *Nouvelles choisies*. By Edgar Allan Poe, Editions Hachette, 1853.

Bosquet, Alain, editor. *Anthologie de la poésie américaine*. Librairie Stock, 1956.

Cabau, Jacques. *Edgar Poe par lui-même*. Editions du Seuil (Écrivains de toujours), 1960.

Caillois, Roger, editor. *Anthologie du fantastique*. Gallimard, 1966, 2 vols.

———. *Fantastique: soixante récits de terreur*. Le Club Français du Livre, 1958.

———. *Puissances du rêve*. Le Club Français du Livres, 1962.

Casanova, Pascal. *The World Republic of Letters*. Translated by Malcolm DeBevoise, Harvard UP, 2004.

Culler, Jonathan. "Baudelaire and Poe." *Zeitschrift fur franzosische Sprache und Literatur*, vol. 100, 1990, pp. 61–73.

Delarue-Mardrus, Lucie. "Oeuvre, vie, amours d'Edgar Poe." *La Revue de Paris*, 15 November 1925, pp. 270–301; 1 December 1925, pp. 578–600.

———, translator. *Six poèmes d'Edgar Poe*. Editions Pichon, 1921.

Eliot, T. S. "From Poe to Valéry." *The Recognition of Edgar Allan Poe*, edited by Eric W. Carlson, U of Michigan P, 1966, pp. 205–19.

Esplin, Emron, and Margarida Vale de Gato, editors. *Translated Poe*. Lehigh UP, 2014.

Filippakopoulou, Maria. *Transatlantic Poe: Eliot, Williams, and Huxley, Readers of the French Poe*. Peter Lang, 2015.

Goimard, Jacques, and Roland Stragliati, editors. *La grande anthologie du fantastique*. Presses Pocket, 1977–1981. 10 vols.

Les grands maîtres de la littérature fantastique. Famot, 1980. 2 vols.

Gutbrodt, Fritz. "Poedelaire: Translation and the Volatility of the Letter." *Diacritics*, vol. 22, nos. 3–4, 1992, pp. 49–68.

Hennequin, Émile, editor and translator. *Contes grotesques*, 3ème edition. By Edgar Allan Poe. Paul Ollendorff Libraire-Éditeur, 1882.

Hughes, W. L., editor and translator. *Contes inédits*. By Edgar Allan Poe, Hetzel, 1862.

Jackowska, Susanne d'Olivera, editor and translator. *La réhabilitation d'Edgar Poe et ses plus beaux poèmes en vers français, avec texte anglais en regard*. Les Amis d'Edgar Poe, 1933.

———. *Le Corbeau de Edgar Poe. Deuxième volume de ses plus beaux poèmes en vers français avec texte anglais en regard*. Les Amis d'Edgar Poe, 1933.

Jaubert, Alain, editor and translator. *Ne pariez jamais votre tête au Diable et autres contes non traduits par Baudelaire*. By Edgar Allan Poe, Folio, 1989.

Juin, Hubert, editor. *Histoires étranges et récits insolites*. Le Livre du Club Libraire, 1965.

Justin, Henri. "The Paradoxes of Poe's Reception." *Edgar Allan Poe Review*, vol. 11, no. 1, 2010, pp. 79–92.

———. "Retranslating Poe into French." *Translated Poe*, edited by Emron Esplin and Margarida Vale de Gato, Lehigh UP, 2014, pp. 203–12.

———, editor and translator. *Contes policiers et autres*. By Edgar Allan Poe, Classiques Garnier, 2014.

Labbé, Mathilde, and David Martens. "Les Collections de monographies illustrées de poche. Une fabrique collective du patrimoine littéraire (xixe–xxie siècles)." *Mémoires du Livre*, vol. 7, no. 1, 2015. doi:10.7202/1035759ar.

Lauvrière, Emile. *Un génie morbide: la vie de Edgar Allan Poe*. F. Alcan, 1904.

———, editor and translator. *Contes et poésies*. By Edgar Allan Poe, Editions de la Renaissance, 1917.

Lavergnolle, G., editor and translator. *Nouvelles américaines*. By Edgar Allan Poe, F. F. Ardant frères, 1879.

Le Dantec, Y-G., editor. *Histoires*. By Edgar Allan Poe, translated by Charles Baudelaire, Bibliothèque de la Pléiade (Gallimard), 1932.

———. *Oeuvres en prose*. By Edgar Allan Poe, translated by Charles Baudelaire, Bibliothèque de la Pléiade (Gallimard), 1951.

Lefevere, André. *Translating Literature: Practice and Theory in a Comparative Literature Context*. MLA, 1992.

Lemonnier, Léon. *Les Traducteurs d'Edgar Poe en France de 1845–1875*. Presses Universitaires de France, 1928.

———. *Edgar Poe et les poètes français*. Impr. Commerciale de Bretagne, 1932.

———, editor and translator. *Poèmes. Première édition complete*. By Edgar Allan Poe, Editions Corti, 1949.

Leyris, Pierre, editor. *Contes inquiétants et sardoniques*. HarPo, 1985.

Mallarmé, Stéphane. *Oeuvres Complètes*. Edited by Bertrand Marchal, Pléiade (Gallimard), 1998–2003. 2 vols.

———. *Selected Poetry and Prose*. Translated by Mary Ann Caws, New Directions, 1982.

———, editor and translator. *Poèmes d'Edgar Poe*. Deman, 1888.

Martens, David, and Mathilde Labbé. "Les collections de monographies illustrées: des sociabilités littéraires à la pluri-auctorialité." *Mémoires du livre*, vol. 7, no. 1, 2015. doi:10.7202/1035767ar.

Mourey, Gabriel, translator. *Poèmes complets d'Edgar Allan Poe*. Preface by Joséphin Péladan, Editions Dalou, 1889.

Mujica, Barbara. "Teaching Literature: Canon, Controversy, and the Literary Anthology." *Hispania*, vol. 80, no. 2, 1997, pp. 203–15.

Naugrette, Jean-Pierre, editor and translator. *Nouvelles fantastiques anglaises / Stories of Mystery*. Livres de Poche, 1990.

———, editor, with the collaboration of Michael Edwards, François Gallix, France Jaigu, and James Lawler. *Histoires, essais et poèmes*. By Edgar Allan Poe, Le Livre de Poche, 2006.

Orban, Victor, translator. *Poèmes complets (suivies de Scènes de Politian, Le Principe poétique, Marginalia)*. By Edgar Allan Poe, edited by Alphonse Seché, Editions Michaud, 1908.

Palou, Jean, editor. *Histoires étranges*. Casterman, 1963.

Poe, Edgar Allan. *The Collected Works of Edgar Allan Poe*. Edited by T. O. Mabbott, Belknap P of Harvard UP, 1969–1978. 3 vols.

Quinn, Patrick. *The French Face of Edgar Poe*. Southern Illinois UP, 1957.

Rabbe, F[élix], editor and translator. *Derniers contes*. By Edgar Allan Poe. Nouvelle Librairie Parisienne-Albert Savine Éditeur, 1887.

Richard, Claude. *Edgar Poe journaliste et critique*. Klincksieck, 1978.

———, editor, with the collaboration of Robert Koppe. *Edgar Allan Poe: Contes-essais-poèmes*. Robert Laffont, 1984.

Rousselot, Jean. *Edgar Allan Poe*. Seghers (Poètes d'Aujourd'hui), 1953.

Sadoul, Barbara, editor. *La dimension fantastique: Treize nouvelles d'Hoffmann à Claude Seignolle*. EJL, 1996.

Semichon, Charles. "Charles Baudelaire's Translations of Edgar Allan Poe." 2003, U of St. Andrews, unpublished MA thesis.

Steiner, George. *Errata: Revisions of a Lifetime*. Yale UP, 1997.

Sternberg, Jacques, A. Grall, and J. Bergier, editors. *Les chefs d'œuvre de l'épouvante*. Planète, 1965.

———. *Les chefs d'œuvre du fantastique*. Planète, 1967.

Thompson, G. R. *Poe's Fiction: Romantic Irony in the Gothic Tales*. Wisconsin UP, 1973.

Todorov, Tzvetan. *The Fantastic: A Structural Approach to a Literary Genre*. Translated by Richard Howard, Cornell UP, 1975.

Vale de Gato, Margarida. "100 Years and Something of Poe in Portuguese Anthologies." *The Anthology in Portugal*, vol. 2, by Patricia Odber de Baubeta, Margarida Vale de Gato, and Maria de Lurdes Sampaio, Peter Lang, 2013, pp. 153–219.

———. *Edgar Allan Poe em Translação: Entre textos e sistemas visando as rescritas na lírica moderna em Portugal*. 2007. U of Lisboa, PhD Dissertation. Repositório da Universidade de Lisboa, repositorio.ul.pt/handle/10451/566.

Valéry, Paul, editor and translator. *Quelques fragments des Marginalia traduits et commentés par Paul Valéry*. 1927. Reprinted by Fata Morgana, 1980.

Van Bockstaele, Anne-Marie. "Traduction ou réécriture des genres? Le cas de Lucie Delarue-Mardrus (1874–1945)." *Palimpsestes*, no. 22, 2009, pp. 149–67.

Vines, Lois Davis. "Poe Translations in France." *Translated Poe*, edited by Emron Esplin and Margarida Vale de Gato, Lehigh UP, 2014, pp. 47–54 and 352–55.

———. *Valéry and Poe: A Literary Legacy*. New York UP, 1992.

Woestyn, H. -R., editor and translator. *Politien. Drame romantique inédit. Suivi de les derniers moments d'Edgar Poe*. By Edgar Allan Poe, Emile Paul Frères, 1926.

CHAPTER FOURTEEN

~

Popular Poe Anthologies in the United Kingdom and France

Christopher Rollason

The literary production of Edgar Allan Poe, and his tales in particular, may be considered to occupy a location somewhere on the fault line between high culture and popular culture, and as such, Poe is an especially suitable candidate for anthologization of a particular kind, namely that by well-known mass-market publishers under inexpensive imprints that focus on literary classics. Such editions may be viewed as popular, or if one is to be more specific, semi-popular or quality popular. Popular does not necessarily mean low-quality: a quality popular edition could be defined as one that is not primarily academic but is well-produced and textually and typographically reliable, and this is the kind of anthology on which the present chapter will focus. Such an edition may be introduced by a leading literary or critical figure. Some may be more academically oriented than others, if they include, to a greater or lesser extent, critical apparatus in the form of notes, bibliography, or other features, but such editions may still be considered popular courtesy of the imprint under which they appear. Two countries where editions of Poe of this type have been especially frequent are the United Kingdom and France.

It is worth recalling that of the imprints represented here, Everyman's Library and Penguin Classics were both conceived as collections with a mission, aimed at democratizing literature and bringing classic works to the masses. Ernest Rhys, the first editor of Everyman's Library, conceived as a "library of a thousand volumes," had a "vision of a large collection of the great books of the world, in a handsome edition that would be affordable by the common man."[1] In the same vein, it has been said of E. V. Rieu, the master-mind behind Penguin Classics, that his 1946 translation of Homer's *Odyssey*, which sold three million copies, was "a major landmark in popularizing the classics," proving that "Homer could be made accessible to anyone" (Yoon). Such statements suggest that book markets can simultaneously enable both popularity and quality.

The present study will offer a comparative analysis of a corpus of representative popular editions published in the literary markets of the United Kingdom and France during the twentieth century. Of the volumes examined, some anthologize tales alone while others offer a more general overview of Poe and also include representative essays and poems. However, in the interest of comparability, the present analysis will essentially confine itself to the respective volumes' choice of tales. The selection of the corpus has taken as eligible the above two anthology types ("tales" and "tales plus"), while excluding others. The following categories of collections of works by Poe are not considered in this chapter: anthologies consisting solely of poems and/or essays, editions of the longer works, illustrated volumes, children's editions, very brief selections or miniature books, and bilingual editions for language learners.

The corpus for this study thus stands at five volumes from the United Kingdom and four from France. Full details for each volume will be given as they are examined in turn. Of the British volumes, one appeared in Everyman's Library (*Tales of Mystery and Imagination*) and one in Collins Classics (*Tales, Poems, Essays*). The remaining three were published by Penguin (those originally issued as *Selected Writings*, *The Science Fiction of Edgar Allan Poe*, and *The Other Poe: Comedies and Satires*). The French anthologies were all published under the Folio imprint of the Paris publisher Gallimard. The first three—*Histoires extraordinaires*, *Nouvelles histoires extraordinaires*, and *Histoires grotesques et sérieuses*—follow Charles Baudelaire's classic translations, replicating their selection, tale titles, and order of texts as well as their generic titles; a fourth volume consists of tales omitted (and thus not translated) by Baudelaire.

Everyman's Library

Everyman's Library, founded in 1906 and published by J. M. Dent of London, was a staple in the world of popular classics over most of the twentieth century. The Everyman selection of Poe's tales published under the title *Tales of Mystery and Imagination* first appeared in 1908 and was republished in various hardback and paperback avatars over the century, the last (and the one consulted here) being in 1971. In its 1971 edition, it consisted of an eight-page introduction penned by the Irish writer Pádraic Colum, a brief bibliography, a table of contents, and the texts of forty-six tales. The edition ran to 527 pages.[2]

This edition marked an early occurrence of the title *Tales of Mystery and Imagination*, which is of course not Poe's own, but had a bright future: it has reappeared over the years gracing various decidedly popular editions, not always of quality. The tales included are not ordered chronologically, although the table of contents gives a minimal publishing history for each tale (year first published and organ of first publication).[3] Colum's introduction is a survey piece combining fair-mindedness with accuracy and defining Poe as a writer "on the margin" (v) and not practicing social realism, while pointing out his marked theatrical bent. The critical apparatus, such as it is, is not error-free (e.g., the editor of Poe's letters, J. W. Ostrom, appears as "J. Ostarm," and *Godey's Lady's Book* is turned into *Godley's Lady's Book*).

The opening tale is "William Wilson," and the closing tale "The Black Cat," choices placing the anthology under the sign of the gothic. The selection is broadly representative, including not only tales of terror and of ratiocination, but also examples of Poe's excursions into science fiction (e.g., "Mellonta Tauta") and humor (e.g., "X-ing a Paragrab"). Thematic coherence applies insofar as the three Dupin tales are bunched together, as are three landscape tales and two angelic dialogues. "Ligeia," "Eleonora," "Berenice," and "Morella" are, logically, grouped together. However, the closely related "The Tell-Tale Heart," "The Black Cat," and "The Imp of the Perverse" are not neighbors, and nor are the mesmerism-themed "The Facts in the Case of M. Valdemar" and "A Tale of the Ragged Mountains." The tales' ordering is thus somewhere between the reasoned and the arbitrary, but the volume as a whole serves as a decent general introduction to Poe as short-story writer.

Collins

The anthology *Tales, Poems, Essays* was first published by Collins Classics, an imprint of the London publisher Collins, in 1952. It was available in two formats, classic hardback and leather-bound. Its 576 pages comprise the following: front matter (biography, table of contents, and a five-page introduction); primary material (thirty-six texts grouped under "Tales," forty-one poems, and sixteen texts—ten of them actually brief "Marginalia" entries—grouped under "Essays"); and end matter (chronology and bibliography). While in no way academic, this anthology fulfilled a certain educational role in providing information about Poe beyond his texts. The introduction was signed by Laurence Meynell, an exemplar of a then abundant class of all-purpose literati that might seem quaintly archaic today. The general ordering of the volume and its primary and secondary material was standard for the Collins Classics series and is paralleled in, for instance, its editions of Dickens.

Meynell's introduction (subtitled "Some considerations on Poe") is a shade ambiguous, opening with a put-down of Poe as poet: "One would have to be dull indeed of imagination," he declares, "to form the opinion that [Poe] was a major poet" (Poe, *Tales, Poems* 13), while going on to acknowledge his merits as storywriter, namely "powerful imagination" and "vigour and originality" (17). Meynell strikes a contemporary note comparing Poe to the twentieth-century gothic writer Mervyn Peake: "he would have revelled in the crepuscular grotesques of [Peake's] *Titus Groan*" (14). He appears, though, only to identify two genres in Poe's fiction, ratiocination and terror—an oversimplification also reflected in the selection, as described below. Meynell does, nonetheless, duly hail Poe as the inventor of the detective story.

The biography and chronology are accurate. The bibliography is copious and advanced for the time, including translations (Mallarmé, but not Baudelaire), the Gustave Doré and Edmund Dulac illustrated volumes, and even critical material in French. The tale count of this edition is thirty-six, or thirty-seven if one classifies as a tale the genre-problematic "Mesmeric Revelation," included here under "Essays." That text apart, the tales are identical in selection and sequence to those in the Everyman volume except that there are eleven fewer. If one compares the two volumes, the omissions in the Collins volume alter the balance. Tales omitted vis-à-vis Everyman include "The Elk," "Shadow," "Silence," "Mellonta Tauta," "Loss of Breath," and "The Devil in the Belfry." This selection thus, in line with Meynell's perspective in the introduction, concentrates overwhelmingly on the tales of terror and those of ratiocination, with Poe's science fiction severely under-represented and only "The Spectacles" unequivocally representing his comic side. As with Everyman, the opening tale is "William Wilson," and the closing tale "The Black Cat." All in all, a gothic-and-detective Poe is constructed via this selection of tales.

Penguin

Penguin Books, the celebrated originators of the paperback book based in the outer London suburb of Harmondsworth, have released a fair number of Poe selections and editions in their time. The most important are the four volumes released from the 1960s through the 1980s under the imprints Penguin English Library/Penguin American Library/Penguin Classics,[4] of which three enter our corpus (the fourth is an edition of *The Narrative of Arthur Gordon Pym*).[5]

The year 1967 saw the publication in the Penguin English Library of the Poe volume *Selected Writings*, edited by David Galloway, which, like the Collins *Tales, Poems, Essays*, anthologized Poe's work across his three principal genres. It was followed in 1976 by *The Science Fiction of Edgar Allan Poe*, edited by Harold Beaver and published in the Penguin English Library, and in 1983 by *The Other Poe: Comedies and Satires*, published in the Penguin American Library and edited, again, by David Galloway. The second Galloway volume consisted of tales only; the Beaver volume included not just tales but also a longer work, namely *Eureka*. All three volumes were later reissued in Penguin Classics, respectively in 1986 (the first Galloway), 1986 again (Beaver), and 1987 (the second Galloway). Two underwent retitling in the new format: *Selected Writings* became *The Fall of the House of Usher and Other Writings*, and *The Other Poe: Comedies and Satires* was relaunched as simply *Comedies and Satires*.

All three volumes straddled the popular and the more studious, their editors being not literati but professional academics linked to British universities. Beaver was at the University of Warwick (and subsequently in Amsterdam), and Galloway was at the University of Sussex (and later in Bochum in Germany). Thus, they both had trajectories combining the United Kingdom and mainland Europe, implying a certain internationalism. Though not conceived from the beginning as a series (indeed, the tale selections show some repetitions),[6] the Galloway/Beaver volumes may be taken as forming an unofficial trilogy, starting with a general overview of Poe (its tale choice inevitably privileging the gothic/detective) and continuing with explorations of his lesser-known work in two other genres, the science fictional and the comic. The three books were also connected by their original front covers, for all reproduced works by the heavily Poe-influenced French symbolist artist, Odilon Redon.

The first Galloway volume (*Selected Writings*) runs to 540 pages and consists of a brief biosketch of Poe, a table of contents, an epigraph from Poe's poem "Alone," an introduction of thirty-seven pages, and a "Note on the Text" (all as front matter); seventeen primary texts grouped under "Poems," nineteen under "Tales," and sixteen under "Essays and Reviews"; and twenty-four pages of notes (including publication history for each tale) as end matter. There is no bibliography. The tale count could rise to twenty if "The Philosophy of Furniture," here classified as an essay, is considered a tale.

The tales are arranged chronologically in order of publication, the first being "MS. Found in a Bottle" and the last, "Hop-Frog." The selection is obviously constrained by the limitations of space (there is less room for tales than in Everyman and Collins) and inevitably concentrates on the best-known tales and on terror and detection, the comic being represented only by "The Man That Was Used Up" and science fiction by "MS. Found in a Bottle," "A Descent into the Maelström," and "M. Valdemar."

Galloway's second volume (*The Other Poe*) has 256 pages and is organized as follows: front matter—a brief biosketch of Poe (the same as in the first volume), a table of contents, a fifteen-page introduction, and a "Note on the Text"; the primary texts of nineteen tales; and end matter which consists of fifteen pages of notes (with publication history for each tale). Again, a bibliography is lacking. The selection of tales is obviously dictated by the book's raison d'être, namely to shine a light on "the other Poe," that is, the writer's relatively little-known comic and satiric face. The sequence is again that of chronological order of publication, beginning with "Lionizing" and ending with "X-ing a Paragrab." Some of the tales could equally be included in other genres (e.g., "Mellonta Tauta" can also be considered science fiction, and "'Thou Art the Man'" as detection). Not every comic tale is included (for instance, "The Duc de l'Omelette" and "Three Sundays in a Week" are absent).

Both Galloway volumes appear more "academic" than their predecessors in most respects: this is visible both in the nature of their respective introductions and in the presence of end-of-volume notes. Galloway's introduction to his first volume is so constructed as to presume some degree of prior knowledge of Poe: it largely eschews potted biography and constructs an image of Poe finely balanced between *poète maudit* and journalism-savvy professional, child of his time and modernist precursor. It avoids an excess of the overly familiar, evoking less obvious connections such as Poe's influence on Debussy or the parallel with Kafka, and it concludes with a Poe hailed as a writer whose work is "among the most popular in the world" (*Selected Writings* 46). The notes, deliberately kept on the brief side, are adequate but clearly subordinated to the texts themselves.

Galloway's second volume is avowedly more specialized than the first, and this is reflected in the introduction and notes. The introduction again presupposes a certain familiarity with Poe, and it stresses both the numerical weight of the comic tales in Poe's short-story canon and the connections between his comic and non-comic tales—between, for instance, "A Predicament" and "The Pit and the Pendulum," or "King Pest" and "The Masque of the Red Death." Galloway concludes that "the comic is . . . an integral part of Poe's fictional achievement" that has been "too long neglected" (*The Other*

Poe 23). The notes are similar in nature and scope to those in the earlier selection. All in all, Galloway's critical apparatus to both volumes frames a Poe who, in their epoch of publication, the 1960s through to the 1980s, was in process of acquiring greater intellectual and academic respectability—specifically in the United Kingdom—than had been the case in the past.

Harold Beaver's anthology, *The Science Fiction of Edgar Allan Poe*, lays its cards on the table with its title—this volume aims from the outset both to showcase a lesser-known side of Poe and to underwrite him in the science fiction world as a pioneer of the genre. It is at the same time several shades more academic in approach than either of the Galloway volumes. Its 429 pages are made up of front matter—a brief biosketch, table of contents, an eighteen-page introduction, a "Note on the Text," and a two-page bibliography on Poe and science fiction—fifteen tales plus the book-length *Eureka*, variously considered by Poe himself as essay and prose-poem; and end matter —ninety-four pages worth of "Commentary," that is, notes plus a chronology of scientific advances in Poe's time.

The primary texts are arranged chronologically in order of publication, the first being "MS. Found in a Bottle" and the last, "Von Kempelen and His Discovery." To a great extent, the tales have selected themselves: *Eureka* apart, the only possibly controversial inclusions are "The Unparalleled Adventure of One Hans Pfaall," which in view of its length (fifty-three pages) and subject matter is sometimes grouped with Poe's longer adventure narratives,[7] and "Mesmeric Revelation," which, as we have seen, the Collins volume treats as an essay.[8] The only tale omitted that has clear science fiction elements is "The Man That Was Used Up."

Beaver's introduction, already foregrounded in chapter 9 of this book by Stephen Rachman for endorsing the "social relevance" of "Poe's blend of the mathematical and the ideal" (176), is something of a work of art. It begins with science rather than Poe, declaring: "Electro-chemistry dominated the early nineteenth century" and placing Poe's speculations alongside the discoveries of the likes of Galvani and Watt in the age of "voltaic cells, electrodes, Leyden jars" (*Science Fiction* vii). Beaver reclaims Poe as a predecessor of Jules Verne and H. G. Wells, a pioneer in a new genre, and he relates Poe's scientific and technological interests to his metaphysical preoccupations. The reader is also reminded that discourses such as phrenology and mesmerism were at the time considered part of science, and the text concludes with the foreboding image of Poe's tomb from Mallarmé's poetic tribute, "Le tombeau d'Edgar Poe," a granite mass that (though Beaver does not say so) might recall the famous monolith from Stanley Kubrick's film *2001: A Space Odyssey*. The sense of engagement with Poe evident in the introduction carries over into the notes, which—far more detailed than Galloway's—are at the same time factual (with full publication details for each text, including, where relevant, those for Baudelaire's translations, and a tale-by-tale critical bibliography), illuminative (delving into the various scientific contexts), and charged with the fascination of a Poe devotee. Of the five British volumes in our corpus, Beaver's *Science Fiction* may be considered both the most audacious and the most successful, framing a neglected side of Poe in a way that makes the volume a critical achievement in its own right.

Folio

Beaver's mention of the Baudelaire translations serves to remind us of the vital role played from the beginning by those renderings in the much-studied area of the reception of Poe in France, and it should come as no surprise to find those translations exerting a determining force over the four Gallimard Folio anthologies that we will now consider.

The first Folio volume, *Histoires extraordinaires*, appeared in 1973, with a preface signed by Julio Cortázar and translated by Laure Guille-Bataillon. It was followed in 1974 by *Nouvelles histoires extraordinaires*, with a preface by Tzvetan Todorov, and in 1978 by *Histoires grotesques et sérieuses*, prefaced by Sylvère Monod. Together, the first three volumes reproduce the Baudelaire translations of the tales in their totality.[9] They were complemented in 1989 by a volume bringing together almost all the tales that Baudelaire did not translate, with a preface by Alain Jaubert and entitled *Ne pariez jamais votre tête au diable et autres contes non traduits par Baudelaire*.

A number of points may be made about this series as a whole before examining its component volumes. The determining influence of the Baudelaire versions is evident from the fact that the first three volumes reproduce the three selections published in book form in Baudelaire's lifetime, not only textually but also in the volume titles, the tales' individual translated titles, and their sequencing—Baudelaire's original ordering is treated as sacrosanct. If the first three volumes constitute a Poe-Baudelaire triptych, the fourth is defined by being Poe but *not* Baudelaire. Both the first three volumes and the full four volumes can thus be seen respectively as complete sets, depending on one's point of view. The umbilical link to Baudelaire is further reinforced by the reproduction in the first two volumes of two of Baudelaire's own essays on Poe.

The volume entitled *Histoires extraordinaires*, published in 1973, is a multi-author product consisting of material variously by Poe, Baudelaire, Cortázar, and a part-identified, part-anonymous publisher's team. It has 370 pages and is arranged thus: front matter—an eight-page preface signed by Cortázar, a reproduction of the title page of the first edition of *Histoires extraordinaires* from 1856, Baudelaire's essay, "Edgar Poe: Sa vie et ses oeuvres" (which accompanied the 1856 edition), and Poe's poem, "To My Mother," translated by Baudelaire, as a kind of extended epigraph (again as in the 1856 edition)—thirteen of Poe's tales as primary texts, and end matter (a six-page "Note sur l'édition de Baudelaire,"[10] an eleven-page chronology, two pages of bibliography, and the table of contents).[11] The chronology is signed by Germaine Landré; the remaining end matter is unsigned. The Landré chronology is detailed but somewhat subjective, with more on Poe's personal life than on his works. There are no editorial notes to the tales,[12] nor are publishing details given for either the tales or the translations.[13]

The Cortázar preface proves, on investigation, to be surprisingly problematic—though arguably well-suited to the context, as it has elements of a Poe-like hoax. The Folio edition gives no indication as to its provenance, but research reveals that it is actually a translation of a single section of a pre-existing and much longer essay by the Argentine writer. It corresponds verbatim to the section "La página en blanco" ["The blank page"] of the text "El poeta, el narrador y el crítico" ["The poet, the narrator and the critic"], which first appeared in 1956 as a preface to the original edition of Cortázar's two-volume translation of Poe's fiction and was subsequently republished various times in the Spanish-speaking world. Folio nonetheless, in an ingenious act of sleight-of-hand, presented this text by default as if it were a dedicated contribution by the celebrated Argentine.

Baudelaire's sequencing and titling of the tales continues to merit attention today, for despite their nineteenth-century date-stamp, these elements have remained standard in France in modern times.[14] The selection opens with "The Murders in the Rue Morgue" and closes with "Metzengerstein." The sequencing is not chronological but thematic: Baudelaire successively groups tales of ratiocination ("Rue Morgue" is followed by "The Purloined Letter"), science fiction ("Hans Pfaall" follows "The Balloon Hoax"), mesmeric tales (all three), and gothic narratives ("Morella" and "Ligeia"). In some cases, the French title differs from the original: "The Murders in the Rue Morgue" becomes "Double assassinat dans la rue Morgue," and "A Tale of the Ragged Mountains" mutates into "Les souvenirs de M. Auguste Bedloe." Such title changes impact the reader's understanding of the texts: Baudelaire's retitling of "Rue Morgue" stresses the story's theme of the double as the original does not, while in the case of "A Tale of the Ragged Mountains," the rewritten title comes down in favor of the authenticity of Bedloe's "memories," with the original title's neutrality discarded. The selection presented in *Histoires extraordinaires* is, as a first sample, representative and trans-generic—deliberately so, from what we know of Baudelaire's intentions (see more in Vale de Gato's chapter 13 in this book)—and it does not fall into the trap of presenting an all-gothic image (indeed, it even excludes "Usher"!).

It may be asked how much of this volume is Poe and how much it is Baudelaire, for the elements of the French poet's 1856 edition are reproduced in full—not only the translated tales, their titling and their sequencing, but Baudelaire's ancillary material too. Cortázar nonetheless marks an alternative voice, and this irrespective of any issues around the provenance of his text. The Argentine offers an overview of Poe as short fiction artist, stressing his simultaneous, and paradoxical, centrality and marginality. He reads Poe as, variously, a writer alien to the conventions of realist fiction, his work dominated by the notion of "the abnormal" (*Histoires extraordinaires* 13), a textualist whose writing bristles with quotation and allusion, and a visionary science fiction precursor.[15] The French translation is not error-free: the American writer James Russell Lowell is referred to as "Russel Lowell,"[16] and two tales are inaptly given non-Baudelairean titles ("The Man of the Crowd" becomes not "L'Homme des foules" but "L'homme de la foule," and "The Angel of the Odd" not "L'Ange du Bizarre" but "L'ange de l'étrange"). Beyond the familiar Poe-Baudelaire dyad, Cortázar's presence, with its hoaxical element—as far as we know, an editorial creation which at the same time reflects something of Poe's penchant for elaborate deception—may be considered a coup, bringing Poe into a triad alongside his two most celebrated translators of all time.

The Folio edition of *Nouvelles histoires extraordinaires*, Baudelaire's follow-up of 1857 to his first Poe collection, appeared in 1974. It emulated its predecessor insofar as it offered a preface by an eminent collaborator, this time the Franco-Bulgarian literary critic and expert in the fantastic genre, Tzvetan Todorov. This choice suggests a French approach more academic than the British, Todorov as a professional scholar not fitting into the "man of letters" category of Colum or Meynell. The 375-page volume consists of front matter (Todorov's fifteen-page preface, a reproduction of the original title-page from 1857, and Baudelaire's essay, "Notes nouvelles sur Edgar Poe," which prefaced the original edition); twenty-three of Poe's tales; and as end matter an eleven-page chronology (Landré's, reproduced verbatim from the Folio *Histoires extraordinaires*), thirty-two pages of notes by the Baudelaire scholar Yves-Gérard Le Dantec (taken over from the 1951 edition of his Pléiade volume of Poe's works, also published by Gallimard),[17] and a two-page bibliography (a slightly revised update of that of *Histoires extraordinaires*).

The only significant difference from the first Folio volume is the presence of editorial notes.

Baudelaire's sequencing and titling are, again, replicated. The first tale is "The Imp of the Perverse," the last, "The Oval Portrait"; one again notes Baudelaire's thematically oriented arrangement with, for instance, "Usher" (now included) following on from "Berenice," the three angelic dialogues grouped together, and "Silence" leading on from "Shadow." Poe's comic and science fictional sides are represented through, for instance, "Lionizing" and "Some Words with a Mummy." The French titles do not diverge significantly from Poe's.

Todorov's preface in practice introduces not so much the twenty-three tales of this edition as the totality of tales translated by Baudelaire, but nonetheless concentrates throughout on Poe. Like Cortázar, Todorov stresses the multigeneric character or "extreme variety" (Nouvelles histoires extraordinaires 7) of Poe's short story corpus; and like Cortázar again, he reads Poe as a voice from the edge, from the realm of the exceptional, dedicated to "the systematic exploration of limits" (11) and estranged from realist criteria.

If the Todorov text certainly focuses on the American author, Le Dantec's notes are quite heavily Baudelairean—perhaps unsurprisingly, as he was also Pléiade's editor for its collected works of Baudelaire.[18] There are annotations to "Notes nouvelles sur Edgar Poe" as well as to the tales, but no publication details for either tales or translations. Explanations of Poe's references sit cheek-by-jowl with speculative connections between Poe's texts and writings of Baudelaire considered influenced by them. All in all, this edition of Nouvelles histoires extraordinaires is, even more so than its Folio predecessor, arguably as much Baudelaire as it is Poe—a two-for-the-price-of-one production whose bicephalous nature may certainly have gratified many of its French purchasers.

The third Folio volume, Histoires grotesques et sérieuses, appeared in 1978 and brings into the collection Baudelaire's third volume of translations, originally published in 1865. Its 342 pages consist of: a twenty-page preface by the Paris-based academic and Anglicist, Sylvère Monod, as the only front matter; eleven tales or quasi-tales, beginning with "The Mystery of Marie Rogêt" and ending with "The Philosophy of Furniture";[19] "Le Genèse d'un Poème" and a short text from 1864 also by Baudelaire, "Avis du traducteur," as primary texts;[20] and ten pages of chronology (again Landré's), thirty-five pages of notes (signed not by Le Dantec but by Geneviève Bulli), this time including publication details for both Poe and Baudelaire as well as explanatory notes,[21] three pages of bibliography (different from that of the first two

Folio volumes), and the table of contents as end matter. The volume resembles Folio's second but not its first volume in including editorial notes.

Baudelaire's sequencing of course remains, and it is notably genre-oriented, bundling respectively ratiocinative, comic, and landscape tales. His "Avis du traducteur" concerns not so much this volume as the totality of his translations of a writer whom he saw as "a part of myself" (*Histoires grotesques et sérieuses* 288). Monod's preface, unlike the more general Cortázar and Todorov texts, focuses specifically on the volume in hand, noting that *Histoires grotesques et sérieuses* represents Poe's tale-writing in its multigeneric "astonishing variety" (7), and going on to analyze and contextualize each of the twelve texts. Bulli's notes are informative and accurate, and they offer more than Le Dantec's insofar as they indicate publication and translation details for the individual texts. This third volume may be considered a worthy successor to its predecessors: it is also a shade less Baudelairean than either.

The Folio Poe-Baudelaire triad was complemented in 1989 by a fourth volume, *Ne pariez jamais votre tête au diable et autres contes non traduits par Baudelaire*, translated, edited, and introduced by the French novelist and film director, Alain Jaubert. The hegemony of Baudelaire is paradoxically both subverted by the non-Baudelairean material, and maintained by a title that, even if negatively, continues to define Poe by referring to the French poet. The book's 509 pages consist of a preface of sixty-three pages by Jaubert and a note on the text as the book's only front matter; the preface to *Tales of the Grotesque and Arabesque*, the framing narrative for *Tales of the Folio Club*, and twenty-five tales as the primary texts; and a four-page chronology (this time new), fifty-nine pages of notes on the individual tales (including publication details), and the table of contents as end matter. There is no bibliography as such, but the introduction includes bibliographical footnotes.

The volume is unusually homogeneous in terms of editorial matter, being effectively Jaubert's single-handed production. The tales comprise all but one of those not translated by Baudelaire—"The Journal of Julius Rodman" is excluded on grounds of length. Few, it must be said, would consider the majority of these non-Baudelairean tales as falling among Poe's major works. The editor, for once in Folio, had a free hand and opted for a chronological organization, thus diverging from Baudelaire's thematic orientation. The first tale proper is "Le duc de l'Omelette" (its original French title unchanged), the last the unfinished "The Light-House." The translated titles eschew the controversial; the near-untranslatable "X-ing a Paragrab" becomes the equally strange "Ixage d'un paragrab." The chronology is adequate and more text-centered and less biographically oriented than Germaine Landré's earlier effort; the notes are useful and informative, offering precious detail enabling the French reader to situate such less obvious tales as "Mellonta Tauta" or "Von Kempelen and His Discovery" and, in a case like "The Man That Was Used Up," admitting that textual features such as puns may be untranslatable (*Ne pariez jamais* 472).

Jaubert's preface is the longest and most detailed in our corpus; it also, interestingly, cites the Todorov, Beaver, and Galloway (*Comedies and Satires*) editions/prefaces and their insights (51, 67n). It covers both Poe's work in general and the specific content of the volume (Jaubert, ingeniously, adopts an ad hoc typographical device, asterisking the references to the tales of his volume). The preface explores multiple aspects of Poe's writing, from the hoaxical through the intertextual to the comic and science fictional. Jaubert underscores the continuing hegemony of the Baudelaire translations, observing notably the privileged status, "forever untouchable" (65), of the generic titles of the three Baudelaire volumes. It may be concluded from this edition that Jaubert has made a valiant effort to complement the Baudelairean image of Poe with further and, ultimately, fuller data.

The publishing history of popular editions of Poe in the United Kingdom and France, as examined through the above nine-volume corpus, reveals both convergences and divergences between the literary systems of the two countries in the twentieth century. In both, one notes a tendency over time for editions to become more academic in approach and to include a more substantial critical apparatus; this would be in line with the gradual institutionalization of American Studies at university level in both countries, but in France somewhat before the United Kingdom.[22] Meanwhile, if national stereotypes might lead to expect a more systematic and programmatic French methodology and a more empirical, ad hoc British approach, the volumes show that neither Penguin nor Folio followed a fixed and identical model in their different de facto series, with much depending on the editor's discretion. The issue of genre appears as particularly central in both British and French contexts, impinging on both textual sequencing (chronological or generic?) and the presentation of Poe in introductions that, as time goes by, tend to lay greater stress on his multigeneric production: there is a visible shift over time in both countries away from an overly gothic (or gothic-detective) view of Poe, with much greater emphasis on his comic and science fictional facets (the latter most notably, but not only, in Beaver's *Science Fiction*). Finally, the French selections studied offer a key ontological divergence from their British counterparts by being devoted wherever possible as much to Baudelaire as to Poe. Baudelaire is followed to the letter, not only in his translations, but also in the aspects of volume titling, tale titling, and tale sequencing, with his introductions and notes carrying over. Even his absence is a kind of presence. In the twentieth century at least (things would be rather different in the twenty-first), a unique posthumous literary collaboration finds Charles Baudelaire's shadow floating over the French literary market in Edgar Allan Poe, as if—or so it must have seemed to many—to be lifted nevermore![23]

Notes

1. See the presentation of Everyman's Library at http://everymanslibrarycollecting.com/site_index.html.

2. Everyman's Library later added a second volume by Poe, *Poems and Essays*, first published in 1927 and introduced by the Scottish man of letters and folklorist Andrew Lang.

3. The sequencing of the tales in this volume does not appear to reflect that followed in any of the main earlier collected editions of Poe and may have originated with Everyman.

4. The history of these imprints is somewhat complex. The Penguin Classics imprint was established in 1946, and in its first decades only included literature in translation. For English-language classics, Penguin created the Penguin English Library in 1963 (at first it also included American titles), and the Penguin American Library in 1981. The three collections were merged into an expanded Penguin Classics imprint in 1986, and that regime continues today.

5. *The Narrative of Arthur Gordon Pym of Nantucket*, edited by Harold Beaver, was released in the Penguin English Library in 1975 and reissued in 1986 in Penguin Classics.

6. "MS. Found in a Bottle," "A Descent into the Maelström," and "The Facts in the Case of M. Valdemar" appear in both *Selected Writings* and *Science Fiction*; "The Man That Was Used Up" is included in both *Selected Writings* and *The Other Poe*.

7. *Pym* and "The Journal of Julius Rodman."

8. Also included as an essay in the Everyman *Poems and Essays* mentioned above.

9. Baudelaire translated a total of forty-six short texts by Poe, of which three ("Mesmeric Revelation," "The Philosophy of Furniture" and "Maelzel's Chess-Player") are, as we have seen for the first two, classified by others as essays, while "The Philosophy of Composition" (which he accompanied with the text of "The Raven") is certainly an essay. He also translated *Pym* and *Eureka*.

10. This note includes the text of a (never-sent) letter addressed by Baudelaire to Maria Clemm, dated 1856 and not included in Baudelaire's original *Histoires extraordinaires* (*Histoires extraordinaires* 353–55).

11. For this volume as for the others published by Folio, we should recall that the conventions of French book presentation are not always the same as those in the United Kingdom; in France, the table of contents invariably appears not as front matter but as end matter.

12. Baudelaire's original notes to the tales are included as footnotes.

13. The "Note sur l'édition de Baudelaire" does include some explanatory notes, but only to "Edgar Poe: Sa vie et ses oeuvres" (essentially correcting Baudelaire's errors of fact).

14. See the detailed analysis in the previous chapter of this book, by Margarida Vale de Gato.

15. Unless otherwise noted, all translations from French are my own.

16. Cortázar's Spanish original has, correctly, "Russell Lowell" (though without "James").

17. Baudelaire's own notes also appear as footnotes to the tales, as in *Histoires extraordinaires*.

18. See Vale de Gato's chapter 13 in this book.

19. Of which two, "Maelzel's Chess-Player" and "The Philosophy of Furniture," may also be considered essays (see chapter 13 in this book).

20. "Le Genèse d'un Poème" is a composite text made up of an introduction by Baudelaire and his translations of "The Philosophy of Composition" and "The Raven." Geneviève Bulli explains in her notes that "Avis du traducteur" was intended as an introduction to *Histoires grotesques et sérieuses* but that it was not published in Baudelaire's lifetime. It was discovered by Yves-Gérard Le Dantec and first published in 1934 (*Histoires grotesques et sérieuses*, 334–35).

21. Baudelaire's notes appear once more as footnotes to the tales.

22. For instance, Cambridge University only introduced American literature as a course on Part II of the English Tripos in the mid-1970s. American writers such as Walt Whitman had meanwhile featured on the French *agrégation* programme for some time before that.

23. In the twenty-first century, see the work of Henri Justin (as both critic and translator) marking a move away from the automatic privileging of the Baudelaire translations ("Retranslating Poe").

Works Cited

Baudelaire, Charles. *Oeuvres complètes*. Edited by Yves-Gérard Le Dantec, Gallimard (Pléiade), 1961.

Cortázar, Julio. "El poeta, el narrador y el crítico." *Obras en Prosa*, by Edgar Allan Poe, translated by Julio Cortázar, vol. 1, Revista de Occidente and Editorial Universitaria Universidad de Puerto Rico, 1956, pp. lv–xcvii.

Justin, Henri. "Retranslating Poe into French." *Translated Poe*, edited by Emron Esplin and Margarida Vale de Gato, Lehigh UP, 2014, pp. 203–20.

Poe, Edgar Allan. *Comedies and Satires*. Edited and introduced by David Galloway, Penguin, 1987.

———. *The Fall of the House of Usher and Other Writings*. Edited and introduced by David Galloway, Penguin, 1986.

———. *Histoires extraordinaires*. Translated by Charles Baudelaire, preface by Julio Cortázar (translated by Laure Guille-Bataillon), Gallimard (Folio), 1973.

———. *Histoires grotesques et sérieuses*. Translated by Charles Baudelaire, preface by Sylvère Monod, Gallimard (Folio), 1978.

———. *The Narrative of Arthur Gordon Pym of Nantucket*. Edited and introduced by Harold Beaver, Penguin, 1975.

———. *Ne pariez jamais votre tête au diable et autres contes non traduits par Baudelaire*. Translated and with preface by Alain Jaubert, Gallimard (Folio), 1989.

———. *Nouvelles histoires extraordinaires*. Translated by Charles Baudelaire, preface by Tzvetan Todorov, Gallimard (Folio), 1974.

———. *Oeuvres en prose*. Translated by Charles Baudelaire, edited by Yves-Gérard Le Dantec, Gallimard (Pléiade), 1951.

———. *The Other Poe: Comedies and Satires*. Edited and introduced by David Galloway, Penguin, 1983.

———. *Poems and Essays*. 1927. Introduction by Andrew Lang, Dent (Everyman's Library), 1969.

———. *The Science Fiction of Edgar Allan Poe*. Edited and introduced by Harold Beaver, Penguin, 1976.

———. *Selected Writings of Edgar Allan Poe: Poems, Tales, Essays and Reviews*. Edited and introduced by David Galloway, Penguin, 1967.

———. *Tales of Mystery and Imagination*. 1908. Introduction by Pádraic Colum, Dent (Everyman's Library), 1971.

———. *Tales, Poems, Essays*. Introduction by Laurence Meynell, Collins, 1952.

Yoon, Sun Kyoung. "Popularizing Homer: E. V. Rieu's English Prose Translations." *The Translator*, vol. 20, no. 2, 2014, np. http://www.tandfonline.com/doi/abs/10.1080/13556509.2014.968990.

~

CHAPTER FIFTEEN

Under the Spanish Eye

Illustrated Poe Editions in Spain

Fernando González-Moreno and Margarita Rigal-Aragón

Edgar Allan Poe's literary reception in Spain has been widely examined, from the early contributions by John Eugene Englekirk (1934) and Pedro Salinas (1941) to the more recent work by David Roas Deus (2011), Santiago Rodríguez Guerrero-Strachan (2011), and Margarita Rigal-Aragón (2011).[1] However, an aspect neglected by Spanish scholars up to this point has been how illustrators—under the supervision and control of editors—approach Poe's works in Spain. Poe was anthologized in Spain as early as 1858 when a Poe collection heavily influenced by Baudelaire, *Historias extraordinarias*, first appeared in print.[2] The small volume contained translations of five of Poe's stories ("Hans Pfaall," "The Murders in the Rue Morgue," "The Gold-Bug," "The Purloined Letter," and "The Facts in the Case of M. Valdemar," presented in this order) and a short story by a very well-regarded Spanish writer, Cecilia Böhl de Faber.[3] Between 1858 and 1887, other collections followed, including another *Historias extraordinarias* edited by José Trujillo in 1860 in Madrid, with ten stories, and yet another collection with the same title edited by Manuel Cano y Cueto in Sevilla in 1871 with thirteen tales.

Poe's tales and poems have been an endless source of inspiration for graphic artists, as proven primarily by Burton R. Pollin (1989) and Barbara Cantalupo (2014). Spain has not been an exception. Spanish illustrators have played a significant role in "translating" Poe's words into images, and scores of illustrated Poe compilations demonstrate how Spanish artists render their visual understanding of Poe's works. Nevertheless, no academic studies have offered a general panorama of the main illustrated editions of Poe in

Spain. This is the primary purpose of our chapter: we take the reader on a journey through twelve illustrated editions from the last quarter of the nineteenth century to the commemoration of Poe's birth bicentenary. All these editions, chosen as the most representative in their decades, will allow us to determine how Poe was read in Spain, which tales were in higher demand among readers, and which episodes were taken as the most iconic. These aspects were conditioned by and clearly reflect the historical backgrounds in which each illustrated edition was created: 1) the unstable period of the Bourbon Restoration (1875–1931), 2) the Second Republic (1931–1936)—which promoted cultural and educational advances, 3) the Spanish Civil War (1936–1939), during which, surprisingly, Poe continued to be printed, 4) the postwar years under the long Francoist regime, and 5) the much more fruitful Democratic phase that we enjoy today.

We consider illustration—as Poe himself did—as an interpretative tool of narration. Poe built and maintained his ideas on this matter over a long period of time. For instance, in his review of Oliver Goldsmith's *The Vicar of Wakefield*, Poe distinguishes this illustrated edition as a piece of art, calling it a comprehensive work in which not only the text but also the format, typing, paper quality, printing, and illustrations, deserve attention (9). He does not contemplate the illustrations as simple embellishments or as distractions for the reader but defends the informative value of an image. According to Poe, the scarce interruption that the reader can get from an illustration is balanced by the gratification it affords, since it provides the possibility of comparing the conception of the author's designs with those of the artist (8–9). In this sense, an illustration might achieve a second task: to inspire the fantasy of the readers so that they can reach a deeper understanding of the text. Throughout his life, Poe argued that illustrations must not be plain adornments, and he insisted on well-executed images in agreement with the text; the different brochures of his imagined literary journals always conveyed this assertion.[4] In the same way, we defend the study of illustrations as an element in dialogue with the text—following it in some cases, completing it in others, or even contradicting it—a dialogue that, after all, reflects the way that Poe was presented by Spanish editors and understood by readers.[5] The works of these illustrators allow readers to focus their attention on specific aspects within individual Poe tales and condition the readers' experiences with those tales. Interpreting these illustrations lets us demonstrate how Poe was received at different times in Spain. As a way of demonstrating this evolution, many of the illustrations we choose to accompany our study refer to the same tale—the only one selected by all but one of the publishing houses whose editions we examine—"The Tell-Tale Heart."

Early Illustrated Editions through
the End of the Spanish Civil War

The first illustrated Poe edition entered the Spanish literary scene as early as 1887 (Pollin 204). Pondering Baudelaire's influence on Poe's reputation in Spain, it should come as no surprise that this book came to light only three years after the Quantin illustrated edition of 1884 was published in Paris. Poe already appealed to Spanish readers, writers, editors, translators, and publishing houses before the 1887 illustrated edition, but from that time until today, he has continued to appeal to Spanish illustrators and to all of the aforementioned parties—whether they be producers and mediators of literature, or the audience at which the illustrated editions are aimed.

The 1887 illustrated collection was titled *Historias extraordinarias*, published in Barcelona by Daniel Cortezo & C. in the Biblioteca de Arte y Letras series. The stories were translated by Enrique Leopoldo de Verneuil, who translated from Baudelaire's French rather than Poe's English. De Verneuil also included Baudelaire's 1857 prologue for his *Nouvelles histoires extraordinaires* in this edition. The compilation contains eleven tales that seem to have been perfectly chosen to show the different faces of Poe: the grotesque, the humorous, the adventurous, the macabre, the arabesque, and the rationalist. They were illustrated by the Barcelonan artist, Fernando or Ferran Xumetra Ragull, who specialized in fantastic and romantic subjects. Xumetra had already illustrated Hoffmann's *Fantastic Tales*, so he was particularly appropriate to take on Poe's work. Each Poe story includes one headpiece, one tailpiece, and one or two full-page illustrations, for a total of thirty-seven illustrations, plus an allegorical portrait of Poe.[6] Xumetra's illustrations had the merit of providing visual renditions for tales that, to our knowledge, until then had not inspired other images, such as "The Tell-Tale Heart" and "The Cask of Amontillado." From this first illustrated edition, the inclusion of both tales was standard in later collections, and these became two of the most represented and iconic stories in Spain. The other tales that Xumetra illustrated would enjoy different fortunes. The so-called stories of ratiocination, "The Murders in the Rue Morgue" and "The Gold-Bug," keep appearing with certain regularity, as do the following tales of terror and/or the supernatural—"The Black Cat," "A Descent into the Maelström," "The Pit and the Pendulum," and "Ligeia." Other stories, including "Hans Pfaall," "William Wilson," and "Metzengerstein," have suffered the progressive disinterest of both editors and illustrators in Spain.

Xumetra's illustrations—described by Pollin as "conventional but skillful" (21)—unite two different ways of approaching Poe that later artists have followed as opposing paths. On the one hand, several illustrations have been resolved in a very literal way, taking Poe's texts word by word and transforming them into melodramatic scenes. This tendency—more traditional and less risky—can be observed in the episodes depicted for "The Black Cat," "William Wilson," "Cask," "Ligeia," and "Metzengerstein." In all these cases, the characters seem like nineteenth-century actors declaiming on a stage, recalling the illustrations included in the *folletines* that were so popular during this time period.[7] However, Xumetra also offers a deeper reading through different scenes; in keeping with late-nineteenth-century Decadentism, he tries to suggest the atmosphere—oppressive or menacing—of the narration. In this sense, two of the illustrations stand out from the others. The first case is the headpiece for "The Tell-Tale Heart" (figure 15.1), in which we can see the old man sleeping, unaware of the menacing presence of a skeleton wrapped in a floating cloth and holding a scythe. It is the allegorical image of Death symbolizing the assassin's obsession, rather than the flesh-and-blood killer himself, that threatens the old man—a menace that we perceive and that makes us feel a deep and disturbing sense of powerlessness. The second, the headpiece for "William Wilson," presents an unusual composition. It is not a literalistic representation of any of the passages, but a personal, symbolic, and free reading: Xumetra retakes the traditional Christian iconography of the Sacred Heart of Jesus—together with a scythe, a quill piercing the heart, and a laurel branch—to evoke the remorse of the character; William Wilson writes his story as a kind of confession to purge his dishonest deeds, and Xumetra understands it as a symbol of Christ's forgiveness.

The continuity of these two different tendencies—one more literal and "folletinesca," and the other more symbolic and suggestive—can be traced in the 1908 edition of *Narraciones extraordinarias*, published by Saturnino Calleja in Madrid, and in *Cuentos*, published in Barcelona by Araluce circa 1914.[8] The first was published both as an independent volume with a pictorial cover depicting Poe's portrait, and as part of the series, La Novela de Ahora, (no. 41), favoring the image of these tales as *folletines* sold in weekly installments. Eight stories are included here, and they were translated and introduced by Alfonso Hernández Catá.[9] Due to his interest in literature in general and in short story writing, it comes as no surprise that he translated and prefaced these stories by Poe. Again, Baudelaire shines as the most likely source when Catá recognizes Poe as the poet of the disturbing, the truculent, the fiendishly miraculous, the extremely terrifying, the macabre, and the abnormal.[10]

The illustrations in this edition were by Manuel Picolo López, Elías Corona, J. Cuevas, Isidro Gil y Gavilondo, and Evaristo Barrio, leading illustrators and perennial collaborators in the editions by Calleja.[11] The style of

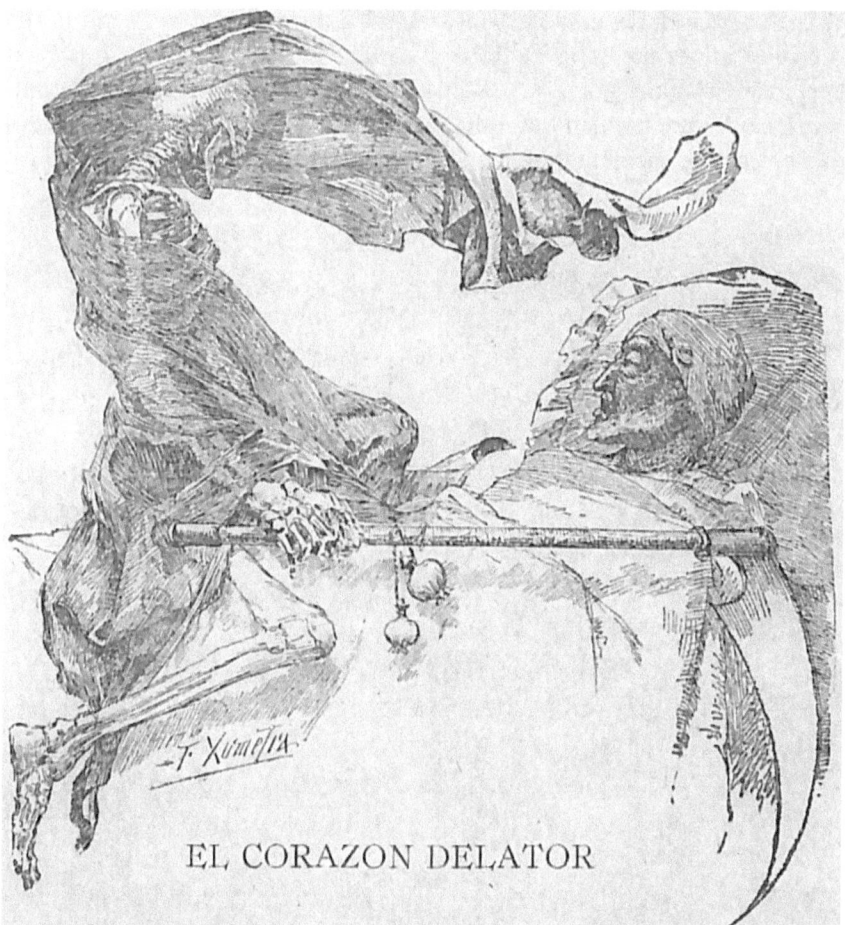

EL CORAZON DELATOR

Figure 15.1. "The Tell-Tale Heart," by Fernando or Ferran Xumetra Ragull (Daniel Cortezo, 1887, p. 221).
Courtesy of the Universidad de Castilla-La Mancha.

these images, according to the editor's purpose of offering popular and accessible editions, is mainly descriptive and literal; for example, the vignettes in "The Oval Portrait" and "The Black Cat" refer to fairly mundane moments in the narration. Some of these illustrations are resolved with a picturesque character, almost folklorist—the female figures for "Berenice" and "Hop-Frog" look like regional Spanish girls—denoting the training of some of these illustrators as genre painters. We may perceive a certain interest in the romantic and mysterious aspects of some tales—"The Premature Burial" or "Berenice." A slight glimpse of the grotesque and the macabre, which had

been so very well described by Hernández Catá, can barely be found in the
two illustrations for "The Tell-Tale Heart." The first, although showing a
later moment of the story, is a headpiece with the killer hiding the old man's
corpse under the wooden floor; the second emphasizes the victim's vulture-
like eye at the moment when the narrator enters the room (figure 15.2),

Figure 15.2. "The Tell-Tale Heart," by Manuel Picolo (Casa Editorial de Saturnino
Calleja Fernández, 1908, p. 19).
Courtesy of the Universidad de Castilla-La Mancha.

startling and waking his victim. Choosing this very instant, Manuel Picolo proves to have recognized the initial climax of the narration; however, the image is little more than a limited attempt to equal Poe's effect.

For its part, the 1914 edition of *Cuentos* by Edgard Allan Poe [sic] comprised five short stories which, according to the publishing house, were "adapted" by Manuel Vallvé for "children."[12] The volume contains a brief, unsigned, and error-ridden introduction about Poe's life. However, the comments on Poe's writing style are unexpectedly avant-garde for the Spanish scenario of the time: Poe's work "is distinguished by an extraordinary fantasy, an exquisite mastery in the art of producing a deep impression on the mind of the reader, as proved by his 'Gold-Bug'" (ix).[13]

Regarding the illustrations, this 1914 edition turns out to be more original and promising than the edition from 1908. Josep (José) Segrelles Albert was a gifted and talented illustrator, earning early success thanks to his work for Araluce. In fact, the eight illustrations in color are among his first productions for this publishing house. It is true that, bearing in mind the exceptional capacity Segrelles Albert demonstrated in his later works to suggest evocative and mysterious atmospheres, some of these illustrations underwhelm the viewer. This is especially the case with the three illustrations he offers for "The Gold-Bug": the Scarabaeus, the well-known discovery of the treasure, and the narrator holding the old parchment by the fireplace. However, three other illustrations must be highlighted since they prove that Poe's texts were a source of inspiration that spurred Segrelles's pictorial talent at his best. First, the old man from "The Tell-Tale Heart" appears in a deeply psychological portrait in which Segrelles succeeds in depicting the iconic value of the vulture eye. Second, the scene from "The System of Doctor Tarr and Professor Fether," including the members of the orchestra playing with eccentric and superhuman energy, indicates that Segrelles grasped the comic nature of this tale. And finally, perhaps the best of all, is the terrible appearance of the Red Death before Prince Prospero (figure 15.3). Segrelles has resolved the scene in complete darkness, highlighting with effective theatricality both characters and a basic setting with red cat-eye like windows and a clock. We, the readers, occupy the same position as Prince Prospero, looking into the face of the Red Death. In this way, the illustrator equates us with the Prince and reminds us that we, too, will be victims of Death. From his first approach to Poe onward, Segrelles would remain captivated by his work, offering new and more mature visual readings on later occasions.[14]

Figure 15.3. "The Masque of the Red Death," by Segrelles (Casa Editorial Araluce, 1914, facing p. 20).
Courtesy of the Research Group LyA, Universidad de Castilla-La Mancha.

On How Poe Rode Out the Francoist Regime

Just three years after the end of the Spanish Civil War, and with the most severe part of the postwar era as a backdrop, Joaquín Gil published a new illustrated edition of Poe's writings in Barcelona. This work was one of the projects dedicated to re-establishing a quality editorial market in Spain. In this sense, and as a way of conferring to the book an additional artistic value, the editors went back to including illustrations produced by traditional techniques. This 1942 edition was titled, once again, *Narraciones extraordinarias*, and the prologue and translations of the sixteen tales included were by Josep (José) Farrán y Mayoral.[15] It is interesting to note that, even though the title provided was, again, *Narraciones extraordinarias*, "The Raven," "To Helen," "To——," and "Annabel Lee" were included at the end of the book. In the prologue, Farrán claimed that he was rendering directly from Poe's English into Spanish. This claim seems true, for his prose is no longer similar to that of previous Spanish editions (in which the French versions were followed), but closer to Julio Cortázar's translations of the 1950s.[16] This preface shows Farrán's understanding of what Poe wanted to communicate to the reader: "his ardent and truthful love for beauty . . . exquisite sensibility to feel, to perceive very new and singular shades of beauty" (8). Farrán states that he is not going to write about the artist's life because it was already well-known to everyone (7), although this was certainly not true in Spain at the time. This conscious omission might be understandable in the context of Spain's political situation. Right after the war, and under Franco's dictatorship, ecclesiastic censors were very severe: if the *oeuvre* or life of an author was considered immoral, the publication was forbidden. Thus, Farrán justifies the morality of several of the tales included (10–11), like "William Wilson," and leaves out of the selection others whose main characters do not show any remorse, such as "The Tell-Tale Heart."

The artist in charge of the vignettes that precede every tale in this 1942 compilation was Pedro or Pere Riu Baragnes, a painter, printmaker, and etcher from Barcelona. Riu used xylography to produce these thirty-two images, a technique that bestowed on them a peculiar expressiveness due to the use of well-contrasted red-brown lines. While eight of the tales had already been included and illustrated in previous Spanish editions, another eight were illustrated for the first time: "Eleonora," "MS. Found in a Bottle," "Lionizing," "The Angel of the Odd," "The Colloquy of Monos and Una," "The Conversation of Eiros and Charmion," "The Spectacles," and "The Fall of the House of Usher." The presence of this last story, which will become a tale repeated in Spanish anthologies and editions from that moment forward, must be highlighted. Riu depicts the instant when the traveler-narrator approaches the house of Usher and contemplates it for the first time: a massive construction crossed by a fissure and crowned by pointed conical roofs that highlight its gothic atmosphere, opening up an imaginative space that points to an ideal of fantasy (figure 15.4).

The image recalls Arthur Rackham's earlier representations, although in general, Riu's style—more restrained—has nothing to do with Rackham's

Figure 15.4. "The Fall of the House of Usher," by Pedro Riu Baragnes (Iberia-Joaquín Gil Editor, 1942, p. 95).
Courtesy of the Universidad de Castilla-La Mancha.

openly grotesque and macabre illustrations. In fact, Farrán seems to be criticizing Rackham when he indicates in his prologue:

> We have gone through a luxurious British edition of [Poe's] stories, illustrated with deep theatricality, as it was typical of the decadent style of the *fin de siècle*. We have been unable to avoid a feeling of horror and disgust when confronted with such ugliness. The illustrator has failed to understand Poe. Poe, himself, would have felt outraged with that sinister display of revolting ghosts and terrifying scenes; his intelligence, his exquisite taste, would have led him to exclaim: "What does all of this have to do with the poetics of my work?" (9–10)

Riu's vignettes must be understood from the perspective of this defense that puts the accent on the beauty of Poe's prose, beyond the elements of terror, ugliness, repulsion, and madness that we can find in the narration. To reflect that same idea on how to read these tales, Riu does not include any of the elements that could be considered as indecorous, grotesque, or macabre. On the contrary, he emphasizes the beauty of the xylographic lines and their capacity to suggest haunting feelings. Thus, in "The Fall of the House of Usher," the undulating lines of the clouds, lake, and tree branches surrounding the imposing and massive house are enough to transmit to us a sense of restlessness.

Some fifteen years later, in 1957, another illustrated edition saw the light of print in Barcelona: this edition of *Narraciones extraordinarias* included eight tales with no paratext—no prologue, no introduction, not even the name of the translator was provided. The publishing house was Editorial Juventud, founded in 1923 and still active today. Due to the success of this book, the same house published, in 1968, *Nuevas narraciones extraordinarias*. The nine tales included in this second collection, translated by Mariano Orta Manzano, were accompanied by Baudelaire's 1856 and 1857 prologues. There was, too, a chronological chart, which—surprisingly enough—contained no mistaken data: the birth date was correct, the Byronic trips had disappeared, and so on. Regretfully, from the point of view of the texts, this collection adds nothing new to the Spanish perception of Poe at the time.[17]

The illustrations in the 1957 Editorial Juventud edition could have been very promising. Regardless of the book's lack of any paratextual material, we know that its eight drawings are by José Narro Celorrio. Narro was a constant collaborator with this publishing house during the 1950s and one of the most celebrated illustrators in Spain at that time, despite living in the exile.[18] Already a well-known sketch artist before the Civil War, during the postwar period he specialized in illustrated books. His style of elegant, detailed, and expressive drawing lines was considered a referent to be followed by other artists. However, and unfortunately, these illustrations for Poe's tales may not be counted among his best works; they can only be declared correct and proper. Two stories were illustrated for the first time: "The Mystery of Marie Rogêt" and "The Purloined Letter." The latter highlights the ridiculousness of the prefect of the Parisian Police, Monsieur G——, examining in detail every piece of furniture, but Narro accomplishes little more with either illustration. Among the other tales illustrated by Narro, lacking originality as well, we find "The Tell-Tale Heart," which might show just a glimpse of malice on the murderer's face, but the illustration as a whole barely resembles a crime scene (figure 15.5).

When Editorial Juventud published its second volume, a new illustrator was selected: Jaime Azpelicueta. Today he is almost unknown, but in 1968 Azpelicueta had already enjoyed wide experience illustrating classics. His style, characterized by fine and arabesque drawing lines, is indebted to late Art Nouveau and recalls the tradition inaugurated by Aubrey Beardsley in 1894. The intricate lines of Azpelicueta's designs flourish from the main images, metamorphosing them and giving form to thoughts and obsessions. We can see this in "Morella," whose imaginative intelligence arises from her own head; in "Berenice," in which several monstrous and toothy skulls fly away from the narrator's head; and in "William Wilson" (figure 15.6). This final illustration shows the heads of both men intertwined like two lungs linked by their alveoli as a way of suggesting the symbiotic relationship between the two characters. They are the two sides of human nature; the idea of the double and how our soul is inhabited by the evil and the good, two forces that cannot live without the other and that are fed reciprocally. Azpelicueta's illustrations are moving images that must be included among the best visual approaches to Poe's tales.

We have glossed over Editorial Juventud's 1968 Poe edition, but we cannot leave the 1960s without mentioning, although briefly, the edition *Obras inmortales: Narraciones, Ensayos, Poemas*, published in 1967 by E.D.A.F. This edition compiled *The Narrative of Arthur Gordon Pym*, sixty-three tales, six essays, nine "Marginalia" pieces, and forty-four poems.[19] The prologue, by an unknown author, does not go into Poe's life but reflects wisely on Poe's texts, highlighting, for instance, that when dealing with the author of "Eleonora," we find an accumulation of experiences, a repertoire of overwhelming heartbeats, something similar to realities so vivid, so intense, so extreme, and so amazing, that we live them and incorporate them into our lives, or we will be unable to understand them (xi–xv).

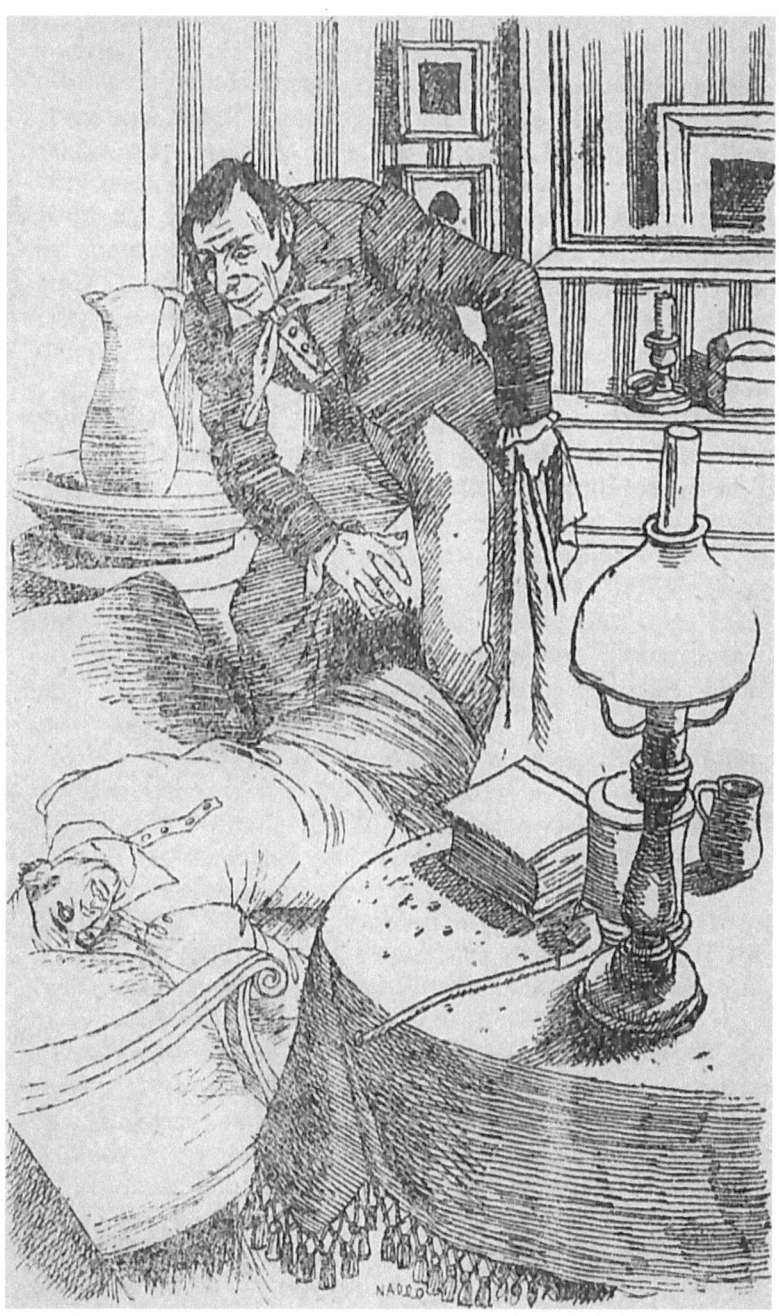

Figure 15.5. "The Tell-Tale Heart," by José Narro Celorrio (© Editorial Juventud, 1957, p. 113).
Courtesy of Editorial Juventud.

Figure 15.6. "William Wilson," by Jaime Azpelicueta (© Editorial Juventud, 1968, p. 117).
Courtesy of Editorial Juventud.

This edition included sixteen illustrations in color by the Madrilenian José Picó Mitjans, a well-known painter and customary illustrator of periodicals such as *Blanco y Negro* and *ABC*. The images, described by Pollin as "crude pictures" (209), fail to capture the feelings resulting from the arabesque or the supernatural terror in the tales illustrated (including "The Fall of the House of Usher," "The Black Cat," and "The Tell-Tale Heart"). In these pieces, most of the expressions do not show more than silly stupefaction. Thus, in "Tell-Tale Heart," we cannot see any trace of madness, anxiety, or fury on the face of the murderer; nor is the iconic eye of the old man highlighted; Picó has even modified the original text, as the assassin should not appear grasping the old man by his neck, but suffocating him with a mattress on the floor (figure 15.7). On the other hand, Picó Mitjans's illustrations of tales connected to the parodic-grotesque have more satisfactory results, including those for "Some Words with a Mummy," "The Devil in the Belfry," and "The Spectacles." This last illustration shows the image of the lady as the "beau ideal" that the narrator believes he sees in the opera box; in this way, the illustrator helps to trick the reader as Poe's text does, not revealing the truth of the woman's appearance.

In 1971, while the Francoist regime was progressing to its end and Spain struggled with fragile attempts toward cultural and social—but not political—*apertura*, or opening, Ediciones Nauta published a new and carefully printed edition of Poe's tales under the title *Obras selectas*. This two-volume edition, translated by María Cristina Reiss Raimundo, included a prologue by Carlos Rojas, forty of Poe's tales, "The Raven" and "The Philosophy of Composition," 108 short "Marginalia" entries, and—probably for the first time in Spanish—"The Journal of Julius Rodman."[20] Rojas appears to have read Marie Bonaparte's 1933 study on Poe, to be familiar with Borges's appreciation for Poe's texts, and to admire *Pym* more than any other of his *oeuvres* (although *Pym* is not included in this selection). It must be pointed out that the inexpensive paperback edition of Cortázar's Poe translations had been circulating in Spain since the previous year (1970) thanks to Alianza Editorial, which makes us think that the publication of this illustrated, hardcover edition, translated and prefaced by writers other than Cortázar, was Ediciones Nauta's unsuccessful attempt to surpass Alianza's pocket edition.[21]

The illustrator selected on this occasion is a perfect example of the situation that the country was living through at the time. Ramón Calsina Baró, a painter, lithographer, and illustrator praised by his colleagues and by a select group of admirers, never enjoyed official recognition due to his ideological past. At the end of the Spanish Civil War in 1939, Calsina went into exile, but he decided to come back and was imprisoned for several months. After

Figure 15.7. "The Tell-Tale Heart" by José Picó Mitjans (E.D.A.F., 1967, facing p. 704).
Courtesy of Editorial E.D.A.F.

his release, Calsina began a career as an independent painter, out of fashion, developing a very particular style of magic figurativism. This personal interest drew him to two writers: Cervantes and Poe. Ediciones Nauta offered him the opportunity to illustrate *Don Quixote* in 1965 and Poe's *Obras selectas* in 1971. The result, faithful to Calsina's style, must be declared to be irregular, but we cannot be as severe as Pollin, who remarked that "the figures all look like wooden puppets and the scenes are lifeless" (210). Calsina approaches most of the tales of the arabesque in a disappointing way: "The Fall of the House of Usher," "The Masque of the Red Death," "The Black Cat," "The Tell-Tale Heart," or "The Pit and the Pendulum," among others, were already well-known tales, and Calsina's illustrations offer little novelty. The aforementioned "Tell-Tale Heart," for instance, depicts the characters—the murderer and the policemen—as caricatures, transmitting a certain tone of parody rather than dementia or psychological terror (figure 15.8). Nevertheless, one striking detail must be pointed out: the inclusion of a heart on the floor, suggesting the beatings that enervate the assassin.

On the other hand, for those tales connected to the grotesque as parody, Calsina proves to be an illustrator of great originality. The images he created for tales such as "The Sphinx," "Bon-Bon," "Never Bet the Devil Your Head," "King Pest," "X-ing a Paragrab," "Some Words with a Mummy," or "The Devil in the Belfry" (figure 15.9)—in which the people from Vondervotteimittiss have been represented literarily as cabbages—show an excellent sense of humor and a very clever interpretation of Poe, a facet of his work that illustrators have commonly disregarded.

The Golden Age of Poe's Illustrated Editions: The Democratic Period

A constant in Poe's reception in Spain—not too distant from that in other countries—is that his tales of ratiocination have usually been perceived as the most appropriate for young readers. In this sense, the editors of juvenile literature counted on the invaluable collaboration of illustrators, who primarily focused on the aspects of these narrations as stories of mystery and adventure. So, when Vicens Vives decided to include Poe as part of its 1988 collection "Aula de Literatura," the stories selected were "The Gold-Bug" and "The Murders in the Rue Morgue." However, the set of illustrations included in this first edition, a reproduction of works by Arthur Rackham, was possibly too adult for the target reader of this collection. Thus, in 1995, the book was re-edited with a new set of ten illustrations in color by the Spanish painter and illustrator Tino Gatagán (pseudonym for Constantino

Figure 15.8. "The Tell-Tale Heart," by Ramón Calsina Baró (Ediciones Nauta, 1971, vol. 2, p. 39).
Courtesy of Mercé Calsina, © Fundació Privada Ramon Calsina at www.fundaciocalsina.org.

Gómez Vidal). Gatagán reinforces the visual reading of the first story as a treasure hunt, while he presents "Murders" without its most cruel details. In fact, the well-known attack of the orangutan is depicted, but without a single drop of blood. The scene does not lack expression, but it differs from previous illustrators' versions, which are usually more gruesome. Vicens Vives completed the presence of Poe in its collection with a new edition in 1996, now including "The Black Cat," "The Facts in the Case of M. Valdemar," "The Cask of Amontillado," "The Masque of the Red Death," "Hop-Frog," "The Pit and the Pendulum," "The Tell-Tale Heart," and "The Fall of the

Figure 15.9. "The Devil in the Belfry," by Ramón Calsina Baró (Ediciones Nauta, 1971, vol. 1, p. 105).
Courtesy of Mercé Calsina, © Fundació Privada Ramon Calsina at www.fundaciocalsina.org.

House of Usher." These 1995 and 1996 editions are intended for high school students. Both contain prologues, notes, and a brief explanation of each of the included tales; some tasks and didactic proposals are also provided for students. The 1995 anthology was prefaced by Javier Fornieles, and the 1996 by Manuel Broncano;[22] the most interesting facts about these two introductions are that Broncano seems to be actually addressing a young public, whereas Fornieles appears to have forgotten about his audience.

Jesús Gabán Bravo, a prizewinning illustrator and a specialist in editions for children and young readers, was in charge of the thirty-six illustrations included in the 1996 edition. The challenge was not minor when considering that the images should be appropriate for young readers, but Gabán succeeded. His images, without being excessively macabre, are captivating and disturbing, especially thanks to his symbolic use of color. Some of his representations should be considered true icons, such as those for "The Tell-Tale Heart" and "Hop-Frog." Regarding "Tell-Tale Heart," there are two illustrations: the first shows the old man, a realistic and expressive portrait characterized by the deep wrinkles, toothless mouth, and vacant deep blue eye—an image that suggests both pity and repulsion. The second, final scene (figure 15.10) depicts the murderer in the foreground, looking toward the empty wooden floor with his hands covering his face as if trying to hide his obsession; the policemen, however, remain chatting in the background, oblivious to this progression of irrationality and self-destruction. Gabán has used a strong and artificial beam of red light, cast on the killer and the floor, to suggest with great success this sense of compulsion.

The edition of Poe's tales published by Galaxia Gutenberg and Círculo de Lectores in 2004 must be considered, without doubt, the most ambitious project in Spain in offering a complete and deep visual reading of this author's literary work. In fact, it was awarded a second prize by the Ministry of Culture as best-edited book. Joan-Pere Viladecans, a self-taught painter and illustrator from Barcelona and one of Spain's most acclaimed graphic artists in recent decades, elaborated more than one hundred drawings to re-create in images sixty-seven of Poe's tales as translated by Cortázar. Thus, this two-volume set deserves the merit it achieved.[23]

Viladecans's illustrations, far from descriptive or literalistic representations, amplify the spirit of the text, offering suggestive images—half-figurative, half-abstract—that accompany us during the reading. They try to evoke feelings and sensations that serve as echoes of the narrations and to establish a perfect dialogue between image and text. Viladecans uses a restricted palette, but in a powerfully symbolic way. He primarily uses red, black, and ochre in the tales of terror—colors linked to blood, night, or death—while green, blue, and violet—tones more associated with imagination—appear in the fantastic and satiric pieces; his use of color guides us unconsciously through all the stories and serves to reinforce the unity of effect that Poe himself defended.

Moreover, Viladecans's forms and colors create a strong organic conception. Readers feel they are holding a treatise on human nature—what Poe's tales are, after all—and this edition ends up bringing to our minds a kind of new Voynich Manuscript, whose organic, botanical, and biological diagrams are a complete mystery. This biological-evocative sense can be appreciated,

Figure 15.10. "The Tell-Tale Heart," by Jesús Gabán (Vicens Vives, 1996, p. 115).
Courtesy of Editorial Vicens Vives.

for example, in the illustration of "Tell-Tale Heart," where we do not see any of the usual images of the old man or the murderer, but a suggestive red heart transformed into an eye-like ovule being fertilized by several spermatozoa—a very original way of indicating how the old man's heart, after his death, remains alive to denounce the killer (figure 15.11). In this way, Viladecans creates an illustration that becomes a pictorial story by itself—an image that accompanies the text, completes it, and expands it. This illustration also reminds us that the genesis of the tale lays in the heart itself.

The last edition we analyze here was published by Anaya in 2009 to commemorate the bicentenary of Poe's birth, and it provokes mixed feelings for us. In regard to the prologue, its author—Luis Alberto de Cuenca Prado—a well-regarded poet, translator, essayist, and Spanish academic—perpetuates several clichés about Poe's life. He states, for instance, that Poe was a psychopath who spent most of his life drinking and who thought that the death of a beautiful and young woman was the "grandest manifestation of universal aesthetics" (5–7), reworking Poe's words to de Cuenca Prado's own purpose of conveying a mystified vision of the author. The twelve tales included, translated by Doris Rolfe in 1983, maintain a good balance between the different "lines" that characterize Poe's narrations.[24]

The illustrations, unlike the prologue, prove that Poe now lives in a Golden Age in Spain thanks to a new generation of illustrators who approach his work without those clichés or conventionalisms. This edition demonstrates that Poe's visual richness is better covered by several artists than by a single one. Anaya has managed to gather an excellent team of artists whose different styles and personalities find a perfect fit in this aesthetic variety. The illustrations for "Ligeia" and "The Black Cat" belong to the illustrator and filmmaker Pere Ginard; his images, which imitate the appearance of antique daguerreotypes and wood engravings, lend a phantasmagoric atmosphere to the texts. Max Hierro, comic author and children's book illustrator, depicts "MS. Found in a Bottle" and "Hop-Frog"; the representation of the buffoon—now pitiful, now hungry for revenge—must be highlighted. "The Fall of the House of Usher" and "The Cask of Amontillado" have been illustrated by Beatriz Martín Vidal, whose personal manner denotes an elegant and sad melancholy. Javier Olivares's unmistakable and always captivating style can be seen in "Berenice" and "The Premature Burial." Gabriel Pacheco is responsible for "Valdemar" and "The Pit and the Pendulum," where the presence of the menacing death has been masterfully resolved. And last but not least, Raúl Allén, a young comic illustrator from Valladolid, provided the illustrations for "A Descent into the Maelström" and "The Tell-Tale Heart."

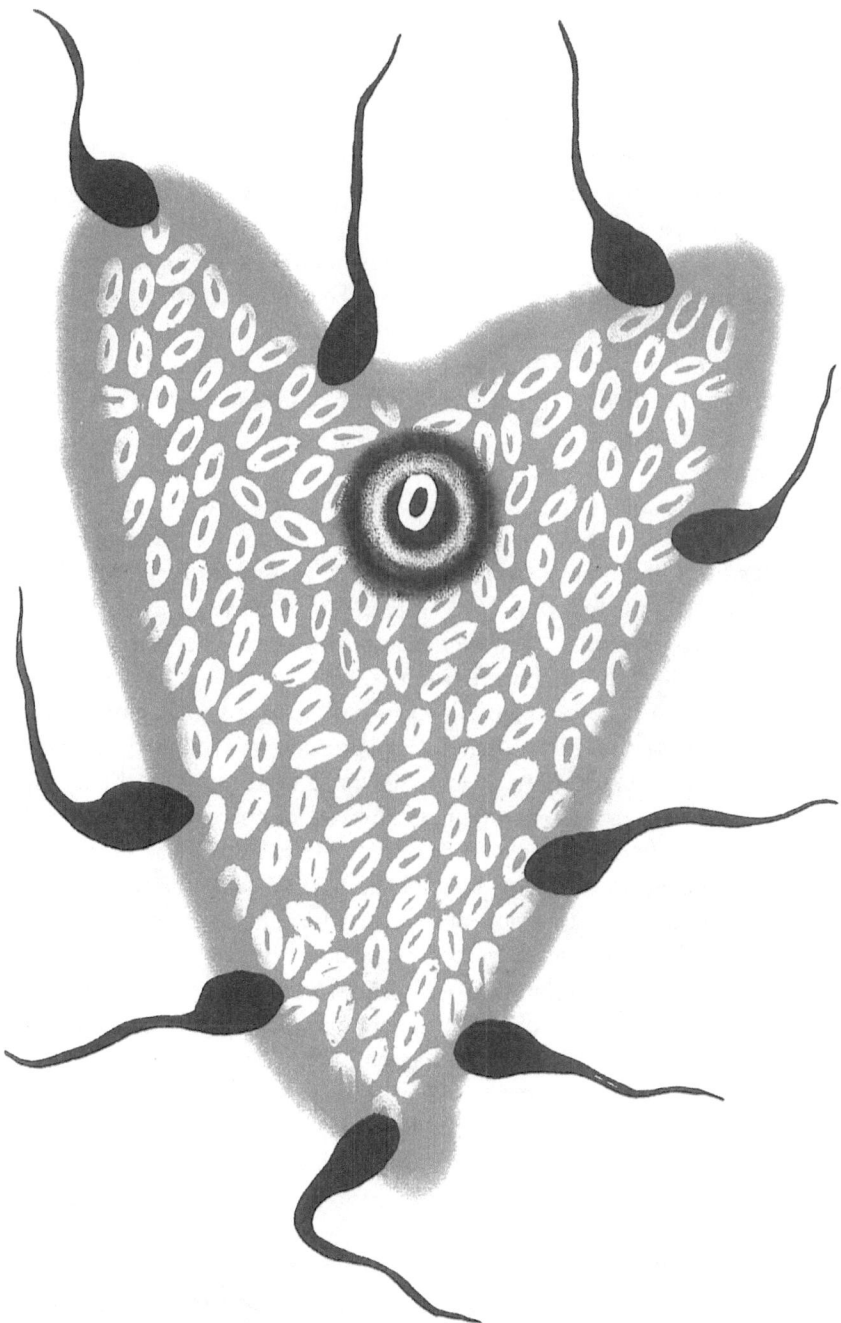

Figure 15.11. "The Tell-Tale Heart," by Joan-Pere Viladecans (Galaxia Gutenberg/ Círculo de Lectores, 2004, vol. 1, p. 115).
Courtesy of Joan-Pere Viladecans.

To complete our journey through the illustrations of "Tell-Tale Heart," we must finish with a brief comment on this last illustration (figure 15.12). Allén's use of a deeply contrasted shadowing confers a remarkable expression to his vulture-eyed old man. This close-up portrait stands up before a plain setting—a minimal *mise-in-scène* is enough to perfectly suggest a gothic atmosphere—and our attention is captivated by the eyeball. In this case, we do not see the pale blue eye with a film over it as described by Poe, but—and here is where Allén's major originality lays—a bright orb that reminds us of its inhumanity and supernatural character. That shining orb inevitably attracts the murderer, as a fly is captivated by a lightbulb and, in the same way, this attraction/obsession will cause the narrator's own death. The murderer extinguishes that light, but he ignites a new obsession that will condemn him: the beating heart.

We have covered a long period of illustrated editions in Spain. Through these key editions, we have been able to explore the main contributions that Spanish editors and illustrators have made for the diffusion and understanding of Poe's tales in this country. We are aware that this is only a part of a more complex panorama, since we have not dealt here with the editions of single tales—a field in which works such as Ángel Bellido's etchings on "Berenice" (1976) must be highlighted—or other types of works, which would require further studies. Nevertheless, our approach is significant enough to answer the main question of this analysis: up to what point do the Spanish illustrated editions provide an original, different, or characteristic reading of Poe's tales? The first illustrated edition by Xumetra (1887) can be read as a complete declaration of intent. Its publication date—just thirty-three years after the first illustrated edition of Poe anywhere in the world (Vizetelly, 1852), and only three years after leading editions such as Stoddard's (1884) or Quantin's (1884)—declares the early and devoted fascination that Spanish editors and readers felt for Poe.[25] Very few countries, with the exceptions of the United States, the United Kingdom, and France, have edited or illustrated Poe's tales as consistently as Spain. From that first moment, we also observe the editorial preference for offering original illustrations, images deliberately designed for each new edition, without depending on foreign illustrators or copying sets from other countries. And finally, as we described above, Xumetra had already established a basic dual way of confronting Poe that would be followed by most artists in varying degrees.

On the one hand, we find a more traditional and less original manner that avoids the most macabre and disturbing aspects of Poe's tales and that focuses on melodramatic scenes represented with dull literality. By the end of

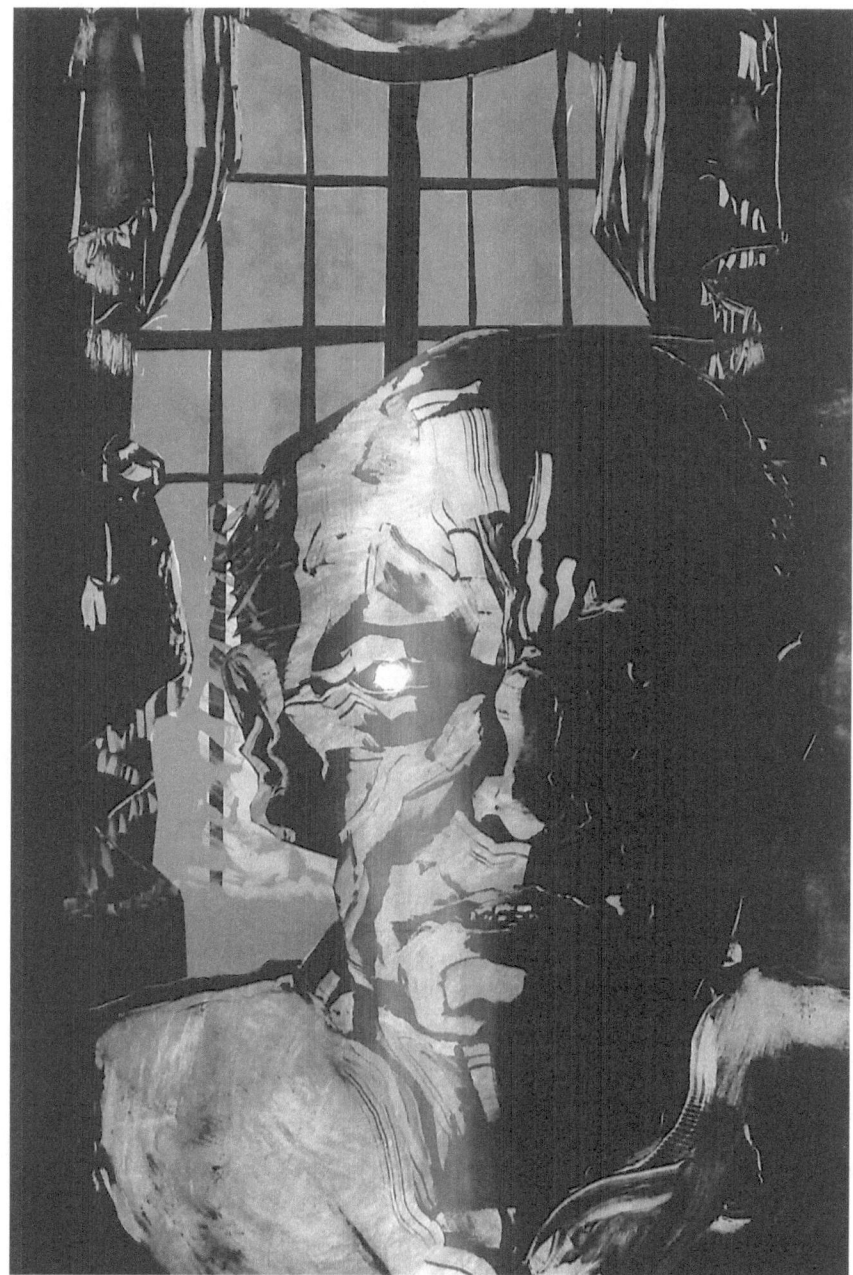

Figure 15.12. "The Tell-Tale Heart," by Raúl Allén (Anaya, 2009, p. 127).
Courtesy of Editorial Anaya.

the nineteenth century and the first decades of the twentieth, this situation was justified by the editors' interests in presenting the tales—most of them of the arabesque type—as mystery plays or as *folletines*, very popular among the public. However, the continuity of this tendency during the Francoist regime can only be understood by the presence of censorship that sought to avoid any kind of immoral, disgusting, or indecent element. Faced with this situation, the artists—especially those persecuted for their political ideas—opted for the tales of the grotesque as parody, those in which the humor can hide a severe social and political critique. It is here that illustrators such as Calsina really shine and where the Spanish artists made their most personal and original contributions.

On the other hand, beginning with Xumetra, we can also find less conventional images that try to penetrate beyond the literality of Poe's words—illustrations that attempt to evoke or to suggest the oppressive atmosphere of the tales, the mental instability of the characters, their deathly obsessions, or the presence of supernatural forces. Xumetra, Segrelles, and Azpelicueta began to trace a path that reached its peak with the more recently published editions. During the democratic period, Poe's texts have been explored both in a wider and deeper way, and Spanish illustrators have tried to cover Poe's vast aesthetic richness, leaving aside old topics and offering personal readings with great originality. Although since the 1980s there has been a multitude of editions conceived for high school students—and therefore, the artists' creative freedom might be subordinated to the adequacy of the images—it is surprising to note the adult style of many of these illustrations. An excellent exception among these editions for the youth is, certainly, the deluxe edition illustrated by Viladecans, an extraordinary example of how Poe's written texts can be translated into evocative images. We long for more editions of this type, artistic publications intended for an adult audience of Poe enthusiasts and/or bibliophiles. In Spain there remains a notable lack of illustrated editions conceived as art works.

There is also a need for more professional introductions, like the one written by Broncano in 1996. It is a misfortune that both students and adults are constantly confronted with mistaken or made-up information about Poe's life and about his works. Printing houses and editors should certainly seek academic prologues. Similarly, there is a critical gap that needs to be filled: the prologues or introductions do not refer to the illustrators or illustrations. There is no explanation for why the reader is being offered a visual interpretation of the texts, and no explanation about why a specific illustration or illustrator is selected. In our opinion, a direct approach, in which the paratext justifies the inclusion of the illustrations and/or examines particular pieces, will better integrate the images and the texts and provide Spanish readers with a clearer and more powerful understanding of Poe.

Notes

1. We would like to thank Emron Esplin and Margarida Vale de Gato for inviting us to participate in the panel they organized on Poe and anthologies for the 2017 annual conference of the American Literature Association. The acquisition of the bibliographical materials needed for this chapter would have been impossible without the financial support of the Spanish Ministry of Economy, through the research project entitled "Edgar Allan Poe on line. Texts and Imagines" (Ref. HAR2015-64580-P). We would also like to thank the members of our research group, LyA (sponsored by the University of Castilla-La Mancha), who always promptly assist us. We are deeply indebted to the people, institutions, and publishing houses for granting free permission to reproduce these illustrations; we acknowledge them each individually in the specific illustration captions.

2. This edition was prepared and prefaced by Nicasio Landa, a medical doctor interested in culture. Baudelaire's 1856 translation, *Histoires extraordinaires*, his biographical essays on Poe, and his later Poe translations were major influences on the reception of Poe in Spain. See Rigal-Aragón's "A Historical Approach to the Translations of Poe's Narrative Works in Spain."

3. Cecilia Böhl de Faber (1796–1877), better known by the pseudonym of Fernán Caballero, was one of the major female literary figures of her time.

4. See, for example, Poe's "Prospectus for the *Penn*" and "Prospectus for the *Stylus*."

5. Erwin Panofsky's *Meaning in the Visual Arts* is a must when approaching the analysis of images. Antonio Monegal's compilation of texts and essays, *Literatura y pintura*, is also very useful to better understand the differences and the relationships between literary and visual languages.

6. Later re-editions, such as the Casa Editorial Maucci edition from Barcelona in 1900, included the same tales but with only twenty-nine illustrations and Poe's portrait.

7. "Folletines" were cheap, popular, and serialized editions of literature that were common in nineteenth-century Spain. They usually included melodramatic pieces.

8. Pollin indicates the year 1923 for this edition, without specifying whether it is the first (205). We have found copies with the date of the original ecclesiastical license ("Nihil Obstat") needed for the publication, October 21, 1914. Therefore, 1914 is the year of the first edition. The year for the second edition may be 1923; the third appeared in 1937, and the fourth appeared in 1952.

9. Catá was a prolific essayist, a writer of short stories, poems, and plays, and a diplomat.

10. This description brings to mind Baudelaire's words: "sufficient to present Edgar Allan Poe in his various aspects as a visionary teller of tales now terrible, now

gracious, in turn mocking and tender, always a philosopher and analyst, a lover of the magic of absolute verisimilitude, a lover of the most detached buffoonery" (Hyslop and Hyslop 95).

11. Most of the illustrations belong to M. Picolo ("Berenice," "The Tell-Tale Heart," "The Gold-Bug," "The Premature Burial," and "Hop-Frog"). E. Corona was in charge of "The Back Cat," I. Gil illustrated "Valdemar," and E. Barrio, "Cask of Amontillado." The headpiece for "The Oval Portrait" can be attributed to J. Cuevas, since the title page indicates "Ilustraciones de Picolo, Corona, Cuevas y Gil" and none of the other illustrations were signed by Cuevas. The tale "Shadow" ("El espectro") is the only one included that is not illustrated.

12. Vallvé was a frequent collaborator of Casa editorial Araluce. We should note that the tales were not actually adapted for children, but told using the same impressive language Poe himself used to describe the macabre and grotesque images depicted in tales such as "The Masque of the Red Death" and "Hop-Frog."

13. Unless otherwise noted, all translations from Spanish into English are our own.

14. A powerful example can be found in the *Illustrated London News* Christmas number of 1935, where Segrelles published six outstanding illustrations of "Berenice," "The Gold-Bug," "The Black Cat," "Masque," "The System," and "Cask."

15. Farrán was a versatile figure of the epoch: a teacher, critic, and well-known writer because of his translations of English authors, among them Shakespeare.

16. It must be kept in mind that Cortázar's translations have been the most anthologized in Spain (Rigal-Aragón 20–21).

17. This information about the 1968 edition, although not particular to that edition's illustrations, is relevant to any discussion of Poe editions in Spain because important advances in Poe studies had been made in Spain during the 1950s. Two brothers, Julio and Ramón Gómez de la Serna y Puig, devoted time and ability to translating and prefacing quality editions of Poe's works.

18. At the end of the Civil War, Narro went into exile and spent two years in the Roussillon concentration camps (France). In 1941, he returned to Catalonia and worked for the editor Josep Janés i Olivé Editorial Juventud, but, due to the repressive Francoist regime, in 1952 he left Spain and settled in Mexico.

19. In this edition, the anonymous editor considers "Mesmeric Revelation" as an essay and "Maelzel's Chess-Player" as a tale. The translators were Ricardo Summers, Aníbal Froufe, and Francisco Álvarez. We have not been able to find reliable biographical information about Ricardo Summers and Francisco Alvárez. Aníbal Froufe enjoyed writing verses and knew English, French, and Italian, which he would have learned in prison, where he spent about twenty years during the dictatorship. He is mentioned as a frequent translator for Aguilar and Editorial Juventud. The translation, when compared to previous ones or to Cortázar's, differs only in some word choices.

20. Carlos Rojas Vila was a prizewinning Spanish novelist.

21. This pocket book publishing house, Alianza, is located in Madrid. It was founded in 1966 and is still a very important Spanish publisher.

22. In the first, Cortázar's translations are used, and in the second Broncano himself and a colleague, Julio César Santoyo, were responsible for the translations of the eight tales.

23. This is probably due to the fact that, since the decade of the seventies, Cortázar has been the most influential translator of Poe in Spain (see Rigal-Aragón). However, it is a pity that the publisher also chose to reproduce Cortázar's long out-of-date prologue.

24. Doris Rolfe was an active translator of Poe and Twain during the 1970s and 1980s.

25. See our study, *The Portrayal of the Grotesque in Stoddard's and Quantin's Illustrated Editions of Edgar Allan Poe*.

Works Cited

Broncano, Manuel. "Introducción, notas y propuestas de trabajo." *El gato negro y otros cuentos de horror*, Vicens Vives, 1996, pp. VII–XLVI and 1–32.

Cantalupo, Barbara. *Poe and the Visual Arts*. Penn State UP, 2014.

Cortázar, Julio. "Vida de Edgar Allan Poe." *Todos los cuentos*, by Edgar Allan Poe, Galaxia Gutenberg/Círculo de Lectores, vol. 1, 2004, pp. 7–37.

Cuenca, Luis Alberto de. "Prólogo." *Cuentos de Poe*, Anaya, 2009, pp. 5–7.

Englekirk, John Eugene. *Edgar Allan Poe in Hispanic Literature*. Instituto de las Españas en Los Estados Unidos, 1934.

Farrán y Mayoral, Josep. "El arte de Edgar Allan Poe." *Narraciones extraordinarias*, Iberia-Joaquín Gil, 1942, pp. 7–16.

Fornieles, Javier. Introducción. *El escarabajo de oro. Los crímenes de la calle Morgue*, Vicens Vives, 1995, pp. VII–XXX.

Gómez de la Serna, Julio, translator. *Cuentos fantásticos*. By Edgar Allan Poe, Editorial Fama, 1953.

———. *Fantasías humorísticas*. By Edgar Allan Poe, Aguilar, 1962.

Gómez de la Serna, Ramón. *Edgar Poe: El genio de América*. Editorial Losada, 1953.

González-Moreno, Fernando, and Margarita Rigal-Aragón. *The Portrayal of the Grotesque in Stoddard's and Quantin's Illustrated Editions of Edgar Allan Poe (1884)*. Edwin Mellen, 2017.

Hernández Catá, Alfonso. "Una breve noticia sobre el poeta norteamericano Edgar Poe." *Narraciones extraordinarias*, Casa editorial de Saturnino Calleja Fernández, 1908, pp. 5–7.

Hyslop, Lois, and Francis E. Hyslop Jr., editors and translators. *Critical Papers: Baudelaire on Poe*. Bald Eagle Press, 1952.

Monegal, Antonio, et al. *Literatura y pintura*. Arco Libros, 2000.

Panofsky, Erwin. *Meaning in the Visual Arts*. Penguin, 1993.

Poe, Edgar Allan. *Cuentos*. Adapted by Manuel Vallvé, illustrated by Josep Segrelles Albert, Casa Editorial Araluce, [1914].

———. *Cuentos*. Translated by Julio Cortázar, Alianza Editorial, 1970. 2 vols.

———. *Cuentos de Poe*. Translated by Doris Rolfe, illustrated by Javier Serrano, Raúl Allen, Pere Ginard, Max Hierro, Beatriz Martín Vidal, Javier Olivares, and Gabriel Pacheco, Anaya, 2009.

———. *El escarabajo de oro. Los crímenes de la calle Morgue*. Translated by Julio Cortázar, illustrated by Arthur Rackman, Vicens Vives, 1995.

———. *El gato negro y otros cuentos de horror*. Translated by Julio-César Santoyo and Manuel Broncano, illustrated by Jesús Gabán, Vicens Vives, 1996.

———. *Histoires extraordinaires et Nouvelles histoires extraordinaires*. Translated by Charles Baudelaire, illustrated by Hermann Vogel, Eugène-Michel-Joseph Abot, François-Nicolas Chifflart, Daniel Urrabieta Vierge, Jules-Descartes Férat, León Pierre Herpin, Henri Meyer, Jean-Paul Laurens, and Fortuné-Louis Méaulle, Quantin, 1884.

———. *Historias extraordinarias*. Imprenta de Luis García, 1858.

———. *Historias extraordinarias*. Edited by José Trujillo, Imprenta de las novedades, 1860.

———. *Historias extraordinarias*. Edited by Manuel Cano y Cueto, Eduardo Perié, 1871.

———. *Historias extraordinarias*. Translated by Enrique Leopoldo de Verneuil and illustrated by Ferran Xumetra Ragull, Daniel Cortezo & C., 1887.

———. *Historias extraordinarias*. Translated by Enrique Leopoldo de Verneuil and illustrated by Ferran Xumetra Ragull, Casa Editorial Maucci, 1900.

———. *Narraciones extraordinarias*. Translated and edited by Alfonso Hernández Catá, illustrated by Manuel Picolo et al., Casa Editorial de Saturnino Calleja Fernández, 1908.

———. *Narraciones extraordinarias*. Translated by Josep Farrán y Mayoral and illustrated by Pedro Riu, Iberia-Joaquín Gil, 1942.

———. *Narraciones extraordinarias*. Illustrated by J. Narro, Editorial Juventud, 1957.

———. *Nuevas narraciones extraordinarias*. Translated by Mariano Orta Manzano, illustrated by Jaime Azpelicueta, Editorial Juventud, 1968.

———. *Obras inmortales*. Translated by Ricardo Summers, Aníbal Froufe, and Francisco Álvarez, illustrated by José Picó Mitjans, E.D.A.F., 1967.

———. *Obras selectas*. Translated by María Cristina Reiss Raimundo, introduced by Carlos Rojas, illustrated by Ramón Calsina Baró, Ediciones Nauta, 1971. 2 vols.

———. "Prospectus for the *Penn*." *Saturday Evening Post*, June 6, 1840, Edgar Allan Poe Society of Baltimore. https://www.eapoe.org/works/misc/prosp002.htm.

———. "Prospectus for the *Stylus*." *Saturday Museum*, Philadelphia, March 4, 1843, Edgar Allan Poe Society of Baltimore. https://www.eapoe.org/works/misc/prosp010.htm.

———. "Review of *The Vicar of Wakefield, A Tale*." *The Complete Works of Edgar Allan Poe*, edited by James Albert Harrison, 1902, vol. 11, pp. 8–10.

———. *Todos los cuentos*. Translated by Julio Cortázar, illustrated by Joan-Pere Viladecans, Galaxia Gutenberg/Círculo de Lectores, 2004. 2 vols.

Pollin, Burton. *Images of Poe's Works: A Comprehensive Descriptive Catalogue of Illustrations*. Greenwood Press, 1989.

"Prólogo." *Obras inmortales*, by Edgar Allan Poe. E.D.A.F., 1967, pp. I–XV.

Rigal-Aragón, Margarita. "A Historical Approach to the Translations of Poe's Narrative Works in Spain." *Translated Poe*, edited by Emron Esplin and Margarida Vale de Gato, Lehigh UP, 2014, pp. 13–24 and 339–44.

Roas Deus, David. *La sombra del cuervo: Edgar Allan Poe y la literatura fantástica española del siglo XIX*. Devenir, 2011.

Rodríguez Guerrero-Strachan, Santiago. "Un persistente recuerdo: La recepción de Poe en España." *Los legados de Poe*, edited by Margarita Rigal-Aragón, Síntesis, 2011, pp. 145–73.

Rojas, Carlos. "Prólogo." *Obras selectas*, by Edgar Allan Poe, Vol. 1, Ediciones Nauta, 1971, p. 10.

Salinas, Pedro. "Poe in Spain and Spanish America." *A Symposium at the Nineteenth Annual Commemoration of the Edgar Allan Poe Society of Baltimore*, edited by John Calvin French, Johns Hopkins UP, 1941, pp. 25–31.

CHAPTER SIXTEEN

~

A Century of Terror, Ratiocination, and the Supernatural

Poe's Fiction in Argentina from Carlos Olivera to Julio Cortázar

Emron Esplin

Edgar Allan Poe holds a firm place in Argentina's literary marketplace and within Argentina's literary system. Argentine bookstores typically stock multiple editions of Poe's works translated into Spanish, and Argentine libraries (from the national down to the municipal level) hold hundreds of books by and about Poe. I have written elsewhere about Poe's overall importance in Argentina,[1] but here I would like to examine how certain literary intermediaries—particularly anthologizers, editors, and translators—have helped to shape the Poe that is most visible in Argentina today. These players all qualify as rewriters of texts in the ways described by André Lefevere throughout his work on literary translation.[2] In *Translating Literature*, he claims that "[t]ranslators, critics, historians, and anthologizers . . . are image makers, exerting the power of subversion under the guise of objectivity" (6–7). Similarly, Leah Price emphasizes the power that rests in the hands of the often overshadowed "mediators" in the literary field: "The work of professional mediators like editors, condensers, and reviewers figures less often in critical text than in scholarly footnotes. . . . Yet competing editorial alternatives (anthology, abridgement, expurgation, collected works) add up to more than a series of accidents in the transmission of particular texts. They also shape a larger generic system" (10). These "image makers" and "professional mediators" decide who and what vast audiences read by choosing whom to anthologize, translate, write about, and publish.

The anthologizers I approach in this chapter appear in various forms, including translators and editors as well as traditional anthology creators.

The question of inclusion/exclusion, an issue that is central to the idea of the anthology and that Margarida Vale de Gato and I have unpacked in our introduction to this volume, is also visible in the work of the editor and the translator, although at varying scales. Anthologizers, translators, and editors all participate in a similar decision-making process when they choose who and/or what to include in the tomes they publish.[3] For the purposes of this chapter, I examine Poe's Argentine editors and translators *as anthologizers*, paying close attention to which Poe pieces they include/exclude in their works and to the ways they justify these decisions in their paratexts.

Poe's fiction has been widely available in Argentina for at least 130 years, but he was primarily read as a poet throughout Spanish America in the late nineteenth and early twentieth centuries.[4] Today, Poe's prose is more visible in Argentina, both in anthologies and in editions or collections of Poe's works. I have analyzed the Argentine and the Spanish American shifts in taste away from Poe's poetry and toward his prose in other venues,[5] but in this chapter I am more interested in the particular types of Poe stories that defined him in Argentina from the 1880s through the 1980s and the connection between this "typing" of Poe and the anthologization process. Not surprisingly, two of the writers who dramatically affected the shift between Poe's Argentine reputation as poet-prophet toward his image as a fiction writer also played major roles in this narrative of anthological power—Jorge Luis Borges and Julio Cortázar. However, Borges and Cortázar are not the only influential Argentine anthologizers/translators/editors of Poe to favor his darker, supernatural, and/or ratiocinative tales. This emphasis began with Carlos Olivera's early collection of Poe translations in 1884, continued through Armando Bazán's editorial work in the 1940s, increased with Borges's translating and anthologizing Poe in the 1940s—then anthologizing him again at least once every decade until Borges's death in 1986—and culminated with Cortázar's extensive translating and editing of Poe's fiction from the 1950s onward. Many other Argentine editors, translators, and anthologizers worked with Poe during the twentieth century, but these four mediators crafted and honed what has now become the dominant image of Poe in Argentina's literary system; their anthologizing strategies favored and maintained a Poe of terror, ratiocination, and the supernatural.

Carlos Olivera: Creating Argentina's First Poe Collection

In 1884, Carlos Olivera released the first Argentine collection of Poe's fiction, *Novelas y cuentos* [*Novels and Stories*], and his proclivities cast a long shadow that is still visible in the selections of Poe's fiction that are most often edited, translated, and anthologized in Argentina in the twenty-first century. Before Olivera's *Novelas y cuentos*, several of Poe's stories were available in Spanish translation (some translated by Olivera himself before the book release) in Argentine literary journals, and Charles Baudelaire's famous French translations of Poe's works were also familiar to the reading public—both in Baudelaire's French and translated from his French into Spanish.[6] The title of Olivera's collection is a misnomer, as he offers translations of thirteen of Poe's stories but does not touch Poe's published novel—*The Narrative of Arthur Gordon Pym of Nantucket*—nor his unfinished "The Journal of Julius Rodman."[7] Title aside, the collection includes a healthy dose of terror, detection, and the supernatural with only a spattering of the comic via Olivera's renditions of the following tales: "The Masque of the Red Death," "Berenice," "Ligeia," "The Murders in the Rue Morgue," "The Mystery of Marie Rogêt," "The Purloined Letter," "The Facts in the Case of M. Valdemar," "The System of Doctor Tarr and Professor Fether," "The Pit and the Pendulum," "Hop-Frog," "The Cask of Amontillado," "Four Beasts in One," and "The Oval Portrait."

Novelas y cuentos maintains a conflicted relationship with Baudelaire that both embraces his influence and attempts to distance the collection from the French poet and translator. All thirteen stories that Olivera includes were previously translated by Baudelaire, but Olivera makes sure to inform his readers that he is translating straight from Poe, not from Baudelaire's translations. Just below the title on the title page, he emphasizes that the stories are "TRANSLATED DIRECTLY FROM THE ENGLISH",[8] and a comparison of the story titles he uses, juxtaposed with Baudelaire's, confirms Poe's English as Olivera's source text.[9] In his prologue to the collection, "Al Lector" ["To the Reader"], Olivera argues that Baudelaire's translation "is undoubtedly a notable work, but not as complete as I believe possible" (i). His suggestion that Baudelaire's translation lacks completeness must be qualitative rather than quantitative, because Baudelaire translated more than triple the amount of Poe's stories than Olivera did. Olivera reads Baudelaire's translation as what he calls "a *free translation*," and he spends the majority of his prologue critiquing such translations and making a powerful appeal for what current translators and translation studies scholars call foreignization. Yet, he happily follows up his prologue with his own Spanish-language translation of one of Baudelaire's biographical essays on Poe, and he makes questions about a French connection to his collection impossible to avoid by publishing the book (clearly marketed for a Spanish-language audience and with its prologue signed in Buenos Aires) in Paris.

In a collection as brief as *Novelas y cuentos*, Olivera had to exclude far more Poe than he included, and these decisions helped produce a particular image of Poe. The thirteen stories Olivera translated demonstrate a marked proclivity for Poe the creator of terror, supernatural, and detective stories over Poe the satirist or comedian, and while Olivera does not explicitly address his selection criteria, his defense of his translation praxis in the prologue provides hints about his reasoning. Olivera claims that "the secret of Edgar Poe's marvelous success" rests in "his conclusions, that is to say, the object that guides him, is always accomplished, inevitably" (v). With this claim, Olivera completely accepts Poe's theory of unity of effect and argues that Poe's genius resides in his ability to know the end from the beginning and to aim the elements of a given tale toward his desired effect for that specific text. In terms that refer to literature in general and not just to Poe, Olivera argues that a text's "delicate details" take the audience to the "peak of joy" or to "the bottom of an abyss of pain and mourning" (iii). With two exceptions—"Tarr and Fether" and "Four Beasts in One"—the Poe texts Olivera translates create either an effect of awe (specifically at Dupin's ratiocinative powers in the three detective tales) or one of terror/bewilderment (as seen in various levels in the eight remaining stories in *Novelas y cuentos*). In the former case, the reader is certainly left on a joyous height to celebrate Dupin's mental powers, and in the latter, Poe drags the reader down into the abyss but creates an aesthetic sense of elation or pleasure in the descent. Perhaps "The Pit and the Pendulum," with its surprise "happy ending," best demonstrates this phenomena as the reader enters the pit with the tortured narrator and, at the very moment of total despair, is snatched from the abyss and placed in an exultant space. In short, Olivera's attraction to Poe relies on Poe's ability to create a desired effect, and Olivera's preferred Poe effect is unmistakably one of terror or awe that creates a type of joy in the reader.

How can we explain, then, Olivera's inclusion of his renditions of "The System of Doctor Tarr and Professor Fether" and "Four Beasts in One"? Poe wrote both pieces in a comic or satiric vein familiar to Poe's contemporaries and to Poe scholars today, but somewhat foreign to many Poe readers (regardless of the language in which they read Poe) who know the author via the editing and anthologizing that has favored his darker side from Griswold onward. Considering the relative dearth of comic or satiric pieces by Poe available in Argentina when Olivera released *Novelas y cuentos* in 1884, these two translations would have seemed particularly odd.[10] Olivera offers his readers a broader, more inclusive portrayal of Poe by including these two stories—indeed, a version of Poe that acknowledges his own pride in being able to write stories of diverse types. However, the overall effect of terror or awe that Olivera seems to be aiming for with *Novelas y cuentos* might be threatened by the comic relief offered by these two tales. At a minimum, his anthological decision not to completely exclude Poe's comic and satiric side interrupts the volume.

Olivera's inclusion of these two stories only offers a brief nod to Poe's humorous writings, and while that acknowledgment refuses to erase this particular Poe from existence in Argentina, the editor/translator successfully contains the laughter via the quantity and, perhaps more importantly, the placement of the other tales. As a part of the foreignizing praxis he puts forth in his prologue, Olivera argues that maintaining the source text's word order is paramount when translating because the reader's "final thought" grows from the "final word read" (v). Only two of the translations in *Novelas y cuentos* end with particularly powerful words—"M. Valdemar" with "abominable purification" (258) and "The Oval Portrait" with "she was dead!" (353). Placing "Tarr and Fether" directly after "Valdemar" immediately softens the effect of Poe's most infamously visceral conclusion, but following "Tarr and Fether" with the opening words of Olivera's translation of "The Pit and the Pendulum"—"I was broken, broken unto death by that long agony" (287)—instantly extinguishes any mirth the reader might have felt while reading "Tarr and Fether." In a similar manner, placing "Four Beasts in One" after "The Cask of Amontillado" pulls the reader out of Montresor's suffocating catacombs, but the fresh air that the lighter story provides gets sucked out by the finale of the following (and collection-ending) tale, "The Oval Portrait," in which an obsessed artist paints the life out of his young bride. The story and the volume end with death.

In brief, Olivera sandwiches the two comic tales between particularly gruesome stories—"M. Valdemar" and "The Pit and the Pendulum" in one case, and "The Cask of Amontillado" and "The Oval Portrait" in the other—with the ghastly "Hop-Frog" sitting between the two sets. Combining this placement with the two trios of stories that open the volume—the first grouping includes three supernaturally infused stories of death ("The Masque of the Red Death," "Berenice," and "Ligeia"), and the second consists of the Dupin trilogy—makes clear that as a translator/editor, Olivera acknowledges the existence of a comic or satiric Poe but buries that Poe alive in his volume. *Novelas y cuentos* heavily stresses the Poe who creates terror and/or awe via the supernatural, death, and/or deduction, and this is the Poe that gains and maintains traction in twentieth and twenty-first century Argentina.

Armando Bazán: Approaching Poe's
Complete Works via Multiple Translators

Poe's reputation continued to grow in Argentina, but no Argentine attempt was made to publish a "complete works" until sixty years after Olivera's collection of translations when, in 1944, Armando Bazán compiled a thick Poe collection and published it as *Obras completas* [*Complete Works*].[11] Containing translations of thirty-eight tales/sketches, *Eureka*, *Pym*, "The Philosophy of Composition," and twenty-three poems,[12] Bazán's edition of Poe's *Obras completas* is not a complete works, but it is clearly the most comprehensive Poe collection published in Argentina before the latter half of the twentieth century. It contains many more of Poe's stories than any Argentine edition before the translations of Julio Cortázar in 1956. Bazán's collection, although more wide-ranging than former editions, does not offer a consistent translation praxis. He cites four different translators for the prose (including Olivera) and five distinct translators for the poetry on the page between his title page and his prologue, yet he fails to identify the individual translator for any of the specific pieces in the collection. Thus, the differences between Poe's own styles or voices when shifting between his terror, supernatural, detective, comic, satiric, hoax, and philosophical pieces can be exaggerated or flattened, depending on the choices and styles of the various named but uncited translators. In terms of paratextual clues about Bazán's organizing strategy for the edition, his prologue is heavy on Poe biography and light on any discussion or ranking of genre.[13] He continually praises Poe, and he does little to direct his reader toward certain Poe texts over others with, perhaps, the exception of "The Gold-Bug" which he mentions more often than any other Poe tale.[14]

Lacking other hints from the prologue to guide us toward Bazán's preferences or judgments about Poe's different story types, we must rely primarily on the edition's contents, lack of contents, and textual order to highlight the continual penchant for terror, the supernatural, and the ratiocinative. Out of the thirty-eight translated tales/sketches, twenty-three of them clearly fit within the realms of terror, the supernatural, or detective tales while one piece has been described as a romantic tale and a terror tale—"The Assignation." The remaining fourteen tales/sketches offer examples of Poe's comedies, satires, romantic pieces, hoaxes, philosophical musings, and landscape portrayals. These latter inclusions certainly do cast Poe as a more varied author than did Olivera's short collection or that of any of the Argentine periodical publications of Poe's work up to this time, but what Bazán excludes reveals an active decision to focus on the darker side of Poe's works. The majority of the Poe stories that Bazán does not include in *Obras completas*—eighteen tales—come from Poe's comedic and satiric veins.[15] Bazán also avoids a trio of landscape pieces,[16] the hoax "Von Kempelen and His Discovery," the conversation between spirits that makes up "The Power of Words," and three stories that might be called parodies[17]—two of terror and one of ratiocination—adding up to a total of twenty-six absent tales from Poe's lighter side. The only stories of terror or the supernatural that Bazán excludes are "Morella," "The Oblong Box," "Mesmeric Revelation," and "Silence." "Morella" is the only surprising absence here, since this tale is so often grouped with "Berenice" and "Ligeia"—two stories Bazán does include. In short, Bazán's inclusions favor Poe's terror, supernatural, and detective fiction but admit that Poe wrote in other modes, while his exclusions help the volume emphasize Poe's darker and more serious reputation.

Bazán also creates a visible hierarchy via the order in which he offers the stories. Twenty-one or twenty-two of the first twenty-five tales/sketches are tales of deduction, the supernatural, and/or terror—with the possible discrepancy depending on how one reads "The Assignation."[18] All of the final thirteen pieces that make up the remainder of the book's offerings of shorter prose represent Poe's other modes, with only two exceptions. The book opens with translations of four detective stories—the Dupin trilogy followed by "The Gold-Bug"—and continues with five of Poe's most well-known tales of terror: "The Black Cat," "The Cask of Amontillado," "The Pit and the Pendulum," "The Masque of the Red Death," and "Hop-Frog." Bazán briefly and only slightly swerves from his routine with "Tarr and Fether" and "King Pest," but then returns to terror and the supernatural with the next nine entries— "Ligeia," "Valdemar," "William Wilson," "The Tell-Tale Heart," "Berenice," "Metzengerstein," "Shadow—A Parable," "The Imp of the Perverse," and "The Man of the Crowd." The inclusion of "Eleonora"—the twenty-first translation in the collection—offers the first real glimpse of a different Poe to the reader, who has been immersed for almost 250 pages in the ratiocinative, supernatural, and terror stories, with the only short break coming from the previously cited "Tarr and Fether" and "King Pest" that, in any case, are also quite dark. The book then returns to Poe's darker side with translations of "The Fall of the House of Usher," "The Assignation," "MS. Found in a Bottle," and "A Tale of the Ragged Mountains" before making its break toward Poe's other styles.[19] The remaining section of fiction juxtaposes all of Poe's other modes, and only nods twice at the Poe that the majority of the collection emphasizes.[20] Bazán gives his reader more Poe variety, but the organizational structure he creates reinforces the emphasis on Poe's detective, supernatural, and terror tales that his inclusions and exclusions already demonstrate.

Jorge Luis Borges: Anthologizing/Re-Anthologizing Poe's Fantastic and Detective Fiction

At the same time that Bazán was preparing his edition for Claridad, in the early 1940s, Jorge Luis Borges was heavily involved in the creation of two significant anthologies of world literature that would resonate throughout Spanish America and the Spanish-speaking world for the remainder of the twentieth century, and both anthologies featured Poe. One anthology collected stories of the fantastic, while the other focused on detective fiction. With each anthology, Borges and his colleagues attacked the realist aesthetics of their contemporaries in early 1940s Argentina.[21] Poe served as a valuable tool in this literary battle because his literature and his persona already carried weight in the Argentine literary system and his fiction—even in its comic, satiric, or other veins that Borges did not anthologize—consistently challenges the limits of realism. Borges's early anthologizing of Poe continually pairs the latter's supernatural and detective tendencies, and his perpetuation of either of these Poe types always simultaneously supports the other. Finally, Borges's last work to anthologize Poe by including him in two multivolume "library" projects more openly discusses Poe as a terror writer while re-emphasizing Poe's detective and fantastic works that Borges had anthologized earlier.[22]

In 1940, Borges, Adolfo Bioy Casares, and Silvina Ocampo released *Antología de la literatura fantástica* with Editorial Sudamericana. The first edition of this anthology contained fifty-four entries from around the globe and from ancient to modern times, including Borges and Bioy Casares's translation of Poe's "The Facts in the Case of M. Valdemar."[23] In the prologue to the first edition, Bioy Casares explains that the organizing principle for what might appear to be an eclectic volume was his, Ocampo's, and Borges's reading pleasure: "To make it we have followed a hedonic criterion. . . . Analyzed with a historic or geographic criterion, it can seem irregular. . . . This volume is, simply, the joining of the texts of fantastic literature that seem best to us" (14–15). He also claims that the book grew out of a conversation the three of them shared in 1937 about their favorite fantastic stories rather than originating from a goal to create an anthology (14).

The specific decision to pick "M. Valdemar," and the inclusion of Poe in the book in general, were probably Borges's choices, as Bioy Casares was a fairly harsh critic of Poe while Borges maintained a complex, life-long literary relationship with Poe and apparently liked this particular story.[24] Borges reveals his preference for "M. Valdemar" in a 1937 review of Edward Shanks's biography of Poe by listing this tale as one of Poe's works that validates "his glory," regardless of some of the weaknesses Borges finds in Poe's literary corpus (*Obras completas* 4: 333).[25] Borges's proclivity for this story's gruesome finale draws a baffled response from Bioy Casares who, in a journal entry from June 10, 1963, quotes Borges's thoughts about his/Bioy Casares's translation of "Valdemar" versus Cortázar's more recent rendition and then states: "Even though this story has a fairly repugnant ending, Borges does not avoid it. It is curious: boldness in the physical circumstances of lovemaking offends him; the most repugnant circumstances of the macabre do not. He has a slightly infantile admiration for this type of audacity. He admires the end of 'M. Valdemar'" (*Borges* 903).

"M. Valdemar" is a strange choice for this anthology for at least two reasons. First, Poe has other tales that more clearly exemplify the mode of the fantastic, especially "The Black Cat."[26] Second, the tale's gruesome finale can easily be read as a shift away from the fantastic toward the basest type of corporeal horror.[27] Placing "M. Valdemar" in an anthology of fantastic fiction shifts the emphasis away from the climax (regardless of Bioy Casares's claim that Borges enjoys this ending) toward the story's supernatural core—the hypnosis of a man on the verge of death and that man's eventual and continual speaking to the living from beyond the grave. In short, the anthological framing of the story changes how readers engage with it; by defining "M. Valdemar" as a fantastic story, the anthology calls attention to the in-between-ness of Valdemar's hypnoses—an experience that lasts for several months—rather than to the sudden putridity that only fills the story's ultimate moments.

For Poe's overall reputation in Argentina, Borges's choice of "M. Valdemar" as the Poe text in *Antología de la literatura fantástica* matters less than the fact that Borges places Poe in this anthology at all. Poe's inclusion and the brief coverage he receives in the anthology's apparatus—the prologue and the short headnote that introduces "M. Valdemar"—cast him as a writer of both fantastic and detective stories. The first "typing," as a writer of fantastic fiction, is not surprising due to the anthology's title and content. Bioy Casares's prologue offers a brief critique of Poe and Guy de Maupassant while acknowledging them as some of the "masters of the genre" (8), and the headnote to "M. Valdemar" claims that Poe "renewed the fantastic genre" (*Antología* 226). The headnote also creates a more surprising Poe type for this particular anthology when it avers that Poe "[i]nvented the detective genre" and lists Arthur Conan Doyle and G. K. Chesterton as two of the writers influenced by Poe (226).

This 1940 coupling of Poe the fantastic writer and Poe the creator of detective fiction stuck, both in Borges's later anthologizing of Poe and in

Poe's current Argentine reputation. The release of *Antología de la literatura fantástica* is considered "a milestone in Spanish American letters" (Zavala Medina 352). The anthology has remained influential from 1940 to the present, undergoing a major expansion of included texts in 1965 and being reissued by Sudamericana several times into the twenty-first century. The latest Sudamericana reprinting of the expanded version occurred in 2014 and, like its predecessors, this printing of *Antología de la literatura fantástica* frames Poe as an early and essential voice of the fantastic and as the creator of the now ubiquitous detective genre.

Borges and Bioy Casares took a more direct route to framing Poe as the inventor of the detective genre in their 1943 anthology, *Los mejores cuentos policiales* [*The Best Detective Stories*]. The first edition of this anthology included sixteen stories (thirteen of which were translations), beginning with Leonor Acevedo de Borges's translation of Hawthorne's "Mr. Higginbotham's Catastrophe" as "La muerte repetida," and continuing with Borges and Bioy Casares's translation of Poe's "The Purloined Letter" as "La carta robada."[28] The original and second (1944) editions of this book contain zero paratext—no prologue, no introduction, no discussion of the authors nor the translators—so the contents themselves serve as the anthologizing apparatus. The inclusion of Hawthorne's "Higginbotham," a somewhat comical and far lesser-known Hawthorne tale, feels out of place as the opener to an anthology that claims to collect "the best" detective stories, especially considering Borges's perennial claims that Poe created detective fiction. Borges revealed his thought process in another anthology he published over forty years later in the prologue he wrote for La Biblioteca de Babel's 1986 printing of a short Hawthorne collection, *El gran rostro de piedra* [*The Great Stone Face*]. In this piece, Borges claims that Poe invented the genre in 1841 but that Hawthorne "anticipates surprises and artifices" from the genre through "Higginbotham" although he "accentuates the comic" (12). In *Los mejores cuentos policiales*, then, "Higginbotham" serves as a precursor to the genre while "The Purloined Letter" arguably represents the best of what Borges sees as the genre's origin in Poe's Dupin trilogy. The anthology's third edition, published in 1947, added brief biographical and bibliographical headnotes for each included author. In Poe's case, Borges and Bioy Casares inserted almost the exact same headnote they had written for Poe in *Antología de la literatura fantástica* seven years earlier, with the addition of two bibliographical references and the adjective "famous" (24) to describe Poe.[29] So while the former anthology nodded to Poe's invention of detective fiction while representing him as a writer of the fantastic, the latter anthology—from its third edition onward—affirmed Poe's rejuvenation of the fantastic while representing him as the original detective story writer.

The publication history surrounding Poe's presence in *Los mejores cuentos policiales* became confusing in the 1950s, obscuring Poe's place, but in 1983 he took center stage when Borges and Bioy Casares finally published a prologue for the detective anthology they had been selling in one form or another for forty years. After the success of the initial anthology's first three editions, Emecé released another detective anthology in 1951, organized by Borges and Bioy Casares and under the same name—*Los mejores cuentos policiales*—in which Poe did not figure. The press only distinguished the 1951 anthology from their original detective anthology by the demarcation "segunda serie" [second series], and this second series was then republished several times from the early 1950s until the 1960s by Emecé in Buenos Aires and then by Alianza in Madrid through the 1970s and early 1980s. Poe is probably absent from all of these "second series" reprintings, but the issue became opaque because when Alianza re-released the original anthology (including Poe) in 1983, they did so by naming that anthology *Los mejores cuentos policiales (2)* while selling it as a two-volume set with the second series anthology that had been renamed *Los mejores cuentos policiales (1)*.

Regardless of this confusion, Borges and Bioy Casares emphasized Poe's importance to the genre in the prologue they wrote in late 1981 and released with the double-volume set in 1983—in the first pages of volume 2, not volume 1. Almost half of the brief prologue focuses on Poe; Borges and Bioy Casares recognize "The Murders in the Rue Morgue" as the original detective story, they discuss Poe's influence on later writers of the genre and, perhaps not surprisingly by this point, they remind us of Poe's experience as a writer of fantastic tales (7–8). In fact, they go as far as to suggest that Poe's first detective story grows out of Poe's fantastic mode: "Poe had the habit of writing fantastic tales; the odds are that when he set out to write ["Rue Morgue"] he only proposed to add, to an already long series of dreams, one more dream" (7). They close the prologue by citing the same anthologizing criterion they had used to organize *Antología de la literatura fantástica* back in 1940—reading pleasure—to justify their choices: "To select the texts of this volume we have followed the only possible criterion, the hedonic criterion. The reading of every one of the pieces that make up this volume was very pleasant for us" (8). With this prologue, Borges and Bioy Casares come full circle and reiterate that when we read either fantastic fiction or detective stories, we do so for pleasure, and that when we dig to the center of each genre, we find Poe.

Borges continued to anthologize Poe in the 1950s and 1960s by shifting his focus to Poe's only published novel, *The Narrative of Arthur Gordon Pym of Nantucket.* Borges often cited *Pym* as his favorite work by Poe, and he an-thologized and re-anthologized two brief excerpts that he had translated from Poe's novel. The first translation appears simply as a quotation that Borges translated and incorporated into the analysis he offered in his 1932 essay, "El arte narrativo y la magia." He then included this excerpt as "Del agua de la isla" in the 1955 anthology he and Bioy Casares published—*Cuentos breves y extraordinarios* [*Short and Extraordinary Stories*]—and as an add-on to the second piece, "El animal soñado por Poe," in the 1957 anthology *Manual de zoología fantástica* and its 1967 expansion, *El libro de los seres imaginarios* [*The Book of Imaginary Beings*]—both with Margarita Guerrero.

As with Borges's earlier anthologizing of two complete tales by Poe, his anthologizing of these *Pym* fragments emphasizes Poe as a writer of supernat-ural and detective stories. *Pym* is primarily a sea adventure, but the passages Borges chooses to translate and anthologize deal with the extraordinary, divisible water that Pym and his companions find on a remote island and with the carcass of a strange land animal they drag out of the ocean. The translation of these particular fragments, from a long and fairly tedious novel, and their inclusion in three anthologies that emphasize the supernatural in their very titles clearly fit within Borges's pattern of casting Poe as a writer of the fantastic. The detective connection is less obvious, but as I have argued in *Borges's Poe*, the specific words Borges uses in this translation—especially his replacement of "dog" with "sabueso" [bloodhound]—combined with Borges's tendency to describe the whole of *Pym* by its last and most mysteri-ous chapters all point these two passages toward the detective genre (75–80). Like *Antología de la literatura fantástica* and *Los mejores cuentos policiales*, these newer anthologies each enjoy several reprints, which allows Borges to con-tinue to typecast Poe as a fantastic and detective writer even while pulling the excerpts from Poe's longest and most cumbersome piece of fiction.

Borges's next and final acts as a Poe anthologizer came very late in his life—in the 1970s and 1980s, when he was asked by various publishers to cre-ate libraries rather than single anthologies. For an author whose own biogra-phy and literary corpus revolved so much around the concept of the library, it should not surprise us that different presses looked to Borges in his old age to help them create multivolume series of literature to be sold as "libraries" to a reading public that now saw Borges as a major writer and a trusted curator of literary tastes, even when his tastes cut against the grain of highbrow literary genres. Borges included a different edition of Poe in each of these libraries, and both Poe editions reiterate Poe's place as a writer of the fantastic and the inventor of detective fiction while more openly including Poe's terror fiction in ways that Borges had avoided in his earlier anthologizing of Poe.

The first of these series—La Biblioteca de Babel—started in the mid-1970s as a collaborative project between Borges and the Italian designer, publisher, and editor, Franco Maria Ricci.[30] The Spanish-language version of this library contained thirty-three titles released by Ediciones Siruela in Madrid between 1983 and 1988, with Poe's La carta robada, the eighteenth volume, published in 1985. The inner jacket of all the books in La Biblioteca de Babel openly calls the series "a collection of fantastic literature," and Borges's prologue once again places Poe in conversations concerning the fantastic and detective fiction. Here, though, he also opens the door more widely to Poe's works of terror by citing Poe's famous response in the preface to Tales of the Grotesque and Arabesque about terror belonging to the soul rather than to Germany ("Prólogo," La carta robada 10) and by using the term "nightmare" to describe the majority of Poe's fiction (12).[31] The book includes translations of one detective story—"The Purloined Letter"—and four stories that can be read in terms of terror and/or the supernatural—"MS. Found in a Bottle," "M. Valdemar," "The Man of the Crowd," and "The Pit and the Pendulum."[32] Borges offers both the corporeal and otherworldly readings of "M. Valdemar," claiming that in this tale, "physical horror is added to the horror of the supernatural," and he explicitly calls "The Pit and the Pendulum" "a gradual exaltation of terror" (12). Most pointedly, Borges waxes nostalgic for his childhood days of reading Poe and recalls countless re-readings of Poe's "The Pit and the Pendulum" (12–13) rather than the detective stories and fantastic pieces he praises elsewhere.

The second series, Biblioteca Personal, consists of seventy-two volumes that Borges published with Hyspamérica beginning in 1985. Like the books in the Biblioteca de Babel series, the volumes in Biblioteca Personal were organized by Borges (and, this time, María Kodama) and include prologues that he wrote for each volume. Borges's general prologue that appears at the beginning of each of these books reveals, once again, an anthologizing strategy based on reading enjoyment and his own "preferences" ("Biblioteca personal" 3). In the prologue to the individual Poe volume, Cuentos, Borges makes the same nod toward Poe's terror fiction that he made in the prologue to the Biblioteca de Babel series by citing Poe's preface to Tales of the Grotesque and Arabesque, but this time he only describes the tales included in the volume either in terms of detective fiction or the fantastic ("Prólogo," Cuentos 9–10). The book contains the same five tales published in the Biblioteca de Babel volume and adds translations of "Maelström," "Rue Morgue," "The Cask of Amontillado," and his favorite Poe essay—"The Philosophy of Composition."[33] The volume includes a selection of Poe's tales of terror, and the prologue references Poe as a terror writer, but it then openly calls

"M. Valdemar," "Maelström," "MS. Found in a Bottle," "The Man of the Crowd," and "The Pit and the Pendulum" "fantastic literature" (9–10) while failing to (or refusing to) categorize "The Cask of Amontillado." This particular selection, in short, acknowledges and includes the three long-running Poe types in Argentine anthologizing and editing of Poe—detective, supernatural, and terror fiction—but it collapses the latter into Borges's own two preferred descriptions of Poe, the inventor of the detective genre and a rejuvenator of the fantastic.

Julio Cortázar: Translating and Ranking Poe's Complete Fiction

Of all of Argentina's anthologizers and editors of Poe's prose, Julio Cortázar did more to give Argentine and Spanish-language readers in general a broad and varied Poe; he also did more to rank or judge Poe's various types of stories. Cortázar accomplished the former feat through a massive translation project that included sixty-seven of Poe's stories, *Eureka*, *Pym*, and a large selection of Poe's literary criticism. He initially published these translations in 1956, and they have been republished, repackaged, and reissued continuously ever since.[34] He achieved the second act of ranking by consciously ordering his translations of Poe's stories and then explicitly describing his praxis in his paratexts. Cortázar's preferences swerve slightly from Borges's, but they also demonstrate the consistent favoring of terror, the supernatural, and detective fiction that Argentine Poe editions and anthologies have favored since Olivera in the 1880s.

Cortázar provided a healthy amount of paratext with his translations, including a particularly insightful "Notas" section that follows up his translations of the stories and develops his criteria for his ranking of Poe genres and his ordering of Poe tales.[35] Cortázar opens these notes by arguing that the ordering of Poe's texts creates a conundrum for the editor because each text functions both individually and as a group, and that to maintain the "deliberately arranged effects," the editor must organize the tales in "the most harmonious way possible" (487). He claims that other Poe editions "commit the sin of arbitrariness" (487), whether organized chronologically or via some other method, by continually ordering Poe's stories in ways that lead to interruptions of the "continuity of atmosphere" (488) between selections rather than allowing that ambiance to grow as the reader moves from one tale to another.

To combat this problem, Cortázar claims to have organized his translations of Poe's stories following a two-tiered approach. The first step concerns how interesting he, as a Poe reader and translator, finds specific modes (or perhaps even genres) of Poe's stories: "In the present edition the stories have been organized by taking, as the essential qualification, the interest of the *temas*, and as the secondary qualification, the comparative value of the stories" (488).[36] While Cortázar uses the word "temas" in this passage—which translates as "themes"—the titles that he gives to the groups themselves and his desire to separate stories with similar "temas" or themes in his second guiding principle demonstrate that the first step in his organizational process is actually one of distinguishing mode or genre rather than theme. Cortázar goes on to suggest that as the modes decrease in interest, so does the quality of Poe's tales. The "eight successive groups" (488) he describes, then, form a ranking of the different types of tales that Poe wrote, and this ranking fits comfortably within previous Argentine models for editing and anthologizing Poe's short fiction: "stories of terror, of the supernatural, of the metaphysical, analytical, of anticipation and retrospection, of landscape, of the grotesque, and satirical. This order takes into account the progressive decrease of interest, as we said, with a parallel decrease of quality" (488).[37]

Cortázar finds more interest in the tales of terror than Borges did and slightly less interest in the detective fiction, but three of his top four Poe modes match directly with the proclivities revealed in Olivera's Poe collection, Bazán's Poe edition, and Borges's various anthologies. The only surprise here rests in the placement Cortázar gives to the metaphysical stories, which take a more prominent place in his esteem than we have seen with previous Argentine anthologizers, editors, and translators. Cortázar, like Borges, is much bolder than Olivera or Bazán in his critiques of Poe's lighter-hearted fiction. He claims that Poe's satiric pieces "have a very minor value in the work of Poe" (488), and he suggests that both the satiric stories and the grotesque tales do not contain "true humor" (488). In fact, Cortázar praises each of the first six groups of stories and marks the shift from the "beautiful" (489) landscape pieces (which he ranks below several other types of tales, but still thoroughly respects) to the grotesques and the satires as the delineation that "signals as well the decline of the quality of the tales" (489).

Cortázar's second tier of organization concerns the order of the specific stories within each of his defined groups, and he bases this order on a strategy that intentionally seeks to avoid thematic or scenic sequence. Using "temas" as "themes" this time around, rather than as genre or mode as he did previously, he states, "within each group, the stories have been arranged in a way that similar *temas* or settings *do not* follow one another" (489). He then provides an example of how he has separated the seafaring tales in the terror section from each another (489). In the first section, Cortázar closely follows this principle. Along with the division of the seafaring stories, the confessional narrators from "The Black Cat," "The Tell-Tale Heart," and "The Imp of the Perverse" are separated from one another by various stories, and Cortázar maintains a substantial distance between the revenge in "The Cask of Amontillado" and the revenge in "Hop-Frog." This type of separation becomes more difficult in the smaller sections as "Eleonora," "Morella," "Berenice," "Ligeia," and "The Fall of the House of Usher"—the majority of Poe's dead beautiful women—all appear in succession in the supernatural section (although we could split hairs here and argue that the women who are buried alive are briefly separated from those who are not). Likewise, "Eiros and Charmion" and "Monos and Una" appear back-to-back in the "metaphysical stories" section while the Dupin tales follow one another in their chronological and plot sequence in the "analytical" grouping.

While Cortázar follows his first organizational principle—that of mode/ genre separation and ranking—better than he follows his second rule of thematic and setting distancing, he almost undermines his own analysis of his purported divisions by not using them within his table of contents, by admitting that several stories could belong to more than one of the groups (489), and by stating that "this does not intend to be a classification" (489). Yet, as he claims earlier in the notes, the order of the stories is of utmost importance because "the reader tends, with logical sense, to read the tales in the order in which the editor presents them" (487). Any ordering of stories, especially in a large collection for which there is no guarantee that the reader will make her way through the whole arrangement, creates a de facto ranking of tales, so Cortázar's notes simply make his thought process or his reasons for his rankings visible to the reader who already experiences those rankings while reading through the volumes.

Even though Cortázar himself sees and understands the problematic nature of dividing Poe's tales into different groups, he prefers making such divisions (at least in his explanatory notes, if not in his table of contents) to following either a chronological or a random ordering of Poe's stories, and he ends up justifying both his mode/genre divisions and his story orderings within those divisions by claiming that he is following Poe's lead. Cortázar quotes an often-mentioned letter that Poe wrote to Philip Cooke on August 9, 1846, in which he praises the "*diversity and* variety" of his own tales, claims that "each tale is equally good *of its kind*," and then picks "Ligeia" as his "*best* tale" because it "is that of the highest imagination" (qtd. in Ostrom et al. 1: 596). Cortázar certainly disagrees with Poe that each of Poe's stories is "equally good" by preferring some types (terror, supernatural, metaphysical, analytical, anticipation and retrospection, landscape) over others (grotesque and satiric), but he claims that his divisions flow from "'the highest imagination" (490) downward and that the collection also honors Poe's "desire of *variety*" (490). In short, Cortázar offers a diverse and nearly complete selection of Poe's short fiction in translation; he orders and ranks that variety in ways that favor Poe's terror, supernatural, metaphysical, and analytic tales and that disparage Poe's satiric and grotesque pieces; and he claims Poe's own authority for doing so. Cortázar's Poe translations have remained in print in various forms from 1956 onward, and they are still considered *the* Spanish-language translations of Poe, but more importantly for this particular chapter, his organizing apparatus remains in place, and readers who approach Poe in Spanish through his translations consume his rankings and ingest his preferences whether they read his notes or not, simply due to the order in which he organized Poe's tales.

An author's established reputation in a given literary system precedes him/ her when new audiences approach the writer's work. In the case of Poe in the Argentine literary system, his status as the creator of the detective genre, as an innovator of the supernatural, and as a master of terror re-creates itself for new generations of readers every time anthologizers, editors, and translators choose to focus on these particular works from his literary corpus. The twentieth-century emphasis on this particular Poe, however, was not simply a natural outcome of what Argentine readers wanted at the beginning of that century. Indeed, Argentine readers of that time period wanted the Poe they been given during the first several decades of his literary presence in Argentina—the melancholy poet. This particular focus emerged from the combined efforts of several editors, anthologizers, and translators (who often simultaneously functioned as editors or anthologizers) who played the part of image creator and took on the role of intermediary between Poe and his Argentine readers. As Cortázar suggests, organizing Poe's stories "poses a problem of taste" (487), and Argentina's editors, anthologizers, and translators of Poe's fiction have consistently preferred the darker and more serious Poe over his lighter and more humorous avatar. The inclusions, exclusions, and explanations of Olivera, Bazán, Borges, and Cortázar created a long-lasting image of Poe—as a writer of supernatural, terror, and detective stories—and this image appears poised to serve as Poe's primary identifier in Argentina well into the twenty-first century.

Notes

1. See Esplin, "'Un muerto vivo': Poe and Argentina" in Philip Phillips's edited volume, *Poe and Place*.

2. Lefevere uses different terms, specifically "rewritings," "refractions," and "rewrites," in separate publications to describe this concept. See *Translating Literature: Practice and Theory in a Comparative Literature Context*, "Why Waste Our Time on Rewrites? The Trouble with Interpretation and the Role of Rewriting in an Alternative Paradigm," and "Mother Courage's Cucumbers: Text, System and Refraction in a Theory of Literature."

3. This claim is more problematic for translators since, depending on the situation, some translators have the opportunity to decide what or who is included in a given translation, while others do not.

4. John Eugene Englekirk suggests that "both French and Spanish versions of Poe's tales began to appear almost simultaneously about a decade after his vogue in the Peninsula, sometime in the late [eighteen] sixties" (20). In the late 1870s and early 1880s, translations of various Poe tales appeared in disparate Argentine periodicals, and Carlos Olivera's translated collection of Poe tales, *Novelas y cuentos*, was published in 1884. Englekirk and several others clearly show that while Poe's fiction was available in the late nineteenth and early twentieth centuries, his reputation in Argentina and in other Spanish-speaking countries in the Americas was that of poet-prophet until at least the 1940s.

5. See Esplin, *Borges's Poe: The Influence and Reinvention of Edgar Allan Poe in Spanish America*, and "From Poetic Genius to Master of Short Fiction: A Map of Edgar Allan Poe's Reception and Influence in Spanish America from the Beginnings through the Boom."

6. See Englekirk (especially pages 15–35) for Baudelaire's presence in and influence on both the Spanish and Spanish American receptions of Poe.

7. In the explanatory headnote that he offers before his translation of "The Mystery of Marie Rogêt," Olivera calls this fairly long story a novel (144), suggesting that the first half of his title probably refers to the two lengthy pieces in this collection—"Rue Morgue" and "Marie Rogêt."

8. Unless otherwise noted, all translations from Spanish to English are my own.

9. Several scholars have noted that the titles of certain Poe tales in other romance languages often reveal that the translators are relying on Baudelaire's French. This is not the case with Olivera's *Novelas y cuentos*.

10. According to Englekirk's bibliography, the only comic or satiric Poe piece published in Argentina before Olivera's *Cuentos y novelas* was a translation of "Tarr and Fether" in an 1869 volume of *Revista Argentina*. Rafael Heliodoro Valle's and Hensley C. Woodbridge's later bibliographies show no comic/satiric Poe translations in Argentina until the early twentieth century, although French and Spanish versions of the few comic pieces Baudelaire translated were certainly available. I would like to thank Juan Pablo Canala of the Salón del Tesoro in the Biblioteca Nacional Argentina for sharing with me his Poe findings in Buenos Aires periodicals of the latter half of the nineteenth century—adding to Englekirk's bibliography and reconfirming this virtual lack of a comic or satiric Poe in Argentina before Olivera's translations.

11. Two shorter Poe publications during this interim are worth noting. In 1903, Biblioteca de la Nación published a small collection under the Hispanicized Baudelaire title, like so many other Poe collections in Spain and throughout Spanish America, of *Historias extraordinarias*. This book included anonymous translations of "The Black Cat," "The Imp of the Perverse," "The Man of the Crowd," "The Tell-Tale Heart," "The Gold-Bug," "The Cask of Amontillado," "The Premature Burial," "Four Beasts in One," "William Wilson," "Some Words with a Mummy," "The Oval Portrait," and "Lionizing." The anonymous editor's inclusion of the adventuresome and ratiocinative tale "The Gold-Bug" rather than the Dupin trilogy demonstrates less interest in Poe's deduction than Olivera's edition. The weekly periodical *Los intelectuales* released a brief Poe edition (under the Hispanicized first and misspelled second name, Edgardo Allam Poe) in February 1923 that contained anonymous translations of "The Purloined Letter," "The Angel of the Odd," "Metzengerstein," "MS. Found in a Bottle," and "Eleonora"—offering a surprisingly balanced portrayal of Poe's works in various genres with two tales of terror, a detective story, a comedy/satire, and an enigmatic romance. This short edition is available in a bound volume with other weekly printings from *Los intelectuales* in the Biblioteca Nacional Argentina under number 000893715.

12. I include "The Unparalleled Adventure of One Hans Pfaall" and "The Philosophy of Furniture" among the thirty-eight tales and sketches, although the first is certainly not short and the latter is sometimes considered an essay.

13. Bazán's prologue is a fairly typical example of an empathetic Poe biography in Spanish America before the middle of the twentieth century. Bazán romanticizes Poe in ways similar to Baudelaire and Rubén Darío that would have been familiar to Argentine readers of Poe by the 1940s. He also repeats or introduces various mistakes in Poe's biography, including suggestions that John Allan adopted Poe (7), that Poe spent time in Greece (8), and that "every time he can he founds magazines with a more or less ephemeral life" (11).

14. Bazán rarely names other Poe stories by their titles in his prologue, but "The Gold-Bug" appears at several key points in Bazán's biography of Poe's life. He calls the recently orphaned Poe "the future author of 'The Gold-Bug'" (7), he notes that Poe won a prize for "The Gold-Bug" and describes the story as "that tale destined to cross all of the world's language frontiers" (11), and he finishes the prologue by referring to Poe as a "storywriter, poet, and philosopher, the author of 'The Gold-Bug,' 'The Bells,' and *Eureka*" (19).

15. "The Duc de L'Omelette," "A Tale of Jerusalem," "Loss of Breath," "Bon-Bon," "Mystification," "How to Write a Blackwood Article," "The Devil in the Belfry," "The Man That Was Used Up," "Why the Little Frenchman Wears His Hand in a Sling," "The Business Man," "Never Bet the Devil Your Head," "Three Sundays in a Week," "Diddling," "The Spectacles," "The Literary Life of Thingum Bob, Esq.," "The Thousand-and-Second Tale of Scheherazade," "Mellonta Tauta," and "X-ing a Paragrab" are all absent from Bazán's edition.

16. "The Landscape Garden," its expanded version titled "The Domain of Arnheim," and "The Elk" (or "Morning on the Wissahiccon") do not appear in Bazán.

17. Bazán does not include "The Premature Burial," "The Sphinx," or "Thou Art the Man."

18. "The Assignation" is difficult to compartmentalize. Mabbott calls it "the most romantic story Poe ever wrote" (148), but Cortázar, while acknowledging the story's "extravagant romantic effusiveness" (500) in his notes to his Poe translations, still groups the story among Poe's tales of terror. Does the reader interpret the double suicide in the story's finale as romantic or terrible?

19. Even if the reader sides with Mabbott's judgment on "The Assignation," it is not a stretch to read this story as a part of the dark Poe that Bazán favors rather than as a second romantic interruption (following "Eleonora") in the first section of *Obras completas*.

20. Bazán publishes translations of "Four Beasts in One," "The Oval Portrait" (nod one), "Some Words with a Mummy," "Lionizing," "The Angel of the Odd," "The Balloon Hoax," A Descent into the Maelström" (nod two), "The Island of the Fay," "The Conversation of Eiros and Charmion," "The Colloquy of Monos and Una," "The Unparalleled Adventure of One Hans Pfaall," "The Philosophy of Furniture," and "Landor's Cottage." Bazán also includes the translations of *Pym* and *Eureka* after "Hans Pfaall" but before "The Philosophy of Furniture" and "Landor's Cottage." He follows the latter two pieces with "The Philosophy of Composition," suggesting (though his table of contents and his prologue do not make this explicit) that he considers "The Philosophy of Furniture" and "Landor's Cottage" as essays rather than tales/sketches.

21. For an analysis of one of these anthologies—*Antología de la literatura fantástica*—as a tool to critique realist literatures of the time period, see Daniel Zavala Medina's *Borges en la conformación de la Antología de la literatura fantástica*.

22. Not all supernatural literature qualifies as fantastic literature, but Borges used the term "fantastic" so loosely throughout his career that his anthologizing Poe as a fantastic writer clearly functions under the longer-running Argentine tradition of connecting Poe to the supernatural. See note 26 for more on this subject.

23. The anthology includes entries as ancient as excerpts from Zhuang Zhou and Petronius and as contemporary as Borges's own "Tlön, Uqbar, Orbis Tertius," which was first published in May 1940, only seven months before the anthology's own printing in late December 1940.

24. In his gigantic collection of journal entries concerning his perennial conversations with Borges, entitled *Borges*, Bioy Casares has little positive to say about Poe. For example, his June 9, 1963, entry includes a critique that Borges offered about Poe's tales of dying women that leads Bioy Casares to call Poe "very ignorant" (901). He agrees with Borges that "Ligeia," "Morella," and "Berenice" "seem absurd"; he criticizes "The Man of the Crowd" (a Poe story that Borges enjoyed); and he claims that *Pym* was Poe's best work (901).

25. Borges also briefly mentions "Valdemar" in a 1943 review—"Leslie D. Weatherhead: *After Death*"—and in his 1967 *Introducción a la literatura norteamericana*, co-authored with Esther Zemborain de Torres.

26. In his treatise on the fantastic, *The Fantastic: A Structural Approach to a Literary Genre*, Tzvetan Todorov defines most of Poe's supernatural pieces as either "uncanny" or "marvelous," but he sees "The Black Cat" as a possible "exception" that can be read as fantastic according to his fairly stringent terms (48). Reading Poe's tales through Julio Rodríguez-Luis's broader framing of the fantastic, which includes both what Todorov calls the fantastic-marvelous and the fantastic-uncanny, brings several of Poe's tales under this larger umbrella of fantastic literature. "M. Valdemar," however, is still a stretch due to the shift in focus caused by the story's horrific finale. See my discussion of some of the confusion caused by Borges's labeling "M. Valdemar" as a fantastic tale in *Borges's Poe* (126–28).

27. Amaryll Beatrice Chanady clearly explains this issue with "Valdemar" in *Magical Realism and the Fantastic: Resolved Versus Unresolved Antinomy*, arguing that the tale's "emphasis is more on the loathsome disintegration of the hypnotized body than on the question of whether mesmerism exists" (142).

28. For more information on the translation of "Higginbotham" and the strange inclusion of this Hawthorne tale as the initial story in *Los mejores cuentos policiales*, see my "Playing the Detective with 'Mr. Higginbotham's Catastrophe' and 'La muerte repetida': Borges, Acevedo de Borges, Poe, and the Translation of Hawthorne's Tale as Proto-Detective Fiction."

29. The newer headnote even kept the errors from the earlier headnote—suggesting that Poe died in New York instead of Baltimore, and adding an extra "the" to the title of Poe's book *Tales of the Grotesque and the Arabesque* (24).

30. The original Italian series—La Biblioteca di Babele—was released between 1975 and 1985, with the first thirty volumes coming out between 1975 and 1981.

31. Borges also disparages Poe's comic work while pointing toward these nightmares: "apart from the occasional misguided incursion into the humorous genre, the word nightmare is applicable to almost all of Poe's narratives" (12).

32. The translations of "M. Valdemar" and "The Purloined Letter" are those previously published by Borges and Bioy Casares. José Luis López Muñoz translated the other three tales.

33. Strangely, Borges does not use his and Bioy Casares's translations of "M. Valdemar" and "The Purloined Letter" in this volume. Instead, those and all other tales in the book are translated by Julio Gómez de la Serna while Ricardo Dessau translated "The Philosophy of Composition."

34. For historical details about the publications and republications of Cortázar's Poe translations, see my essay "'William Wilson' as a Microcosm of Julio Cortázar's Poe Translations" (252–53).

35. The amount of paratext Cortázar offers in his original, two-volume edition of Poe translations in 1956 is certainly atypical for a translation and, frankly, a gold mine for translation studies scholars and scholars of book production and history. The first volume, which houses the translations of the sixty-seven stories, begins with

a ninety-seven-page, bifurcated introduction—the first half a Poe biography and the second half an essay on Poe as poet, fiction writer, and literary critic—and ends with a section of notes about the stories and about Cortázar's organizing method. The second volume, which includes his translations of *Pym*, *Eureka*, and several essays, offers a translator's note for *Pym*, notes for *Eureka* and the essays, an overall note about Poe texts that Cortázar did not translate, and a lengthy bibliography that includes Poe editions (mainly in English but also in Spanish) and Poe criticism and biography in English, Spanish, and French. Editions of Cortázar's translations after 1970 split the initial volume of stories into two separate volumes—*Cuentos*, *1* and *Cuentos*, *2*. The biographical half of Cortázar's original introduction has appeared in *Cuentos*, *1*, and the notes on the stories have been reprinted in *Cuentos*, *2* ever since. For the sake of convenience for a contemporary reader, I cite a current and widely available edition of *Cuentos*, *2* when quoting Cortázar's notes rather than citing the harder-to-find 1956 first edition.

36. In the two citations in this chapter in which I leave "temas" untranslated, the term appears in italics as a marker of language, not as a marker of emphasis in Cortázar's Spanish-language text.

37. Cortázar's explanatory notes categorize and order Poe's tales as follows: 1) Terror stories: "William Wilson," "The Pit and the Pendulum," "MS. Found in a Bottle," "The Black Cat," "The Facts in the Case of M. Valdemar," "The Oval Portrait," "The Tell-Tale Heart," "A Descent into the Maelström," "The Cask of Amontillado," "The Masque of the Red Death," "A Tale of the Ragged Mountains," "The Imp of the Perverse," "The Premature Burial," "Hop-Frog," "Metzengerstein," "The Oblong Box," "The Man of the Crowd," "The Assignation," and "Shadow." 2) Supernatural stories: "Eleonora," "Morella," "Berenice," "Ligeia," and "The Fall of the House of Usher." 3) Metaphysical stories: "Mesmeric Revelation," "The Power of Words," "The Conversation of Eiros and Charmion," "The Colloquy of Monos and Una," and "Silence." 4) Analytical stories: "The Gold-Bug," "The Murders in the Rue Morgue," "The Mystery of Marie Rogêt," and "The Purloined Letter." 5) Anticipation and retrospection stories: "The Unparalleled Adventure of One Hans Pfaall," "Von Kempelen and His Discovery," "The Thousand-and-Second Tale of Scheherazade," "The Balloon Hoax," "Some Words with a Mummy," and "Mellonta Tauta." 6) Landscape stories: "The Domain of Arnheim," "Landor's Cottage," "The Island of the Fay," and "Morning on the Wissahiccon" (or, "The Elk"). 7) Grotesque stories: "The Sphinx," "The Angel of the Odd," "King Pest," "A Tale of Jerusalem," "The Man That Was Used Up," "Three Sundays in a Week," "'Thou Art the Man,'" "Bon-Bon," "The Spectacles," "The Devil in the Belfry," "The System of Doctor Tarr and Professor Fether," "Never Bet the Devil Your Head," "Mystification," "Why the Little Frenchman Wears His Hand in a Sling," "Loss of Breath," "The Duc de L'Omelette," and "Four Beasts in One." 8) Satirical stories: "The Literary Life of Thingum Bob, Esq.," "How to Write a Blackwood Article," "A Predicament," "Lionizing," "Diddling Considered as One of the Exact Sciences," "X-ing a Paragrab," and "The Business Man."

Works Cited

Bazán, Armando. Prólogo. *Obras completas*, by Edgar Allan Poe, Editorial Claridad S. A., 1944, pp. 7–19.

———, editor and compiler. *Obras completas*. By Edgar Allan Poe, Editorial Claridad S. A., 1944.

Bioy Casares, Adolfo. *Borges*. Ediciones Destino, 2006.

———. Prólogo. *Antología de la literatura fantástica*, edited by Jorge Luis Borges, Adolfo Bioy Casares, and Silvina Ocampo, Editorial Sudamericana, 1940, pp. 7–15.

Borges, Jorge Luis. "El arte narrativo y la magia." *Obras completas*, vol. 1, Emecé Editores, 2004, pp. 226–32.

———. "Biblioteca personal." *Cuentos*, by Edgar Allan Poe, compiled by Jorge Luis Borges, translated by Julio Gómez de la Serna and Ricardo Dessau, Hyspamérica Ediciones Argentina S. A., 1987, p. 3.

———. "*Edgar Allan Poe*, de Edward Shanks." *Obras completas*, vol. 4, Emecé Editores, 2007, pp. 332–33.

———. "Leslie D. Weatherhead: *After Death.*" *Obras completas*, vol. 1, Emecé Editores, 2004, pp. 280–81.

———. Prólogo. *Cuentos*, by Edgar Allan Poe, compiled by Jorge Luis Borges, translated by Julio Gómez de la Serna and Ricardo Dessau, Hyspamérica Ediciones Argentina S. A., 1987, pp. 9–10.

———. Prólogo. *El gran rostro de piedra*, by Nathaniel Hawthorne, selected by Jorge Luis Borges, translated by Federico Eguíluz, Ediciones Siruela, 1986, pp. 9–13.

———. Prólogo. *La carta robada*, by Edgar Allan Poe, selected by Jorge Luis Borges, translated by Jorge Luis Borges, Adolfo Bioy Casares, and José Luis López Muñoz, Ediciones Siruela, 1985, pp. 9–13.

Borges, Jorge Luis, and Adolfo Bioy Casares. "Del agua de la isla." *Cuentos breves y extraordinarios*, edited by Jorge Luis Borges and Adolfo Bioy Casares, Raigal, 1955, pp. 165–66.

———. Headnote. *Los mejores cuentos policiales*, Emecé Editores, 1947, p 24.

———. Prólogo. *Los mejores cuentos policiales (2)*, 1983, Alianza, 2002, pp. 7–8.

———, editors. *Los mejores cuentos policiales*. Emecé Editores, 1943.

———. *Los mejores cuentos policiales* (segunda serie). Emecé Editores, 1951.

Borges, Jorge Luis, Adolfo Bioy Casares, and Silvina Ocampo, editors. *Antología de la literatura fantástica*. Editorial Sudamericana, 1940.

Borges, Jorge Luis, and Margarita Guerrero. "El animal soñado por Poe." *El libro de los seres imaginarios*, edited by Jorge Luis Borges and Margarita Guerrero, Kier, 1967, pp. 21–22.

———. "El animal soñado por Poe." *Manual de zoología fantástica*, edited by Jorge Luis Borges and Margarita Guerrero, Fondo de Cultura Económica, 1957, pp. 24–25.

Borges, Jorge Luis, and Esther Zemborain de Torres, editors. *Introducción a la literatura norteamericana*. Columba, 1967.

Chanady, Amaryll Beatrice. *Magical Realism and the Fantastic: Resolved Versus Unresolved Antinomy*. Garland, 1985.

Cortázar, Julio. "Notas." *Cuentos, 2*, by Edgar Allan Poe, translated by Julio Cortázar, Alianza Editorial, 2007, pp. 487–521.

———, translator. *Obras en prosa*. By Edgar Allan Poe, Revista Occidente and Ediciones de la Universidad de Puerto Rico, 1956. 2 vols.

Englekirk, John Eugene. *Edgar Allan Poe in Hispanic Literature*. Instituto de las Españas en los Estados Unidos, 1934.

Esplin, Emron. *Borges's Poe: The Influence and Reinvention of Edgar Allan Poe in Spanish America*. U of Georgia P, 2016.

———. "From Poetic Genius to Master of Short Fiction: A Map of Edgar Allan Poe's Reception and Influence in Spanish America from the Beginnings through the Boom." *Resources for American Literary Study*, vol. 31, 2006, pp. 31–54.

———. "'Un muerto vivo': Poe and Argentina." *Poe and Place*, edited by Philip Edward Phillips, Palgrave, 2018, pp. 321–41.

———. "Playing the Detective with 'Mr. Higginbotham's Catastrophe' and 'La muerte repetida': Borges, Acevedo de Borges, Poe, and the Translation of Hawthorne's Tale as Proto-Detective Fiction." *Translation Review*, vol. 94, 2016, pp. 80–106.

———. "'William Wilson' as a Microcosm of Julio Cortázar's Poe Translations: Horror in the Doubling of the Human Will." *Translated Poe*, edited by Emron Esplin and Margarida Vale de Gato, Lehigh UP, 2014, pp. 251–60 and 410–16.

Heliodoro Valle, Rafael. "Fichas para la Bibliografía de Poe en Hispanoamérica." *Revista Iberoamericana*, vol. 16, 1950, pp. 199–214.

Lefevere, André. "Mother Courage's Cucumbers: Text, System and Refraction in a Theory of Literature." *The Translation Studies Reader*, edited by Lawrence Venuti, 3rd ed., Routledge, 2012, pp. 203–19.

———. *Translating Literature: Practice and Theory in a Comparative Literature Context*. MLA, 1992.

———. "Why Waste Our Time on Rewrites? The Trouble with Interpretation and the Role of Rewriting in an Alternative Paradigm." *The Manipulation of Literature: Studies in Literary Translation*, edited by Theo Hermans, St. Martins, 1985, pp. 215–43.

Mabbott, Thomas Ollive. "The Visionary (The Assignation)." *Tales and Sketches Volume 1: 1831–1842*, by Edgar Allan Poe, edited by Thomas Ollive Mabbott, U of Illinois P, 2000, pp. 148–50.

Olivera, Carlos. "Al lector." *Novelas y cuentos*, by Edgar Allan Poe, Librería Española de Garnier Hermanos, 1884, pp. i–vii.

———, translator and editor. *Novelas y cuentos*. By Edgar Allan Poe, Librería Española de Garnier Hermanos, 1884.

Ostrom, John W., Burton R. Pollin, and Jeffrey A. Savoye, editors. *The Collected Letters of Edgar Allan Poe*. Gordian Press, 2008. 2 vols.

Poe, Edgar Allan. *Historias extraordinarias*. Biblioteca de la Nación, 1903.

Poe, Edgardo Allam [sic]. "Historias grotescas y serias." *Los intelectuales*, year 2, no. 48, 12 February 1923, pp. 1–32.

Price, Leah. *The Anthology and the Rise of the Novel: From Richardson to George Eliot.* Cambridge UP, 2000.

Rodríguez-Luis, Julio. *The Contemporary Praxis of the Fantastic: Borges and Cortázar.* Garland, 1991.

Todorov, Tzvetan. *The Fantastic: A Structural Approach to a Literary Genre.* Translated by Richard Howard, Cornell UP, 1975.

Woodbridge, Hensley C. "Poe in Spanish America: A Bibliographical Supplement." *Poe Newsletter*, vol. 2, no. 1, 1969, pp. 18–19.

Zavala Medina, Daniel. *Borges en la conformación de la* Antología de la literatura fantástica. Miguel Ángel Porrúa and Universidad Autónoma de San Luis de Potosí, 2012.

CHAPTER SEVENTEEN

~

Editing and
Anthologizing Poe in Japan

Takayuki Tatsumi

A Poe Anthology for Juvenile
Readers: Retelling as a Literary Genre

Let me narrate the way a Japanese scholar-critic, who encountered Poe in a
volume for children as an elementary school student in the 1960s, ended up
translating and even anthologizing Poe himself in the twenty-first century.
The Poe collection I first read was entitled *Yurei-sen* [*The Ghost Ship*], edited
by Takehiko Takeda, illustrated by Motoichiro Takebe, and published in
1958 as the twenty-seventh volume of Kaiseisha's Meisaku Boken Zenshu
[Series of Great Adventure Stories]. This series covered major figures of
world popular literature such as Alexandre Dumas, H. G. Wells, Jules Verne,
Arthur Conan Doyle, Maurice Leblanc, Henry Rider Haggard, and others.
My father, a professor of English at Sòphia University in Tokyo, very carefully selected and bought me several volumes from the series. Thus, Doyle's
Sherlock Holmes and Leblanc's Arsène Lupin immediately became my
heroes. What matters here is that the Poe volume, including three pieces—
"The Ghost Ship," "The Purloined Letter," and "The Gold-Bug"—also fas-
cinated me with aristocratic detectives like C. Auguste Dupin and Legrand.

Poe scholars and Poe readers will recognize the latter two titles, but "The
Ghost Ship" does not appear in any of Poe's works in English. All we can
recall here is one of Poe's early tales, "MS. Found in a Bottle," featuring a
spectacle of "a gigantic ship" of approximately "four thousand tons" (*Tales
and Sketches* 140), to which Stuart and Susan Levine add the following note:

"In the legend of the Flying Dutchman, *the ghost ship* is supposed to appear when a ship is going down. Poe's *ghost ship* is right on schedule" (631; emphasis added). However, Kaiseisha's edition of "The Ghost Ship" had nothing to do with "MS. Found in a Bottle." Despite the misleading title, the sensational cover illustration of the volume undoubtedly refers to this particular story. The mystery is quickly resolved when one reads the tale; "The Ghost Ship" is, in fact, Takehiko Takeda's retelling of *The Narrative of Arthur Gordon Pym of Nantucket.*

At this point it is necessary to explain the role of the "reteller" of major works for children in Japan. To put it simply, Kaiseisha's Series of Great Adventure Stories consists of radical retellings, not "faithful" translations. For this project, the publisher invited a number of popular writers and editors to serve as retellers of famous stories for children. Thus, sometimes the name of the reteller is printed on the cover in far larger lettering than the name of the original author. Biographically speaking, Takehiko Takeda (1919–1998), the editor of *The Ghost Ship*, was well-known in the field of Japanese detective fiction. He helped inaugurate a detective fiction magazine, *Hoseki* [*Jem*], in 1946 and served as its editor-in-chief through 1948. Thus, it was very natural for Takeda to start another literary career by retelling for children "The Enormous Darkroom," one of the popular works of Edogawa Rampo, the king of Japanese detective fiction, whose pseudonym mimics the pronunciation of "Edgar Allan Poe."

The rise of Western-style education in Japan ignited such a boom of retelling for children that many publishers tried to expand their market by compiling collections of major world literary masterpieces retold for elementary school pupils. These acts of retelling sometimes reconstruct the original story very radically, even violently. In the case of *The Ghost Ship*, Takehiko Takeda's retellings of "The Purloined Letter" and "The Gold-Bug" are very faithful to Poe's source texts, whereas "The Ghost Ship" radically transforms the whole structure of *The Narrative of Arthur Gordon Pym*, not just its title. The reason is very simple. Retellers were keenly aware of moral codes for children, obeying self-imposed restraints. Thus, "The Ghost Ship" lacks the scene of cannibalism on the Grampus, the adventures on the island of Tsalal, and the death of Pym's friend Augustus, winding up with a happy reunion between the children and Captain Barnard. In Japan, as Judy Wakabayashi suggests, folktales, legends, and religious and moral tales are, at times, related to children in simplified form (227). It is beyond doubt that Takeda retold *Pym* for children, keenly aware of this tradition of censorship.

In this sense, it is possible to set up an analogy between retellers for children in postwar Japan and writers of chapbooks for illiterate people in premodern Anglo-America, for both of them share the ambition of popularizing literature and uplifting people's literacy so seriously as to edit and transform the original text very aggressively. Victor Neuburg claims that chapbooks included "abridged versions of the romances of knights and maidens that, in lengthier and more sophisticated versions, had delighted medieval audiences" (82). The earliest list of chapbooks in the North American colonies included *Robinson Crusoe, Aesop's Fables, Gulliver's Travels, Pilgrim's Progress, Don Quixote,* and other major works (89–90). This list cannot help but remind us of the retold and abridged series of world literature for children such as Kaiseisha's Series of Great Adventure Stories described above.

Of course, the act of retelling for children cannot take place without disfiguring the source text. However, if the reteller succeeds in arousing interest in literature, the juvenile and/or less literate reader will want to read the original sooner or later. Herein lies the significance of retelling for children as a branch of juvenile literature. To tell the truth, until recently I had absolutely no memory of reading "The Ghost Ship" as a child. I picked up the collection once again in order to prepare a keynote address in 2018, and upon re-reading it, I promptly recovered the lost memory and recognized that this is a radically modified juvenile version of *Pym*. This rediscovery of "The Ghost Ship" helped to clarify why I was to write a chapter on *Pym* in my dissertation at Cornell University in 1987, and to translate this novel for Shueisha's Poe edition as the ninth volume of the Pocket Masterpiece series in 2016. I will elaborate on this in my conclusion. What matters now is that, as my case history shows, the most disfigured juvenile version of Poe's novel, published in the 1950s, motivated a child to later read the original text, study it in an academic edition, and even translate it in the twenty-first century.

In the Wake of the Meiji Revolution: The Dawn of Poe Anthologies/Editions in Japan

The Meiji Revolution (1853–1877) served as an incubator for the reception of Western literature and culture. This revolution, along with the Meiji era (1868–1912) that followed it, helped produce a number of talented authors, scholars, and translators in Japan. As I have already pointed out in my chapter, "The Double Task of the Translator: Poe and His Japanese Disciples" in *Translated Poe*, the official origin of the Japanese translation of Poe could well be located in the distinguished journalist of the Meiji era, Shiken Morita (1861–1897), who translated "The Purloined Letter" and "The Pit and the Pendulum." By the same token, however, we should not forget that he also deserves the title of the first editor of Poe in Japan, for he published a book with Hakubunkan Publishers in 1897, *Shuchin Shosetsu: Kan-Ippatsu* [*Pocket Fiction: Narrow Escape*], that included these two stories. Here we should note that "Kan-Ippatsu" ["Narrow Escape"] is, in fact, the first Japanese title for "The Pit and the Pendulum."

Raicho Hiratsuka's aborted Poe collection probably matters more for the late Meiji period. Born Haru Hiratsuka in Tokyo in 1886, she was a proto-feminist philosopher who made every effort to promote women's liberation in Japan and inaugurated the feminist magazine, *Seito* [*Bluestocking*], in 1911 as its major organ. It was in this magazine from 1911 to 1912 that Hiratsuka translated eleven of Poe's works: "Shadow—a Parable," "Silence," "The Power of Words," "The Black Cat," "The Masque of the Red Death," "The Conversation of Eiros and Charmion," "The Oval Portrait," "The Cask of Amontillado," "The Island of the Fay," "The Man of the Crowd," and "A Descent into the Maelström."

From a twenty-first century perspective, it might be difficult for us to understand why an early Japanese feminist would gravitate toward Poe, an author whose portrayals of women are problematic at best. However, we should be aware that in the late Meiji era, Poe was one of the most popular Western writers in Japan. We can assume that after graduation from Nihon Women's University, this proto-feminist, Hiratsuka, came to know Poe's works at a meeting of the Keishu Bungakukai—a literary circle for women—with noted writers and scholars such as Choko Ikuta, Akiko Yosano, Shukotsu Togawa, Toboku Hirata, Kocho Baba, Gyofu Soma, Toson Shimazaki, and Sohei Morita as lecturers. Some of these writers were such big fans of Poe as to introduce and translate his poems and tales in literary magazines. Without the support of Choko Ikuta, the leading figure in this circle, Hiratsuka could not have started *Seito*. In this way, Hiratsuka came to translate Poe's poems and tales in *Seito*, and she also planned to publish a Poe collection. However, the proposed book had to be abandoned as *Seito* itself gradually intensified its feminist tendency. For now, we have only to remember how necessary it was for Meiji feminists like Hiratsuka to engage in serious study of English, with Poe as one of the exemplary texts.

The Taisho era (1913–1926) saw the first boom of Poe editions in Japan. It started with Jitsumaro Okada's translated and edited book, *Kabutomushi, Uzumaki, Botsuraku* [*Beetle, Maelström, Fall*], published in 1913 by Hokubunkan. As clearly seen in the title, this collection includes translations of three tales: "The Gold-Bug," "A Descent into the Maelström," and "The Fall of the House of Usher." While his precursors were all writers and scholars educated in Japan, Okada's decision to study outside of Japan makes his career unique. Born in Hiroshima in 1877 (the year of his death is unknown), Okada studied at Doshisha and Keio high schools and became a newspaper reporter for *Tokyo Jiji Shinpo* [*Current Affairs News*]. However, Okada decided to quit this job and instead study at Oberlin College in the United States in 1902, finishing with a bachelor's degree in English. After returning to Japan in 1904, he started teaching English at the high school level in Kobe and in 1924 took a tenured job at Meiji University in Tokyo. As a teacher, he could speak impeccable English and translated Western literature very beautifully. In short, Okada's is not only the first Poe collection in the Taisho era but also the first Poe edition translated and compiled by a native of Japan who was educated in the United States.

The most important editor of Poe in the Taisho era is undoubtedly Seiji Tanizaki (1890–1971), a professor of English at Waseda University.[1] Tanizaki began his career as a translator by editing (for Taiheikan Shoten, 1913) *The Masque of the Red Death*, a selection of Poe's prose that included thirteen tales—"Shadow," "The Masque of the Red Death," "The Fall of the House of Usher," "William Wilson," "The Domain of Arnheim," "The Premature Burial," "The Oval Portrait," "Silence," "The Tell-Tale Heart," "The Colloquy of Monos and Una," "Morella," "Ligeia," and "Landor's Cottage." He then produced a six-volume set, *Collected Tales of Edgar Poe*, for Shunyodo in 1941, and this set was reprinted by Shunjusha in 1969. While James A. Harrison's *Complete Works of Edgar Allan Poe*, published in 1902, included seventy-one tales, Tanizaki translated sixty-four tales, including Poe's novel, *The Narrative of Arthur Gordon Pym of Nantucket*. Although Tanizaki began his work during the Taisho era, his 1941 edition of Poe appears to be the most comprehensive collection of Poe's tales in the next period—the Showa era (1926–1988).

Tanizaki's *Collected Tales of Edgar Poe* was not the first multivolume edition of Poe's tales in Japan, however. From 1931 through 1933, nearly a decade earlier than Tanizaki, Naojiro Sasaki (1901–1943) published a five-volume set, *Collected Tales of Poe*, with Daiichi Shobo. Born in Komatsu city, Ishikawa Prefecture, Sasaki graduated from the English Department of the University of Tokyo in 1925 and became a professional writer. While Tanizaki's *Collected Tales* includes sixty-four tales, Sasaki's *Collected Tales* featured only forty-seven. Nonetheless, the latter is still highly appreciated by general readers and avid collectors, for Sasaki's translation is more precise than Tanizaki's. For example, Tanizaki interpreted "the after-dream of the reveller upon opium" (397) as the Quixotic "impossible dream" (*Collected* 2: 25) in his translation of "The Fall of the House of Usher," whereas Sasaki correctly understood it to be "the bad condition of hangover" (*The Black Cat* 26). What is more, Sasaki translated the following fifteen Poe works into

Japanese for the first time: "Metzengerstein," "Lionizing," "The Imp of the Perverse," "Berenice," "Hans Pfaall," "How to Write a Blackwood Article," "A Predicament," "Diddling Considered as One of the Exact Sciences," "Mesmeric Revelation," "The Assignation," "Von Kempelen and His Discovery," "The Business Man," "The Sphinx," "Loss of Breath," and "The Literary Life of Thingum Bob, Esq." Eleven years younger than Tanizaki, Sasaki passed away at the age of forty-two. And yet, the essence of his translation of Poe was condensed in Shinchosha's pocket book anthologies, *Murders in the Rue Morgue* (1951) and *The Black Cat and The Gold-Bug* (1951), both of which had long lifespans and were widely read for more than half a century until they were replaced by my new translation in 2009.

For Poe's poetry, the Taisho era saw three editions: Takeji Wakameda's 1922 *Poems of Poe*, including thirty-two pieces such as "The Raven," "The Valley of Unrest," and "To——" as well as a brief biography; distinguished poet Ichiei Sato's 1923 *Collected Poems of Poe*, including forty-seven works as well as Yukimitsu Haruyama's essay on Poe's poetry; and Takanobu Itoh's 1926 *Complete Poems of Poe*, including forty-three pieces (the translator omitted "Al Aaraaf" and included the prose poems "Silence" and "Shadow"). Takashi Miyanaga of Hosei University, a critical bio-bibliographer of Poe, highly appreciated Itoh's translation, which skillfully blends colloquial language with literary style, as is typically exhibited in his rendition of "The Bells" (Miyanaga 192).[2]

The Showa era (1926–1988) saw a variety of sophisticated anthologies of Poe. In 1929, the guru of Japanese detective fiction, Edogawa Rampo (the pen name for Taro Hirai, 1894–1965), published *Stories of Poe and E. T. A. Hoffmann* as the thirtieth volume of Kaizosha's World Popular Fiction series. It was in 1914 that Rampo, as a student of economics at Waseda University in Tokyo, first encountered and seriously read Anglo-American detective stories by Poe, Arthur Conan Doyle, and G. K. Chesterton, which fatefully determined his literary tastes. Thus, he selected for his pseudonym the five ideographs, "Edogawa Rampo" [江戸川乱歩] to mimic the pronunciation of "Edgar Allan Poe," which in Japanese rather decadently suggests one "staggering drunkenly along the Edo River." As I have already pointed out in my preface to *The Edogawa Rampo Reader*, Rampo's first published story, "Nisen Doka" ["The Two-Sen Copper Coin"] succeeded also in further complicating the cryptogrammic tradition that Poe, the father of world detective fiction, had inaugurated with "The Gold-Bug" in 1843. Poe's arabesque, grotesque, and ratiocinative tales exerted great influence upon Rampo's *eroguro-nonsensu* [erotic-grotesque-nonsense] detective fiction, and Rampo's Poe selections for the aforementioned anthology demonstrate this influence.

Rampo very carefully selected the following fifteen stories for this anthology: "The Gold-Bug," "The Murders in the Rue Morgue," "The Mystery of Marie Rogêt," "The Purloined Letter," "A Descent into the Maelström," "MS. Found in a Bottle," "The Oblong Box," "The Premature Burial," "The Pit and the Pendulum," "The Masque of the Red Death," "The Black Cat," "Hop-Frog," "The Tell-Tale Heart," "The Fall of the House of Usher," and "William Wilson." However, while Rampo is credited as translator for these stories, Atsushi Watanabe, the editor-in-chief of *Shinseinen* magazine, ghost-translated them on behalf of Rampo. Therefore, it is safe to say that Rampo played the very role of anthologist who selected the stories and asked the best person to translate them. What made this volume so popular was Rampo's reputation as the godfather of Japanese detective fiction.

Returning to Poe's poetry, we should not ignore the impact of Konosuke Hinatsu's incredibly sophisticated and profoundly archaic translation of "The Raven," in 1936, on the subsequent boom of anthologies of Poe's poems. In the same year, Kobunsha published *Poems of Edgar Allan Poe* with Nagao Sugimoto as the translator, which included thirty pieces such as "The Raven," "To——," and "The Sleeper." In 1940 Iwanami Shoten Publishers published *Poe's Essays on Poetry* with Michizo Masuda as the translator. This volume included Poe's "The Poetic Principle," "The Philosophy of Composition," "The Rationale of Verse," and his review of Longfellow's *Ballads and other Poems*. With the exception of "The Poetic Principle," all of these pieces were first translated into Japanese in this anthology.

In 1950, Kinji Shimada of the University of Tokyo, a distinguished scholar of comparative literature, published the *Poems of Edgar Poe*. Unlike other Japanese translators, anthologizers, and editors of Poe, Shimada was well-versed in French literature and came to know Poe through Stéphane Mallarmé. Shimada had read Konosuke Hinatsu's translations in *The Best Poems of Poe*, especially Hinatsu's splendidly phantasmagoric translation of "The Bells," and then felt compelled to translate the poet himself.

Shimada's career induces us to reconsider the way Poe has been more highly evaluated in France than in the United States. As if to mirror this transatlantic contrast, Poe seems to have been more favorably accepted by Japanese scholars of French literature than by Japanese Americanists. Two different translations of Patrick F. Quinn's *The French Face of Edgar Poe* were published simultaneously in Japan in 1975, one from Hokuseido Shoten Publishers with Akio Matsuyama as the translator, the other from Shinbisha Publishers with Toru Nakamura as the translator. Just as Konosuke Hinatsu influenced the later translators of Poe, Shimada, along with leading critic, Hideo Kobayashi, co-translated Baudelaire's essays on Poe and helped emphasize the European face of Poe in Japan. I still remember that back in the 1980s, Junji Kunishige—a renowned Hawthorne scholar at the University of Tokyo—told me that Poe, unlike Hawthorne and Melville, could not be called a purely "American" writer. It was not until the advent of New Historicism in the late 1980s and 1990s, especially in the work of Shawn Rosenheim and Stephen Rachman's co-edited book, *The American Face of Edgar Allan Poe*, that Japanese Poe scholars began to recognize Poe as a radically *American* writer.

The rise of "Collected Works of Literature" in postwar Japan appears to be a unique happening within the Japanese literary system of the time period. These collections reached their peak in Japan in the 1960s. Kawade Shobo Publishers, among others, was the most significant precursor of this phenomenon, for it started publishing Collected Works of New World Literature in 1940. Kawade Shobo's timing is intriguing. In 1940, the Second Sino-Japanese War had bogged down, and Japan joined Italy and Germany to establish the Tripartite Pact, forming the Axis powers. To put it simply, Japan was facing a most serious crisis that year, radically detached from all other countries apart from these two geographically and culturally distant allies. Kawade Shobo's brave decision to publish these Collected Works from 1940 through 1943 opened a literary window through which the Japanese people could keep in touch with others.

After the war, in 1948, Kawade Shobo inaugurated a new forty-volume series called Collected Works of World Literature, including a volume on Poe (1950) edited by Yoshio Nakano of the University of Tokyo. A major figure of the English Literary Society of Japan, Nakano joined forces with Kinji Shimada, an authority on comparative literature as mentioned above, and other prominent translators such as Naojiro Sasaki and Tomoji Abe to translate sixteen of Poe's tales and eleven of his poems. In 1956 the same Kawade Shobo published another big anthology, *The Black Cat, The Gold-Bug and Moby-Dick*, including seven short stories by Poe and a novel by Herman Melville.[3] While Japanese scholars had long considered Poe as "European," this volume succeeded in emphasizing his American literary kinship for the first time.

Kawade Shobo's ambitious project was followed by Chikuma Shobo Publishers' Complete Works of World Literature, whose thirty-third volume (1959) was devoted to Poe and Baudelaire, with Yoshio Nakano, Tomoji Abe, Konosuke Hinatsu, and others as translators and editors. This anthology once again features Poe's European gothic face by including ten tales such as "Ligeia," "The Fall of the House of Usher," "William Wilson," and "The Masque of the Red Death," but it also includes *Eureka* and parts of

Poe's "Marginalia." It should be noted that a long afterword was written by a leading literary critic, Kenichi Yoshida, who was educated at Cambridge University; he was the first son of Prime Minister Shigeru Yoshida, who signed the San Francisco Peace Treaty in 1951. The included biography of Poe was written by the distinguished Americanist, Masami Nishikawa of the University of Tokyo.

The 1960s began with a three-volume anthology, *Selection of Poe's Major Works*, published by Kagamiura Shobo between 1960 and 1961. The first volume includes eighteen gothic tales such as "William Wilson," "A Tale of the Ragged Mountains," and "Berenice," translated by Motoshi Karita of Sophia University and Yuko Eguchi of Tokyo Women's University.[4] The second volume features eighteen stories covering not only gothic romance but also science fiction, such as "MS. Found in a Bottle," "A Descent into the Maelström," and "Mellonta Tauta," translated by Hideo Ichiriki of Waseda University and Rikutaro Fukuda of Tokyo University of Education, an authority on modernists such as Ezra Pound and Ernest Hemingway. The third volume contains ten pieces with special emphasis on ratiocinative tales, such as "The Murders in the Rue Morgue," "The Mystery of Marie Rogêt," "The Purloined Letter," and "Thou Art the Man," translated by Yukio Suzuki, Yasuo Suga, Hideo Ichiriki, and Motoshi Karita. This selection is followed by Seiji Tanizaki's five-volume collection, *Complete Tales of Edgar Allan Poe: A Definitive Edition* (Shunjusha, 1962), the radically revised version of the six-volume set, *Collected Tales of Edgar Poe* from Shunyodo (1941), mentioned earlier.

To sum up, the early translations of Poe in Japan so deeply imbibed the nutrients of modernization, as if reflecting the popular slogan "Out of Asia and into Europe" [*datsua nyuou*] advocated by major intellectual leaders such as Kentaro Suzuki and Yukichi Fukuzawa in the wake of the Meiji Restoration, as to attempt to locate Poe in the Western context of great literary tradition. This is the reason why post-Meiji publishers made every effort to edit a collection of world literature. Their primary goal of translation was not so much academic professionalism as literary craftsmanship.

The 1970s: A Coincidence between American and Japanese Anthologies

The most significant event in the history of Poe anthologies and editions in Japan is Tokyo Sogensha's enormous three-volume hardcover set entitled *The Collected Works of Poe*, published in 1963. The translators were all distinguished professors of English at major universities, whereas the editors furnished the volumes with Harry Clarke's and Odilon Redon's woodblock prints. Although this collection prints no proper name of any Poe scholar on its covers, it is highly plausible that Shoichi Saeki of the University of Tokyo played the role of general editor, for he contributed a long afterword to the first two volumes. A distinguished professor of English and comparative literature, Saeki had been influential in the 1960s and 1970s. His major monographs included *American Literary History* (Chikuma Shobo, 1969), *A Critical Biography of Ernest Hemingway* (Kenkyusha, 1979), and *The Century of Autobiography* (Kodansha, 1985). His translated (and co-translated) works include Hemingway's *The Sun Also Rises*, Saul Bellow's *Henderson the Rain King*, Philip Roth's *Goodbye, Columbus*, Tony Tanner's *City of Words*, Leslie Fiedler's *Love and Death in the American Novel*, and others. Since he was also very active in the field of literary criticism, he achieved fame not only in academia but also in literary journalism. This may be the reason why he was asked to display leadership in editing the *Collected Works of Poe*.

What makes this project important is that while the first two volumes feature sixty-two tales, including *Pym* (translated by Tadaaki Ohnishi), the third volume covers sixty-two poems and the unfinished play, "Politian"; five essays on poetics; the spiritual conversation trilogy; unclassifiable texts like "Maelzel's Chess-Player," "The Philosophy of Furniture," and "How to Write a Blackwood Article"; the prose poem *Eureka*; and selections from "Marginalia." Sogensha's volumes contain sixty-eight tales—if we count the spiritual conversation trilogy and unclassifiable texts—two texts more than the sixty-six offered in Tanizaki's collection. Nonetheless, what makes this collection remarkable in the Japanese tradition is that the editor-in-chief made an insightful decision to divide the text by genre, placing all of the fiction in the first two volumes with poems, essays, reviews, and unclassifiable texts in the last volume.[5] While modern Japan was constructed in the age of *Pax Britanica*, importing British culture as represented by its constitutional monarchy, it is through the spectrum of literary genres that postwar Japan cultivated the American sense of literary market.

The boom in the collected works of world literature, which had been ignited by Kawade Shobo, kept expanding in the 1970s. In 1970, Shueisha published the eighteenth volume of its World Literature Series, entitled *"The Fall of the House of Usher" and "The Black Cat"* and including twenty-four Poe stories, with Kenichi Yoshida, Saichi Maruya, Reiji Hikawa, Yoshio Nakano, Kazuo Ogawa, and Shoichi Saeki as translators. In 1971, Chuo-Koronsha published the seventh volume of A New Collection of World Literature, entitled *Poe and Hawthorne*, and consisting of fourteen of Poe's tales, translated by Yoshida and Maruya, as well as Hawthorne's novel, *The Scarlet Letter*, with an afterword by Akio Atsumi of Gakushuin University.

As already noted, major publishers asked these same professors to join their respective Collected Works series. It is simply because they were highly reputed that Yoshida and Saeki, in particular, participated in a number of collected works of world literature from different major publishers. And yet, this tendency made a difference in the mid-1970s. Having published his edited and translated collection, *The Gold-Bug, The Black Cat and The Fall of the House of Usher* from Kodansha in 1971, Toshio Yagi of Seijo University joined forces with Shoichi Saeki and Koji Oi of Kobe Women's College to translate twenty-two tales by Poe for the thirty-second volume of Kodansha's Collection of World Literature published in 1974.[6]

It was in the mid-1970s that I became favorably impressed with a couple of Poe editions, one in Japan and the other in the United States: Tokyo Sogensha Publishers' five-volume pocket book anthology, *The Collected Works of Poe* (1974–1979), based on the three-volume hardcover anthology published in 1963 that I mentioned above, and Stuart and Susan Levine's edited *The Short Fiction of Edgar Allan Poe* (1976). On the one hand, the Japanese paperback edition, like its 1963 hardcover precursor, covers nearly all of Poe's tales, poems, and critical essays, and its reprinting of Saeki's afterword portrays Poe not as a romantic genius, but a skillful parodist who made use of literary precursors with his highly mannerist *ars combinatoria*. On the other hand, the Levines' edition pays keen attention to the development of Poe's sense of literary genres, redefining Poe as an innovative editor. Despite the differences between the Japanese and American editions, both were published in the 1970s, and they share a deep interest in the evolution and revolution of Poe's mannerist literature. To be more exact, given that Saeki's afterword was originally written in 1963, the Japanese insight into Poe's fiction as the product of editorial patchwork predates the Levines' efforts by thirteen years. What matters here is that in the mid-1970s, both of these editions were affordable and easily accessible to young students in Japan like me. Without them, I would not have decided to pursue Poe studies.

In retrospect, the 1970s saw a new phase of Poe criticism. Developing his revolutionary monograph, *Edgar Poe: Seer and Craftsman*, Stuart Levine states in his introduction, "The New Image of Poe," that by the 1970s new approaches to the author had accumulated such that the old image of Poe came to be questioned. Indeed, the old pathological image was easy to visualize: "a creepy chap, somewhere in an attic, bats flapping about his head as he sits at his desk, writing. A candle sputters in a wine bottle, perhaps, casting shadows which magnify his size on the cobwebby walls and ceiling. A second bottle on the cluttered desk holds unwholesome-looking liquor" (xv). However, Levine dismisses this old image of Poe as a well-wrought myth fabricated by Rufus

Griswold, Poe's fellow editor, rival, and eventual literary executor, if not executioner. Although the older generation of critics had been obsessed with the romantic myth of Poe, new Poe scholars, with recently discovered materials, started redefining Poe as an artist and/or artisan, whose editorial career invited him to very consciously craft literary works of art, marketing them as popular commodities. Thus, Levine concludes: "We see far stronger ties to his place and age than we used to; we see somewhat less 'mad genius' and somewhat more 'commercial craftsman.' More wit, erudition, and philosophical consistency are evident in the new Poe, and far less compulsion" (xxi). His re-vision is not inconsistent with Saeki's re-portrayal of Poe as self-conscious parodist, magazinist, and even histrionic diddler. The new image of Poe created in both 1970s America and Japan undoubtedly led us to relocate him in the literary genealogy from gothic romance through postmodern metafiction.

As Saeki gradually shifted his attention from American literature to Japanese literature in the late 1970s, it was Toshio Yagi who inherited Saeki's legacy and took over the hegemony in Poe studies as well as Poe anthologies in Japan. Very sensitive to the rise of Franco-American criticism as represented by structuralism, semiotics, and deconstruction, as well as to the rise of science fiction studies influenced by post-Marxist criticism in the 1970s, Yagi published a two-volume anthology called *Poe's Science Fiction* with Kodansha in 1979 and 1980. This set included fifteen stories that Yagi translated himself. Given that Harold Beaver had already published *The Science Fiction of Edgar Allan Poe* in 1976, whose selection of sixteen stories does not differ largely from Yagi's (Yagi only excluded "Von Kempelen and His Discovery"), there is no doubt that Yagi imbibed the spirit of Beaver's anthology in editing his own. However, we have to note a critical point between 1976 and 1979: the worldwide boom of *Star Wars*, premiering in the United States in 1977 and in Japan in 1978. The year 1979 also saw the publication of distinguished science fiction scholar-critic Darko Suvin's post-Russian formalist and post-Marxist monograph, *Metamorphoses of Science Fiction: On the Poetics and History of a Literary Genre*, which redefined science fiction as a literary genre of "cognitive estrangement."

Mirroring the rise of science fiction in the late 1970s, a cutting-edge cultural magazine, *Cahiers*, featured Edgar Allan Poe as one of the founding fathers of science fiction in its September 1979 issue (with Yagi as one of the contributors) and in "From Science Fiction to Contemporary Literature" in its December 1978 issue, featuring Stanislaw Lem and J. G. Ballard. In the meanwhile, the literary journal *Eureka* focused on science fiction in its April 1980 issue—translating theoretical essays by Darko Suvin, Robert Scholes, and Eric Rabkin. To put it another way, the late 1970s saw a coincidence between the boom of science fiction ignited by *Star Wars* and the rise of science fiction criticism influenced by postformalist and poststructuralist theory. Of course, Beaver's and Yagi's inclusion of "The System of Doctor Tarr and Professor Fether" in the category of science fiction might sound strange. However, it is also true that the rise of theory helped redefine science fiction as a branch of speculative fiction as represented by Lem, Ballard, and Philip K. Dick—all of whom showed interest not so much in outer space symbolized by NASA's Apollo project as in inner space cultivated by turn-of-the-century modernists, including Dada-Surrealists and post-Freudian psychiatrists. From this perspective, "The System of Doctor Tarr and Professor Fether," which dramatizes the revolution within a French mental hospital, could well be called a prototype of modern speculative fiction. Therefore, Beaver's and Yagi's selection of the tale unwittingly illuminated the possibility of speculative fiction overlapping with the frontier of postmodern literature.

Twenty-First Century Poe Anthologies in Japan

Even in the twenty-first century, Toshio Yagi kept editing Poe anthologies. Having translated Nathaniel Hawthorne's *The Scarlet Letter* in 1992 and Herman Melville's *Moby-Dick* in 2004, he edited an anthology of Poe's criticism for Iwanami Shoten in 2009, consisting of nine essays and Poe's reviews of James Fenimore Cooper, Hawthorne, Henry Wadsworth Longfellow, and Charles Dickens. Given his talent for translation and his academic expertise, Yagi's translations and annotations of English-language literature are highly readable and deeply erudite.

Of course, Poe's gothic romance stories are still so popular as to be re-translated into Japanese time and again. For example, distinguished scholar of English and past president of the English Literary Society of Japan, Yoshi-yuki Fujikawa, published a pocket book anthology, *The Black Cat*, in 1992, which includes eight stories. In addition, Takayoshi Ogawa's two paperback anthologies of Poe, *The Black Cat/The Murders in the Rue Morgue* (2006) and *The Fall of the House of Usher/The Gold-Bug* (2016), brilliantly showcase the author's gothic taste. What is more, distinguished writer and translator Ken Nishizaki, the winner of the Japan Fantasy Novel Award in 2002, published an anthology of Poe's tales, including seven stories such as "William Wilson" and "The Tell-Tale Heart."

To close this chapter, I will come full circle to discuss my own Poe anthology and one from a colleague of mine. My own three-volume pocket anthology of Poe was published by Shinshocha between 2009 and 2015. This project was designed to celebrate the bicentennial of Poe's birthday in 2009.

Deeply influenced by Stuart Levine's criticism, I attempted to emphasize the generic outline of Poe. Accordingly, the first volume, *The Black Cat/The Fall of the House of Usher*, includes six "gothic romance" stories. The second volume, *The Murders in the Rue Morgue/The Gold-Bug* contains six "detective fiction" stories. And the third volume, *A Descent into the Maelström/The Light-House*, consists of seven "science fiction" stories. Moreover, I also tried to give a twist to the existing sense of literary genre by adding "The Man of the Crowd" and "Hop-Frog" to the second volume and "The Domain of Arnheim" and "The Light-House" to the third volume.

My three-volume set was followed by the ninth volume of Shueisha's Pocket Masterpiece series, *E. A. Poe*, edited by noted translator Yukiko Konosu and major writer Kazuki Sakuraba, the winner of the 138th Naoki Award, with the help of Yoko Ikesue as bio-bibliographer. This anthology consists of three poems, sixteen tales, and a novel. Although Konosu is a professional translator, she does not translate all of the pieces. For two poems, "Anabelle Lee" and "Eldorado," the editors reprinted Konosuke Hinatsu's archaic translations, while they reprinted Saichi Maruya's translations of the Dupin trilogy. What made the book much heftier is Poe's novel, *Pym*, which I was asked to newly translate. Of course, it is unusual to include this novel in a Poe anthology. And yet, I felt honored to be a translator of *Pym* in Japan, following in the footsteps of Tanizaki (Shun'yodo Publishers, 1948), Tadaaki Ohnishi (Tokyo Sogensha Publishers, 1957), and Yuichi Takamatsu (Kodansha Publishers, 1969), as very few Japanese translators have wanted to translate this particular work. What is more, unlike my precursors, I was in a position to refer to the 1994 reprinting of Burton Pollin's annotated edition of *Pym*, as well as to Richard Kopley's 1992 edited collection of insightful articles, *Poe's Pym: Critical Explorations*. With the help of these academic resources and internet search engines, I found it easier to translate the otherwise unintelligible parts of the text. It is undeniable that the development of technology as well as the sophistication of translators in the twenty-first century has remarkably enhanced the quality of Poe editions and anthologies in Japan. As Japan went through the stages of post-Meiji modernization—as represented by "Out of Asia and into Europe"—and the postwar democratic cultivation supported by academic intellectuals, the nation has demonstrated its intellectual sophistication through the anthologization of Edgar Allan Poe.

Notes

1. Tanizaki's older brother, Jun'ichiro Tanizaki, was a candidate for the Nobel Prize in Literature, and his art for art's sake drew him to Poe. He brilliantly translated "The Fall of the House of Usher" in 1917.

2. Before moving to the Showa era, I should note in passing that Shukotsu Togawa (1870–1939) of Keio University published the first annotated edition of Poe, entitled *A Tale of the Ragged Mountains*, in 1922. This book, which includes the title story and "The Oblong Box," has the English text on one page and the Japanese translation and footnotes on the facing page.

3. This is the first Japanese version of *Moby–Dick*, translated by Tomoji Abe. It was also published by Iwanami Shoten in the same year.

4. Eguchi also published *A Comparative Study of Edgar Poe and Akutagawa Ryunosuke* with Sobunsha in 1968.

5. Furthermore, this collection also included D. H. Lawrence's article on Poe in the first volume and Allen Tate's essay on the author in the second volume.

6. Yagi also published an epoch-making monograph, *A Study of Edgar Allan Poe: Destruction and Creation*, from Nan'Undo in 1971, and he served as the first president of the Poe Society of Japan in 2007.

Works Cited

Abe, Tomoji, and Yoshio Nakano, editors. *The Black Cat, The Gold-Bug and Moby-Dick*. By Edgar Allan Poe and Herman Melville, Kawade Shobo, 1956.

Abe, Tomoji, Nakano Yoshio, Hinatsu Konosuke, et al., translators. *Poe and Baudelaire*. Afterword by Yoshida Ken'ichi, chronology by Nishikawa Masami, Chikuma Shobo Publishers, 1959.

Beaver, Harold, editor. *The Science Fiction of Edgar Allan Poe*. Penguin, 1976.

Edogawa Rampo, editor. *Stories of Poe and E .T. A. Hoffmann*. Kaizosha, 1929.

Eguchi, Yuko. *A Comparative Study of Edgar Poe and Akutagawa Ryunosuke*. Sobunsha, 1968.

Fujikawa, Yoshiyuki, editor and translator. *The Black Cat*. By Edgar Allan Poe, Shueisha, 1992.

Hinatsu, Konosuke, translator. *The Best Poems of Poe*. Senshin Shorin, 1947.

———. *The Raven*. By Edgar Allan Poe, Koshokan Shoten Publishers, 1936.

Ichiriki, Hideo, and Rikutaro Fukuda, translators. *Selection of Poe's Major Works*. Vol. 2, Kagamiura Shobo, 1960.

Itoh, Takanobu, translator. *The Complete Poems of Poe*. Kougyokudo Shoten, 1926.

Karita, Motoshi, and Yuko Eguchi, translators. *Selection of Poe's Major Works*, vol. 1. Kagamiura Shobo, 1960.

Konosu, Yukiko, Kazuki Sakuraba, and Takayuki Tatsumi, translators. *E. A. Poe*. Shueisha, 2016.

Kopley, Richard. *Poe's Pym: Critical Explorations*. Duke UP, 1992.

Levine, Stuart. *Edgar Poe: Seer and Craftsman*. Everett Edwards, 1972.

Levine, Stuart, and Susan Levine. "Notes." *The Short Fiction of Edgar Allan Poe*, edited by Levine and Levine, The Bobbs-Merrill Company, 1976, pp. 630–31.

———, editors. *The Short Fiction of Edgar Allan Poe*. The Bobbs-Merrill Company, 1976.

Masuda, Michizo, translator. *Poe's Essays on Poetry*. Iwanami Shoten Publishers, 1940.

Matsuyama, Akio, translator. *Poe and Baudelaire* [*The French Face of Edgar Poe*]. By Patrick F. Quinn, Hokuseido Shoten Publishers, 1975.

Miyanaga, Takashi. *Poe and Japan: A History of Reception*. Sairyusha, 2000.

Morita, Shiken, editor and translator. *Shuchin Shosetsu: Kan-Ippatsu*. By Edgar Allan Poe. Hakubunkan Publishers, 1897.

Nakamura, Toru, translator. *Poe and France* [*The French Face of Edgar Poe*]. By Patrick F. Quinn, Shinbisha Publishers, 1975.

Nakano, Yoshio, editor. *World Literature: Edgar Allan Poe*. Kawade Shobo, 1950.

Neuburg, Victor. "Chapbooks in America: Reconstructing the Popular Reading of Early America." *Reading in America: Literature and Social History*, edited by Cathy Davidson, Johns Hopkins UP, 1989, pp. 81–113.

Nishizaki, Ken, editor and translator. *The Short Stories of Edgar Allan Poe*. Chikuma Shobo Publishers, 2007.

Ogawa, Takayoshi, editor and translator. *The Black Cat/The Murders in the Rue Morgue*. By Edgar Allan Poe. Kobunsha, 2006.

———. *The Fall of the House of Usher/The Gold-Bug*. By Edgar Allan Poe, Kobunsha, 2016.

Okada, Jitsumaro, editor and translator. *Kabutomushi, Uzumaki, Botsuraku*. By Edgar Allan Poe, Hokubunkan, 1913.

Poe, Edgar Allan. *The Collected Works of Poe*. Tokyo Sogensha, 1963. 3 vols.

———. *The Collected Works of Poe*. Tokyo Sogensha, 1974–1979. 5 vols.

———. "MS. Found in a Bottle." 1833. *Tales & Sketches Volume 1: 1831–1842*, edited by Thomas Ollive Mabbott, U of Illinois P, 2000, pp. 135–48.

Pollin, Burton, editor. *The Imaginary Voyages: The Narrative of Arthur Gordon Pym, The Unparalleled Adventures of one Hans Pfaall, The Journal of Julius Rodman*. 1981. Gordian Press, 1994.

Rosenheim, Shawn, and Stephen Rachman. *The American Face of Edgar Allan Poe*. Johns Hopkins UP, 1995.

Sasaki, Naojiro, editor and translator. *The Black Cat and The Gold-Bug*. By Edgar Allan Poe, Shinchosha, 1951.

———. *Collected Tales of Poe*. Daiichi Shobo, 1931–1933. 5 vols.

———. *Murders in the Rue Morgue*. By Edgar Allan Poe, Shinchosha, 1951.

Sato, Ichiei, translator. *The Collected Poems of Poe*. Shueikaku, 1923.

Shimada, Kinji, translator. *Poems of Edgar Poe*. Kantosha Publishers, 1950.

Sugimoto, Nagao, translator. *Poems of Edgar Allan Poe*. Kobunsha, 1936.

Suvin, Darko. *Metamorphoses of Science Fiction: On the Poetics and History of a Literary Genre*. Yale UP, 1979.

Suzuki, Yukio, Yasuo Suga, Hideo Ichiriki, and Motoshi Karita, translators. *Selection of Poe's Major Works*, vol. 3. Kagamiura Shobo, 1961.

Takeda, Takehiko, editor. *Yurei-sen*. By Edgar Allan Poe, illustrated by Motoichiro Takebe, Kaiseisha, 1958.

Tanizaki, Seiji, editor and translator. *The Masque of the Red Death*. By Edgar Allan Poe, Taiheikan Shoten, 1913.

——. *Collected Tales of Edgar Poe*. 1941. Shunjusha, 1969. 6 vols.

——. *Complete Tales of Edgar Allan Poe: A Definitive Edition*. Shunjusha, 1962. 5 vols.

Tatsumi, Takayuki. "The Double Task of the Translator: Poe and His Japanese Disciples." *Translated Poe*, edited by Emron Esplin and Margarida Vale de Gato, Lehigh UP, 2014, pp. 163–74 and 387–90.

——. "Preface." *The Edogawa Rampo Reader*. Edited by Seth Jacobowitz, Kurodahan Press, 2009, pp. 1–8.

——, translator. *The Black Cat/The Fall of the House of Usher*. Shinshocha, 2009.

——. *A Descent into the Maelström/The Light-House*. Shinshocha, 2015.

——. *The Murders in the Rue Morgue/The Gold-Bug*. Shinshocha, 2009.

Togawa, Shukotsu, editor and translator. *A Tale of the Ragged Mountains*. By Edgar Allan Poe. ARS, 1922.

Wakabayashi, Judy. "Foreign Bones, Japanese Flesh: Translations and the Emergence of Modern Japanese Children's Literature." *Japanese Language and Literature*, vol. 42, no. 1, 2008, p. 227–55.

Wakameda, Takeji, translator. *Poems of Poe*. Etsuzando, 1922.

Yagi, Toshio. *A Study of Edgar Allan Poe: Destruction and Creation*. Nan'undo, 1971.

——, editor and translator. *The Gold-Bug, The Black Cat and The Fall of the House of Usher*. By Edgar Allan Poe, Kodansha, 1971.

——. *Poe's Criticisms*. Iwanami Shoten, 2009.

——. *Poe's Science Fiction*. Kodansha, 1979–1980.

Yagi, Toshio, Saeki Shoichi, and Oi Koji, translators. *Poe and Hawthorne: The Gold-Bug and The Black Cat/The Scarlet Letter*. Kodansha, 1974.

Yoshida, Kenichi, and Saichi Maruya, translators. *Poe and Hawthorne*. Chuo-Koron-sha, 1971.

Yoshida, Kenichi, et al., translators. *"The Fall of the House of Usher" and "The Black Cat."* By Edgar Allan Poe. Shueisha, 1970.

Index

Italicized page numbers indicate figures.

~

About the Editors and Contributors

Jana L. Argersinger is an independent scholar and long-time editor of journals and essay collections focused on nineteenth-century American literature and culture, including *Poe Studies*; *ESQ: A Journal of the American Renaissance*; *Poe Writing/Writing Poe* (2012, with Richard Kopley); *Toward a Female Genealogy of Transcendentalism* (2014, with Phyllis Cole); and *Hawthorne and Melville: Writing a Relationship* (with Leland Person, 2008). She has published in the *Edgar Allan Poe Review*, contributed a chapter to *Edgar Allan Poe in 20 Objects* (2016, a companion volume to a Johns Hopkins University exhibit) and, as co-editor of *Poe Studies*, undertaken collaborative features on subjects as wide-ranging as affect theory, nineteenth-century medicine, trauma studies, and single-author studies. Her interest in American women writers of the nineteenth and twentieth centuries has produced scholarship on Susan Warner, Sophia Peabody Hawthorne, Rose Lathrop Hawthorne, Elizabeth Stoddard, and Carol Ryrie Brink, published in such journals as *American Literature* and *Documentary Editing*. She is a past president of the international Council of Editors of Learned Journals and a current vice president of the Margaret Fuller Society.

Emron Esplin is associate professor of English at Brigham Young University where he teaches courses in U.S. literature and inter-American literary studies. He is the editor, with Margarida Vale de Gato, of *Translated Poe* (2014), and he edits the journal *Poe Studies: History, Theory, Interpretation*. His first monograph, *Borges's Poe: The Influence and Reinvention of Edgar Allan Poe in*

Spanish America, was published in 2016. He received the 2013 James W. Gargano Award from the Poe Studies Association for his article "Borges's Philosophy of Poe's Composition," published in *Comparative Literature Studies*. He has also published articles on Katherine Anne Porter, Nellie Campobello, Pancho Villa, William Faulkner, Julio Cortázar, and Nathaniel Hawthorne. He is currently working on a book-length project on the English-language translations of Jorge Luis Borges's short fiction.

Fernando González-Moreno holds a PhD in art history and is an associate professor at the University of Castilla-La Mancha in Spain, where he teaches Art History. His research interests focus on iconography, the relationship between image and text, and illustrated book history. In this sense, he has mainly studied the illustrated reception of three authors, Cervantes, Edgar Allan Poe, and Mary W. Shelley. His publications include *The Eduardo Urbina Cervantes Collection in the Cushing Memorial Library and Archives, Texas A&M University Libraries* (2010), *The Portrayal of the Grotesque in Stoddard's and Quantin's Illustrated Editions of Edgar Allan Poe (1884)* (2017), and "Beyond the Filthy Form: Illustrating Mary Shelley's *Frankenstein*" in *Global Frankenstein* (2018), among others. He is co-editor of the online catalog of illustrated editions "Textual Iconography of *Don Quixote*," and he currently co-directs the interdisciplinary research group "LyA" and the research project "Edgar A. Poe on-line. Text and Image" (ref. HAR2015-64580-P), funded by the Spanish Ministry of Economy and Competitiveness.

John Gruesser is a senior research scholar at Sam Houston State University and a Visiting Fellow at Texas A&M's Melbern G. Glasscock Center. He is a former president of the Poe Studies Association and the author of six books, including *Edgar Allan Poe and His Nineteenth-Century American Counterparts* (2019) and *Race, Gender and Empire in American Detective Fiction* (2013). He is also the editor of five books, including *A Century of Detection: Twenty Great Mystery Stories 1841–1940* (2010) and a scholarly edition of John E. Bruce's 1907–1909 novel, *The Black Sleuth* (2002). In addition to working on *Man on the Firing Line: A Literary Life of Sutton E. Griggs, 1872–1933*, he is currently editing the essay collection *Animals in the Classics: How Natural History Inspired Great American Fiction* and (with Alisha Knight) a Broadview edition of Pauline E. Hopkins's 1901–1902 novel, *Hagar's Daughter: A Story of Southern Caste Prejudice*.

Michelle Kay Hansen received her PhD in English with a literature focus from the University of Nevada, Las Vegas in 2012. Her main research interests are American gothic and horror fiction and film, focusing on the concepts and definitions of "monstrosity," "art-horror," Julia Kristeva's theory of "abjection," and horror and postmodernism in popular culture. An active member of the Popular and American Culture Association (PCA/ACA) since 2008, Michelle has presented her research on several panels and as an invited roundtable panelist at various regional, national, and international conferences. Her published work can be found in *Adapting Poe* (2012) and *New Worlds, Terrifying Monsters, Impossible Things* (2016). She is currently working on a number of projects about Shirley Jackson, including Jackson's cartoons and uncollected works. Michelle currently teaches English at Utah Valley University.

J. Gerald Kennedy is Boyd Professor of English at Louisiana State University and former chair of the English department. His sixteen books include *Strange Nation: Literary Nationalism and Cultural Conflict in the Age of Poe* (2016) and the co-edited *American Novel to 1870* (Oxford 2014). He was a Writing Residency Fellow at Bellagio, Italy, in 2017 and a Taylor Fellow at the University of Virginia in 2017 and 2018. He has appeared in several documentaries on Poe, including *Edgar A. Poe: Buried Alive* (PBS, 2017). He edited the *Portable Edgar Allan Poe* (2006) and was co-editor of the *Oxford Handbook of Edgar Allan Poe* (2019). His latest project is a trade book titled *Peering into Darkness: Edgar Poe and our Culture of Fear*.

Bonnie Shannon McMullen is an independent scholar based in Oxford, England. She taught English at the University of Pittsburgh, at the University of Toronto, and in Sapporo, Japan before tutoring undergraduates for degrees in English at a number of colleges at the University of Oxford. Her research and writing have concentrated on the fiction of Britain and the United States in the nineteenth and twentieth centuries, with a particular focus on transatlantic cultural influences, travel literature, and the short story. She has published widely on George Eliot, Edith Wharton, F. Scott Fitzgerald, and others. Her article, "Lifting the Lid on Poe's 'Oblong Box'" was published in 1995 in *Studies in American Fiction*. "'A Desert of Ebony': Poe, *Blackwood's*, and Tales of the Sea" appeared in 2010 in the *Edgar Allan Poe Review*. In addition, her publications on Wharton and Fitzgerald examine the hidden allusions and cross-currents between their writing and Poe's, demonstrating the often unconscious indebtedness of these authors to Poe's pioneering work. An earlier version of her chapter in this book was presented at the International Poe and Hawthorne Conference in Kyoto in 2018.

Travis Montgomery is associate professor of English at Oklahoma Christian University. Secretary of the Poe Studies Association, he is active in Poe scholarship, serving on the editorial board of *Poe Studies* and regularly reviewing books for the *Edgar Allan Poe Review*. His publications include articles in journals such as *Gothic Studies* as well as a chapter in *The Cambridge Companion to American Gothic*. With John Gruesser, Montgomery wrote an essay about the figure of Poe in Melville's "Bartleby, the Scrivener," and that piece appeared in the 2016 volume of *Poe Studies*.

Scott Peeples is professor of English at the College of Charleston and author of *Edgar Allan Poe Revisited* (1998) and *The Afterlife of Edgar Allan Poe* (2004), which received the Patrick F. Quinn Award from the Poe Studies Association. With J. Gerald Kennedy, he edited *The Oxford Handbook of Edgar Allan Poe* (2019), and from 2008 to 2013 he edited the journal *Poe Studies* with Jana L. Argersinger. He has also published numerous essays and book chapters on Poe and nineteenth-century American literature. His biographical study of Poe, *The Man of the Crowd: Edgar Allan Poe and the City*, will be published in 2020.

Philip Edward Phillips is professor of English and associate dean of the University Honors College at Middle Tennessee State University. He is the editor of *Prison Narratives from Boethius to Zana* (2014) and *Poe and Place*, which received the 2018 J. Lasley Dameron Award from the Poe Studies Association. Other related publications include articles in *Approaches to Teaching Poe's Prose and Poetry* (2008), *Edgar Allan Poe in Context* (2013), *Deciphering Poe: Subtexts, Contexts, Subversive Meanings* (2013), *Edgar Allan Poe in 20 Objects* (2016), and *The Oxford Handbook of Edgar Allan Poe* (2019). He has held research fellowships at the Boston Athenæum, the Newberry Library, and the W. T. Bandy Center for Baudelaire and Modern French Studies. He is a member of the editorial board of the *Edgar Allan Poe Review* and a past president of the Poe Studies Association.

Harry Lee Poe serves as Charles Colson Professor of Faith and Culture at Union University in Jackson, Tennessee. He is the author of seventeen books. His work on Edgar Allan Poe includes two books, *Edgar Allan Poe: An Illustrated Companion to His Tell-Tale Stories* (2008), for which he won an Edgar Award in 2009, and *Evermore: Edgar Allan Poe and the Mystery of the Universe* (2012); contributed chapters in *Edgar Allan Poe in 20 Objects* (2016) and *Poe and Place* (2018); and a number of articles. He served for ten years as president of the Edgar Allan Poe Museum in Richmond and is descended from Edgar Allan Poe's cousin, William Poe. A lover of books, like C. Auguste Dupin and Lord Peter Wimsey, Hal collects first editions, ephemera, and memorabilia related to Edgar Allan Poe and the Inklings of Oxford. His Poe collection has been on display in a number of major libraries, including the National Library of Russia in St. Petersburg in 2009. He is married to Mary Anne, who serves as dean of the School of Social Work at Union University. They have two daughters: Rebecca, who is married to Joshua Hays, and Mary Ellen.

Stephen Rachman is associate professor in the Department of English, former director of the American Studies Program, and co-director of the Digital Humanities Literary Cognition Laboratory at Michigan State University. He is the editor of *The Hasheesh Eater* by Fitz-Hugh Ludlow. He is a co-author of the award-winning *Cholera, Chloroform, and the Science of Medicine: A Life of John Snow* and the co-editor of *The American Face of Edgar Allan Poe*. He has written numerous articles on Poe, literature and medicine, cities, popular culture, and an award-winning website on Sunday school books for the Library of Congress American Memory Project. He is a past president of the Poe Studies Association and is currently completing a study of Poe entitled *The Jingle Man: Edgar Allan Poe and the Problems of Culture*.

Margarita Rigal-Aragón holds a PhD in English Studies. She is an associate professor in the Humanities College (Facultad de Humanidades, Albacete) at the University of Castilla-La Mancha in Spain, where she teaches classes in English and North American literatures and English language courses. Her main field of research is the American Renaissance period. Her book-length publications include *A Descent into Edgar Allan Poe and His Works: The Bicentennial* (2010), *Los legados de Poe* (2011), and *The Portrayal of the Grotesque in Stoddard's and Quantin's Editions of Edgar Allan Poe* (2017, together with Fernando González-Moreno). She has published chapters in *Translated Poe* and *Fragmentos de Realidad: los autores y las poéticas del cuento en lengua inglesa*, and her articles appear in several academic journals, including the *Edgar Allan Poe Review* and *Revista de Filología Inglesa*. She is also the first president of the Edgar Allan Poe Spanish Association (EAPSA).

Christopher Rollason (MA, Trinity College, Cambridge; PhD, University of York) is an independent British scholar living in Luxembourg and a former member of the Department of Anglo-American Studies at the University of Coimbra, Portugal. He is the author of a doctoral thesis on Poe, on whom he has also published numerous articles, book chapters, and reviews—including contributions to the *Edgar Allan Poe Review*. He was active in the series of Poe bicentennial conferences held in Spain in 2009 (*inter alia* with papers on Poe and Borges and on Poe and psychoanalysis). He has also given conference papers on Poe and Dickens (Dickens bicentennial, Lisbon 2012), Poe in Spanish translation (American Comparative Literature Association, Harvard 2016), and Poe and Carlos Fuentes (International Association of Inter-American Studies, Coimbra 2018). In addition, he has published articles on Walter Benjamin, Bob Dylan, Portuguese literature, Latin American literature, translation studies, and Indian writing in English.

Jeffrey A. Savoye is an independent scholar, long and closely associated with the Edgar Allan Poe Society of Baltimore. He is also an honorary member of the Poe Studies Association. As the co-editor of *The Collected Letters of Edgar Allan Poe* (2008), the standard edition of Poe's correspondence, and the author of dozens of articles, published chiefly in the *Edgar Allan Poe Review* and *Poe Studies/Dark Romanticism*, he has deeply explored various aspects of Poe's life and writings. He is also the driving force behind the well-regarded website of the Poe Society: https://www.eapoe.org.

Takayuki Tatsumi has taught American literature and critical theory at Keio University, Tokyo, since 1989. He has served or is serving as president of the American Literature Society of Japan (2014–2017), president of the Poe Society of Japan (2009–), president of Keio University's Society of Arts and Letters (2018–), and vice president of the Melville Society of Japan (2012–). He is currently a member of the editorial board of the *Journal of Transnational American Studies* (2009–). His book *Full Metal Apache: Transactions between Cyberpunk Japan and Avant-Pop America* won the 2010 IAFA (International Association for the Fantastic in the Arts) Distinguished Scholarship Award. Co-editor of *The Routledge Companion to Transnational American Studies* (2019), he has also published a variety of essays in *PMLA*, *Critique*, *Extrapolation*, *American Book Review*, *Mechademia*, *The Oxford Research Encyclopedia of Literature*, and elsewhere on subjects ranging from the American Renaissance to post-cyberpunk fiction and film. His recent collaborations include *The Cambridge History of Postmodern Literature* (2016), and his most recent monograph is *Young Americans in Literature: The Post-Romantic Turn in the Age of Poe, Hawthorne and Melville* (2018). His latest edited collection is *Trans-Pacific Cultural Studies* (four volumes; 2019).

Alexandra Urakova is a senior researcher at the A. M. Gorky Institute of World Literature of the Russian Academy of Sciences, Moscow, and also a core fellow at the Helsinki Collegium for Advanced Studies, University of Helsinki. She is the author of *The Poetics of the Body in the Short Fiction of Edgar Allan Poe* (2009, in Russian), editor of *Deciphering Poe: Subtexts, Contexts, Subversive Meanings* (2013), and co-editor, with Tudor Sala and Tracey A. Sowerby, of *The Dangers of Gifts from Antiquity to the Digital Age* (forthcoming). She has published on Poe, antebellum gift books, and nineteenth-century American literature in *New England Quarterly*, *Nineteenth Century Literature*, *Edgar Allan Poe Review*, *Poe Studies*, and *American Periodicals* as well as in the edited volumes *Poe's Pervasive Influence* (2013), *Poe and Place* (2018), and *The Oxford Handbook of Edgar Allan Poe* (2019).

Margarida Vale de Gato translates, writes, teaches, and researches. She is an assistant professor in the areas of translation and U.S. literature in the School of Arts and Humanities at the Universidade de Lisboa, and she co-coordinates the American Studies Group of ULICES. As a literary translator, she has produced versions of French and English canonical texts into Portuguese (Sarraute, Michaux, Carroll, Yeats, Twain, Kerouac, Munro). Her most recent academic publications include a chapter for *The Oxford Handbook of Edgar Allan Poe* titled "Poe and Modern(ist) Poetry" and an article in META on her translation of *Lolita*. She has published poems and short stories in national and international journals and anthologies, as well as the poetry collections *Lançamento* (2016) and *Mulher ao Mar* (2010), with the enlarged editions *Mulher ao Mar Retorna* (2013) and *Mulher ao Mar e Grinalda* (2018). For the stage, she wrote (with Rui Costa) the play *Desligar e Voltar a Ligar*, published in 2011.